ADVANCE PRAISE FOR *MY FIRST TIME IN HOLLYWOOD*

"Through the first-person voices of some of the most fascinating, insightful, funny, ego-maniacal, and brilliant people, Cari Beauchamp's *My First Time in Hollywood* chronicles the years when Los Angeles became the Hollywood of the world's imagination and movies our internationally shared mythology. Essential reading for anyone interested in film history."

—**John Landis**, director of *National Lampoon's Animal House*, *The Blues Brothers, Trading Places*, and Michael Jackson's *Thriller*

"A delight and a revelation. Cari Beauchamp, one of the great writers on early cinema, helps us re-see Hollywood. Its creation is between these pages. Its early days come alive like never before. *My First Time in Hollywood* is a treasure, and a fascinating read."

—**Mark Cousins**, writer and director of *The Story of Film: An Odyssey* and *A Story of Children and Film*

"If ever a book could act as your own personal time machine and make you feel the Tinseltown dust beneath your feet, it's *My First Time in Hollywood*. In their own words, actors, directors, writers, and others give vivid accounts of arriving in a young town to create and work in a brand-new industry, and at least half of them are women. As entertaining as it is informative, this is a book I will refer back to forever."

—**Allison Anders**, director of *Orange is the New Black*, *Sex in the City*, and *Gas Food Lodging*

"What a priceless parade of evocative and highly entertaining memories. Once you start reading you won't want to stop."

—**Leonard Maltin**, film critic and historian

"*My First Time in Hollywood* puts us in the heads of dozens of remarkable people who fell in love with moving images on a screen and set off to put themselves 'in the picture.' Cari Beauchamp has curated a gallery of hopes, illusions, and keen observation, notable for its portrait of early Hollywood and its insight into our human longing to be part of something transcendent."

—**John Sayles**, writer and director of *Lone Star*, *The Brother from Another Planet*, and *Eight Men Out*

"Ace Hollywood chronicler Cari Beauchamp reminds us with scrumptious detail that even the greatest, when they went West, faced insecurities and challenges in finding their place in the world of filmmaking. *My First Time in Hollywood* makes you laugh out loud while pulling at your heartstrings."

—**Anne Thompson**, founder and editor of Indiewire's Thompson on Hollywood

"What every film fan yearns for—first-hand, eyewitness accounts of a Hollywood none of us can remember and all of us wish we'd known. Completely fascinating."

—**Kevin Brownlow**, Academy Award-winning film preservationist, historian, and author of *The Parade's Gone By*, *Napoleon: Abel Gance's Classic Film*, and *David Lean: A Biography*

My First Time in Hollywood

ALSO BY CARI BEAUCHAMP

Without Lying Down:
Frances Marion and the
Powerful Women of
Early Hollywood

Joseph P. Kennedy Presents:
His Hollywood Years

Adventures of a Hollywood Secretary

Anita Loos Rediscovered

Hollywood on the Riviera:
The Inside Story of the
Cannes Film Festival
(with Henri Behar)

My First Time in Hollywood

Stories from the Pioneers, Dreamers and Misfits Who Made the Movies

CARI BEAUCHAMP

ASAHINA & WALLACE

LOS ANGELES

2015

WWW.ASAHINAANDWALLACE.COM

Introduction, annotations, and volume compilation © 2015 by Cari Beauchamp

Published in the United States by Asahina & Wallace, Inc.
www.asahinaandwallace.com

ISBN: 978-1-940412-14-6
Library of Congress Control Number: 2015931846

For Randy Haberkamp of the Academy of Motion Picture Arts and Sciences, Mary Lea Bandy of the Museum of Modern Art, Charlie Tabesh of Turner Classic Movies, Madeline Matz of the Library of Congress, Ned Comstock of the USC Cinematic Arts Library, and all the librarians, archivists, programmers, and preservationists who work to save and share the history of the movies and the people who made them.

There is no such thing as an old movie if you haven't seen it before.

CONTENTS

Introduction   i

1909
Hobart Bosworth   1
A stricken Broadway actor discovers a new career.

1910
Mrs. D. W. Griffith (Linda Arvidson)   5
A director's wife helps birth a business.

Mary Pickford   15
Hollywood's first female mogul turns ringlets into riches.

1912
Frances Marion   19
She enters as an actress but triumphs as a writer.

1913
Henry King   29
A chance encounter turns a stock actor into a star director.

Harold Lloyd   35
A character actor finds his glasses and stardom as America's Everyman.

Lillian Gish   40
This fragile waif has a backbone of steel.

Karl Brown   48
A journeyman cinematographer goes from color to black and white.

Lionel Barrymore   57
The need for a steady paycheck launches a film dynasty.

Virgil Miller   61
A Kansas professor electrifies Hollywood.

Cecil B. DeMille   64
Grandiosity has its beginnings in a barn.

1914

Raoul Walsh   73
A cowboy is hired to herd actors.

Anita Loos   81
This smart brunette creates the quintessential dumb blonde.

Elsie Janis   89
Vaudeville's sweetheart leaves the stage…but never her mother.

Marie Dressler   93
A surprising source explains the economics of the film business.

Agnes de Mille   98
The legendary choreographer first dances in the Hollywood hills.

1915

King Vidor   106
A Texas tornado turns his talents to directing.

DeWolf Hopper   113
Only in Hollywood: Broadway's famous Voice goes before the silent cameras.

Hedda Hopper   118
A Hollywood wife becomes the Talk of the Town.

1916

Evelyn Scott   126
A screenwriter's daughter soaks it all in.

Gloria Swanson   133
"I was the golden girl…everyone said so."

Colleen Moore   142
A starstruck teenager becomes a star.

1918

Myrna Loy 150
A Montana girl finds culture in Culver City.

Budd Schulberg 158
A Hollywood prince surveys his kingdom.

1919

Lenore Coffee 168
A cosmopolitan writer discovers the charms of a frontier town.

Alice Guy 180
"America takes back everything it gives you."

1921

Winfrid Kay Thackrey 186
A set director proves herself in a man's world.

1922

Sam Jaffe 198
Then as now: Brother-in-law of a studio chief gets the job.

Will Hays 204
The man who came to Code.

1923

Norma Shearer 217
On her first day in town, the future Queen of M-G-M meets her King.

Mary Astor 222
A seventeen-year-old has an affair to remember.

1925

Louella Parsons 229
An ambitious writer boosts her career by boosting Hollywood.

Valeria Belletti 235
A wide-eyed studio secretary tells all.

1926

Ben Hecht   240
The man who loved to hate Hollywood.

Sergei Bertensson   247
For the Russians, Hollywood gets lost in translation.

Robert Parrish   255
Skill with a pea shooter launches a multifaceted career.

1928

Maurice Rapf   261
It's good to be young, rich, and live in Malibu.

Salka Viertel   267
A European émigré creates a safe haven for others.

Laurence Irving   277
His job interview is with a naked Douglas Fairbanks.

Maurice Leloir   286
An intellectual Frenchman is enchanted by Hollywood.

Ralph Winters   291
Making the cut from silents to talkies.

1929

Noël Coward   300
"Don't be frightened, dear—this—this—is Hollywood!"

Acknowledgments   303

Sources   307

Index   311

About the Author   330

Hollywood in 1910: The Hollywood Hotel is at the far left, on Hollywood Boulevard; Hollywood High School is at the top center, at Highland and Sunset. (Courtesy of Marc Wanamaker/Bison Archives)

Introduction

"There's America…and then there's Hollywood," said Noël Coward in the early 1930s, for even then the word "Hollywood" was the internationally recognized synonym for the movies, emblematic of glamour, excitement, and most of all, possibilities.

These first-person reminiscences by future film greats about their arrival in Southern California resonate with that sense of possibility. Of course at the time, they didn't know what their future held or, for that matter, what would become of Hollywood. Each of these journeys was unique, but all these newcomers shared a passion for the work they wanted to do and a deep-seated belief in their abilities. As always, serendipity played a role in the process.

These pioneers represent a wide variety of cultures and backgrounds. They came from the South, the Midwest, the East Coast, and as far away as London, Paris, and Moscow. Only a third of them appeared in front of the camera, the rest were of that great group of romantics, inventors, and visionaries who toiled behind the camera as directors, writers, cinematographers, editors, costumers, lighting designers, and set decorators in this most collaborative of art forms.

A precious few were actually in the film business when they arrived in California. D. W. Griffith and his Biograph troupe came in pursuit of warm sunshine so they could film in the winter months. Others were searching for a place as far away as possible from the dreaded "Trust," the name commonly given to the Motion Picture Patents Company, a consortium of companies headed by Thomas Edison, who held most of the patents on motion picture cameras and projectors. When Eastman Kodak joined the Trust, the monopoly was complete and license fees were demanded for almost everything to do with making movies, down to the sprocket holes on a strip of film. New York and New Jersey were the hubs of early filmmaking, so renegade companies—buying equipment from Europe or wherever it could be found—fled to Florida, Cuba, and California to dodge the thugs hired by the Trust to maintain its lucrative control.

In those early days, movies were an idea one week, in front of the camera the next, and in theaters within a month. There were no clear paths to follow and no rules to break. With only a few taking movies seriously as a business, the doors were wide open to women and Jews, unwelcome in more established and respectable professions, and Hollywood become a magnet for the creative and entrepreneurial misfits who fill these pages. By the time women won the right to vote in 1920, they had been thriving for over a decade at every level of moviemaking—as directors, producers, editors, and writers. Women wrote half of all films made before 1925.

With the exception of Florence and King Vidor, who dared to drive the rutted dirt roads between Texas and California in 1915, everyone came by train. Most of the travelers had not been far from their birthplaces and, whether that was New York or Europe, had never seen anything like the Great Plains, the Rocky Mountains, or the deserts of New Mexico and Arizona. And their excitement and anticipation only grew as they neared Southern California.

Over the years, porters had tossed wildflower seeds along the tracks from the back of trains as they neared Los Angeles, and the result was what actress Leatrice Joy called "two yellow streams like ribbons ... It was like heaven saying welcome to California." Then there were the feather-duster palm trees and of course the fragrant orange groves. Wherever these dreamers had come from, they knew they weren't in Kansas anymore.

It would not be until the opening of Union Station in 1939 that all three major train lines came into the same Los Angeles depot. Before that, most passengers, whether they were greeted by hordes, a few colleagues, or found their way into town alone, disembarked at Pasadena. As Evelyn Scott remembered, "We got off the train at Pasadena, not Los Angeles a few miles farther on, because our hostess wished to take us out to Hollywood by 'the pretty way,' not the ugly one from the main depot."

Hollywood was the antithesis of glitter and glamour then. Established in the late 1880s by Harvey Wilcox, a prohibitionist and real estate man from Kansas, and his wife, Daeida, Hollywood was one of forty incorporated towns within the Los Angeles area. After Harvey died in 1891, Daeida remarried and carried on her first husband's mission: to build a community that would attract what he considered the right kind of people. In addition to giving land to churches, she lured the renowned French watercolorist Paul de Longpré to Hollywood by giving him property on which to build a mansion and a sprawling, tourist-attracting garden. The selling of liquor in Hollywood was forbidden as were public drunkenness, poolrooms, bowling alleys, and "other such morally and physically polluting businesses." (Alphonzo Bell, the founder of nearby Bel Air, proclaimed another grandiose and eventually futile attempt at neighborhood control when he told actor Fred Thomson, "I've made it a law—not one acre of my land is to be sold to actors or Jews.")

One hundred years after Franciscan friars had cut a swath through the native villages and built a mission there, Los Angeles was still a frontier town in many ways. The land boom of the late 1800s began to change that as potential buyers came west on the recently completed intercontinental railroads. Midwestern families joined together to purchase large tracts of land so that they could move en masse to create their own communities, infused with their own values. The discovery of oil in 1892 spurred the development of ports and changed the look of the land; wells pumped away amid orange trees, churches, a few hotels, and small clusters of houses and shops.

Los Angeles was first introduced to the "flickers" in 1897 when the lights dimmed at the Orpheum Theater and, on a large white sheet, the image of a life-sized Annabelle Moore performed her Sun Dance for a few precious moments. The Lumière brothers in France are credited with the first public screening of short films in late 1895 and the following spring, Thomas Edison, who had introduced the Kinetoscope, displayed a film in which waves pounded toward the audience.

Edison's primary focus was on the equipment, cameras, and projectors, not the creative product that could result, and the same was true for the Gaumont Company in Paris. However, Gaumont's secretary, Alice Guy, had other ideas, and when she finished her daily chores she was given permission to use the company's cameras to create short dramatic films that would ignite an industry. At the same time in Paris, George Méliès was experimenting with double exposure, which would lead to his magical fantasy films such as *A Trip to the Moon*. In 1903, Edwin Porter in New

Jersey edited a dozen shots into a several-minute narrative called *The Great Train Robbery*. Throughout American vaudeville theaters, one reel of film, five to ten minutes in length, began to be shown as a "chaser" between acts to clear out the theater for the next show. Yet the movies soon gained such popularity that proprietors built separate venues for them, and by 1910 there were ten thousand nickelodeons throughout the country, all desperate for product.

Movies were a cheap form of entertainment aimed primarily at the lower classes until Adolph Zukor, a Hungarian immigrant furrier turned arcade owner, had the bright idea to import a French film, *Queen Elizabeth*, starring Sarah Bernhardt. By carefully presenting the almost hour-long film and selling the rights to distribute it state by state, Zukor quadrupled his investment. Then George Kleine screened the eight-reel Italian epic *Quo Vadis* at the Astor Theatre in New York, where it ran for several months at a dollar a ticket. It didn't take long for first-class theaters to be built exclusively to show films, and the Strand in New York opened its doors in 1914 with the premiere of one of the first American-made feature-length films, *The Spoilers*. The next year, there were lines around the block to see D. W. Griffith's shockingly racist, cinematically innovative, and technically brilliant *The Birth of a Nation*.

And when people wanted to know the names of the actors they were starting to recognize from one film to the next, fan magazines—beginning with *Photoplay* in 1912—became an auxiliary industry.

Films played a pivotal role in turning an isolation-inclined nation into one that proactively supported America's entry into World War I. Blatantly promoting the Allied cause, *Johanna Enlists* encouraged soldiers not to return until they had "taken the 'Germ' out of Germany." The enemy was demonized in the none-too-subtle *To Hell with the Kaiser* and *The Kaiser—The Beast of Berlin*, with audiences urged to "come and hiss." Newsreels informed the nation of the war's progress, and when Mary Pickford, Douglas Fairbanks, Marie Dressler, and Charlie Chaplin made personal appearances to sell war bonds, they nearly caused riots.

The intense popularity of the stars and the way the public considered them their own came as a surprise to everyone, including the actors themselves, and with the Armistice in November 1918, there was no doubting either the power or the patriotism of the film industry. As historian Kevin Brownlow writes, "The movies had clearly shown the effectiveness with which they could exploit a nation's latent hatred and the box office had shown its profitability." That "latent hatred" helped inflame an anti-immigrant fever that resulted in the Palmer Raids—mass arrests by the government of suspected radicals spearheaded by President Wilson's Attorney General, Mitchell Palmer—which led to the deportation of thousands and the passage of laws that effectively closed Ellis Island. But then, as now, filmmakers didn't credit or blame themselves for cultural or political change; they were too busy making the next movie.

World War I also had a cataclysmic effect on the business of films. Before the assassination of Archduke Ferdinand in Sarajevo in 1914, the quality of European films, particularly those from France and Italy, far surpassed those made in America. But the conflict demanded all available men and material be devoted to the cause; production facilities were shut down and theaters taken over to house occupying armies. At war's end, European filmmaking was crippled, and American movies dominated the international market.

The Supreme Court declared an armistice of a different kind in 1917 when the justices ruled against the Trust and ended its attempt to monopolize filmmaking and exhibition. The two big winners were the independent moviemakers and Los Angeles, where more than one hundred movie companies were listed in the 1920 city directory. Southern California had become the center of filmmaking—for America and the world.

The locals, who had been none too thrilled to see women walking the streets in heavy makeup or men sitting under trees in Biblical costumes, soon realized that the movie business was becoming the city's largest employer, and the ripple effect on hotels, restaurants, and stores was not only appreciated but depended upon. Films and film stars were the best advertising Southern California could have asked for, and tourism was flourishing.

Movies helped spark the Jazz Age and, along with the increasing availability of automobiles, a cultural revolution. It is difficult to overstate the influence of films on Americans, particularly those in the hinterlands. Different mores, fashions, lifestyles, and foreign lands were all seen for the very first time. Oh, you could read about them in books if you sought them out, but suddenly the world beyond the horizon was there to behold on the local screen. Newsreels showing suffragettes marching built support for women's right to vote. Films such as *A Girl's Folly* revealed both the tangible benefits and the emotional price of living the high life, and Margaret Sanger's advocacy of birth control was promoted in *The Hand That Rocks the Cradle.*

Imagine a young Midwestern woman in 1922 who has never been more than a few miles from her birthplace. She feels isolated in her community and wonders what is wrong with her for wanting something more. She goes into a darkened theater to see *Back Pay*, and there is Matt Moore telling Seena Owen that he loves her in her little gingham dress. When Seena responds in frustration, "But I have a crepe de chine soul!" that young woman knows she has found a kindred spirit; she is no longer alone. (The title *Back Pay* comes from the scene in which Seena, partying madly, dancing on a table, and drinking champagne announces: "If there are any wages to sin, some of us have a lot of back pay coming!")

No wonder so many people wanted to come to Hollywood. In 1910, Los Angeles was home to three hundred thousand people; by the midtwenties, one hundred thousand were pouring into the city each year. Roads of loose dirt and gravel were soon smoothly paved, and the hills above this hive of activity were graced with the huge HOLLYWOODLAND sign, constructed to promote yet another housing development.

Working out of barns and filming on empty lots gave way to more permanent locations, and by 1924 large studios sprawled throughout the area. Along Melrose, the Brunton-United Studio, about to be taken over by Paramount, abutted the much smaller FBO Pictures. The Pickford-Fairbanks Studio was nearby at Santa Monica Boulevard and Formosa, Warner Brothers was up on Sunset Boulevard, and Universal City had been flourishing in the San Fernando Valley for almost a decade. Metro-Goldwyn-Mayer had just opened its gates in Culver City that spring, and Cecil B. DeMille was about to take over the former Thomas Ince Studio down the street on Washington Boulevard.

Over the years between 1909 and 1929, films went from ten-minute-long sketches to cinematic masterpieces such as *The Crowd, The Wind*, and *The Big Parade*. Innovations in lighting, cameras, lenses, editing, and storytelling were constant. Exhibition evolved from one-reelers shown on a sheet in a hall accompanied by a piano player to epics screened in majestic theaters with full orchestras.

No one personified the grand theater owner more than Sid Grauman, the son of vaudeville performers and a natural-born promoter. He opened his Million Dollar Theatre on Broadway in downtown Los Angeles in 1918 and took notice when a clever businessman dragged two army-surplus searchlights to advertise his store. Grauman jumped on the idea and lights flooded the sky for the premiere of Douglas Fairbanks's *Robin Hood*, on the opening night of Grauman's Egyptian Theatre on Hollywood Boulevard in 1922. Too much is never too much in Hollywood: eight years later, two hundred searchlights heralded the debut screening of *Hell's Angels*. Grauman's Chinese Theatre opened in 1927 and became a tourist attraction after Mary Pickford's dog Zorro, as the story goes, left his paw prints in wet cement, inspiring the showman to put stars' hand- and footprints in cement in the theater's forecourt.

The press began reporting on the activities and opinions of film stars as if they were kings and queens. And in Los Angeles, a city without many prominent families or a deeply rooted power structure, the luminaries of the movie business became the elite. Douglas Fairbanks and Mary Pickford ruled from Pickfair, their estate in Beverly Hills; Frances Marion and her husband, Fred Thompson, created their Enchanted Hill at the very top of a Beverly hill with a mahogany-floored stable and 360-degree views; and Harold Lloyd added a waterfall, an Olympic-sized pool, and a nine-hole golf course to his Green Acres. Opulence reigned and at times, wealth and taste actually came together. Yet, as Anita Loos would note, many of the newly affluent "were the peers" of their servants "in everything but sex appeal. To place in the limelight a great number of people who ordinarily would be chambermaids and chauffeurs, give them unlimited power and instant wealth, is bound to produce a lively and diverting result."

As exciting as the fan magazines made Hollywood seem, day-to-day life was rather mundane. Dinner parties at Pickfair ended by ten, with cups of Ovaltine passed to the guests as a signal that the evening was over. Monday through Saturday, workdays began at six in the morning and often did not end until well after dark. The actress Marion Davies would occasionally encourage her cast and crew to head to the beach with her for a picnic or an impromptu dinner party at her ocean-side estate, but as the companion of press baron William Randolph Hearst, she could get away with such carefree behavior and was the exception to the rule.

For the adventurers whose stories fill this book, there was an innocence, excitement, and energy to those early years. Their community was small and close-knit, with real and enduring friendships. As the screenwriter

Lenore Coffee remembers, "It was like a carnival or the way one feels when the circus is coming to town, only the circus was always there."

This book ends with the dawning of sound, but talkies did not happen overnight after Al Jolson announced, "You ain't seen nothing yet." It was a several-year process, resisted for multiple reasons, some artistic, most economic. In many ways, sound films brought the reinvention of the film business, and with it an influx of new talent, such as experienced stage actors, playwrights, musicians, and engineers. But those stories are for the next volume.

Cari Beauchamp
Los Angeles, 2015

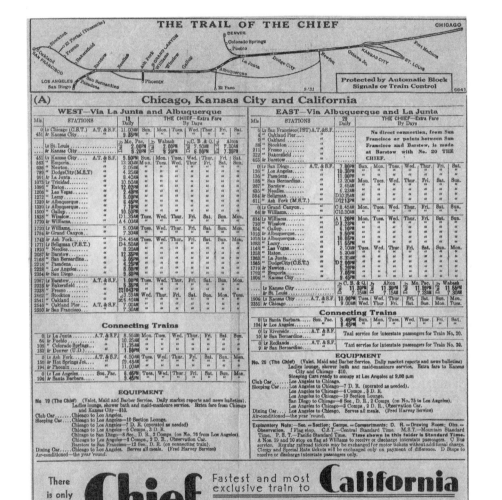

THE TRAIL OF THE CHIEF

CHICAGO

Protected by Automatic Block Signals or Train Control

(A) Chicago, Kansas City and California

WEST—Via La Junta and Albuquerque

Mls.	STATIONS		19 Daily	THE CHIEF—Extra Fare By Days
0	Lv Chicago (C.S.T.)	A.T. & S.F.	11.00AM	Sun. Mon. Tues. Wed. Thur. Fri. Sat.
451	Ar Kansas City	"	9.35PM	
	Lv St. Louis		2.00PM	Mo. Pac. 2.00PM Wabash 2.00PM C.B.&Q. 7.50AM Alton 7.30AM
	Ar Kansas City		5.20PM	9.20PM 6.50PM 7.35PM
451	Lv Kansas City	A.T. & S.F.	9.50PM	Sun. Mon. Tues. Wed. Thur. Fri. Sat.
563	" Emporia	"	12.20AM	Mon. Tues. Wed. Thur. Fri. Sat. Sun.
686	" Newton	"	2.05AM	
789	" DodgeCity(M.S.T.)	"	4.25AM	
991	Ar La Junta	"	8.40AM	
1073	Lv Trinidad	"	10.40AM	
1096	" Raton	"	12.02PM	
1206	" Las Vegas	"	4.50PM	
1272	" Lamy	"	5.50PM	
1330	Ar Albuquerque	"	6.45PM	
1330	Lv Albuquerque	"	7.10PM	
1509	" Gallup	"	10.50PM	
1628	" Winslow	"	D1.35AM	Tues. Wed. Thur. Fri. Sat. Sun. Mon.
1720	Ar Williams	"	A 4.00AM	
1720	Lv Williams	"	5.00AM	Tues. Wed. Thur. Fri. Sat. Sun. Mon.
1784	Ar Grand Canyon	"	7.30AM	
1742	Ar Ash Fork	"	D4.45AM	Tues. Wed. Thur. Fri. Sat. Sun. Mon.
1771	Lv Seligman (P.S.T.)	"	D4.50AM	
1920	" Needles	"	8.30AM	
2087	Ar Barstow	"	12.35PM	
2168	" San Bernardino	"	1.05PM	
2218	" Pasadena	"	2.05PM	
2228	" Los Angeles	"	2.30PM	
2314	Ar San Diego	"	5.30PM	
2087	Lv Barstow	A.T. & S.F.	12.10PM	Tues. Wed. Thur. Fri. Sat. Sun. Mon.
2228	Ar Bakersfield	"	5.35PM	
2335	" Fresno	"	10.43PM	
2462	" Stockton	"	6.10AM	Wed. Thur. Fri. Sat. Sun. Mon. Tues.
2541	" Oakland	"	6.40AM	
2549	" Oakland Pier	"	7.00AM	
2550	Ar San Francisco	"	7.30AM	

Connecting Trains

Mls.				
0	Lv La Junta	A.T. & S.F.	8.55AM	Mon. Tues. Wed. Thur. Fri. Sat. Sun.
64	Ar Pueblo	"	10.25AM	
108	" Colorado Springs	"	11.35AM	
183	Ar Denver (U.D.)	"	1.50PM	
0	Lv Ash Fork	A.T. & S.F.	4.50AM	Tues. Wed. Thur. Fri. Sat. Sun. Mon.
150	Ar Hot Springs Jct.	"	9.48AM	
194	Ar Phoenix	"	11.00AM	
0	Lv Los Angeles	Sou. Pac.	6.45PM	Tues. Wed. Thur. Fri. Sat. Sun. Mon.
194	Ar Santa Barbara	"	9.45PM	

EQUIPMENT

No. 19 (The Chief) (Valet, Maid and Barber Service. Daily market reports and news bulletins). Ladies lounge, shower bath and maid-manicure service. Extra fare from Chicago and Kansas City—$10.

Club Car.... Chicago to Los Angeles.
Sleeping Car.. Chicago to Los Angeles—10 Section Lounge.
Chicago to Los Angeles—7 D. R. (operated as needed)
Chicago to Los Angeles—6 Comps., 3 D. R.
Chicago to San Diego—8 Sec., D. R. 2 Comps. (on No. 76 from Los Angeles)
Barstow to San Francisco—12 Sec., D. R. (on connecting train).
Dining Car.... Chicago to Los Angeles. Serves all meals. (Fred Harvey Service)
Air-conditioned—the year 'round.

EAST—Via Albuquerque and La Junta

Mls.	STATIONS		20 Daily	THE CHIEF—Extra Fare By Days
0	Lv San Francisco (PST)	A.T. & S.F.		No direct connection, from San Francisco or points between San Francisco and Barstow, is made at Barstow with No. 20 THE CHIEF.
9	" Oakland Pier	"		
6	" Oakland	"		
88	" Stockton	"		
211	" Fresno	"		
322	" Bakersfield	"		
403	Ar Barstow	"		
0	Lv San Diego	A.T. & S.F.	7.00PM	Sun. Mon. Tues. Wed. Thur. Fri. Sat.
120	" Los Angeles	"	10.30PM	
136	" Pasadena	"	10.50PM	
186	" San Bernardino	"	12.20AM	Mon. Tues. Wed. Thur. Fri. Sat. Sun.
267	" Barstow	"	2.45AM	
435	" Needles	"	6.23AM	
584	Ar Seligman	"	D10.35AM	
611	" Ash Fork (M.S.T.)	"	D12.13PM	
0	Lv Grand Canyon	"	C 8.45AM	Mon. Tues. Wed. Thur. Fri. Sat. Sun.
64	Ar Williams	"	C10.30AM	
634	Lv Williams	"	A 1.20PM	Mon. Tues. Wed. Thur. Fri. Sat. Sun.
720	" Winslow	"	D 3.28PM	
854	" Gallup	"	6.10PM	
1016	Ar Albuquerque	"	9.45PM	
1016	Lv Albuquerque	"	11.55PM	
1083	" Lamy	"	12.55AM	
1148	" Las Vegas	"	2.20AM	Tues. Wed. Thur. Fri. Sat. Sun. Mon.
1268	" Raton	"	6.15AM	
1363	" La Junta	"	8.35AM	
1565	" DodgeCity(C.S.T.)	"	D 2.00PM	
1719	Ar Newton	"	5.05PM	
1792	" Emporia	"	7.05PM	
1904	" Kansas City	"	9.45PM	
	Lv Kansas City	C.B.&Q. 11.30PM Alton 11.59PM Mo. Pac. 11.59PM Wabash 11.55PM		Daily
	" St. Louis	7.15AM 7.23AM 7.15AM 7.30AM		
1904	Lv Kansas City	A.T. & S.F.	10.00PM	Tues. Wed. Thur. Fri. Sat. Sun. Mon.
2355	Ar Chicago	"	9.00AM	Wed. Thur. Fri. Sat. Sun. Mon. Tues.

Connecting Trains

Mls.				
0	Lv Santa Barbara	Sou. Pac.	5.45PM	Sun. Mon. Tues. Wed. Thur. Fri. Sat.
194	Ar Los Angeles	"	8.45PM	
0	Lv Riverside	A.T. & S.F.		Taxi service for interstate passengers for Train No. 20.
10	Ar San Bernardino	"		
0	Lv Redlands	A.T. & S.F.		Taxi service for interstate passengers for Train No. 20.
9	Ar San Bernardino	"		

EQUIPMENT

No. 20 (The Chief) (Valet, Maid and Barber Service. Daily market reports and news bulletins. Ladies lounge, shower bath and maid-manicure service. Extra fare to Kansas City and Chicago - $10.
Sleeping Cars ready to occupy at Los Angeles at 9.00 p.m

Club Car.... Los Angeles to Chicago.
Sleeping Car... Los Angeles to Chicago—7 D. R. (operated as needed).
Los Angeles to Chicago—6 Comps. 3 D. R.
Los Angeles to Chicago—10 Section Lounge.
San Diego to Chicago—8 Sec., D. R., 2 Comps. (on No. 75 to Los Angeles).
Los Angeles to Chicago—3 Comps., 2 D. R., Observation Car.
Dining Car.... Los Angeles to Chicago. Serves all meals. (Fred Harvey Service)
Air-conditioned—the year 'round.

Explanatory Note:—Sec. = Section; Comps. = Compartments; D. R. = Drawing Room; Obs. = Observation. f Flag stop. C.S.T. = Central Standard Time. M.S.T. = Mountain Standard Time. P. S. T. = Pacific Standard Time. Time shown in this folder is Standard Time. A Nos. 19 and 20 stop on flag at Williams to receive or discharge interstate passengers. C Bus service. Regular railroad tickets may be exchanged for motor tickets without additional charge. Clergy and Special Rate tickets will be exchanged only on payment of difference. D Stops to receive or discharge interstate passengers only.

There is only ONE Chief — Fastest and most exclusive train to **California**

- The SANTA FE is the shortest line between Chicago and California.
- Fred Harvey Air-conditioned Dining Car—the year 'round.

Hobart Bosworth and Stella Adams filming *In the Sultan's Power* at the Sing Zee Laundry drying yard in Los Angeles. (Courtesy of Marc Wanamaker/Bison Archives)

Hobart Bosworth 1909

H obart Bosworth, born in Marietta, Ohio, on August 11, 1867, claimed to be a direct descendant of Miles Standish and the first Dutch settlers of Manhattan, but his childhood was hardly patrician. After his mother died and his father married a woman with whom Hobart clashed, he ran away to New York and signed on as a cabin boy, eventually spending several years at sea. He returned to New York and acted with the Augustin Daly Company for a decade, touring Europe half a dozen times. By 1900, he was an acclaimed Broadway actor, appearing in Shakespearean plays and costarring with Minnie Maddern Fiske in Hedda Gabler. When he was struck with tuberculosis around 1905, he lost his voice and a third of his weight in the course of three months. Desperate and scared, he headed to the West, known for its dry, warm weather, to regain his health. By the time he settled in Los Angeles in 1908, he was forty years old and, while stronger physically, his once-powerful voice was still weak. He thought his acting days were behind him.

I was trying to make both ends meet with a little dramatic school which Oliver Morosco[1] and I had established when, on the morning of May 6, 1909, a quiet gentleman in fashionable clothes called at my office in the school and asked me to act in a motion picture.

I hardly knew what that was. I had seen only one—a fight between Mr. Jeffries and Mr. Sharkey—and did not know anything about the dramatic pictures.

I was shocked, and insulted and hurt by turns. He tried to salve my wounds by telling me that I would never be seen by any of my friends, as the picture would only be shown in the little Main Street nickelodeons; that my name would never be shown or used.

He tried to tell me that his director had hopes for the future of the silly business that might ultimately take it out of these despised nickelodeons and make it worth while.

I remained deeply insulted. I was quite sure that Augustin Daly, my old New York manager for ten years, would turn over in his grave were he to feel that I had debased my art so completely.

But alas, my code of ethics fell before the onslaught of Capital.

He offered me more money for two days' work than I had ever received in my life of devotion to the drama. I had been a Broadway star, but I had also been ill for many years with T.B. [and] being very human and very poor, I fell. "Nobody will ever know it," the tempter whispered. I would do just a few foolish things before a foolish box that I had never seen, the picture would be over in two days. I would act at most thirty or forty seconds per scene (those days scenes never ran over fifty or sixty feet or seconds), it would all be in the sunshine whether we acted in interiors or exteriors, it would all be easy and pleasant—AND $125.00 for two days' work! The prostitution of art began then. I was the first to fall.

On Saturday, May 8, 1909, I went to a vacant lot—the drying yard of a Chinese laundry—on Olive Street near Eighth. Here I found the quiet, exquisitely dressed gentleman, who was James L. McGee, the business manager of the company.

He introduced me to a still quieter little gentleman with the bright smiling eyes I was destined to know and love so well. This was Francis Boggs, the director, who made me comfortable at once and put me at my ease.

The members of the company were Betty Hart, a sweet, brown-eyed little woman; big, golden-hearted Tom Santschi, the stunt man; Jimmy Crosby, the cameraman, who showed me the funny-looking black box that was to accomplish these miracles.

I think these were the original members of the small company sent out by Colonel William N. Selig, of the Selig Polyscope Company of Chicago, to tour a bit and pick up some "location stuff."

* * * *

The Sultan of Turkey at that time was occupying much front-page space. Mr. Boggs had stopped over to make a timely picture (something on the order of our present news reel, shall we say), had written a script over night called, "In the Sultan's Power," and engaged a special company to play the other parts.

2

That is how I came to play the lead in it. Stella Adams, a local actress, played the lady in the Sultan's power, and Frank Montgomery, who afterwards directed so long for the Bison Company and for Selig, was the heavy.

So far as I know, it was the first complete picture ever made in the southwest. Its interest to me was intense and remained so. It was a very, very small grain that started moving the overwhelmingly vast industry in Los Angeles today.

It was a strange, never-to-be-forgotten experience. I, who had spent so many years before audiences and had grown to look to them for all my inspiration as an actor, had to emote before a black box with the thick end of a beer bottle, as it looked, for the lens, and a careless chap who chewed gum, looked at everything but us, the actors, chiefly cocked his eye at the sun to see if there was apt to be any light change in the scene that would cause what we Selig actors called, "a make-over." That is what you will all recognize in your certain knowledge of much motion pictures slang as a "re-take."

I came afterwards to get all my inspiration from that same lens when I began to realize that it was recording my every movement for millions of eyes all over the world at the same time, such audiences as had never been played to before by any human being. Of course, to you youngsters with your knowledge of conditions, that thought means nothing, but to us in 1909, beginning to receive fan mail from India, China and South Africa, it was overwhelming!

You hear now of changes of camera angle, and close-ups, iris out and fade in, and screen tempo, ad infinitium [*sic*]. No such things in those days—no changes in camera angle, no close-ups, no careful rehearsal for days. We had to shoot a thousand feet inside of one day if we could, but positively inside of two. And it had to be done in full sunshine or the director was out of luck and the company could go where it listed.

We averaged twenty-five to thirty-five scenes, the footage of each could not exceed forty or fifty feet. All was hurried, make-shift, and in a measure confused. And I, accustomed to the traditions of the leisurely legitimate stage, where we rehearsed weeks and played the same piece for months, watched the development of this story, each little scene telling its part, with open-mouthed astonishment. The scenes were shot, not in rotation, but according to the location. You know about that today—it still stands for the sake of expediency, but we did finish with some scenes at the then unfinished Hotel Wentworth in Pasadena—and I got my check!

In the Sultan's Power *was released June 17, 1909. Hobart Bosworth went on to appear in dozens of films before establishing his own studio in 1913, where he directed and occasionally appeared in feature-length films based on the works of Jack London. Future greats who worked at Bosworth's studio include Lois Weber, Frances Marion, and the cinematographer/director George Hill. In 1916, with his health failing again, Bosworth merged his company with Paramount and returned to acting, eventually appearing in over 250 films, and working with such directors as Clarence Brown, King Vidor, John Ford, Ernst Lubitsch, Frank Capra, and Michael Curtiz. Bosworth died of pneumonia at the age of seventy-six on December 30, 1943, in Glendale, California.*

[1]Oliver Morosco was the adopted son of the San Francisco–based theatrical impresario Walter Morosco, who introduced Oliver to the art of theater management at a young age. Oliver moved to Los Angeles in 1899 and managed a series of theaters before building the opulent Morosco Theatre in 1913. While many of the actors who starred in his plays toured the country, Morosco founded his dramatic school with Bosworth to ensure he had quality local actors for his own shows, and their troupe became an important source of actors for the burgeoning film industry.

Mrs. D. W. Griffith (Linda Arvidson) 1910

L inda Arvidson was born in San Francisco in 1879. She had been acting *locally for over a year when she met an actor touring under the name of* *Lawrence Griffith. They appeared together in a play at the San Francisco Grand* *Opera House in 1905. She won his heart, not just with her good looks but because* *she listened to his poetry and took his dictation during his stay in the city. Griffith* *was back East when Arvidson wrote him in April of 1906 that she had lost every-* *thing in the Great San Francisco Earthquake. Griffith responded by wire, telling* *her to meet him in Boston. She jumped at the offer. They were married there* *on May 14, 1906, and settled in New York, where they both found acting work* *while he wrote in his spare time. He applied for jobs as a writer at several of the* *new film studios popping up in New York and New Jersey, but he was hired first* *as an actor in early 1908 before going to Biograph, where he quickly became its* *preeminent director. He shot over fifty short films in the last half of that year* *alone, making fifty dollars a week. Linda was acting at Biograph as well as other* *studios, and to avoid any conflicts, the couple kept their marriage secret from all* *but their closest friends. It wasn't until 1910, as they were preparing for their* *first trip to Los Angeles that they confessed their legal status to their bosses. That* *same year Griffith, when signing his new and improved contract with Biograph,* *felt he was successful enough to drop the "Lawrence" and use his real name,* *David Wark Griffith.*

After shivering through one Eastern winter, trying to get the necessary outdoor scenes for our pictures, we concluded that it would be to our advantage to pack up the wardrobe, the cameras, and other paraphernalia, get a little organization together, and with a portmanteau of Western scripts hie ourselves to the city of Los Angeles.

We weren't the first to go there. Selig already had a studio there. Frank

Boggs had brought a little company of Selig players to Los Angeles in the early days of 1908. The next company that reached the coast was that of the New York Motion Picture Patents Corporation, making the Bison brand of pictures. They had arrived in Los Angeles about Thanksgiving, 1909—seventeen players under the command of Fred Balshofer.

* * * *

News was already being broadcast that it was quite O.K. down at the Biograph if you got in right—that they were doing good things and were going to send a company to California for the winter, which would mean a regular salary for the time away.

Who was to go to California and who wasn't? Ah, that was the question! Some husbands didn't care to leave their wives, and as they couldn't afford to take them, they were out. Some didn't mind the separation. Some of the women had ties; if not husbands, mothers; and the California salary would not be big enough to keep up two homes. Some didn't want to leave New York; and some who should have known they didn't have a ghost of a chance wept sad and plentiful tears whenever the director looked their way. One of these was [actress and future screenwriter for Cecil B. DeMille] Jeanie Macpherson. Jeanie didn't go along this first time.

A few days after Christmas was the time of the first hegira to the land of the eucalyptus and the pepper tree. It was a big day.

We were going to Los Angeles to make moving pictures, and Hollywood didn't mean a thing. Pasadena the company knew about. Like Palm Beach, it was where millionaires sojourned for two months during the Eastern winter. San Gabriel Mission they'd seen photos of, and counted on using it in pictures. They understood there were many beaches accessible by trolley; and residential districts like West Adams; even Figueroa, the home of Los Angeles's first millionaires, was a fine avenue then; and Westlake and Eastlake Parks which were quite in town. But they didn't know Edendale from the Old Soldiers' Home at Sawtelle. San Pedro? Yes, that was where the steamers arrived from San Francisco. San Fernando? Well, yes, there was a Mission there too, but it was rather far away, and right in the heart of a parched and cactus-covered desert. Mt. Lowe was easy—there was the incline railway to help us to the top.

Four luxurious days on luxurious trains before we would sight the palms and poinsettias that were gaily beckoning to us across the distances.

The California Limited heads to Los Angeles. (Collection of Patt Morrison)

Hollywood Boulevard in the early teens. (Collection of Patt Morrison)

Let us away!

The company departed via the Black Diamond Express on the Lehigh Valley, which route meant ferry to Jersey City. A late arrival in Chicago allowed just comfortable time to make the *California Limited* leaving at 8 P.M.

The company was luxurious for but three days.

It was only Mr. R. H. Hammer [Griffith's secretary], my husband, and myself who had been allotted four full days of elegance. We *de luxe'd* out of New York via the Twentieth Century Limited. I had come into my own.

Mr. Powell was in charge of the company and so he checked them off on arrival at the ferry—Marion Leonard, Florence Barker, Mary Pickford, Dorothy West, Kate Bruce, the women; George Nichols, Henry Walthall, Billy Quirk, Frank Grandon, Charlie West, Mack Sennett, Dell Henderson, Arthur Johnson, Daddy Butler, Christie Miller, Tony O'Sullivan, and Alfred Paget, the men. There were three wives who were actresses also, Eleanor Hicks, Florence Lee (Mrs. Dell Henderson), and Mrs. George Nichols. And there were two camera men, Billy Bitzer and Arthur Marvin; a scenic artist, Eddie Shelter; a carpenter or two, and two property boys, Bobby Harron and Johnny Mahr.

No theatrical job had come along for Mary Pickford, and the few summer months she had intended spending in "the pictures" would lengthen into a full year now that she had decided to go with us to California. Her salary was still small: it was about forty dollars a week at this time.

* * * *

It was a pleasant trip, especially for those who had not been to California before. Some found card games so engrossing that they never took a peek at the scenery. Some, especially Mary and Dorothy West, oh'd and ah'd so that Arthur Johnson, thinking the enthusiasm a bit overdone, began kidding the scenery lovers. "Oh, lookit, lookit," Arthur would exclaim when the gushing was at its height.

The "Biograph Special" we were. We had rare service on the train. We had every attention from the dining-car steward. Had we not been allowed three dollars per day for meals on the train? And didn't we spend it? For the invigorating air breathed from the observation platform gave us healthy appetites.

At San Bernardino, we each received a dainty bouquet of pretty, fragrant carnations. Flowers for nothing! We could hardly believe our eyes.

At last we were there! Mr. Hammer gallantly suggested, although it was afternoon, that the women of the company go to a hotel at the Biograph's expense, until they located permanent quarters. So the ladies were registered at the Alexandria, then but lately opened, and shining and grand it was. Although they made but a short stay there, they attracted considerable attention. One day Mary Pickford stepped out of the Alexandria's elevator just as William Randolph Hearst was entering. Seeing Mary, he said, "I wonder who that pretty girl is." And one night at dinner, between sips of his ale, indicating our table which was but one removed from his, Mr. Hearst wondered some more as to who the people were.

The players were quite overcome at the company's hospitality. It was quite different from traveling with a theatrical road show where you had to pay for sleepers and meals, and where you might be dumped out at a railroad station at any hour of the cold gray dawn, with a Miners' Convention occupying every bed and couch in the town, and be left entirely to your own resources.

* * * *

On Grand Avenue and Washington Street, hardly ten minutes by trolley from Broadway and Fifth, and seven by motor from our hotel, mixed in with a lumber yard and a baseball park, was a nice vacant lot. It was surrounded by a board fence six feet or so in height, high enough to prevent passers-by from looking in on us. Just an ordinary dirt lot, it was. In the corners and along the fence-edges the coarse-bladed grass, the kind that grows only in California, had already sprouted, and otherwise it looked just like a small boy's happy baseball ground. It was selected for the studio.

A stage had to be rigged up where we could take "interiors," for while we intended doing most of our work "on location," there would have to be a place where we could lay a carpet and place pieces of furniture about for parlor, bedroom—but not bath. As yet modesty had deterred us from entering that sanctum of tiles, porcelain, cold cream, and rose-water jars. Mr. C. B. DeMille was as yet a bit away in the offing, and Milady's ablutions and Milord's Gillette were still matters of a private nature—to the movies.

A load of wood was ordered from our neighbor, and the carpenters set about to fix up a stage and some dressing-rooms: we couldn't dress and make up in our hotels, that was sure, nor could we do so in the open spaces of our "lot."

Our stage, erected in the center of the lot, was merely a wooden floor raised a few feet off the ground and about fifty feet square, of rough splintery wood, and when we "did" Western bar-rooms—*au naturel*—it was just the thing.

Two small adjoining dressing-rooms for the men soon came into being; then similar ones for the women. They looked like tiny bath-houses as they faced each other across the lot. They sufficed, however. There were no quarrels as to where the star should dress. When there were extras, they dressed in relays, and sometimes a tent was put up.

Telegraph poles ran alongside the studio and after our business became known in the neighborhood, and especially on days when we were portraying strenuous drama and got noisy, up these poles the small boys would clamber and have a big time watching the proceedings and throwing us friendly salutations which didn't always help along the "action."

A place had to be found where our camera men could develop the film and we could see the results of our work, for when a picture left Los Angeles it must be complete and ready for release, so down on Spring Street and Second, a loft was rented for a few dollars a month. It was a roomy, though dingy, barn of a place, but it served our purpose well. A tiny dark room was boarded off and fixed up for the developing, and a place set apart for the printing. The huge wheels on which the prints were dried stood boldly apart in the room. There was a little desk for cutting and splicing. At the head of the room furthest from the windows a screen was set, and a sort of low partition about midway the length of the lot hemmed in the projection room.

When things had settled into a routine, and on rainy days, we rehearsed and worked out scenarios up in our loft. We also had the costumes delivered there. The loft was always accessible, and we spent many evenings seeing projections and getting our things together for an early morning start.

Across the street from the loft was a famous old eating place, Hoffman's, where my husband and I dined when we returned late or too weary to dress for the more pretentious hotel dining-room. It was a bit expensive for some of the company, but convenient to our headquarters was one of those market places, indigenous to Los Angeles, where violets and hams commingled on neighborly counters, that served good and inexpensive food on a long white enameled table where guests sat only on one side on high, spindly stools. It was patronized generously by the actors for breakfast and lunch, when we were working in the downtown studio. Here Mary Pickford and brother Jack and Dorothy West were regular patrons.

While the studio was being put in shape, the members of the company had been scooting about looking for suitable places to live. Salaries were not so large, but that economy had to be practiced, even with the fourteen dollars a week expense money allowed every member of the company.

Mary Pickford had brother Jack to look after, and she decided that if she clubbed in with some of the girls and they all found a place together it would be cheaper, and also not so lonely for her. So Mary, with Jack and two of the young girls—Dorothy West and Effie Johnson—thirty-dollar-a-weekers, found shelter in a rooming house called "The Lille." It was on South Olive and Fifth Streets, and the four had rooms here for three and a half per week per person.

* * * *

The men of the company were all devoted to little Jack. He would sit around nights watching them play poker, sometimes until 3 A.M.; he didn't want to be forever at the movies with his big sister. Mary allowed Jack fifty cents a night for his dinner; he'd connect up somewhere or other with his pals, and they would make a night of it.

We were to be no proud owners of an automobile, but rented one by the hour at four dollars for car and chauffeur. The director and his camera man and persons playing leads would travel by motor to location while the others would trolley. As Los Angeles had, even then, the most wonderful system of trolleys in the world, there were few places, no matter how remote, that could not be reached by electric car.

Sunday came to be a big day for the automobile, for on that day we scouted for the week's locations—that is, after David had made out his weekly expenses, his Sunday morning job.

Here is a sample, recorded in almost illegible pen-and-ink longhand:

Luncheon (30 actors)—$7.50
Carfare (30 actors, location both ways)—$15.00
Automobile (so many hours $4. per)—$100.00

Locations (gratuities for using people's places)—$20.00
Incidentals—$17.00
Extras (not actors, not incidentals either)—$11.00

Those sufficiently interested may add.

We would not have been true to the traditions of the Golden State had we not used a Mission in our first picture. We meant to do our very best right off and send back a knock-out.

So to San Gabriel we went to get the lovely old Mission atmosphere in a picture called *Threads of Destiny.*

We spread ourselves; we took the Mission front, back and sideways, inside and out; we used the worn old stairway, shaded by a fragrant pepper tree, that led to the choir loft: we even planted lilies—or rather, Mary Pickford as Myrtle, the orphan girl of San Gabriel, planted lilies—along the adobe wall of the old cemetery where slept baptized Indians and Mexicans.

It was pleasant sprawling about in the lazy sunshine. We who were "atmosphere" wandered about the cemetery, reading the old tombstones, and had the priest guide us through the Mission showing us its three-hundred-year-old treasures. And across the way we visited the curio shop where we bought pretty post-cards and ate tamales, real Mexican tamales.

We would experiment on this Mission picture. We wanted a dim, religious light, and here it was, and we wanted to get it on the screen as it looked to us, the real thing. One little window let in an afternoon slant of soft sunshine that fell directly upon the pulpit where Christie Miller, playing an old priest, was to stand and bless the congregation. If we could light up Christie, the devout worshipers could be mere shadows and it would look fine—just what we wanted. Billy Bitzer would "get" it if it could be got, that we knew. So while Billy was tuning up his camera, Bobby Harron came and gathered in the congregation from the curio shop and cemetery, and we quietly took our places in the chapel and did our atmospheric bit. We did pray—we prayed that it would be a good effect.

We rather held our breath at the picture's first showing until his tricky scene was flashed on the screen. Then we relaxed; it was all there!

Spanish California was not to be neglected this trip, and our next picture, a romance of the Spanish dominion, called *In Old California* is historical as the first Biograph to be taken in Hollywood. The Hollywood Inn was at this time the only exclusive winter resort between the city and the ocean. We needed rooms where we could make up and dress, and Mr. Anderson, the genial young proprietor, welcomed us cordially.

As we came out of the hotel in our make up and Spanish finery and quietly drove off into the foothills, guests were lolling on the broad front porch. With a start they came to. Whatever in the world was happening! "Did you see those people? What is it? What's going on? Let's get our motor and follow them and see," said they.

We had selected what we thought a remote and secluded spot in the foothills, but soon in ones and twos and threes the guests appeared. For a time they seemed well-behaved spectators; they kept quiet and in the background. But Miss Leonard's dramatic scenes proved too much for them. They resented the love-making and began making derogatory comments about movie actors, and one "lady" becoming particularly incensed, shouted loudly, "Well, I wouldn't dress up like a fool like that woman and act like her, no, not for all the money in the world." That off her chest, she turned on her heel, and left us flat.

Paul de Longpré, the famous flower artist, lived only a few blocks from the Inn on Hollywood Boulevard. Many years ago he had left his native France and built a lovely chateau in the broad stretches of young Hollywood. In his gardens he had planted every variety of rose. A tangled profusion of them covered even the walls of his house. We offered fifty dollars a day for the use of the gardens. M. de Longpré went us one better. He offered to let us work if we'd buy a corner lot for three hundred dollars. But what could we do with a corner lot? We had no idea we would work six days and pay the three hundred dollars just in rental. But that we did. What we didn't do was take title to the corner lot. Had we done so we would have laid a foundation for fortune.

I recall M. de Longpré as the first person we met on location in California who seemed to appreciate that we were at least striving for something in an art line. To him we were not mere buffoons as we were to the ladies of the Hollywood Inn.

The Griffiths returned to California with the Biograph troupe for the winter of 1911, but by then D.W.'s womanizing was taking its toll on Linda. While one of Griffith's biographers, Richard Schickel, calls Linda "intelligent and certainly strong-minded," one of the actresses in the company, *Blanche Sweet*, remembered Linda as being "very quiet" and not joining in the studio life. By this time, Griffith was making three thousand dollars a month and had become used to his role as ultimate authority figure. When Linda, who had appeared in over one hundred Biograph films, found a love letter to her husband from another actress, he not only admitted the affair but wrote Linda a note saying "there were others before her and there are sure to be others…"

With that ammunition, Linda wrested a separation agreement, signed on December 28, 1916, that gave her fifteen percent of Griffith's income, but not less than four hundred dollars a month. Unfortunately for all concerned, getting that fifteen percent became Linda's raison d'être for the rest of her life. In her memoir, written in 1925, she gave little hint that she and Griffith were estranged and authored the book under the name of Mrs. D. W. Griffith. The couple finally divorced in 1936, and later that year Griffith married twenty-seven-year-old Evelyn Baldwin.

D. W. Griffith died in Los Angeles at the age of seventy-three on July 23, 1948, only months after divorcing Evelyn. His estate was valued at under fifty thousand dollars, and neither of his former wives was listed in his will. Linda passed away the following year in New York City, on July 26, 1949, at the age of seventy.

Mary Pickford 1910

G ladys Smith was born in Toronto, Canada, on April 8, 1892. Her father died when she was very young, and by the time she was eight, "Little Gladys" was a stage actress and the primary breadwinner for her mother and younger siblings, Lottie and Jack. Gladys taught herself to read during train rides with touring companies and found Broadway success at fifteen in The Warrens of Virginia, written by William de Mille and produced by David Belasco. It was Belasco who decided Gladys needed a new name, and once she had become Mary Pickford, the rest of her family, already so dependent on her and confident of her success, adopted Pickford as well. Theaters closed in the summer then because there was no air conditioning, and the family needed to be supported year-round, so in 1909, Mary Pickford found her way to Biograph Studios, located in a brownstone at 11 East 14th Street in New York City, and was hired by D. W. Griffith at ten dollars a week. She had been at Biograph for a few months when she made her first trip to California.

Our film caravan arrived like a band of hardy pioneers in the thinly populated village of Los Angeles with its eucalyptus palms and heady orange blossoms.

Our studio consisted of an acre of ground, fenced in, and a large wooden platform, hung with cotton shades that were pulled on wires overhead. On a windy day, our clothes and curtains on the set would flap loudly in the breeze. Studios were all on open lots—roofless and without walls, which explains the origin of the term "on the lot." Dressing rooms being a non-existent luxury, we donned our costumes every morning at the hotel. Our rehearsal room was improvised from a loft which Mr. Griffith rented in a decrepit old building on Main Street. A kitchen table and three chairs were all there was of furniture. Mr. Griffith occupied one of the chairs, the others being reserved for the elderly members of the cast. The rest of us sat on the floor. Surveying his squatters one day, Mr. Griffith announced he needed a split or half reel.

"Anybody got a story in mind?" he asked.

Three or four of us dashed for paper and pencil and were soon scribbling like mad. During my first weeks at Biograph I had quite unashamedly sold Mr. Griffith an outline of the opera *Thais* for $10. This time I ventured a plot of my own, and to the great annoyance of the men he bought it. It was called "May and December," and I received a check for fifteen dollars. When Mr. Griffith, shortly after that, rejected a thousand-foot story and a split-reel comedy of mine, Jack and I rented horses and went out to see Mr. Spoor of Essanay.[1] Mr. Spoor gave me a check for forty dollars for the two stories. My greatest competition in this literary sideline was Mack Sennett, who used to claim, teasingly, that my scripts were sold "on the length of my blond curls."

"Let me put your name on my stories," he offered, "and for every one we sell I'll give you five dollars commission on the split reels and eight dollars on the features."

"That's a deal," I said, "but on one condition—I'll have to read and approve of the stories before lending my name to them."

Mack Sennett agreed. A few days later he brought me a story which I heartily disliked. It was overrun with policemen engaged in grossly undignified behavior.

"If you want me to put my name to that story," I said, "you'll have to change all those policemen into private detectives. Their behavior is scandalous!"

He refused indignantly, and that was the end of our collaboration, and the beginning, of course, of the Keystone Cop series.

What with my growing outside earnings Jack and I were soon nursing visions of fabulous wealth. My salary remained forty dollars a week, augmented by a liberal stipend of fourteen dollars for expenses. And it wasn't very long before Jack was working six days a week too, at the standard pay of five dollars a day. The poor little fellow had to fall off horses and out of windows as a double for all the young girls in the company. By spring we had accumulated the unbelievable hoard of $1200. I suddenly could not wait to get back East to see Mother and surprise her with our savings.

In April, 1910, Jack and I arrived in New York only to find that Mother and Lottie had not returned yet from an engagement on the road in *Custer's Last Stand*. I promptly went to the cashier of the Biograph Company and asked her to change my hoard into twenty-four new, crisp fifty-dollar bills. Jack and I then bought Mother a handsome black handbag into which we tucked the bills. The moment Mother stepped into the house we presented her with the bag. She was delighted, but it was agony for us to wait till she opened it. Instead of the astonishment we expected when she looked inside all we saw was a pleasant smile.

"Oh, stage money," she said simply.

Mary Pickford in *Ramona*, one of the dozens of short films she made in Southern California. (Courtesy of AMPAS)

Mother had never seen a real fifty-dollar bill in her life, and neither had the rest of us. When Jack and I assured her that this was the real business, she counted the bills in a voice of mounting excitement. No sooner had she finished than that rascally brother of mine pounced on them and began throwing them in the air. Mother started chasing Jack around the room, and Lottie and I joined in the pursuit, till we got all the bills away from him. That was the beginning of affluence for the Pickford family.

Mary Pickford left Biograph in 1912, married fellow actor Owen Moore, and began jumping between studios, increasing her salary substantially with each move. By late 1914, her marriage was already unraveling, but she was making one thousand dollars a week with Adolph Zukor and Jesse Lasky's Famous Players. After playing waifs, Indians, and young wives, Pickford became "America's Sweetheart" with films such as Poor Little Rich Girl, The Little Princess, *and* Rebecca of Sunnybrook Farm, *in roles written for the screen by her best friend, Frances Marion. In 1919, Pickford joined her soon-to-be husband Douglas Fairbanks, Charlie Chaplin, and D. W. Griffith in forming their own company, United Artists. With their marriage in 1920, she and Fairbanks became Hollywood royalty, ruling from their Beverly Hills home, Pickfair. Pickford was a pioneering actress, producer, studio owner, and philanthropist, as well as a founder of the Academy of Motion Picture Arts and Sciences. She won an Academy Award for her first talkie,* Coquette, *in 1930 and was awarded an Honorary Oscar for "her unique contributions to the film industry" in 1976. She died in Los Angeles on May 29, 1979, at the age of eighty-seven.*

[1]George K. Spoor and Gilbert M. Anderson (better known as Broncho Billy Anderson) formed their Essanay (S and A) film company in 1907. Their home studio was in Chicago, but they, like Biograph, traveled west during the winter in search of sun.

Frances Marion 1912

Marion Benson Owens was born on November 18, 1888, in San Francisco. Her parents were listed in San Francisco society's Blue Book, and the likes of Enrico Caruso and Jack London visited their home. Marion went to public and private schools before enrolling in the Mark Hopkins Art Institute at sixteen. In 1906, the Great Earthquake destroyed much of San Francisco, including the Art Institute and her father's buildings and businesses. Within months, Marion married her art instructor Wesley de Lappe and tried jobs such as peach pitter and telephone operator, before becoming a model and assistant to photographer Arnold Genthe. She also worked as a commercial artist and a reporter for the San Francisco Chronicle. However, the life of two struggling artists soon lost its appeal, and the couple divorced in 1910. Marion then married Robert Pike, the son of a wealthy steel baron. When Robert was sent to Los Angeles to establish a branch of his father's firm, Marion accompanied him. The Pikes' marriage dissolved quickly after their move south.

When I was twenty-one, and a fairly successful commercial artist, I made this notation: "Leave tomorrow for Los Angeles to do Oliver Morosco's theatrical posters. I shall refrain from mentioning to our southern neighbors that San Franciscans look upon the City of the Queen of the Angels as California's floating kidney transplanted from the Middle West."

The approach to Los Angeles was impressive. Hundreds of acres abounded with orange and lemon groves, many originally planted by the Spaniards whose vast holdings had been deeded to them by the King of Spain, and who ruled there until the Americanos came along and unceremoniously said, "This land is ours, and out you go!" And out they went, leaving the heady scent of citrus blossoms to remind us of their parting.

After you left the squat dingy railroad station there was little of interest to be seen beyond the old Spanish Mission on the Plaza and a few adobe houses marked by oleander trees and overshadowed by giraffe-like palms. Obviously the city had sprung up helter-skelter without any pattern, for there was more evidence of haste than taste. True, San Francisco was not famed for its architecture, but it was set like a glittering crown on its fog-mantled hills, and here nothing seemed to glitter except the dust motes in the brazen sunlight. It wasn't ten o'clock in the morning and I was already sizzling with the heat. However, before reporting to Mr. Morosco, I decided to find an apartment which I could convert into a studio of sorts. There were vacancies galore but tacked over many of the rental signs was this ominous edict: "No Jews, actors, or dogs allowed." My blood boiled! I had come from a cosmopolitan city where Jews were revered for their contribution to the arts, science and industry. Where actors were welcome as holidays. Where we gaily quoted "Every good little dog deserves a boy." Irately I scratched in my diary, "What a provincial town this is! I'll finish my job in a hurry, clear out of here, and never come back again!"

* * * *

I learned from Mr. Morosco that the barring of actors from the apartment houses referred only to performers in the movies. "Flickers," he called them. "Those locusts are swarming into Los Angeles, building ramshackle studios from the beach to the mountains. Literally, thousands are trekking west and this is resented by large groups of people, mostly churchgoers, who are forming committees to keep these ragtags and bobtails off the streets and out of our parks. These damn flicker outfits have even built more nickelodeons! Which are filled to the rafters," he added ruefully, as if he sensed danger ahead to the theatre owners.

How instinctively one turns toward the underdog. Weeks later, when I read in an editorial that a committee yclept The Conscientious Citizens had over ten thousand signatures on a protest to force the invaders out of Los Angeles, I immediately dubbed them The Constipated Citizens and hoped the civil war would end in triumph for the movie-makers. How could anyone resent the lively fun they had brought into this dull environment? You encountered their gypsy-like caravans wherever you went. Indians in full war paint rode hell-bent for leather across the dusty riverbeds. Mack Sennett's cops leapt aboard the cable car that climbed a midget hill known as Angel's Flight. Even the little parks became outdoor stages.

Frances Marion as an actress for Lois Weber. (Courtesy of
Cari Beauchamp)

During the noon hour you were apt to see Bluebeard and all his wives
cozily eating ham sandwiches and hard-boiled eggs, while the Apostle
John sat under a pepper tree with his arm around a bathing beauty.

* * * *

Before the year ended, Los Angeles was beginning to reap a considerable
harvest; the interlopers had to be fed, clothed, and housed. Cafés, shops
and beach resorts were prospering. Wily landlords removed those obnox-
ious signs and doubled their rents. The Constipated Citizens had hit the
dust.

An ornate nickelodeon opened and we trooped into it to watch the figures on the screen, silent as ghosts, with their moods interpreted by amateur pianists who played "Hearts and Flowers" when heroines wept, "The Anvil Chorus" when all hell broke loose in some hysterical melodrama. We roared with laughter at the subtitles interspersed on the film to point out the passage of time or to explain the action: "Came the dawn, treading like a modest maiden"..."Tell me the truth, Mother, I beseech you. Is Reginald Macintosh really my father?" Yet there were some films we didn't ridicule and these bore the stamp of A. B. [Biograph] and were directed by a man named David Wark Griffith. A great many featured a young girl with long curls whom we called Goldilocks. She stood apart from the others and supplied a sense of reality even to weak stories, carrying the rest of the cast with her.

Were the movies a passing fad or here to stay? I asked the opinion of my closest friend, Adela Rogers St. Johns, a bride just out of her teens and already making her mark as a newspaper reporter. Her decisive answer came like the silencing thud of a judge's gavel. "They are here to stay."...

Frances Marion and Mary Pickford at work on a script. (Courtesy of MOMA)

Our group consisted of a wide selection of characters, all earnest career seekers, over whom Adela presided protectively like a lioness over her cubs.

There was Sessue Hayakawa, a Japanese interpretive dancer, who had come to America with high hopes for success and had sown his seed upon alien soil. Engaged to him was Tsuru Aoki, an exquisite Japanese girl whom I had known since my boarding school days, and whose father was Japan's foremost painter. Adela had taken them under her wing, and when she heard that a *Madame Butterfly* type of picture was to be made at the Thomas Ince studio she set up an appointment for Sessue and Tsuru. Both were given roles, which were their first steps up the ladder of fame.

One of the most puzzling members of our group was Erich von Stroheim who had come to California because he heard there was a future in the movies for a man of his appearance and education. He wore a monocle and tight girdle, affected the goosestep, bragged about his social position, his fortune tied up in Austria, and lived meagerly off what he could borrow from the rest of us. His preposterous stories entertained us, though we didn't think he had a chance to succeed as an actor in the movies; the average leading men bordered on what one might call pretty, their faces covered with a light pinkish makeup, their mouths a Cupid's bow.

* * * *

My chance to escape from Los Angeles came unexpectedly: the cost of lithographs had tripled and Mr. Morosco decided against the expense of reproducing posters. Did I sing "Home Sweet Home"? I did not! I accepted a job with an advertising firm. The truth was, I had no intention of leaving; the movie bug had stung me. Grandchild of four pioneers, I sensed a future in this fascinating if cock-eyed business. But how to get into a studio when you weren't an actress was my puzzler until I met Owen Moore at a New Year's Eve party. He had seen several of my posters and was confident that his wife, Mary Pickford, would like to have me make one of her. In fact, he would arrange to have us meet.

On the day of my interview with Mary Pickford, as I came out of the apartment house, a violent wind, which the natives call a Santa Ana, was blowing a gale of dust from across the desert into the city. Seeing those tall palms nodding recklessly to each other, I realized how impossible it would be to carry my large portfolio filled with sketches unless I wanted to look like a hen in a cyclone. So I left the samples of my work, which were the excuse for the interview, and sallied forth.

The studio was a series of nondescript barns and sheds, yet when the man in charge opened the gate you felt as if you had looked through an opaque rock candy Easter egg into a multicolored vista beyond. This impression was due to the skeletons of various buildings which served as backgrounds for scenes, the bustle and excitement of actors in polychromatic costumes, their brightly painted faces making them perfect examples of the undertaker's art.

"We're shooting three pictures here today," said the office boy who was escorting me to Miss Pickford. "Guess all this is new to you, you look like an outsider." My sullen nod admitted it; I hated being a stranger in this fascinating world. "Miss Pickford ain't in her dressing room," he rambled on. "She's splicing some film in the cutting room. Guess that stumps you outsiders," he added with the smugness of Knowledge speaking to Ignorance. "There's the cutting room straight ahead. Just knock on the door."

"Come in! I've been expecting you," said a firm, clear voice, and in a deeper tone than one would associate with the childlike image Miss Pickford presented on the screen.

The door opened and she stood before me, dressed in a simple frock, with a large towel turban on her head; obviously she had just washed her long curls and rolled them on rags. Shorter than my five feet two, and not many years younger, she seemed such a little girl that I felt more like putting my arms around her than shaking hands formally. "You're Frances," she said, extending her hand. "Hello."

"Hello, Mary." I stood there, holding her slender little hand in mine, all the charming compliments I had prepared fleeting before the frank appraisal in her eyes. And as she looked at me, I became aware that a strange watchfulness lay behind her steadfast gaze, a penetrating analysis which enabled her to see past the outward shell and read your character as clearly as if it were etched upon a stone tablet.

"I think we're going to be friends," Mary said, breaking the long silence that had fallen on us.

"Thank you, Mary," I mumbled, feeling exactly as if I'd just had my brain X-rayed.

To bridge my self-consciousness, she held a ribbon of film to the light and explained how scenes had to be cut when they ran over-length, how close-ups were spliced in, and that it was Mr. Griffith who had conceived the idea of moving a camera close to the actors' faces so the public would get to know them intimately instead of their remaining tiny figures, such as one sees on a stage from the top gallery.

We skirted lightly over many subjects, then Mary said, "Owen tells me that you're an artist."

Here was the open door I had been waiting for, but I guess salesmen are born, they don't spring into being overnight. "Yes, I am—after a fashion."

"It must be a lot of fun to paint."

"A lot of hard work."

"What isn't hard work if you want to succeed? I get up at the crack of dawn. All day we're out in the hot sun and working under the most trying conditions. It's not easy to thrust your own personality into the background and play another character, often foreign to your own. As we rush from one role to another, I scarcely have time between pictures to become Mary Pickford again." Into her eyes came a wistful expression which revealed the sadness that had already scarred this young life. "When I was a child I used to retreat into a dream world and hide from reality. Unfortunately, as we grow older we learn that there is no escape."

We were interrupted by a photographer who had some proofs to show her. Because it was such a small room, she excused herself and stepped outside. The door was slightly ajar and I overheard her say, "Destroy this one of Mr. Moore and me, it's too intimate a pose. For publicity we use only the stills of ourselves taken on a set when we're in a picture together."

"Yes, Miss Pickford."

Miss Pickford. It occurred to me then that in all the articles I had read about her she was never referred to as Mrs. Moore. In fact, I couldn't recall even in interviews where she or the interviewer had ever alluded to her love affair with Owen Moore or her marriage. Was it because there was little congeniality in their relationship? Was he jealous that her star was shining brighter than his? Or were the studio heads determined to keep America's Sweetheart forever a young girl? Would she seem less desirable, less virginal, if visualized in the arms of a man? What a nutty business, I thought. But that's what made it so provocative.

When she came back into the cutting room I rose. "Mary I'm sorry I interrupted your work, and I mustn't keep you any longer, you've been very kind to—"

"But I really enjoyed our visit. Working since I was five years old, I haven't had time to make new friends. There's a kinship between us, so please come to see me again when I return to California, I'm sure before the year is out."

As I took her outstretched hand in mine, and once more held in that moment of silence by her truth-searching gaze, I can't explain what suddenly moved me but my eyes filled with tears. I hurried out of the cutting room for fear she might notice them. Still, I could not be sure whether I had succeeded; as I glanced back, she was standing in the doorway waving to me. Lordy, I've made a fool of myself, I thought; she must think I'm a sentimental ass.

* * * *

For months I had felt the twinge of personal interest in the picture business, but now, fired by Mary's description of her hard though rewarding work, my interest had kindled, and the longing to become enmeshed in that life kept stirring my roots. How could I achieve this? What could I do? I had muffed my chance with Miss Pickford. If only she had seen some of my portraits ...

One morning, after Adela had congratulated me for having been made head of the art department in the advertising firm, I confessed my nagging desire to get into the movies. "You're off your trolley! You always have been! But that's your charm!" She reached for the telephone. "Now you have named your poison—I'll send you to an old friend of mine, Lois Weber, the only woman director in the picture business. She will give you some darn good advice, which you probably won't take. Anyway, happy hunting!"

Two days later I was ushered into Lois Weber's office by her secretary. Through the window we could see the stage where a scene was in full swing. About forty costumed actors were milling about, the women shaking their fists, the men brandishing axes and swords, all roaring in a deafening chorus. "They're storming the palace of Versailles," explained the secretary, calling my attention to the painted backdrop which bore little resemblance to the photographs I had seen of the royal palace. "When the whistle blows, the mob scene will be over and our gracious lady will be here to greet you." She stressed the "lady" with such fervent ardor that I wondered if I would be expected to genuflect when I met Miss Weber.

Finally the whistle blew, the mob dispersed, and the director left the set. "Sit down, my dear," Miss Weber said, when taut nerves made me rise stiffly as she entered the room. "I'm very happy you came to see me. I'm sure Mrs. St. Johns told you why I was interested in you. One of the most fascinating sidelights in the art of making motion pictures is the search for new talent. Some directors demand previous experience in the young people they sign, but I believe in taking amateurs and teaching them all I have learned during my years in the theatre. In this way, I can build their acting careers toward ultimate success." She was smiling warmly. "I have a broad wing, would you like to come under its protection and—"

"Miss Weber," I interrupted, "I seem to be here under false pretenses. I'm not an actress. I haven't the slightest desire to become one. But I do want to get into the picture business. Frankly, I can't understand why I have such a fierce urge when I really have so little to offer to it. All I can do is paint. I'm a fair artist. That might help with the sets and costumes. My newspaper experience didn't spark but I've sold quite a few magazine stories. Perhaps your press department might be interested in seeing what I can whip up along the publicity line. But I could never learn to act, even if Svengali hypnotized me, I'm too—"

Her laughter silenced me. "You're doing a fair piece of acting right now. My dear, if you don't want to work before the camera until you know your way around the studio and are acquainted with everyone, I'll find plenty for you to do."

By this time I was so dizzy there were half a dozen Lois Webers floating around the room. Two hours later I signed a contract. The only fly in the ointment came when she remarked, "How ambitious you are for such a young girl."

"But I'm not a young girl. I'll be twenty-four in November. I've been married and divorced."

"Goodness!" I thought it was a gasp of disapproval at my rejected wedding ring until she added, "Twenty-four! You don't look that old. I thought you were still in your teens." Her hand patted mine. "Soon as you come to work here never mention your age. In spite of your protests, we might shape your destiny and turn you into an actress. An actress never tells her real age."

Thus I entered the Bosworth studio as: Frances Marion. Actress. Refined Type. Age 19.

Lois Weber had changed Marion Owens's name, but Frances Marion's passion remained writing, and she found success adapting some of Mary Pickford's greatest hits, including Poor Little Rich Girl, The Little Princess, Pollyanna, *and* Rebecca of Sunnybrook Farm. *Marion wrote and directed* The Love Light, *starring Pickford and the love of Marion's life, her third husband, the preacher turned actor Fred Thomson. She wrote films for Marion Davies, Norma Talmadge, and Jean Harlow, and by 1928 had been Hollywood's highest-paid screenwriter for over a decade. That same year, Fred Thomson was second in popularity only to Tom Mix (Pickford's husband, Douglas Fairbanks, was number eight), but Thomson died of tetanus that December, leaving Marion with two young sons to raise. She went on to become the only woman ever to win two Academy Awards for original screenwriting:* The Champ *in 1930 and* The Big House *in 1931. She was a founder of the Writers Guild, served as its first vice president, and in addition to screenwriting, wrote several novels, a textbook on film writing, a collection of short stories, and her autobiography. Marion, who stayed lifelong friends with Pickford, Adela Rogers St. Johns, Anita Loos, and Lillian Gish, was also an accomplished pianist, painter, and sculptor. She died in Los Angeles on May 12, 1973, at the age of eighty-four.*

Henry King 1913

enry King, whose Irish ancestors had come to America in the 1680s, was born on January 24, 1886, in Christiansburg, Virginia. Leaving school at fifteen, he worked on the railroads for several years before joining the Empire Stock Company as an actor. He traveled the country with them and was happy on the stage, but a chance encounter changed all that.

After *The Minister's Daughter* closed I went to Michigan to join the company of [the play] *Common Law*, which eventually returned me to New York. One night I was having dinner at the Bathalday Inn, a very famous old theatrical hotel, with Helene Hamilton, the daughter of Mr. Osmond, owner of the Osmond Stock Company, and Pearl White. Miss Hamilton was going over to the Putnam Building, diagonally across Times Square, to see a man about a motion picture engagement. I had never seen a motion picture so I went over with her and stood in the hall while she had her meeting.

After a while, the door opened and she and a man came out. She introduced him as Wilbert Melville. He was an independent producer who sold films to various companies, usually to the Lubin Film Manufacturing Company. When he learned I was an actor, he asked, "Why don't you go into motion pictures?"

I said, "Oh, no, I have blue eyes. They tell me they won't photograph."

"Oh," Melville said, "we overcame that a long time ago." I went to his hotel the next day to talk it over. By the end of that conversation I signed up with him and agreed to come to California.

I had been discussing acting in *Top o' the Morning* with Henry W. Savage but decided to take a chance on the movies. I always felt that I could never afford not to work. I was trying to get all the experience I could and also make a living. I was always looking for a job. And I will say this: in all my years in the business I've never been out of a job two weeks, because I was always looking. I never went on the basis of "How much can I get?" but of "When can I start?" I would come in from a road show at $75 a week and made no bones about going directly into a stock company for $25 a week. I needed experience.

I got plenty of experience, good and bad. At Lubin, they didn't shoot pictures in sequence, they shot scenes as they came to the location. Generally, the screenplays were written so that one page equaled one scene. An average screenplay was on four or five sheets of paper, sometimes as many as ten.

When we were filming *The Mate of the Schooner Sadie* (1913), we worked in San Pedro for two or three days on the deck of one of those big two-mast schooners that hauled lumber. We were waiting for the schooner to sail so that we could shoot a sequence at sea and they said, "The ship is going to sail at two o'clock tomorrow." The next day we arrived there at about ten a.m. and no ship. They said, "Why, the ship sailed at two this morning!"

We took a speedboat and skirted out after them. We caught the schooner about fifty miles from shore. It was between Catalina and the other islands, on its way to Yokohama or someplace. We needed the ship for a fight sequence that we hadn't finished. I was to break away and run out to the spar, fighting this group off. At the end, my feet slip out from under me and I go off the bow and drown.

We expected to do this scene just outside the breakwater rather than fifty miles from shore. But I did it. I was a good swimmer so I went out on the spar, my feet slipped out from under me and I turned and went into a dive into the water. I did a shallow dive and when I came up, I'll tell you, the ship looked as tall as a fifty story building coming right over me....I swam as hard as I could and as the ship started to pass me, it started drawing me into it. I would kick it with my feet and dive and come up away from it and I'd be drawn back and have to kick away again. I did that four or five times. Then an actor named Henry Stanley, who knew something about ships, grabbed onto one of those doughnut-shaped life preservers and threw it to me and I grabbed it. The life preserver had a line on it and Stanley took that line and made fast on the rail. I was so exhausted now from swimming with my clothes on that I hooked my hands through the

Actor Henry King became a legendary director. (Courtesy of MOMA)

life preserver and just held on. The Captain ran aft and threw a big two-inch hauser-line over the stern and told me to hold onto that until he could get a boat down to pick me up. ...

I was with Lubin's West Coast company in Los Angeles for about three months, acting in three-reel pictures. After working so hard in the theater, I found movies kind of rough going. You might work from nine to eleven on Monday morning, then not again until Tuesday noon. I couldn't stand it. It was getting on my nerves, so I had a table brought into my dressing room, and started writing, just to keep myself occupied. I would write screenplays, which was easy since I had played in all those repertory shows and I knew thirty or forty plays—I could take a little of this and a little of that and I could get a pretty good story out of it. I had learned the form of script writing from reading the ones we were using and thought, "Heavens, I can do better than that!" I would take an old play, take one section out of it and turn it into a three-reel picture.

* * * *

Soon, I got a chance to direct. In 1914, a very popular picture called *The Spoilers* came out. In it, Tom Santschi and William Farnum had a ferocious fight and, after that, it seemed as though every picture had to try and equal or out-do that fight. I was working on a picture with Bert Bracken that called for a fight scene. I told Bracken, "For heaven's sake, please let's not do another one of those *Spoilers* fights like Bill Farnum. I've seen that same fight in half a dozen pictures."

"What other kind of a fight is there?" Bert asked.

I said, "Well, let's do something that will be as original for us as that was for them. I don't work today and you're going on location. Suppose I sit down and write out a fight scene for you. I think I know what I'm doing and I'll work it out for you if that's agreeable to you."

"That's fine," Bert said. "You write it out and we'll do it, if it's any good."

When I was about eight years old, in Elliston, Virginia, just about three miles from Lafayette, I saw the man who took care of the baggage at the train station get into a terrible fight with another colored man. They fought as no one had ever fought before. I didn't know what they were fighting about, but it was brutal. They fought right up to unconsciousness. That fight left a very vivid impression in my mind. It had stayed with me. I could picture all the details, watching this fight in my mind, and that's what I based our fight in the picture on. I wrote it out just as I remembered it, even to the degree of having one man pick up a stone and beat the other on the head with it, so that the stone ended up covered in blood.

I wanted close-ups of a stone and a hand coming in trying to get hold of it. And when the stone struck flesh, I wanted the blood to spurt all over it.

When Bert got back from location, I showed them this scene I had written. Bert said, "How in the world did you do this? This is just a jumble of scenes. I have no idea what to do with the thing." I got down and showed him how the players would go about it, what the cameras would do. I directed the first part of the fight, then the next scene and the next. Finally, Bert just sat back and I directed the whole thing—and acted in it, too.

I put the camera in close for a close-up of these fingers, the hand and the stone, the hand trying to get hold of the stone—all in great big close-up— the blood spurting. Finally, I finished the fight scene—the first thing I'd ever directed other than those pick-ups I had done for Melville at Lubin.

I sent the film to a laboratory. The next day the cutter who was the sister of the man who ran the laboratory [cameraman Joseph Brotherton] came to Bert and said, "I have a lot of scenes over here, some of them a foot long, some two feet long, and I haven't any idea what to do with it." Bert Bracken looked at me as if to say, "There you are."

I said, "I know exactly what to do with it." I went over to the cutting room and sat down with her and said, "You put this here and this here," and I went all the way through it until she had it all assembled. She said, "You have scenes here not a foot long; some of them are only eight or nine frames."

"Well, maybe they should be less than that," I replied.

She shook her head. "How are you going to see a scene that's less than three feet?" she asked. "It has to be at least three feet before you can see it."

"Is that a rule?" I said. "If it is, we'll change it." The girl and I took the film into the projection room and ran it. I never saw anyone so excited in my life. She thought it was terrific. She said, "I've never seen anything like this in film before!"

I said, "Come on, let's go back to the cutting room."

"Oh, no," she said. "I wouldn't touch one frame of it for anything in the world."

"Now let's don't be silly," I said. "We've got a couple of things that are a little too long. We can cut a few frames. See where this piece comes down and it touches there? When you cut that, it's going to give it that little jab. You're going to see the speed, the force of it." I made a couple of little changes like that. Well, when the Horkheimers saw it, they thought it was exciting. Then I sent for Bert Bracken and I asked him to look at it. He did and told me, "Boy, this is something! I never dreamed it would come out like that." That's what made them decide that I could direct. I was getting $75.00 a week for acting, so they gave me $25.00 additional for directing.

Henry King was soon directing full time and went on to make more than one hundred films over the next fifty years. His Tol'able David, *starring Richard Barthelmess, won Photoplay's Gold Medal (the forerunner of the Oscars) for best picture in 1921. He then directed* Romola *and* The White Sister, *both filmed in Italy and starring Lillian Gish. In the midtwenties, King worked with producer Sam Goldwyn and the screenwriter Frances Marion, and directed* Stella Dallas, Partners Again, *and* The Winning of Barbara Worth. *King earned his pilot's license in the teens and was dubbed "the flying director," often doing his own location scouting. In 1930, King joined Fox where he stayed for thirty years, directing almost every genre of film with actors such as Gregory Peck, Ava Gardner, Spencer Tracy, Henry Fonda, Tyrone Power, Shirley Jones, Susan Hayward, and Ronald Colman. King was one of the original founders of the Academy of Motion Picture Arts and Sciences and was nominated for Best Director for* The Song of Bernadette *in 1944 and* Wilson *in 1945. Other classic films he directed include* Twelve O'Clock High, Carousel, *and* The Sun Also Rises; *his final film was* Tender is the Night *in 1962. He was honored with a Lifetime Achievement Award by the Directors Guild in 1956 and died of a stroke in Toluca Lake, California, on June 29, 1982, at the age of ninety-six.*

Harold Lloyd 1913

Harold Clayton Lloyd was born in Burchard, Nebraska, on April 20, 1893. His parents divorced when he was young, and Harold and his father headed to Colorado and then California. They landed in San Diego, where Harold had some schooling before his father's entrepreneurial efforts failed and Harold found occasional work on the stage.

When I came up from San Diego in the spring of 1913, my father, who was working part time in a shoe store, and I moved into the Belmont, a theatrical hotel on Main Street next to the Hippodrome, a big ten-and-fifteen-cent vaudeville house. Gaylord [Harold's older brother], who had been homesteading to discouraging results in Wyoming, joined us and became the Belmont's night clerk, while I was bell boy and relief clerk when not making the rounds of the stock companies or bucking the movie extra lines. ...

There was a moment in the early Los Angeles days when I considered turning chorus man. I played with the Morosco Stock Company in three bills in small parts, one of them a member of the student corps in *Old Heidelberg*, parent of the musical *The Student Prince*. The wages for such parts were never more than twenty-five dollars a week, that including a week's rehearsal without pay. For one bill that survived only a week I rehearsed two weeks, making my pay $8.33 a week.

It was an extraordinary stock company—the best I ever knew...But the better the company, the less opportunity for a youngster.

So I called up the Edison people at Balboa. Yes, they were using some people; come on down. I worked with them at three dollars a day on such days as extras were needed until the company returned to New York in midsummer. In one picture I had a small bit in a barn-dance scene.

When the film was shown at a Main Street ten-cent house owned by Gore Brothers, who rose later to proprietorship of the West Coast chain of theaters, I saw myself on the screen for the first time. Vanity never took a worse wallop. The shock that comes with the first glance at the proofs the photographer mails you after the sitting is something like it. None of us photographs as he imagines himself, and of the two likenesses, the camera's is not the flattering one. ...

Disgusted as I was with the movies, nothing else offered. Universal was at its original California lot at Sunset Boulevard and Gower Street, Hollywood, and there I went. The lot was the birthplace of pictures in Hollywood. In October of 1911 David and William Horsley, of the old Nester company, had set out from New Jersey to join the movement Selig, Bison and Biograph had led to the coast. Hollywood, a place of 5,000, had been annexed to Los Angeles the year before. Land there was much cheaper than in the city proper. So they went direct from the Los Angeles station to Hollywood and, without looking further, leased the old Blondeau tavern and stable at Gower and Sunset. In May, 1912, Universal had bought the studio.

Those who never have been to Southern California—and a few remain—cannot understand and are curious, I find, about the distinction between Hollywood and Los Angeles. Hollywood lies in the Cahuenga Valley, which stretches twenty miles from the original pueblo of Los Angeles to the sea at Santa Monica. Originally most of it was a cactus thicket given over to cattle and sheep. A great drought in 1879, if you will pardon a moment of drought, ruined the cattle trade and led to the first experiments with citrus trees and Chinese truck gardeners. In 1883 Horace H. Wilcox came out from Topeka, Kansas, where he had made money in real estate, and bought an apricot and fig orchard at Hollywood and Cahuenga Boulevards, now the heart of the town, as a country home. His wife named the place Hollywood, after an estate of a friend in the East.

In the midst of Los Angeles' wildest boom in 1887 Wilcox platted the estate, but sold few lots and died land poor in 1893. When the town was incorporated in 1903 its population was only 700 and one of its first ordinances prohibited the driving of sheep in flocks of more than 2000 through the streets. Seven years later, unable to command its own water supply, it succumbed to Los Angeles. When I first knocked on the Universal's gates in 1913, there still was a reach of open country between the city and the

Balboa, now a part of Newport Beach, was the site of several studios in the teens and early twenties. (Collection of Allison Burnett)

Harold Lloyd as Lonesome Luke, one of several characters he developed before finding his glasses. (Courtesy of Suzanne Lloyd)

studio; from Hollywood to the sea, a long gap, there was only the village of Sawtelle.

Four companies were working on the Universal lot. For extras there was a casting window and a bull pen with benches where you sat all day unless you could get through the gates and dog the heels of an assistant director.

The gatekeeper was a crabby old soul who let me understand that it would be a pleasure to keep me out. As I lurked about I noticed that at noon a crowd of actors and extras drifted out in make-up to eat at a lunch counter across the way, passing the gatekeeper without question each way. The next morning I brought a make-up box. At noon I dodged behind a billboard, made up, mingled with the lunch-counter press and returned with them through the gate without challenge. Once inside, I was assumed to be an extra on the job. I got no work—hardly expected to get it—but I did learn useful things about studio routine, meet older heads among the extras, learn the names of directors and assistant directors and after a time begin to register on their memories as a regular. On the way out I made a point to speak to the gateman, and on future entrances, if he looked the least suspicious I would say, carelessly, "With Smalley"—Phillips Smalley being one of the directors.

* * * *

The ruse of slipping through the gates in make-up with the returning lunchers had the disadvantage of not being workable until midday, by which time all parts would have been given out. Once acquainted with the guaranty actors, however, they let me through a window of their dressing room before the cameras started the morning grind, and I began to get work.

The masters of our destinies were the assistant directors. The director himself had too much on his mind to bother casting more than the leads. The minor and background roles were filled by his assistant, and if it was necessary to call upon the casting window for more extras, it was he who entered the bull pen and weeded out the waiters. Like second lieutenants, assistant directors were apt to be young and top-heavy with new authority; and though I escaped the bull pen early, more than one assistant director wiped his shoes upon my self-respect. My armor was pasteboard and my wounds were many.

Harold Lloyd and his friend Hal Roach began making short films together in 1915, which they sold to Pathé, with the sale price based on the number of feet of film that was accepted. Lloyd created various characters in complex disguises, but it was when he finally settled on the simple addition of round glasses that he found stardom.

As the Everyman who overcomes each mishap that he encounters, Lloyd was turning out several shorts a month. In 1919, he was looking for props to use during a photo session when he pulled out what he assumed was a fake bomb and lit the fuse with a cigarette. The bomb exploded, taking his thumb and forefinger with it. Part of Lloyd's success had been due to his daredevil stunts, and many assumed his career was over. Lloyd went from doctor to doctor, but it was Sam Goldwyn's uncle who designed the prosthetic glove that allowed Lloyd to continue acting. His stunt climbing and hanging from the clock in Safety Last *in 1923 is testament to his determination—and the glove's efficacy.*

Lloyd rivaled Chaplin, Keaton, and Pickford in popularity, was in fact more prolific, and because he owned most of his own films, accumulated a fortune in the process. He spent several years building what many still consider the ultimate Beverly Hills estate, Green Acres. He married his costar Mildred Davis in 1923, and they had three children. Lloyd also supported both his parents for the rest of their lives. While Lloyd transitioned to sound films, he went on to other interests including photography; he was an early proponent of Technicolor and 3D photography, amassing over two hundred thousand 3D slides. He was a philanthropist and active in heading up the Shriners' Children's Hospital. He also endowed scholarships and chairs at UCLA, USC, and Loyola Marymount, and was an early supporter and funder of the American Film Institute. Harold Lloyd died in Los Angeles on March 8, 1971, at the age of seventy-seven.

Lillian Gish 1913

L illian Gish was born in Springfield, Ohio, on October 14, 1893. Her father, James, deserted the family when Lillian and her younger sister, Dorothy, were small, and her mother, Mary, took to the local stage to support her girls, who soon joined her in the theater. They traveled with stage companies around the East Coast and one summer shared an apartment with the Smiths, another fatherless family in similar circumstances. Several years later, Lillian and Dorothy were at the movies when they saw their old friend Gladys Smith in the film Lena and the Geese. When the Gishes were next in New York, they tried to find her at the Biograph studio, but no one there answered to the name Gladys Smith. They soon learned that she had changed her name to Mary Pickford and was Biograph's biggest star (although still without her name in the credits of her films). Pickford was about to return to Broadway, but first she introduced the Gish girls to her director, D. W. Griffith, who hired them on the spot. Lillian and Dorothy had been with Griffith for only a few months when the Gish family made its first trip to California.

It was a five-day journey overland from New York City to Los Angeles. In contrast to bleak and blustery Manhattan, Los Angeles was warm and inviting that day in February 1913. The city smelled like a vast orange grove, and the abundance of roses offered a cheery welcome.

The climate was obviously agreeing with Mother. Dorothy was her usual bouncing self, full of amusing stories about film work. Mother was immediately concerned with my health. She hurried me off to a doctor. He told her: "Your daughter is badly run down. The tests show pernicious anemia."

His prescription for my recovery was simple: sunshine, rest, proper nutrition, and, for a tonic a California red wine called Zinfandel—two tumblers a day at lunch and dinner. He wanted me to drink the cheapest kind, at 50 cents a gallon. The taste was sour, particularly to my palate, which thrived on chocolate ice-cream sodas. But I soon regained my health, although I remained pale and underweight.

When I went to see Mr. Griffith, he put me to work on the same terms he had offered me in New York.

Although this was our first winter in California, Mr. Griffith and his company had spent the last three there. In New York, Mr. Griffith had often found the weather a handicap to production. Moreover, he needed a variety of backgrounds for his films, which eliminated New York as a year-round headquarters. After a visit, he had decided to make Los Angeles his winter quarters. Other film-makers had already discovered the virtues of the area. Los Angeles, then a residential city of about 300,000 people, had wide boulevards, churches and Spanish-style houses. Nearby were ocean and desert, snow-capped mountains and green valleys, Spanish missions and fruit farms. Although he was to spend much time there in the next few years, he was loath to call it his permanent quarters. He considered the climate marvelous for the body but bad for the mind and soul, and he always punctuated his stays with frequent trips.

He lived at the Alexandria Hotel, where Mack Sennett, his most devoted disciple, was also a resident. During the first year, according to Sennett, working quarters had been a vacant lot on Twelfth Street and Georgia, where Mr. Griffith had set up tents for dressing rooms.

Mary Pickford was not among the Biograph players in California my first year. She was still playing in [the Broadway production] *The Good Little Devil* when she and her mother discussed a new contract with Mr. Griffith. Mrs. Pickford had decided that Mary deserved at least $500 a week, which Mr. Griffith considered out of the question.

"Three hundred," Mr. Griffith countered. "That's the best I can do."

"You'll be sorry, Mr. Griffith," Mrs. Pickford said. "Mary can get five hundred."

He let Mary go. He had an ambivalent attitude toward his protégées. He helped them to achieve success, and when they wanted to leave he let them go without a restraining word. He was happy for them.

* * * *

Mother took a small apartment for us only a block from the studio, so that we could walk to and from work. There were two rooms and a kitchen;

A typical open-air set, where sheets and tablecloths would often blow in the wind. (Collection of Allison Burnett)

Dorothy and I shared one room, and Mother used the other, which also served as dining and living room. The apartment had Murphy beds. There was a mirror on the wall, and when it was pulled down a bed was visible behind it and behind that a cupboard for hanging clothes.

Dorothy was already a promising comedienne, and Mother no longer had to work so hard; now she only occasionally came to work at the studio.

The Biograph studio on Pico Street was really nothing more than an open-air stage. Without walls or roof, it consisted solely of a large wooden floor built on the site of an abandoned streetcar barn. The shed nearby was sectioned off into dressing rooms, Mr. Griffith's office, and a one-rack costume department. We had only daylight to work in. When interiors were filmed, the set was unprotected from wind, and often while we were shooting scenes in the dining room the curtains and tablecloth would billow gently. Audiences must have thought it a drafty house. Because the whole process was so makeshift, Mr. Griffith's results seem all the more remarkable.

When it rained we all congregated in the rehearsal hall. There Mr. Griffith conducted rehearsals of not only his own current story but those of other directors as well. Often there were five or six stories in various stages of preparation. Mr. Griffith's powers of concentration were so great that he could watch a rehearsal, read notes, and talk to his staff at the same time. At times he would look at you without actually seeing you ….

In rehearsals we were expected to visualize the props—furniture where none stood, windows in blank walls, doors where there was only space. Our physical movements became automatic and our emotions completely involved.

Most rehearsals were open—that is, the whole staff, actors, workmen, and the men from the laboratory were free to come and watch. Often there would be visitors on the set. Mr. Griffith loved the presence of an audience while his company rehearsed—and rehearsed so effectively that at the end of the scene, the onlookers would be in tears. Later, we learned to withhold, not to give as much as we would if the camera were operating. Film was expensive, and a scene was shot only once, so we conserved our strength for that one take.

When Mr. Griffith was hungry he would turn to us and say, "Hungry? Well, now you may eat."

During lunch he would help those who happened to be eating with him. If an actor did not know what to do with a character, if he was baffled and could not get insight, Mr. Griffith would say: "Well, haven't you seen someone like this in your life? Go find him. Go get an idea from someone, and bring it back to me, and let me see if it's any good. I can't think of everything! I'm writing the whole story. You have only one character to worry about, so you try to round it out and make it real and whole!"

Many times, if the shooting were going well, or the light was good, he wouldn't break for lunch but continue taking one scene after another. Sunlight often controlled his plans. If it looked as though a mist was forming or the light would dim later, he would keep going. We would often get so hungry we'd think we were going to collapse. Sometimes we had to play our most important scenes on empty stomachs. We worked long hours every day, sometimes late into the night. We filmed all day if the weather permitted, rehearsed after the light failed, then watched rushes. But we never thought to complain. We considered it a privilege to work for Mr. Griffith. With him, we never felt we were working for a salary. He inspired in us his belief that we were involved in a medium that was powerful enough to influence the whole world.

* * * *

Our California work schedule was similar to the one in New York. Four o'clock rising was not unusual during location trips. While it was still dark we would board the trolley car that would take us to the country. When we had leading parts we came by car, which the company hired. Mr. Griffith was driven by car too. I remember that he was always carefully dressed in a neat business suit, an immaculate white shirt, and a dark tie.

On location we did what was expected of us without fuss. One day I might have a leading role; the next day I could be working in the background, playing several small parts. Within a few hours I could be a village belle decked out in curls and ruffles; an Indian brave riding bareback on a wild pony, rushing to attack the belle's home; and a cowboy, my curls under a Stetson, racing to the belle's rescue. Doubles and stunt men were unknown.

I knew how to ride a horse backward and forward. Furthermore, youth and ignorance made me fearless.

I was playing in a western opposite Raoul Walsh, one of our handsomest actors as well as directors. In the scene he and I and George Siegmann—a dear, gentle man who usually played villains—were to gallop past the camera on our steeds. One of the horses we were to use was wild and unmanageable, and everyone passed him up.

"I'll ride him," I offered.

We were supposed to go up the road and then turn around in order to the pass the camera. My mount behaved as we went up the road, but once we had turned in the other direction, toward what he considered home, he took off like a wild creature. I could not stop him. We dashed past the camera and continued toward the woods. He meant to dislodge me under low-hanging tree branches and then to return to his stable. I was screaming. My shouts for help awakened Eagle Eye, a member of the company who was asleep in the bushes. He leaped up, caught the horse, and saved me.

Nonchalantly I slid off, found another animal, and went through the scene again.

Someone standing nearby remarked: "God looks after actors. They're his favorite children."

Lillian Gish (far right) as an extra with Mary Pickford in *The New York Hat*. Mary's brother, Jack, is in the background. (Courtesy of MOMA)

Chatsworth Park was the location where our westerns were usually filmed. It was called "the home of the rattlesnakes." Snakes were abundant there in spring, so each of us was supplied with a vial of antidote for snake bite. In one film I was to play a scene with snakes. Never having been on intimate terms with reptiles, I did not relish the prospect. But I rode out in the automobile with several snakes on my lap. I expected to find them cold and clammy, but they were surprisingly warm, even affectionate. They curled up and went to sleep in my lap. Later we played a very good scene together.

* * * *

Mr. Griffith often went in search of his locations. Once he had found what he wanted he would send an assistant to ask about renting a front porch, a lawn, or an entrance—whatever was necessary for the film. Five or ten dollars was the usual sum offered in payment, and it was usually gladly accepted. Not many movies had yet been made, and people were delighted to have their properties used as locales. They would usually come out to watch the filming, and their comments were often painfully unflattering. We much preferred the bedlam of carpenters building sets at the studio to being out on the street watched by strangers who talked about us as we tried to concentrate on our scenes.

But not all spectators were offensive. We had devoted followers too. There were always certain familiar faces among the watchers. We did not know who they were, but a small loyal band of them would find out where we were on location and track us down. Mr. Griffith was always pleasant and often joked with them.

Lillian Gish became Griffith's muse, starring in such films as Judith of Bethulia, Birth of a Nation, *and* Intolerance. *Unlike other actors who worked with Griffith for a year or two and then left for higher salaries, Gish stayed with "the master" as she called him for over a decade, starring in such classics as* Broken Blossoms, Way Down East, *and* Orphans of the Storm. *She also directed a film starring her sister and written by Dorothy Parker,* Remodeling Her Husband. *Lillian wanted everyone working on the film to be female, but failed to find a woman cinematographer. The film is lost but most of the feature films Gish starred in are preserved and available.*

While she often played the delicate waif, her friend Frances Marion said that

Lillian was "as fragile as a steel rod." In 1925, Gish came to M-G-M and made La Bohème, *followed by incredible performances in* The Scarlet Letter *and* The Wind, *both adapted by Marion. Louis B. Mayer however did not appreciate Gish because he preferred actresses with what he considered to be sex appeal, and after almost twenty years of working nonstop in front of the camera, Gish returned to the stage, making only occasional films, over the next two decades. She was one of the first distinguished actresses to perform on live television in the late 1940s and '50s. She was featured on programs such as* The Defenders, The Alfred Hitchcock Hour, *and* The Love Boat. *Well into her eighties, she appeared in Robert Altman's* A Wedding. *Her final film performance was in* The Whales of August, *costarring Bette Davis, in 1987. Gish lived in New York, where she was an active participant in the cultural life of the city, often dining and seeing films with old friends such as Frances Marion and Anita Loos. Lillian Gish left much of her estate to the Museum of Modern Art when she died on February 27, 1993, at the age of ninety-nine.*

Karl Brown 1913

K arl Brown was born on December 26, 1896, in McKeesport, Pennsylvania. His parents, William and Lucille Brown, were actors and, after a stint in New York, the family moved to Hollywood for the year-round work that the movies offered. Karl, fifteen at the time, and his parents found work at Kinemacolor, one of many film companies that skyrocketed to success only to crash and burn with equal speed during the teens, and one of the earliest to experiment with color film. Karl worked in the lab, but took every opportunity to soak up the knowledge of Kinemacolor's experienced and international cadre of cinematographers. Karl bought a camera at a pawnshop and learned all he could about lenses, shutter speeds, and color film.

Kinemacolor, which had brought me, a kid in short pants, from New York to Hollywood, which had taught me all the closely guarded secrets of color cinematography, was in the year 1913 dying, a forlorn victim of box-office malnutrition.

Why? Because Kinemacolor required the expert care of specially trained technicians to make its glories come to life. It had begun with royalty no less, having recorded in full faithful color the great Durbar [a ceremonial gathering] staged in India to commemorate the accession of George the Fifth. Every true Briton throughout the empire felt bound to see this picture, if it took his last farthing. It took time—two years at least, because the color could be shown only with a specially designed projector—as the film traveled the world from London to Cape Town and from New Jersey to Sydney.

The profits were so huge that the Kinemacolor Company decided to go into commercial production. In that decision lay the cause of its eventual downfall, for Kinemacolor was expensive. There were not enough theaters equipped with the Kinemacolor projectors, or enough projectors, or enough free grand spectacles to be filmed. What Kinemacolor really needed was another Durbar, but George the Fifth was in remarkably good health.

The one theater in the Los Angeles area equipped to show Kinemacolor pictures was the California, at Ninth and Main. I went there regularly to see our pictures, because my job of developing negative kept me literally in the dark as to what was happening outside on the open stages. Our little one-reel pictures were made to exploit color for color's sake. There was one about a hospital fire, showing lots of flames; another, from a Hawthorne story about a pumpkin that becomes a man, showed up the golden yellow of the carved jack-o'-lantern very well indeed.

The audiences at the California seemed to care nothing about our beautiful colors. What they wanted was raw melodrama and lots of it, and what seemed to stir them most of all was the steady flood of pictures made by a man named D. W. Griffith, formerly of Biograph but now, late in 1913, a free agent making his own way and sweeping all opposition away by the sheer audacity of his conceptions. This fellow Griffith seemed to delight in scorning tradition.

There was *Judith of Bethulia*, in which the lushly opulent Judith gets a monstrous giant dead drunk, after which she cuts off his head with his own sword. The huge figure of the wine-guzzling Holofernes fascinated me. I had never before seen so much man in one piece. He towered over everyone in the picture. I wondered who he was and where they'd found him. In some circus, I supposed, but when I mentioned this at the studio, everybody laughed at me. This "giant" was Henry Walthall, a small man made to seem huge by the magic of Griffith's cameraman, Billy Bitzer. No, they didn't know how it was done, but only that Bitzer was a wizard who could do anything with a camera. So now I had to find out, any way at all, how this particular trick had been done. I was sixteen, and as curious as a dog's nose about everything, whether it concerned me or not. It was the sort of itch that Kipling poeticized as "Something hidden. Go and find it."

Meanwhile, I was a regular patron of the California out of loyalty to Kinemacolor. One night I bought my ticket and took my place at the end of the line. There was a big, specially featured Biograph picture, *The Battle at Elderbush Gulch*, directed by that same everlasting D. W. Griffith. His pictures kept cropping up everywhere you looked, there was no avoiding them; if you dodged *The New York Hat* in one movie house, you'd run bang

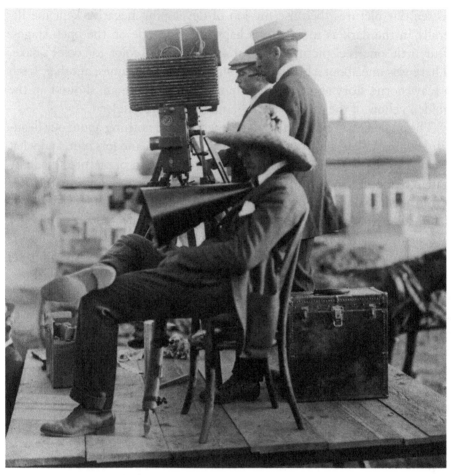

From back to front, Karl Brown, Billy Bitzer, and D.W. Griffith. (Courtesy of AMPAS)

into *Pippa Passes* in another. I disliked this fellow Griffith for the way he hogged all the audiences. Then I saw something that made me despise him all the more. For the first time in weeks, the California was *not* showing a Kinemacolor. They'd taken it off to make room for this big two-reel special—by Griffith, of course. I seethed.

* * * *

And so Kinemacolor died. The final rites were conducted by old man Wiener, the front-office boss, who sat at a desk in the big, two-story, chalet-type building that had been our laboratory and handed out the final paychecks to all of us waiting in line. Fair to the last, Kinemacolor offered free transportation back to New York to all who wanted it. Nobody wanted it. Hollywood was becoming the Hollywood of pictures, with little studios springing up all over the place. And besides, it was the off-season for the theater in New York, where no shows of any consequence would be opening until well into the end of the year.

So my father and mother and I took our money and went back home. It was a good home, too, the best we'd ever had—six rooms and a service porch; a part-time maid named Ida Belle; a pet dog named Lily, who had come to us out of nowhere and who had adopted us as her very own; a large garden full of flowers and grapevines and fruit trees. No, we'd take our chances in Hollywood.

And the chances were good, too. The gold rush of ambitious amateurs to Hollywood, hoping for a sudden bonanza of discovery and stardom, was well under way. But experienced people were in very short supply. We had the advantage there, because we were all as well trained as a trio of performing seals in a vaudeville act.

My father and mother went to work elsewhere, here, there and wherever a job was to be had. My father was big and fat and carried himself as a personage of the greatest possible importance. He could play anything from a ruffian to a ruler, a sailor to a saint. Long years on the stage had taught him this versatility. My mother was equally talented.

I was not. I had a head full of theories, but who wants to listen to the theories of a sixteen-year-old kid who was just then getting used to wearing long pants...Then a ray of hope broke through when the news seeped out that the great D. W. Griffith was moving his entire company to Hollywood. He had taken the Kinemacolor lot as his studio, not more than a hundred steps from our front door.

Unknown to Griffith, the greatest living master of suspense, a harrowing suspense situation was being played right in our home. It was: how could we wangle our way into his organization and have steady jobs in our old studio located practically at our doorstep? No carfare; makeup at home; come home for lunch; be within call at any moment, day or night. Perfect. The problem: how to work it?

My father made the rounds, finding out about Griffith's every move. Thanks to this one-man espionage bureau, we knew when Griffith was coming, when he would leave New York, when he would arrive at the Arcade station. Should we meet him at the train? No; too many reporters, too many job hunters. He'd have to come to the studio. We'd trap him there at the only entrance, the flight of steps leading up from Sunset Boulevard.

The great day arrived after a sleepless night. We were gathered, all three of us, at what we considered the most strategic spot—the steps. He'd have to go up that little flight of seven steps from the Sunset Boulevard level to the lot itself. So there we planted ourselves and there we waited.

My plans were all made. I'd get hold of Billy Bitzer, as soon as I found out who he was, and take him on a grand tour of the studio, showing him all the wonderful things we had built. Quite incidentally, as a careless side mention, I'd managed to drop a word or two of the part I had played in bringing all this about. I felt this would be the most dignified way to make the approach. I did not dare hope for anything like immediate acceptance into the bosom of the Griffith family. I would plant the seed, and who knows? Maybe someday ...

People kept gathering. My father knew most of them, because there wasn't a studio in town, however sketchy, that he didn't visit. It was an article of faith with him to get to know as many people as possible, because he kept telling me over and over again, "It isn't *what* you know, but *who* you know."

The people were from all over the picture world. Everyone who was not actually on a set shooting was there: cameramen, directors, actors, and a swarm of people who hoped to be actors someday—all waiting for the great man to make his entrance.

A high-bodied limousine purred around from the curve of Sunset Boulevard. A uniformed driver was at the wheel. A man and two young ladies and a very young gentleman were seated in back. All eyes followed the car as it pulled to a stop just beyond the steps where we were standing.

The driver got out and opened the door. A tall, spare man got out. He held his hand to help his two young lady guests out. The very young gentleman followed.

"That's Griffith," said my mother softly. "And that's Lillian and Dorothy Gish with him, and Robert Harron."

"Are you sure?" I asked, unable to believe that this slender gentleman could possibly be the giant of the industry. "Why, he can't be more than—than thirty."

"Why, yes, I'd judge him to be in his thirties. What do you think, Will?"

We looked around. My father was gone. We searched for him with our eyes. There he was, shaking hands with Frank Woods, the company's supervisor, and being very, very jovial. Woods advanced toward Griffith, my father in tow. Woods was greeted warmly by Griffith. He introduced my father, who took Griffith's proffered hand warmly. There was nothing shy or diffident about my father. He might have been the owner of three railroads and a couple of munitions factories.

"Looks as though we're in," said my mother happily. "Trust Will to be Johnny-on-the-spot when the box is open."

People were crowding in to smile their prettiest on the new arrivals. It was hard enough for me to swallow the fact that these three young-sters with Griffith really were the famous Gish sisters and the Robert Harron we'd all seen in so many Griffith pictures. But what was impos-sible to believe was that anyone so obviously young, so boyishly slender, so unmarked by the battles of the world, could possibly be the one and only, great, and world-famous D. W. Griffith. He must have started when—well, when he was not so very much older than I was. The miracle was not that he had done so much, but that he had done so much so young.

Another car drew up, this one a big, seven-passenger open touring car. It was crowded with men. The man in the front seat got out. He walked to the place where a sidewalk would be someday, followed by the others, who grouped around him as they looked the place over.

"That's Billy Bitzer," said my mother. "The chubby one with the cloth hat. Go on. Ask him for a job."

I felt suddenly all weak and helpless. "You mean—*now*?"

"Of course. Go on. Hurry up. Get to him before all the rest of the mob does."

"Couldn't we wait until he's—not so busy?"

"Look, if you don't get to him now, you'll never get to him, because the jobs'll all be gone. Do as your father did, walk right up and speak your piece as if you owned the place."

I still hung back. My mother shook my arm and snapped, "Karl!" in a tone that could not be mistaken. I made a quick appraisal. The worst Bitzer could do would be to say no, but if I didn't go, I'd have to live with that woman. I decided to go, but somewhat slowly. I thought that any unseemly rush would be undignified.

I approached the king of cameramen and asked, "Mr. Bitzer?"

He looked around from the men he was talking with. Bitzer was a round man with a round face and a round neck that bulged a little over his collar. He was also a brown man, with brown eyes, a brownish skin, and definitely brown lips, of all things. He looked at me and said, as though annoyed by an unwelcome intrusion, "Yes?"

Well, I did my usual rush act, named all the people I'd worked with, my latest job as still man for Alvin Wyckoff, and then I paused to give him his turn to talk.

He looked me up and down disapprovingly and said, "So?"

I couldn't think of an apt answer off the bat. While I was trying to think of one, he spoke rather sharply, in a don't-bother-me-can't-you-see-I'm-busy tone of voice. "Well, out with it. What do you want?"

"Well, I'd sort of like a job." This didn't strike me as being particularly brilliant, but was out and there was no changing it now.

Bitzer came right to the point. "Look. We've got our own laboratory and we've brought all our help. I take all the stills. And as for your many qualifications, I'd think you'd do well to apply elsewhere, because I do all my own photographic work as well. Does that answer you?"

I made one last try. "Couldn't I be your assistant or something? I don't cost much and I work long hours. Ask Al Wyckoff, or Johnny Leezer. Ask anybody!"

He smiled for the first time, shaking his head in advance of the no I was sure was coming. But he did qualify it. "Look, kid. All I require of an assistant is a strong back and a weak mind, and you just don't strike me as being the type. Sorry."

Griffith's voice called, "Billy!"

"Right away, Mr. Griffith." He started to move away. I ran after him, keeping pace as I pleaded, "Please Mr. Bitzer! I know I'm not wanted but before you go will you please tell me how you managed to make Hank Walthall look so big in *Judith of Bethulia*?" He stopped now and stared at me. I continued, recklessly, now that the game was lost. "I asked Johnny Leezer and he didn't know and he said I'd have to ask you, so I'm asking you, and if you'll please tell me I won't ever bother you any more, honest I won't." It all came out pretty fast, but I knew he was in a hurry.

His face softened into kindness. "Sure, be glad to. But it'll take a little time. Report to work at nine tomorrow morning and I'll show you what you have to do."

Griffith repeated his call. Bitzer hurried to join him. I stood there, trying to make myself believe that what I'd heard was true. Suddenly, I believed, and in that instant I whirled and made a headlong dash toward my mother, so suddenly and so unexpectedly that I all but knocked down a dignified lady who was walking toward the steps.

I apologized, got a sniff for my pains, and I then hurried to tell my mother the miraculous news.

I never got a chance to open my mouth. She was furious. "Do you know who that was you nearly knocked down? Mary Alden, the actress! When will you *ever* learn to look where you're going?"

All the joy seeped out of my life. "I dunno."

"What did Bitzer say?" There was no real interest in her voice. She had been watching and knew a turndown when she saw one.

"He said I wouldn't do. But I was to report for work at nine tomorrow morning anyway."

"He said *what*?"

"That's what he said."

"Then you are *in*! Do you realize that? You're *in*!" She was wide-eyed with amazement. I suddenly became wide-eyed with amazement, too, as the realization finally hit home with a jarring, delayed impact.

It was hard to believe, but I was in—actually, honestly, really in. Things like this were forever happening to somebody else. But now, incredibly, it had happened to me. Nothing I could think of to say could possibly do justice to the situation, so I simply murmured, "Well, whadda ya know," and let it go at that.

Karl became Billy Bitzer's assistant and worked his way into the role of second cameraman on films such as Intolerance, *for which Brown is credited with inventing the double printing process used in the crucifixion scene. When Griffith returned to New York in 1919, Brown moved to Famous Players-Lasky where he won acclaim for his work on films such as James Cruze's* The Covered Wagon *in 1923. Always inspired by Bitzer and his giant Holofernes, Brown was constantly innovating and worked to perfect methods for magnifying models and projecting miniatures, seven decades before CGI.*

In the late 1920s, Brown directed his first feature, Stark Love, *and from then on moved between writing and directing. In the 1950s Brown wrote for television, including programs such as* The Millionaire *and* Death Valley Days.

Brown retired in 1960, and film historian Kevin Brownlow, who says that Brown's photography "combined qualities of Mathew Brady and Frederic Remington," spent considerable time trying to ascertain his whereabouts (the Cinematographers Guild told him that Brown had passed away years before). Brownlow eventually located Karl Brown and his wife at their home in North Hollywood, enjoying what the cinematographer said was "obscurity on a comfortable income." Brownlow not only recorded him for his groundbreaking documentary, Hollywood, *but also helped shepherd the publishing of Brown's memoirs,* Adventures with D. W. Griffith, *a unique, clear-eyed, humorous, and richly detailed history of those early years. Karl Brown died in Woodland Hills, California, at the age of ninety-three on March 25, 1990.*

Lionel Barrymore 1913

L ionel Herbert Blythe was born on April 28, 1878, in Philadelphia, the eldest child of Maurice and Georgina Drew, actors who used Barrymore as their stage name. Lionel was brought into the business as an infant and made his Broadway debut at twelve. He had never known anything but acting when, in his twenties, he decided to go to Paris to study painting. That lasted several years, but financial realities led him to return to New York. Film work was more dependable and often more remunerative than the stage, so Barrymore went to work for Biograph in New York in 1911. He first came to California two years later.

To begin with, the valley which Hollywood and most of the studios now share was the home of saber-toothed tigers, imperial elephants fifteen feet high, vultures larger than condors, eagles, wild turkeys, rabbits and the Cahuenga Indians. Proof of this can be found in the La Brea Tar Pits wherein the wretched bones of these beasts and Indians are still antiseptically preserved. It seems appropriate that they were the forerunners of our town. We can only hope as time and history pass that the skulls and tibia of certain saber-toothed gossip columnists and perhaps the elephantine hides of a producer or so will become likewise embalmed.

The first white man to find what is now Hollywood was Governor Gaspar de Portola, subdivisor for the King of Spain. The Royal Governor, according to the records, took one supercilious look at the vermin-ridden, rabbit-fed Indians, and hurried away. He sought greener fields to carry out his twofold assignment, which was prophetic: his job was to spread the Gospel and to grab real estate, the twin projects in which Southern California still excels.

When Horace Henderson Wilcox and Daieda Wilcox came on the scene with their Arabian horses "Duke" and "Royal" they bought up 120

Peacock Tea Room.

Lobby, Hotel Alexandria, Los Angeles, Cal.

The lobby of the Alexandria, the premiere downtown hotel in the teens, where many movie people stayed and even more socialized. (Collection of Patt Morrison)

acres of land from John Bower for $12.50 an acre. There were a few people here ahead of them: Christian Duen, a Danish sailor; Herman Newman, a German; Ivar A. Weid, a Dane; and José Mascarel, a Frenchman. They owned and farmed the land which now constitutes Hollywood.

Horace and Daieda wrote back to Topeka and urged their Prohibitionist friends to come on out; and they did, and bought land, preferably from Horace. The Wilcox ranch itself centered upon what is now bounded by Hollywood and Cahuenga Boulevards, and the boundaries were marked up to a few years ago by the pepper trees they set out.

The Wilcoxes eventually died broke and land-poor, and left no legacy to Hollywood save only their name on one of the principal streets, and the name of the place itself. And the origin of that name is in dispute. The California Historical Association believes that Mrs. Wilcox named her ranch after a farm owned by a friend in New England. Another theory is that she mistook the toyon berries, which are still prevalent in the hills, for genuine holly. At any rate, a place name that has attained connotations as gaudy as any in the world, from Babylon on, was the whim of Daieda Wilcox, Kansas Prohibitionist.

Faye Thomas Frederick, a teacher at the Selma Avenue Public School in Hollywood, says that the main social organization of the town during the Wilcox era was the Hollywood Club, and that its principal entertainment was a May Day fete. In 1909 the Hollywood Club's innocent celebration was drowned by torrential rains and the revels were canceled at considerable financial sacrifice. The Prohibitionists hurried home to steam their feet and ward off colds with foot baths and hot toddies and never again emerged in the public eye. I think we can suggest with some certainty that Hollywood has not been the same since.

We made pictures not in Hollywood but on a vacant lot at Pico Boulevard and Georgia, on any other vacant lots from which we could dispossess the small boys, and principally the streets of downtown Los Angeles. Canvas dressing rooms were ranged around the edges of our own lot.

One of the first problems that smote Griffith when he came to California was the scarcity of cheap actors for mob and crowd scenes. There had always been no lack of hungry ones in New York. Here he was forced to make overtures to the Oliver Morosco stock company, offering small sums for the daytime services of the Morosco people. One of the Morosco players was a girl named Marguerite Marsh, who was working in a musical number, *My Gal Irene*, with Charles Ruggles. Marguerite appeared in the picture *The Mender of Nets*, among others, the first year, worked with us again when Griffith trekked out the second time, and produced her little sister Mae, a school girl, who refused to be chased from the lot.

Finally somebody said, "Get a look at the kid. Just like Billie Burke." That started Mae Marsh in pictures.

We lived where we could, in rented rooms or in hotels which took an indulgent attitude toward the poor, and we congregated at the Alexandria Hotel bar which was in unintentional competition with the Hoffman House for the free-lunch patronage of motion picture actors. There were lush weeks when, having succumbed to steady employment, I earned as high as one hundred and twenty-five dollars, but most of the time I did not get that much money. Griffith himself was paid seventy-five dollars a week at this time with a percentage guarantee of only two hundred dollars. (It has been estimated that he spent thirty million dollars producing his great spectacles over the years that followed.)

I played, let us phrase it, several important parts in Griffith's *Judith of Bethulia*, the first four-reel feature made in America, with Blanche Sweet and Henry B. Walthall. This picture was modeled on the four-part technique Griffith invented for his previous *Pippa Passes,* and was actually the front runner for his masterpiece *Intolerance.* I am, therefore, proud to have worked in it; but beyond recalling that Harry Carey was crucified upside down and that I appeared more than once in various disguises, I do not remember much about what I contributed to this work.

* * * *

At about this time, which I believe after thinking hard must have got us up to about 1913, I had a major quarrel with Harry Carey, who had become enchanted with the geranium and citrus-growing prowess of the Southern California climate and declared his intentions of homesteading. I dissuaded him from taking over for a pittance the property which is now the site of the Beverly Hills Hotel.

Donald Crisp, a prudent and astute actor who undoubtedly held onto the first dollar he ever earned, did invest in real estate and made money. He got hold of a piece of undeveloped property out in the ranch regions which he turned over for eight thousand dollars, a pretty profit. The property is now the locale of the Taft Building in the heart of Hollywood, probably worth eight million dollars. I had nothing to do with such enterprises or investments and have never had anything to do with them all my life, worse luck. In one way or another I earned enough—well, not enough, but sufficient—for the exceedingly simple requirements of my life. These requirements hinged around a little night music, a little painting, a good deal of beer, and escape from the rigors of acting on the stage.

Between 1913 and 1926, the year he signed with M-G-M, Lionel Barrymore divided his time between films and the stage. His theater training made him a natural for talking films, and he won the Academy Award for Best Actor in 1931 for his performance in A Free Soul. *He worked consistently, playing a broad range of characters in films such as* Grand Hotel, Dinner at Eight, Captains Courageous, You Can't Take it with You, It's a Wonderful Life, *and* A Christmas Carol. *Barrymore made one film—*Rasputin and the Empress*— with both his siblings, John and Ethel, and appeared with John in four others. Lionel Barrymore was also a prolific composer, directed occasionally, and continued to paint. Plagued with two broken hips and arthritis, he acted and directed on crutches or from a wheelchair during the last twenty years of his life. Barrymore died on November 15, 1954, at the age of seventy-six, in Van Nuys, California.*

Virgil E. Miller 1913

B orn in Coffeen, Illinois, on December 20, 1886, Virgil Miller graduated
from Kansas State University and stayed on for a few years to teach physics
and electrical engineering. He came to California in 1908 and was working as
an electrician in Riverside when he heard about a possible job at Universal, so he
headed to Los Angeles.

Why a teacher of physics and electrical engineering in Kansas State
University, and subsequently an operator in the plant of a big electrical
corporation, should be standing with other curious people on the corner
of Sunset and Gower in 1913 must be answered in the first person, since I
was the teacher who had been drawn into this vortex, this new and totally
different business, a business that apparently held little opportunity for an
electrical engineer, a business in which sunshine was the key to success.

In this new business, pen stages were designed for a maximum of sunlight; adjustable "diffusers" of bleached muslin, strung on overhead wires,
enabled the photographers to vary or modify the amount of light and shade
on the actors, painted sets, and backgrounds; reflectors of tin and silver
leaf reflected light from floor levels. Pictures were made only when the sun
shone. When unusual weather prevailed, such as an "Oregon mist" or an
almost unheard-of fog, pictures could not be photographed—and thereby
hangs a tale.

I had heard that Universal Studios was guilty of an almost treasonable
thought; they were contemplating the use of electric lights to supplement
the sunlight that had brought them to California. That was the rumor
that had brought me to Sunset and Gower on that memorable morning
in 1913. I learned from the old gateman, whose eagle eye watched over
those privileged to enter those sacred portals, that a Mr. Isadore Bernstein

was the general manager; I was also told to see Mr. Frank Ormston and Bob Ross, his assistant, before bothering Mr. Bernstein, as he was a very busy man. Eventually the gateman pointed out Mr. Ormston, and I, taking the bull by the horns, barged over to him and quickly explained that I'd heard of their desire to hire an electrical engineer and was looking for the job. Evidently my story interested him; he took me to his office where I met Mr. Ross, and the two of them, after hearing my story, introduced me to Mr. Bernstein, with a recommendation that I be given a try. I thus became head of the first electrical department in a motion picture studio on the West Coast—no office, no equipment, no help, and not much of a salary. I was to report to Ed Jahrus and his son Don. They were not my superiors, but since they were in charge of prop making they knew where everything electrical was on the lot, and could give me a rough idea of their locations. I was then given a small office and told by Mr. Ormston to get all data relating to lamps and lighting equipment of sufficient "actinic" value to supplement daylight "shooting" and eventually light scenes at night. I immediately got in touch with Billy Rimpau, then of Pacific States Electric Company, and secured a few of the then new and untried nitrogen-filled incandescent lamps of one thousand candlepower. Later, we obtained these in blue glass, to ease the strain on the actors' eyes. From New York I obtained a few Klieg arcs and broads, plus a couple of arc spots, and was ready for business.

My first tests were directed by Joseph DeGrasse; Lon Chaney, Sr., and Pauline Bush were the actors. Fortunately, the tests proved successful; I was "in," and the first electrical department on the West Coast was on its way.

Virgil Miller quickly became a renowned innovator and was one of the first to use electric lights for interior shots and to film at night. After several years at Universal, Miller became a cinematographer and invented a variety of filters, including those that allowed nighttime scenes to be shot during the day. Between 1917 and 1950, Miller was the cinematographer on over 150 films, during which he survived two plane crashes and two train wrecks. His films included the Sherlock Holmes series at Universal, Charlie Chan at 20th Century Fox and The Falcon at RKO. (He was uncredited for his work on Universal's The Hunchback of Notre Dame *and* The Phantom of the Opera.*)*

In the late 1940s and early '50s, Miller traveled the globe for a series of M-G-M documentaries, and in 1952 he was nominated for an Academy Award for his cinematography on Navajo. *Miller then moved to television and spent several years as director of photography for Groucho Marx's show* You Bet Your Life. *Miller was married twice and had five sons. He died in Hollywood on October 5, 1974, at the age of eighty-six.*

A scene being shot with cloth diffusers draped across the ceiling to control the sunlight. (Collection of Allison Burnett)

Cecil B. DeMille *1913*

C ecil Blount DeMille was born in Ashfield, Massachusetts, on August 2, 1881. His playwright father, Henry de Mille, died before Cecil was a teenager, and his mother, Beatrice, wrote plays and taught acting to support Cecil and his older brother, William. Cecil attended a military school and then entered the New York Academy of Dramatic Arts, making his stage debut at nineteen. He appeared in many plays over the next decade, including The Warrens of Virginia, written by his brother and starring Mary Pickford. In 1902, Cecil married the actress Constance Adams, who was seven years his senior. In 1913, he joined Jesse Lasky and Samuel Goldfish[1] to form the Jesse L. Lasky Feature Play Company. He soon found himself on a train heading west with fellow director Oscar Apfel.

I was convinced that the future lay with what, in the name of our company, we called "feature plays"; pictures several reels long, telling a well-constructed story, well acted, and intended not as conglomerate items on the daily changing programs of the nickelodeons or as "chasers" in the vaudeville houses, but precisely as "feature" attractions which could stand on their own merits as a real and new form of the drama. In this aim we were charting a new course in American motion picture production ....

Oscar Apfel and I were very conscious of all this, as we settled down on the train to write a shooting script from the play *The Squaw Man*. We were conscious too that the possible pitfalls were not only literary and photographic. We hoped that Flagstaff [Arizona] might escape the notice of the Trust's strong arm squads and that we might finish the picture with our Pathé camera intact. But I had a revolver in my luggage, just in case.

A shooting script today is likely to run to several hundred typed pages. By the time our train was chugging over the last miles of Arizona desert,

Oscar Apfel and I had perhaps as many as 20 pages of penciled script and the hope that we could find a typist in Flagstaff, cheap. Apfel knew a great deal about motion pictures, 1913 vintage. I was supposed to know something about dramatic construction. The script, we hoped, embodied the best of both. No two parents ever clutched a precious only child tighter than we did that penciled script, when we stepped off the train at the Flagstaff station ....

Our story was laid in Wyoming. We knew that, in the fall of the year, Arizona was warmer and sunnier than Wyoming, so we had come to Arizona. It was warm enough. It was sunny. But some of us had been in Wyoming; and knowledge is always the enemy —or is it rather the friend?—of innocence. With one accord, we saw and knew that for our purposes Arizona, beautiful, healthful, sunny Arizona, was all wrong. It did not occur to us to rewrite the script and send the young man in the play, to let us say, North Africa instead of Wyoming; perhaps there were no squaw men among the North African tribes anyway. It would, of course, never occur to a motion picture producer to place a story in Arizona just because he happened to be in Arizona and have a script, star and camera with him.

There was little time for second thoughts in any case. The train was beginning to practice puffing its lungs and pulling itself together, the way trains used to do, before continuing its westward journey. There was time only for a very quick decision.

I remembered that at the end of the railroad line was Los Angeles and that other picture makers had been working there on and off for some years. The California climate was good, there was a great variety of scenery there and it was that much farther away, so we thought, from the minions of the Trust, in case any of that inquisitive fraternity decided to take too personal an interest in what we were doing.

The quick decision was made. When the train puffed out of the Flagstaff station, we were back on it. Some more of the Jesse L. Lasky Feature Play Company's capital assets were in the conductor's pocket, for our fares to the end of the line. All unknown to its corporate officers in New York, the Company was on the move; and all unknown to a quiet village of orange groves and pepper trees, out there to the northwest of Los Angeles, "Hollywood" was about to be born.

* * * *

Cecil B. DeMille directs a *Squaw Man* interior scene out of doors. (Courtesy of AMPAS)

The Lasky Famous Players barn turned studio in Hollywood. (Courtesy of MOMA)

No doubts, however, appeared on the brave faces we wore when we stepped off the train and went, of course, to the elegant splendors of Los Angeles' leading hotel, the Alexandria.

We knew not a soul in the city, but the Hollywood grapevine must have been in existence before Hollywood existed as a cinema center. It was just about as accurate then as now. The word soon spread that a group of rich easterners had landed at the Alexandria, dripping dollars and panting to make pictures. We soon had many, many friends.

Among our visitors were two enterprising gentlemen named L. L. Burns and Harry Revier. They owned, they told me, a little laboratory about ten miles out. They would like to develop our film. In the course of conversations something else must have developed, namely the fact that while we did have film and a camera too, we were still looking for some place, other than the Alexandria Hotel's baggage room, to use them. Messrs. Burns and Revier had an answer for that, too. In and around the building that housed their laboratory there was space that could be rented for a studio. There was a stage, equipped with diffusers, and room to build another one if we wanted it. I forget whether I nodded wisely at the mention of diffusers or whether I really knew then that diffusers were the strips of cloth hung above an outdoor stage to control in some measure the brilliance of the California sun.

If I have sometimes been mistakenly called the father of the Hollywood film, Burns and Revier deserve to be called its obstetricians. After a long drive through the straggling outskirts of Los Angeles and then through a stretch of open country, they delivered me at last to the somnolent village of Hollywood, to have a look at their laboratory and studio. Turning off the sparsely settled main thoroughfare, grandly called Hollywood Boulevard, we drove down a broad, shady avenue more appropriately named Vine Street, and there it was.

It was a barn. Unmistakably, it was a barn. That did not bother me, though. I was not unfamiliar with stables. In Pompton [New Jersey], as a boy, I had lived over the stable for awhile. Besides, I expected to be working like a horse; what did it matter being housed like one?

On the credit side, it was a surprisingly large barn. L-shaped, one of its yellowish heat-beaten wings ran along Vine Street and the other stretched back, parallel with Selma Avenue, into an orange grove. The owner was a man named Jacob Stern, who lived in a white house near by. Gently, the news was broken to me that while Mr. Stern was entirely willing to let us devote most of his barn to the art of the cinema, for a reasonable consideration, he did reserve the right to keep his carriage and horses there.

While I was coming to terms for the use of the barn and the laboratory services of Burns and Revier, back in New York Jesse [Lasky] and Sam [Goldfish] had begun to worry. Worrying in the New York office about what the studios are doing in Hollywood has since become a firm tradition in the motion picture industry; but I must admit that Jesse and Sam had cause. Sam had already begun to sell exhibition rights to our first picture. Buyers had bought, laying cash deposits on the line. And all Sam and Jesse knew was the director-general had gone beyond Flagstaff, beyond the end of the line, to a barn in a place they had probably never heard of called Hollywood. With a prudent warning to make no long term commitments, however, they approved the renting of part of the barn. Soon a large sign announced to the occasional traveler along Selma Avenue that the Jesse L. Lasky Feature Play Company had acquired a local habitation as well as a resounding name.

A partition was set up within the barn to form a small room, a desk was brought in for the director-general and a kitchen table for his as yet non-existent secretary, and we were ready for business. The most important article of furniture, however, I found to be the wastebasket. It provided a very convenient refuge for my feet whenever Mr. Stern washed his carriage and the water ran under my desk.

Our first employee engaged in Hollywood was a secretary bookkeeper, a little young lady named Stella Stray. She sat behind the kitchen table, perched on a straight wooden chair, with a couple of city directories added so that she could reach the typewriter keys. Stella was thoroughly capable; but she was a victim of one of the first of the economy waves which periodically take their rise in the New York offices and sweep over the Hollywood studios. Someone decided that the salary I was paying Stella, $15 a week, was much too high. A good male secretary, I was told, could be had for less. Stella was given her choice of taking a cut or taking leave of the company. A spunky little person, with more experience in the motion picture business than any of her employers, Stella chose to go. Everybody was sorry. She was sorry too; but she knew her worth. What neither she nor I knew, until she started to leave the office, was that she had a secret weapon. When she started to leave, she picked the typewriter up off her table and began to stagger through the door with the heavy load in her arms. Only then did I learn that it was her own machine. Where she went, it went. Economy or no economy, she was rehired on the spot.

* * * *

I still keep in my safe a small red leather covered notebook, whose ruled pages are now gray with age and frayed at the corners. On them, in pencil, are names and notations, some so faint and smudged that they can hardly be read. They are my first record of the actors and extra players and technicians who were called to or sought us out at the barn to become part of the cast and crew of *The Squaw Man* ....

Inside the front cover of the notebook are the two addresses that formed the two poles of my Hollywood world. One reads: "Studio—6284 Selma Ave." The other is: "Home: 6136 Lexington." Though Mrs. de Mille and [daughter] Cecilia were still in New York, I did not live alone. My companion was young, faithful, graceful, and, so I was assured by the newspaper advertisement through which I found her, quite tame. She was a gray prairie wolf. I bought her for a scene in *The Squaw Man*. The people, not to mention, the horses, around Mr. Stern's barn were perhaps less trustful of her advertised virtues than I was. Because she made them rather uneasy, I kept her at home except when she was working, when she accompanied me to the studio on the end of leash. 6136 Lexington was never bothered by burglars. Night after night, after the wolf and I had dined on my cooking, I turned her loose in the living room. While I read and as often as not fell asleep in my easy chair, the wolf would pace the four sides of the room, silently, intently, hour after hour through the night. I suppose she slept sometimes, but never while I was wakeful.

So we moved, stars, extras, technicians, director-general, and wolf, toward the first day of shooting—December 29, 1913. It was a clear, sunny day. If it had not been, there would have been no shooting. The history of motion pictures, on the technical side, is largely like the history of any science: a chronicle of steps by which nature is made to work with man or prevented from working against him. The sun was California's great asset in the making of early films; but it does rain in California at times. Until, later on, we built glass walls and ceilings around our outdoor sets, rain meant that work stopped and cast and crew enjoyed a friendly game of cards or some knitting or chatting or reading, while the payroll kept rolling along. But our first day was a good day. As I look back on it, it was a very good day.

Just before shooting began, we all lined up outside the barn for a still photograph of the entire company. I have a print of that picture on the wall of my office, and next to it a picture of Paramount studio as it is today, so huge it can only be photographed from the air. As I look at that old picture of *The Squaw Man* company, I can still identify many of those in it. Of those who have slipped out of memory's grasp, there is at least one whom I wish I could identify by name. He was the man who, without knowing it, taught that director-general a lesson that saved the company from ruin.

He had been standing around looking on one day, smoking a cigarette, while Al Gandolfi and I were loading the camera. A bit of the film got twisted. Al tore it off and threw it on the ground. The unknown idler, as I probably thought him to be, picked up the piece of film and touched it with the lighted end of his cigarette. Puff! It was gone, in a vanishing whiff of smoke. Was that how fragile the result of all our work was going to be? Was that how quickly our investment, not to mention the cash we were already taking in from exhibitors, could literally go up in smoke? I made a quick decision and gave Al Gandolfi a startlingly extravagant order. We would shoot two negatives of every scene in the picture. I would leave one at the barn and take one home with me every night. Then, if the barn or my home burned, we would be protected by the other negative.

I was thinking only of possible accident. Since then, as I look over that old picture of *The Squaw Man* company, I wonder if there are in it any of the people who had other thoughts. They were around somewhere, as I soon had reason to discover. Had they been sent or bribed by the Trust? Or were they just disgruntled? I say "they" but I do not even know if there were more than one. If there was only one, he was busy—for he, or they, or someone somewhere, was determined that *The Squaw Man* would never be finished.

That someone first showed his hand, or more accurately his heel, after we had been shooting for some days. Our film was processed in the dark little laboratory next to the barn. One morning when I went in there, before my eyes had become accustomed to the dim light which was all we could use in the laboratory, my feet scuffled over something that made a rustling sound. I picked it up. When my fingers touched it, I did not need light to tell me what it was. It was our film—it was *The Squaw*

Man—unwound, thrown in a heap on the floor, and, as fingers and eyes soon told me, scraped, pitted, disfigured, as if someone had put it on the floor, put his heel on it, and dragged it between heel and floor. It was completely ruined. So would our company have been, if I had not had the extra negative at home.

We went on shooting, and we took extra precautions about the laboratory. I had a bed put in it, and sometimes worked around the clock, taking catnaps at odd hours, partly to speed the production and partly to provide that the inquisitive someone would never be sure when he might have a clear field for another *danse macabre* on our precious film.

Working and sleeping in the laboratory had still other drawbacks, though. The roof leaked. However, I had an umbrella and Mamie Wagner. Mamie was our film cutter. When the rains came, if I was working, Mamie would leave her cutting and hold the umbrella over me. If she was working at her job, I would gallantly return the compliment. Somehow we managed to stay dry enough, by turns anyway, to keep the laboratory work abreast of each day's shooting. No more attempts at sabotage were made upon the film. It was not that our enemies were so easily discouraged. They were only waiting for another and better chance at us.

* * * *

I decided to bring Mrs. de Mille and Cecilia to Hollywood, circa early 1914. When I happened to mention that they were coming, Winifred Kingston, Dustin Farnum's leading lady and later his wife, protested that I certainly wasn't going to bring them to live with a wolf in that house on Lexington, was I? That would not do, she said; and, being a lady of decision, she scouted around and found a house out on Cahuenga Boulevard, which she said was much more suitable for the director-general's wife and child. Winifred was right, of course. The house was little more than a cottage, but it was in lovely open country, in the Cahuenga Pass between Hollywood and the San Fernando Valley.

The day Mrs. de Mille and Cecilia arrived at the end of their long train ride from cold and wintry New York, I met them in an open touring car, the back of which I had filled with violets. At five cents a bunch, the violets were an extravagance, but I could not think of anything better than fresh flowers in January to symbolize my welcome and California's to the two new Californians. Five-year-old Cecilia, in her brown fur collar and muff, I remember, took it all with the unexcited dignity which has never deserted her.

The Squaw Man *almost didn't make it to theaters because of problems with the sprocket holes, but Sam Goldwyn tracked down a friend of a friend who miraculously fixed the film, and it earned enough money to pay for their next film. DeMille would make a dozen more movies with Lasky and Goldwyn, including directing Mary Pickford in* The Little American *and* The Romance of the Redwoods. *He went on to direct Gloria Swanson in such films as* Don't Change Your Husband, Male and Female, *and* The Affairs of Anatol, *making her a star. Lasky and Adolph Zukor merged their companies into Paramount, Sam Goldwyn went out on his own as a producer, and DeMille directed the biblical epics* The Ten Commandments *and* King of Kings *that define him to this day.*

Dubbing himself "director general" from the time of The Squaw Man, *DeMille's hubris and grandiosity were part of his persona, enhanced by his habit of carrying an omnipresent megaphone and having an entourage of assistants trailing in his wake, including a man with a chair who walked behind him, at the ready if the great man wanted to sit down. DeMille also wore a "uniform" of jodhpurs or riding breeches, often including puttees, straps of cloth or leather wrapped around the calves to protect the lower legs from bramble, bushes, and snakes. He lived by his own rules and carried on long affairs with several women, including his screenwriter Jeanie Macpherson.*

Cecil and Constance DeMille had a daughter, Cecilia, and adopted three other children, including Richard, who was the biological son of Cecil's brother, William, and the screenwriter Lorna Moon. (Richard was raised believing he was unrelated to the clan and was told the truth by Cecil after William's death in 1955.) Not all of DeMille's films were successes, but he continued to work and was introduced to a new generation of filmgoers in 1950 by appearing as himself in Sunset Boulevard, *which reunited him with Gloria Swanson. Cecil B. DeMille died in Los Angeles on January 21, 1959, at the age of seventy-seven.*

[1]Born Schmuel Gelbfisz, he changed his name to Samuel Goldfish when he arrived in America at nineteen. After breaking with Lasky and Zukor, Goldfish went into partnership with the Selwyn theatrical family, and they combined their names to create the Goldwyn Company. However, Sam decided he liked the name so much—and it was generating enough publicity—that he legally changed his name to Goldwyn in 1918. That partnership soon broke up as well, and Goldwyn would find success as a solitary independent producer, financing each of his films from the profits of the last.

Raoul Walsh 1914

Raoul Walsh was born in New York City on March 11, 1887. He attended several schools, including Seton Hall in New Jersey, before dropping out, working his way to Europe on a cattle boat, and heading to Texas, where he worked briefly as a cowboy. He suffered a leg injury and discovered the stage during his recuperation. Walsh soon was acting in films and put his experience with horses to work in westerns (filmed in the East) for Pathé.

Near Fort Lee [New Jersey] there was an inn called Oliver's that claimed to have been founded before the Revolution. It was popular with the picture people not only for the cheap food and good service but because it was a handy place to rest while waiting for the sun to shine. At that time, sunlight was the only illumination available. No sun, no picture. I never met a director who did not hate clouds.

Christy Cabanne (pronounced Cabanay) was a good man in every way. He had been a good actor, worked up to be a good director, and became my good friend. He was directing for Biograph when I met him.

Our meeting took place while I was working with a rope in front of Oliver's after an overcast had interrupted shooting. A few people were watching me and I had not noticed the sharp-eyed man in the cap and tweed jacket until he spoke. "That's the best rope-handling I ever saw." His tone seemed to hold genuine interest. "Where did you learn how?"

I was good and I knew it, but something about the way he said it pleased me. I stopped long enough to tell him a little about my experience as a cowboy in Texas.

The upshot of our meeting was that he offered me a job. I had seen a couple of Biograph pictures. They were not as God-awful as the stuff Pathé was making. Both the directing and the acting seemed superior to anything I had so far experienced.

Cabanne put me to work right away and I acted in some one- and two-reelers, several of them featuring Blanche Sweet and Dorothy and Lillian Gish. In one I was a newspaper reporter. My part was so small that I went to see the picture twice to make sure that I was in it. There was another very pretty girl playing the lead. I asked her name. It was Mary Pickford.

Another two-reeler I was in starred Lionel Barrymore. Mr. Barrymore cracked the space barrier between the legitimate stage and motion pictures. Before him, no theater actor would have been found dead in a movie. He led the way and many another great name followed. H. B. Walthall, George Siegmann, and Donald Crisp were among those directed by Cabanne at Biograph.

I was sulking around the studio one day, feeling disillusioned because I had not been featured as often as I had hoped...when Cabanne introduced me to D. W. Griffith, the leading director of the company. "Things are happening," Cabanne told me after the meeting. "Mr. Griffith is leaving Biograph to form his own company. It will be called Fine Arts Studios and we'll go out to the Coast. Keep it to yourself." He turned as he was leaving and added, "By the way, your name is on the list."

* * * *

Griffith's advance men had built a big outdoor stage at the intersection of Vermont and Sunset Boulevard in Hollywood. Griffith called us together the first day and Frank Woods walked out into the middle of the stage and made a speech. He asked us to remember that people in California were not yet used to motion pictures and screen actors. "I hope you'll all behave like ladies and gentlemen now that you've left the four-letter words and the tantrums back in New York." He thanked us for listening and we applauded and some of the cast promptly went out and got drunk. But we blended well enough with the locals. In all my association with Fine Arts, I can recall no major problems with the public. Naturally, we refrained from steeplechasing through cemeteries and otherwise enraging the citizenry. Once people became more conditioned to seeing a bunch of strangers in breeches and turned-around caps cranking cameras and bawling through megaphones, we were more or less accepted, at least professionally. And so Hollywood was born at sixteen frames a second, with the blessings and hopes of many and the dark predictions of a few. The precocious infant was destined to achieve universal fame until middle age, then decline steadily from a complication of ailments.

Raoul Walsh in his days as a stage
actor. (Courtesy of AMPAS)

At that time, most of the real estate around Fine Arts was cow pasture
or under citrus cultivation. On the south end of the lot were four or five
houses and a barn, with a dirt road leading into an orange grove. Some of
the company took up residence in the houses and Frank Woods stocked
the barn with gymnasium equipment. This was an inducement to physical
workouts to keep us in condition and out of trouble until we were needed.
The bars and rings and weights kept some of the more energetic ones off
the streets and out of the saloons.

The popular idea current in the East that motion pictures would never
progress beyond the silent one- and two-reelers persisted in Hollywood.
Releases continued to play in small theaters and nickelodeons and the only
advertising was on the lurid posters around the ticket offices. There were
no screen credits and most of the personnel, including myself, regarded
our job as a meal ticket and good fun. Actors provided their own props
like horses and saddles and costumes. Makeup was an individual chore
and some of the results, as may be imagined, were ludicrous and horrible.

So we began, with no lights, no interiors, and very little money. Except
for the guts and determination of Griffith and Woods and Cabanne and
some of the other directors, Fine Arts would have folded before it started.
In order to cut production costs to the bone and still find public acceptance of its pictures, Griffith decided to go in heavily for Westerns. We
ground out a few of them, then ran short of riders.

Frank Woods sent for me and said, "You're a cowboy. You talk their language. Do you have any suggestions about finding some better ones than the drugstore variety who fall off their horse every time it farts?"

I mentioned the Los Angeles stockyards as a possible source of supply. Trail drivers from Arizona, Utah, and Nevada often brought herds there. It was worth a try. "What sort of pay can I offer?" I asked. Woods frowned and said, "If you go above five a day, you're fired."

I borrowed the Pierce-Arrow, one of the studio's two rented automobiles, and managed to drive it down to the stockyards without killing anyone. As I expected, there was a herd of range cattle in the pens and some drivers sitting on a fence rail. When I got out of the car and made my pitch, they grinned at each other as though they thought I was crazy.

"You mean you'll pay us just to ride around while you take pictures of us?" I found out later that the speaker was Vester Pegg, the foreman.

"That's the general idea." Then I fired my second barrel. "You'll make five a day." Extras got paid only three dollars unless they brought costumes or special equipment. The extra two dollars was called "dress extra." These men would be bringing their horses and saddles, so I figured I was safe from the paymaster's wrath.

That did it. All of a sudden, they were ex-cowpokes. They came off that rail in a hurry and I knew I had all the leather-pushers Frank Woods needed. I got back in the car and drove off as though I owned it. Today, pay like that seems trivial but those cowboys had been eating dust for weeks and drawing down thirty a month, four dollars a day less than I had offered. I knew, I had been that route myself. No wonder one of them asked, "Say, pardner, where's your gold mine at?"

Eight riders showed up that morning. I singled out Vester Pegg and suggested they find a place to stay with a telephone, so they could be called when any of the three directors filming horse pictures needed them. Pegg and his crew left and six more showed up. Frank hired them and said that was enough. He was giving the orders and the studio was paying the wages, but I like to think that at least I had a hand in introducing cowboys to motion pictures. Wasn't I one myself? ...

The cameras were scheduled to roll on another Western, using the new help, at eight the next morning. The sun was shining and the light was perfect until some clouds blew in from the sea and stopped the action. The head cameraman used his blue glass to estimate the density of the overcast and figure how fast the clouds were traveling. When he said, "Forty minutes," everybody took a break. I knew Woods's nose was out of joint because, besides the rest of the company, fourteen riders were sitting on their rumps, doing nothing to earn their pay.

While I was waiting, I noticed a clean-shaven, husky man walking around the set. At first I thought he must be from one of the three lending companies who advanced money to Fine Arts for production. He was dressed in a blue business suit—a strong, athletic-looking fellow who could have been a football player. When he made no effort to locate Griffith or Frank Woods, I put him down as just another visitor and forgot about him until Buck Friedman, the gateman, came over and told me he was Jim Collins, a lieutenant of detectives from the central office. "He's trailing a burglar," Buck said. "He thinks the guy may be one of the extras."

Out of curiosity, I walked over and asked the lawman if I could help. I told him that we would finish shooting in about an hour after the sun came out and that none of the cast would be allowed through the gate until quitting time. He said he would wait. When the camera stopped rolling, he moved in on one of the extras and handcuffed him and took him away.

That was my first meeting with James Finlay Collins. Afterward, I saw a lot of the detective. He kept coming back and asking questions about picture-making and I persuaded Cabanne to give him some bit parts.

I was directing a Western when Jim stopped at the studio to see if I wanted to ride with him. Work was over and I had nothing planned, so I went along. We ate dinner at a fine restaurant in Chinatown, but the deferential owner would accept no payment. "That yellow son of a bitch controls the gambling," the lieutenant said as we were leaving. "We know it, but we have nothing that would stand up in court. These Chinks don't talk."

Part of his territory was the SP [Southern Pacific] freight yards. We drove there and all seemed quiet. Presently Collins stopped the car by a string of flats with a caboose at one end. There was a faint sound of hammering. "Something's going on in there." He told me to sit tight and I lost sight of him, then spotted him sneaking up on some boxcars on the far side of the flats. I watched him stop as though listening. Then he got down and crawled under one of the boxcars and I lost him again.

The next thing I heard was three shots blasting the night. I was worried and I got out of the car, but had enough sense not to go investigating.

Collins showed up after a few minutes, grinning as though pleased with the world. "Looters," was all he said. He finished reloading his revolver, then added, "There were two of them. One got a shot off before I plugged them both."

We got back into the patrol car and drove around the end of the flats and I saw the two bodies lying beside the tracks. We drove on to a telephone and he called the station to send the wagon. After it arrived and took the dead robbers away, Collins said he was hungry. We left the freight yards and went to a chili stand, where he ate two big bowls and a handful of crackers. For a man who had just killed two people, he had a fine appetite. When he had finished, he got behind the wheel and grunted, "I just remembered something." We drove back to the yards and he asked, "Can you drive a car?" I told him that Eddie Stafford, who had leased the two automobiles to the studio, had given me lessons and that I had taken Blanche Sweet and the Gish girls to and from work twice that day.

Jim stopped the car alongside another that was parked not far from where the shooting happened. When we got out, he bowed to me and pointed to the second car. "It's all yours," he said. "The owners won't be needing it any more."

That was how I became the proud proprietor of a Stutz Bearcat and the first Hollywood actor-director to own an automobile. Thirty-five to forty dollars a week left nothing over for such a luxury. I think my detective pal was trying to say thank you for the big parts I had given him. Anyway, nobody asked questions and I drove the Stutz until I went back East. When I showed it with pardonable pride to Jack Pickford, he said, "It's all right, but it's a 1911. He might have shot someone who owned a later model." Jack, of course, could afford to be choosy. Mary and his mother were always sending him checks. But I did not have that kind of money.

* * * *

Levy's Tavern on Spring Street was a gathering place where motion-picture people congregated every Sunday night, and where the Keystone comedians liked to show off their antics.

Charlie Chaplin had just come to Hollywood, and it was on one of these Sunday evenings that I first met him. He was a likeable little fellow with a Cockney accent. While we were chatting, he told me about his early life in England, where he was brought up in a rough and tough district called

Limehouse. When it was time to say good-night, I offered to drive him home. While we were on our way there, he admired my car, asking me how much it cost. I told him it was given to me by two friends who lived in California and were never coming back. Chaplin said, "I have ninety dollars saved up, do you know where I can buy one?" I told him I knew an actor who sold used cars down on Figueroa and Santa Barbara Avenue and, if he wasn't working Saturday, I'd drive him down there. He thanked me again and got out of the car.

On Saturday morning I pulled up in front of the Keystone studio and noticed that the gates were closed. No one was about but Patty Driscoll, the gateman, who was sitting in a chair reading a newspaper. I went up to him and asked, "Patty, what's going on—nobody working today?" He answered, with a wry smile on his face, "No, and I'll be tellin' you why." In his Irish brogue, Patty gave me the facts.

"Six months ago a lady came to the studio with her daughter, who was about seventeen years old—and she was a pretty one indeed. The young girl played several small parts, and they say she had the makings of being a pretty good actress, only she got pregnant. Then her mother went to the district attorney. But Mack Sennett had a good friend in the D.A.'s office, Jack Malloy, who phoned the studio and left word, 'If anybody had anything to do with the girl, tell him to get out of town for a few days.' And would you believe it, the whole studio took off."

I asked, "Did Chaplin go?"

Patty quickly responded, "Go—he was the first to leave."

Other motion-picture companies began to come out from New York about this time. Thomas H. Ince bought a hundred acres at the ocean end of Sunset and built Inceville studio there. Real estate in that area was selling for fifty dollars an acre. The price today is fifty thousand. Ince gave us real competition by making Westerns and pictures of the Barbary Coast and the Klondike in gold-rush days. His top stars, Dorothy Dalton and William S. Hart, played in most of them.

In the same year, Jesse Lasky and Cecil B. DeMille leased a property on Vine Street and built a large production stage. Lasky was the producer and DeMille directed until he began to make his own pictures. This was the West Coast launching of Famous Players, which later became Paramount. And, of course, over in Edendale, Mack Sennett was introducing the public to the Keystone Cops. Hollywood was on its way.

D. W. Griffith was a genius when it came to making a motion picture. He was a quiet man, almost shy until he picked up a megaphone. He called every male member of the company "Mister" and discouraged familiarity. Some of his biographers have accused him of arrogance and unfairness, of being "Mr. Unapproachable." I always found him ready to listen to opinions, and he was the first to offer help when any of his people got into trouble. Whenever I had the chance, I watched while he directed, and tried to remember everything he said and did. Not many people are lucky enough to have a genius for a teacher, and the lessons were free. All I needed to do was keep my eyes and ears open.

Later, when I became a director myself, I profited greatly from the things this master taught me. Cabanne and the other Fine Arts directors were all competent, but none of them had the touch and the superb sense of the dramatic which were evident in everything Griffith made. When he produced and personally directed *The Birth of a Nation*, the world acclaimed his artistry and paid belated tribute. This spectacle changed the history of movies and for the first time put them on a par with all other forms of art. And its nationwide box-office success made movies big business.

Raoul Walsh stayed with D. W. Griffith for several years, learning his craft. Walsh switched between directing and acting, playing the role of John Wilkes Booth in The Birth of Nation. *Walsh directed Douglas Fairbanks in* The Thief of Bagdad *in 1924, and costarred with and directed Gloria Swanson in the then very risqué Sadie Thompson in 1928. That same year, Walsh lost an eye from shattered glass in a car accident when a rabbit went through his windshield. He sported an eye patch from then on, focused on directing, and excelled at it for the next thirty-five years. In 1930, he cast the unknown Marion Morrison, billed as John Wayne, in a major role in* The Big Trail. *Dramas, romances, westerns, historical sagas, and crime films—Walsh directed them all. He worked with actors such as James Cagney, Errol Flynn, Marion Davies, Mae West, Clark Gable, Humphrey Bogart, Jack Benny, Olivia de Havilland, Laurence Olivier, and Rita Hayworth, yet he was never nominated for an Academy Award.*

Raoul Walsh died at the age of ninety-three on December 31, 1980, in Simi Valley, California.

Anita Loos 1914

C orinne Anita Loos was born on April 26, 1888, in Etna, a small town at the base of California's Mount Shasta. Her father, R. Beers Loos, a charming small-time entrepreneur, dragged Anita, her mother, Minnie, her older brother, Clifford, and younger sister, Gladys, along on his near constant search for greener pastures, first to San Francisco, briefly to Los Angeles, and finally to San Diego. He managed a theater there, and Anita and Gladys were child actors on his stage. One-reel films were shown between acts and Anita quickly saw that Biograph films were the best; she began sending stories to the address on the film cans: 11 E. 14th Street, New York. In 1912, she received her first check for twenty-five dollars for The New York Hat, which would be the last film that Mary Pickford made for Biograph. Anita continued to mail off her short scenarios and occasionally receive release forms and checks in return. But, at twenty-five, she was so disenchanted with her life in San Diego that she was considering marriage—or as her suitor said, to "wear the ring"—when we pick up her story.

As I was just about to give in and "learn to wear the ring" of a "loving sweetheart" who used the word "bum" as an adjective, something happened that canceled out the whole deal: a letter that was more poetic in my eyes than any mash note Abelard ever wrote to Héloise.

New York
January 6, 1914

Dear Madam,
I shall be in Los Angeles on Tuesday, January 13th, for a short stay, so if you happen to be in that city I would like to have a personal interview with you at the Biograph Studio, Georgia and Gerard Streets.

81

Trusting you will favor me with a call, and wishing you a very prosperous New Year, I remain,

Very truly yours,
T. E. Dougherty

Dougherty's letter came from the business office of the Biograph Company in New York, but by this time the studio itself was permanently located in Hollywood, a mere two-hour train trip from where we lived. It seems highly apathetic of me not to have thought of invading that studio until Dougherty's invitation arrived. But we were completely settled in our little rut: Pop satisfied, as always, with being a big shot in a small world; Mother so timid that any move at all required superhuman effort; and I aimlessly wasting time among people with whom I was disenchanted. But all of a sudden I was overcome by a desire to meet those shadowy characters who acted in my screenplays. I talked Mother into agreeing to the trip—chaperoned, as always, by herself. Leaving Pop happy, no doubt, to enjoy a couple days of freedom, we took off from San Diego to enter a world of the most fabulous mummery ever devised by man.

We arrived in Los Angeles and checked in at an obscure hotel, and the next morning I telephoned Dougherty at the studio. I was told to come out right away, that both he and Mr. Griffith would be pleased to meet me. This being my phase of copying the stark good taste of royalty, I put on my best white sailor suit (they used to be called "Peter Thompsons," probably after some dress manufacturer), and my hair, in a pigtail tied with wide black taffeta bows, seemed the essence of girlish refinement. But although I was a teenage femme fatale in Coronado, in the flashy locale we were about to enter I must have seemed a schoolchild of about twelve in the charge of a rather meek governess.

As our streetcar entered Hollywood that morning, we found it the same dilapidated suburb it had been when we lived in Los Angeles. Our main purpose in ever going there had been to ride to the end of the line and take lunch at the old Hollywood Hotel, a rambling edifice painted the same dun color as the hills, with a veranda where elderly seekers after sunshine, mostly from the Middle West, sat in big red chairs and rocked their uneventful lives away. Across from the hotel was a shoddy business district; there were a few bungalows interspersed with vacant lots, and

Anita Loos, shortly after going to work for D. W. Griffith. (Courtesy of MOMA)

The Hollywood Hotel. (Collection of Patt Morrison)

that was all. Nobody dreamed a day was close at hand when that one word, Hollywood, would express the epitome of glamour, sex, and sin in their most delectable forms.

* * * *

Mother and I got off the streetcar under the blinding sun and betook ourselves to the Biograph Studio. It consisted of a row of one-story buildings that were scarcely more than sheds; on a center door was painted BIOGRAPH COMPANY—MAIN OFFICE, the sign of which speeded up my already rapid circulation. But now Mother, ordinarily so timid, forged ahead of me. She must have sensed that she was in danger of forever losing her honeybunch, and wanted to investigate what sort of world it was that might gobble me up.

We came into a long narrow office partitioned by a counter, behind which two minor employees in their shirtsleeves were engaged in desultory conversation. One of them asked what we wanted, and Mother said that Miss Loos was there to see Mr. Dougherty. Polite, but not very interested, the man gestured toward a bench, told us to take a seat, and then disappeared through the back doorway. Presently a large pleasant Irish-American in a summer-weight suit emerged and mistaking Mother for his authoress, approached her genially.

"Well, Miss Loos," he said, "it's nice to meet you after all this time."

"But I'm Anita's mother," she corrected him. "This is Anita."

At which moment the door opened and the movies' first real genius entered from the back lot. Up to that time David Wark Griffith had been merely a name scrawled on my vouchers; most of my correspondence had been with Dougherty, who seemed the more important of two unknowns.

Tall, bronzed, and rangy like a cowboy, Griffith was in his shirtsleeves and wore a battered straw sombrero tied under his chin with a black shoestring; the ridiculous get-up didn't detract one bit from his enormous distinction. Griffith must have been in his early thirties, but he had an authority that seemed to deny he had ever been young. His highly arched nose belonged on some Roman emperor; his pale eyes, in sharp contrast to the tan of his complexion, shone with a sort of archaic amusement, as if he were constantly saying to himself, "What fools these mortals be!" But that morning it was Griffith's own turn to be fooled, for he passed right by me and advanced to greet my Mother.

"You're shaking hands with the mother of your authoress," Dougherty spoke up. "It's this little lady who's been writing our scenarios."

Turning to look at me, Griffith's expression went blank, as had Dougherty's, while I was still so impressed by his Jovian dignity that I could only stammer I was pleased to meet him; after which there didn't seem to be anything more for either of us to say. And then Mother, for the first time in her entire life, boldly spoke up to save her child.

"Good-bye gentlemen," she said. "Come along, Anita."

We walked out of that office, with Mother feeling we had escaped from a nest of hobbledehoys. I knew it was my childish appearance that had stunned them into silence; but, even so, to be allowed to leave after so brief a welcome made me feel bitterly frustrated and disappointed.

We had gone about half a block toward the streetcar line when we heard a booming voice call, "Miss Looze!" (Griffith would always pronounce our name "Looze" and drag it out as if it were in two syllables. He had his own pronunciation for words, an affectation which in him seemed natural. Griffith never did or said anything in the same manner as ordinary people.) Not sure the summons was for us, we turned and saw Griffith standing on the sidewalk, beckoning with his long arms for us to come back. Even under that ridiculous sombrero he looked so compelling and fateful that Mother's hackles must have risen; she must have known that this might be good-bye forever to her little girl. But, like an invincible magnet, Griffith pulled her back, with me in tow.

Without any explanation of his strange first greeting, Griffith invited us onto the lot. What we saw in the glare of that raw insolent sun was startling. On the unroofed stage was an ancient pavilion of great splendor; enormous braziers were filling the air with incense, and the set was teeming with characters dressed in biblical costumes. Prominent among them were dancing girls wearing little more than beads, their faces dead white, with black smudged eyes and violent red lipstick. Their semi-nude state was a shock, even to me for, as I have said, when Gladys and I played in *Quo Vadis* we had modestly worn tights. Griffith demanded a chair for Mother and a high stool for me, from which I could oversee the entire stage. Sitting in that place of honor next to Griffith's camp chair, I had the first experience of movies in the making, while Mother tried to look at the shocking spectacle without actually seeing it.

The picture was *Judith of Bethulia*, a daring innovation; for it was to take four reels in the telling, and up to that time two reels had been the limit of any film. The scene that day involved Holofernes' seduction by Judith. I recognized both the stars, although I still didn't know their names. Holofernes proved to be Henry B. Walthall and Judith was Blanche Sweet. She was small, fragile, blond, with a compact little face and a highly arched nose. Blanche Sweet seemed rather unsure of herself, as did all Griffith's young actresses; he wanted no positive traits to prevent them from being passive instruments on whom he could improvise.

Many of Griffith's actors were in fact not actors at all, for he picked people up whenever he was impressed by their looks, as the great Italian film directors were to do later on. Frequently a mere bit player supplied Griffith with an unforgettable scene. There is a close-up in *The Birth of a Nation* of an uncouth Union soldier gazing soulfully at the frail Southern belle, played by Lillian Gish, in a way that will be stamped forever on the memory of anyone who ever saw the picture. Griffith had a camera-man with an amazing control of that apparatus; a slovenly, uneducated German-American named Billy Bitzer, who gave the Master any effect he desired without protesting that there was no possible way to do it.

While Griffith was directing Blanche Sweet that day he stepped onto the set from time to time to demonstrate some tactics of seduction, which he did with a sense of fun that prevented any harm to his male dignity. Sometimes he put his arms about the semi-nude Miss Sweet and whispered in her ear, obviously to save the young actress the embarrassment of his criticism's being overheard. But to Mother those embraces looked like sheer license, and she felt more and more that we were in an anteroom of hell.

When time came for the company to troop off for lunch, Griffith invited Mother and me to the corner drugstore, and there, in the seclusion of a booth, he proceeded to quiz me, with Mother sitting by in stony silence. I told him of having inherited an aptitude for writing from my father and also mentioned my experience as an actress; on hearing this, Griffith's eye lit up, putting Mother instantly on the alert, but I was too engrossed to note the danger signal. Expanding under the attentions of that remarkable man, I confessed to the cramping effect of my home life and explained that my only escape from boredom was the library.

"What do you read?" asked Griffith.

I proceeded to sound off with some intellectual name-dropping: Plato,

Montaigne, Spinoza, et al. It was obvious that he was as lacking in education as I was, but I had had more time to read, and now the great man began
to pick my small brain for scattered bits of information. I had recently discovered Voltaire, and Griffith wanted to know something about him. But
Voltaire's cynicism, as expounded by A. Loos, didn't necessarily convince
Griffith, and he remarked with a benign smile that the human race might
possibly be nicer than that arch pessimist conceded. In return, I felt perfectly at ease to criticize Griffith's own preferences. His idol, it appeared,
was Walt Whitman. I impudently argued that Whitman was hysterical.
"Hysteria has no place in great writing," said A. Loos. "Shakespeare is
never hysterical, neither is Goethe. Walt Whitman is as uncontrolled as
Ella Wheeler Wilcox!" Griffith laughed and was probably as much amused
by my impertinence, as I was intent on trying to set him straight.

I can't say I fell in love with Griffith that day over a sandwich in a corner drugstore, but our session provided the sort of cerebral excitement
that makes the bohemias of the world, the Greenwich Villages and Sohos
and Left Banks, so much more sexy than any other places. Our discussion
continued so long that finally the studio's efficiency expert, a little man
who bristled with *lèse-majesté*, barged in to tell the Master that if he didn't
get back to the set he'd never finish the day's schedule. On our way to the
studio Griffith said to me, "I think we'll have to get you out of San Diego."

*Anita Loos returned to San Diego where she separated the men from the boys
and "purposely chose a boy." The marriage lasted only a few months, but that was
enough to reassure her mother that Anita had at least tried to be respectable. Still,
Minnie insisted on accompanying Anita back to Hollywood and they ensconced
themselves in the Hollywood Hotel. She was welcomed at Griffith's new Triangle
studios where she met her future husband, the director John Emerson, and wrote
very successful physical comedies for Douglas Fairbanks.*

*She continued as an in-demand screenwriter and playwright after she and
Emerson moved to New York in 1919, but her international success came in 1925
when she authored* Gentlemen Prefer Blondes. *First serialized in* Harper's
Bazaar, *the book was eventually published in over a dozen languages and is still
in print. Lorelei Lee, the prototype for the classic smart dumb blonde, went on to
be portrayed in a play, a Broadway musical, and two films. Loos and Emerson
took the fortune she amassed and lived the good life in Europe, New York, and
Palm Beach until the Depression, combined with Emerson's bad investments,*

forced her to return to work. She was happy to join M-G-M in the early 1930s, where she specialized in writing smart, wisecracking female characters in films such as Red Headed Woman, San Francisco, *and* The Women. *Emerson lived out his days in a sanitarium where his chronic hypochondria was catered to, and in the early 1940s, Anita moved to New York where she wrote plays such as* Happy Birthday *for Helen Hayes,* Gigi, *and the book for the musical version of* Gentlemen Prefer Blondes. *She lived across from Carnegie Hall on West 57th Street, became a New York institution, and frequently attended film and museum openings. She died in New York on August 18, 1981, at the age of ninety-three.*

Elsie Janis 1914

B orn *Elsie Jane Bierbower on March 16, 1889, in Columbus, Ohio, "Little Elsie" was on the stage at age five and performing solo acts three years later. She made her Broadway debut, as Elsie Janis, at sixteen and, with her gift for impersonations, was an instant success. She was performing in London when the First World War broke out, and she returned to America. Making movies was a logical next step in her career.*

Elsie was tied at the hip to her mother, Jenny, who went everywhere with her and insisted everyone call her "Ma." When Janis said "we," she was usually referring to herself and "Ma." Friends simply called them "The Jani."

Jack Barrymore had made his début in the moving pictures with sensational success, which had started a phobia on the part of the picture producers to lure theatre stars into their still comparatively unimportant industry. Everyone thought Jack was made to go into the "movies." It was the beginning of the end. Of course, no one could foresee which end! But when they offered me thirty thousand dollars and three drawing-rooms to and from California, we chucked the idea of playing vaudeville until the play was ready, and joined the younger Barrymore in his so-called madness! Frank Garbutt, then the head of Bosworth, Inc., was the tall, white-haired, smiling Mephisto who lured us. He could lure most anyone even without thirty thousand additional "lurettes" and with them—well, we signed the contract one day and were ensconced in the three drawing-rooms en route for California three days later!

Douglas Fairbanks was being "lured" but he was not quite ready to "give up his career" for any monetary consideration. I think he wanted to see just how badly I got wrecked. Anyway, he resisted for a few months!

The three drawing-rooms were not just a "swanky" gesture, for we had

Elsie Janis and Phillips Smalley, Lois Weber's husband, on location. (Courtesy of MOMA)

Hallie [their cook], Josephine my French maid, whom we had brought back from Europe, two dogs, three birds, tennis racquets, golf clubs, a portable gramophone, in fact all the usual Janis impedimenta!

I wrote the scenario for my first film on the way out. It was *The Caprices of Kitty*. When we arrived, we were met by Mr. Garbutt, Phillips Smalley (who was to be my director), newspaper men, cameras, and flowers! Certainly I was going to "destruction" de luxe! Mr. Garbutt had taken a house for us at 323 New Hampshire Avenue in Los Angeles. Hollywood and Beverly were still too much out of things, in fact Beverly Hills was considered "country."

The night of our arrival, Mr. Garbutt and Phil Smalley dined with us in our latest "home." I read the scenario to them and they approved of it. Inside of three days we were "shooting" the picture. Courtney Foote and Frank Elliot were my two leading men. Dustin Farnum was working at the studio, which had practically no roof as we depended almost entirely on sunlight.

I had a lovely, chintz-decorated dressing-room and was treated like a Queen on a holiday. After Mr. Garbutt saw the first scenes, he asked me to make two more pictures. After I saw them, I wanted to take the veil, but nevertheless I wrote the second scenario and preparations were started while I was making the first, which took us nine days.

I simply adored the work, even when we played scenes in the streets and were surrounded by hundreds of spectators! In those days, a murder on a street corner would not have caused any more interest than a moving picture company at work!

My second film was called *Betty in Search of a Thrill.* They wanted Owen Moore, who was then married to my little friend Gladys Smith, by that time Mary Pickford and the undisputed Empress of the films, for my leading man, but he was in New York and "hard to get." I wired Mary saying, "Will you please lend me your husband for one picture?"

Word drifted back to New York that when one saw the Janises they saw Owen Moore, and one day while we were on location, Owen was sitting in the car between Mother and me, holding a hand of each, when we heard a honk, honk behind us. A large car drew along beside ours, and sitting in it was Mrs. Owen Moore! She had loaned him to me for one picture and we were making the third one together. Mary and I often laugh over it now, but at the moment it was a situation not in my scenario! ...

* * * *

Hobart Bosworth, after whom the picture company was named and who was the "big shot" of the studio, both as an actor and a director, liked the third scenario I wrote well enough to direct it and play my father!

Lois Weber, who was Mrs. Smalley in private life, and one of the few women directors who ever really directed, needed Phil in her current productions so Hobart and I started to work on mine. *Nearly a Lady* was the title. It might have been called *Nearly a Good Picture*!

There was a pretty blue-eyed girl very much in evidence around the studio. It was difficult to find out just what her job was, for she did a little of everything. She played in a picture one week, helped "cut" the next, wrote a story the next, and in her spare moments handled the publicity. I told Mr. Garbutt that she would be heard from some day. The last time I heard from her, she had just signed a new contract for thirty-five hundred dollars a week and had written scenario, continuity, and dialogue of three of the biggest pictures of 1931. Her name was, and (though she has had several others, due to a weakness for "marrying the man") still is, Frances Marion! ...

Sidney Franklin, now a great director, was the young man who used to follow me around the "set" saying, "You had your handkerchief in your left hand in the last 'shot,' Miss Janis!" I nicknamed him George Detail and he still answers to it when I meet him out here!

Mr. Garbutt was a glutton for punishment so he asked me to make a fourth picture. I was a glutton for work, so I wrote it and Hobart Bosworth again directed. It was called *'Twas Ever Thus!* The theme was love through the ages, and Owen had to make love to me in five different characters, including prehistoric! Making a cave man of Mary's easy-going, handsome, but somewhat lazy husband was a feat that only Jenny's daughter would attempt!

Alfred Butt, having been informed that we had decided not to return to England for *The Passing Show of 1915*, wrote to say that he not only insisted on my fulfilling my contract, but that he would like me to come as soon as possible. And by this time we were beginning to get the "London Blues," so it was agreed with Charley [Broadway producer Charles Dillingham] that I would go to London and return the next autumn to do the play for him, which was called *Miss Information*.

Right after Christmas, which was a great thrill to me, never having picked roses on Christmas Day, we left California and as nice a crowd of friends as any to whom we had ever tendered one of our tearful farewells!

Elsie Janis returned to Europe, and when the United States entered the First World War in 1917, she was the first American entertainer to go to France to sing and dance for the troops. "Ma" of course went too, as Elsie spent almost a year performing near the front lines. She was dubbed the "Sweetheart of the AEF" (American Expeditionary Forces). After the war, Janis returned to the stage and film, but never with the same success. However, she stayed busy and was credited with writing more than fifty songs. Frances Marion was a lifelong friend, as was Mary Pickford, who met her future husband Douglas Fairbanks at Janis's New York home in 1915.

Janis's mother died in 1930, and two years later Elsie married Gilbert Wilson, a stockbroker at least a dozen years her junior. She continued to work with veterans; her final Broadway appearance was in the musical review Frank Fay's Show *in 1939 and her last film role was in* Women in War *in 1940. Mary Pickford was at Elsie's deathbed in Los Angeles when she passed away on February 26, 1956, at the age of sixty-six.*

Marie Dressler 1914

B orn Leila Maria Koerber in Cobourg, Ontario, on November 9, 1868, Marie Dressler took her stage name in part to separate herself from her estranged father, with whom she had never gotten along. She was a young teen when she left home to join a traveling stock company, and although no beauty and always heavyset, Dressler managed to support herself by acting and singing throughout America's heartland over the next ten years. In 1892, she arrived in New York with her broad physical comedy style firmly established. A decade later, she signed a three-year, fifty-thousand-dollar contract with the vaudeville producers Weber and Fields and became a star as "Tillie," the oversized "ugly duckling," a character she would play for the next dozen years. Mugging and singing songs such as "A Great Big Little Girl Like Me," Dressler became a vaudeville sensation and explained her popularity by saying that "a tired man finds relaxation in seeing me make a fool of myself." She toured the country regularly, playing the larger vaudeville stages of the time, working herself to exhaustion, and then taking time off to rest.

I was convalescing in Los Angeles and went with my nurse to a movie show, as I am very fond of pictures, although I do not think they are in the right hands. Indeed, I consider the picture game the first Woolworth idea since the ten cent store. When it is understood that one hundred prints were made of each film and between ninety to ninety-five of these strips were running every day at $25 each, thus making the earning power of each individual film about $2250 per day or about three quarters of a million per year, it is to know that it was a great game. Furthermore, all communities used to have their little film houses where a woman could go with four children and rest and think she was in a theater.

* * * *

Marie Dressler (left) with Frances Marion on the set of *Min and Bill*, 1930. (Courtesy of MOMA)

Well, as I said before, my nurse and I sought a picture show. As we went in I saw a man looking at me and I remarked:

"There's a man who wants his fare back to New York. He's going to speak."

Sure enough the man with him came up to me and said, "We'd like to talk to you."

"I'll see you at my hotel," I replied, for I was in no mood for a hard luck story and was not equal to standing to listen to it.

The man I had first noticed waited with wild eyes and let the other do all the talking, but after the picture he accompanied the speaker to my hotel and I learned that he was Mack Sennett and his friend was [cofounder Charles O.] Bauman of the Keystone pictures.

They announced, "We want to get into good houses. We believe we can do so with a name like yours."

It was all so unexpected that I did not know what to say and the following day they came again. They made me the proposition that I was to own half the picture when made: that it was to be leased but never sold: they were to put it on and send me a statement every week. When I finally agreed, I went up on the lot and looked around till I found Charlie Chaplin, who was then unknown. I picked him out and also Mabel Normand, to whom I had taken a fancy, and started in to make the picture, known to most of the fans, called *Tillie's Punctured Romance*.

I think the public will agree that I am a good picker, for it was the first real chance Charlie Chaplin ever had and he has since proven his worth while Mabel Normand is one of the most capable and conscientious actresses on the screen. Many a time I have seen her brave a director—and directors won't allow anyone to tell them anything—and say just as they were starting to shoot a scene, "I don't feel that. If I do that, why do I do it? Perhaps the other girl was right in her view. I'm just trying to get it," which showed that she was doing her utmost to get the best out of herself and the picture.

A great many people do not film well and never understand the mechanics of pictures. Fortunately for me I became camera wise immediately. The thing was as alive to me as an audience and I loved it. We had such a good time making this picture that Charlie Chaplin and Mabel Normand cried when we were through with our fourteen weeks labor on it and I was ready to leave Los Angeles.

After the picture was made, I returned to New York and saw the darned thing hawked about for nine long weeks. As fast as it was shown in the projection rooms it was turned down. Nobody would take it, perhaps because the comedy was somewhat in advance of the times and then a little new. I was sure it would make good sometime, and was reminded of my brother-in-law Richard Ganthony's experience, when his ultimate triumph, *A Message from Mars*, laid in Charles Frohman's office for seven years before it was produced.

Meantime, the makers of my first picture were hard pressed for money and things looked exceedingly black. Finally we received a hearing and the minute it was shown in an actual theater it was a triumph. I have heard of lines several blocks long standing to get into the second matinee and evening performance of this picture and eight men have told me that *Tillie's Punctured Romance* built their theaters.

In spite of this success I was eventually obliged to go to the law over a division of the profits. When it came to a settlement, I said I wanted $50,000 and the return of the picture after five years. Everybody thought this was very amusing, as the picture would be dead by then, but the terms were granted. I let the film lie for two years and then leased it again. According to my new agreement I was to receive $25,000 down and a weekly royalty, but again the picture has turned out a hoodoo as far as receipts go, as I cannot get any accounting from the second producer, although the film is still being shown. Anyway, the business side of the moving picture business has always been too complicated for me. There are too many middlemen.

After filming Tillie's Punctured Romance, *Marie Dressler returned to New York, and when America entered the World War in 1917, her fame was such that she joined Mary Pickford, Charlie Chaplin, and Douglas Fairbanks at the White House to kick off their national tour to sell millions of dollars of war bonds. Back on Broadway in 1919, Dressler was elected President of the Chorus Equity Association of America. She was a headliner, but she was outraged that chorus girls had no pay during rehearsals, low pay when a show opened, nothing if it closed, and often had to provide their own wardrobe. Their strike resulted in Broadway going dark for a month and improvements in working conditions being made, but producers balked at working with Dressler after that. When she tried to produce her own version of* Tillie's Nightmare, *it was an expensive failure.*

The coming of the Jazz Age, with its emphasis on youth and glamour, made Dressler's form of comedy out of date, and by 1927, she was living in poverty. A New York friend wrote Frances Marion, who, as a reporter for the San Francisco Chronicle, *had met Marie fifteen years earlier. Marion was now Hollywood's highest-paid screenwriter. She convinced Irving Thalberg, M-G-M's head of production, to give Marie Dressler a contract, and she played in several low-budget comedies, often costarring with the comedienne Polly Moran. When Marion suggested Dressler for a supporting role in* Anna Christie, *the film Marion was adapting for Greta Garbo, Thalberg agreed. Marie's success in the role led Marion to write* Min and Bill *for Dressler; her performance as Min brought her an Academy Award for Best Actress. Dressler went on to star in films such as* Tug Boat Annie *and* Dinner at Eight, *and in 1932, while the Depression circled the globe and hit Hollywood hard, it was the success of Marie Dressler films that helped make M-G-M the only studio to operate in the black.*

After a long battle with cancer, Dressler died in Santa Barbara, California, with Frances Marion at her bedside, on July 28, 1934, at the age of sixty-five.

Agnes de Mille 1914

A gnes George de Mille was born in New York on September 18, 1905, the daughter of playwright William de Mille and Anna George, whose father was the British economist and social-reform advocate Henry George. (William chose to stay with the family tradition of spelling his name with a small "d," while his younger brother Cecil used DeMille professionally and de Mille personally.) Agnes was almost nine when she arrived in Los Angeles with her mother and six-year-old sister, Margaret, to join William, who was already there working with Cecil.

Father's brother, Uncle Cecil, had gone to California the year before, in 1913, an adventure considered by the rest of the family as the purest folly. But Cecil had little to lose. He had had uneven success in acting and playwriting, and his ventures with business had failed as well. On departure for the West he asked Father for five thousand dollars. But Father had staked him too often fruitlessly and this time was being cautious. It has since become clear that Father's decision was not a profitable one, that five thousand dollars would have entitled him to one-eighth interest in Paramount Pictures, Inc. The company was founded around a lunch table in New York. Jesse Lasky, an ex-cornet player who had made a small name in vaudeville with his band of beautiful red-headed girls, gave his name— The Jesse L. Lasky Feature Play Co.; Sam Goldfish [Goldwyn], a glove merchant and Lasky's brother-in-law, lent his talents as business manager. He later changed his name to Goldwyn.

Uncle Cecil went West, young, good-looking, open-minded, and furnished with very nearly unlimited ambition. He raised the cash he needed for his partnership in bits and pieces. His staff he picked up haphazardly wherever he thought he'd found ability. His assistant director, for instance, sold Navaho jewelry for Fred Harvey on board the Santa Fe trains until the day his peddling brought him into contact with Uncle Cecil.

The tales that drifted back from the West were hair-raising. Uncle Cecil had bitter rivals who were intent on doing him down; the exposed film had been trod underfoot and he had sat up all night covering the developers with loaded guns; he had been shot at in the dark as he hurried home with the reels under his coat to the bungalow he shared with a pet wolf (these were not press stories; these were Uncle Ce's letters to his anxious wife); he had overcome his rivals and the first full-length feature was finished; he sent for real actors from the East and for his wife and child.

* * * *

Cecil, who established himself immediately as Director General of the Lasky company, begged Father to join him. They were settled very nicely, he wrote, in what had been a stable on Vine Street. Business was expanding rapidly; the work was pioneering and picturesque; Father was literate and would, therefore, Cecil pointed out, find unique opportunities. So Father agreed to go.

He wrote back every single day from Hollywood and sent photographs: Cecil and himself in director's costumes, riding breeches, and puttees to protect their legs on location work. Cecil in his early thirties, balding already, stocky, with the dynamism of a young bull, his head lowered to gaze straight into the camera, his beautiful teeth flashing; Father, the older brother, thoughtful, intelligent, practiced, waiting slightly to the rear. There were photographs of rattlesnakes crawling over the dressing-room steps, of Hollywood and cowboys, of actresses in tangles of hair, their black-rimmed eyes squinting in the white sun.

Mother decided to close up the New York flat and follow him out with my sister and me. We planned to stay for six months and then we would come back so that Father, well rested, could write another successful play.

Mother started to pack: I looked ahead. I would, I hoped, go to school with an Indian boy. I would have a horse and ride with the cowboys. I would, please God, be allowed to act in the movies.

Hollywood was different from what I thought, anticlimactic after the momentous trip west. Where were the deserts cut and gullied by pale blue rivers? The red and orange Indian mountains we had left behind in Arizona? The ancient villages glimpsed fleetingly as the tracks clicked

Agnes de Mille around age eleven. (Courtesy of MOMA)

behind too fast? From a Pullman window I had seen two Navahos, scarlet and purple, riding quietly down a path to the shadowed arroyo, just as though it had been three hundred years ago, just as though a train were not going by in front of them with little girls eating their lunch of lettuce and Thousand Island dressing en route to join their handsome young father in Hollywood.

The trip was a belated homecoming for Mother. For Father, Margaret and me it was a voyage into pure adventure. We stayed the first few nights with Uncle Cecil but Mother quickly found us a dear little ugly house of our own, snuggling at the foot of a hill and boasting a banana tree and a rose garden.

Hollywood was merely a country town, like many in the East, with palms instead of maples and chestnuts. The hills, though steep, were plain colored. The people were just ordinary.

There were absolutely no Indians, but there was a hermit, which was even rarer, complete with sackcloth, bare feet and staff. Kids said he lived in a cave in the hills.

There were also a good many theosophists and folk of religious bent whose costume was not so easily discernible. I learned to know them by their batik scarves, their strings of beads, their unpowdered noses, their nervous, cheerful expressions and their readiness to come to Mother's teas.

And there were some cowboys. They kept largely to themselves out on the Lasky ranch, coming in only occasionally to the studio to play caballeros or knights or Civil War cavalry or themselves. Occasionally they would show up in a group of six or eight in Uncle Ce's back yard and take us for a good thumping gallop around the block astride their saddlebows. They smelled of sweat and leather and they laughed with great male laughs which we found pleasantly terrifying. We used to come upon groups of them riding down the back streets where the asphalt was soft under their horses' feet.

The scenery was unrefreshing to an Easterner. Geraniums hung unnaturally out of the palm branches. Magenta bougainvillea matted the shingles and waved shoots and tendrils over the roof tops, struggling in suffocating embrace with the Cherokee roses. Roses flattened the poinsettias against the windowpanes. The gross, succulent grass grew rank to one's calves unless one mowed and mowed, and as long as one watered. But right where the last drop of moisture fell there the green comfort stopped, the bare earth showed. Not a clover leaf, not a bit of moss vouchsafed spontaneous relief, not one tender unearned green blade offered itself. A gray, scratching growth took over, unlovely to the foreign eye and terrible to the ankle, which concealed no part of the uncompromising earth.

The main thoroughfare, Hollywood Boulevard, was a shambling, drowsy street of box stores and shingled houses under the dusty crackling palms and pepper trees. The stores had been thrown together in a week, but the houses were substantial, built by citizens of the Middle West who had come to the Coast to die at ease in the sun. A cross between Swiss chalet and Japanese temple, they reflected a cautious exoticism not in evidence in the Tudor-Moorish villas with striped awnings and plentiful cross-timbering which later replaced them. The houses seemed taken unaware by a business street across their front lawns. Backed up into their trees they appeared to yield yard by dusty yard of grass before the crowding of upstart shops. A trolley clanged down the eight miles from Laurel Canyon to the heart of Los Angeles, and this was the only public conveyance. On it every morning rode the entire working staff of the studio carrying their lunch boxes. Only the Director General, my uncle, and the producer, Jesse Lasky, rode to work in cars. Actors, directors and writers went by trolley. And when the family had Uncle Cecil's car or when he came home to dinner with Pop, they walked. I used to see them, crossing the vacant lot in the red sunset, their putteed legs scratching through the dried yellow grass. They carried briefcases and talked with head lowered.

"Anne," called Father, "I've brought Cecil home."

"Cecil?" said Mother in a fluster. His effect on the womenfolk was always that of a cock in a barnyard, and Mother, like all his female relatives, looked upon every chance to serve him as an indulgence on his part.

"William," she said, "you might have warned me." And she rushed to make the table look prettier.

They sat long after dinner and talked of the studio. I was asleep by then, but I woke to hear their voices. They talked with fervor. They were in love with their new work. In the first year, Pop stayed away from the studio only seventeen days, including Sundays.

The studio was a converted stable on Vine Street, a pleasant broad avenue, beautiful with pepper trees that hung in cascades of feathery fronds, pluming and pouring down before the great fruit gardens and arched date palms. The studio building itself was a dingy, dark green wood, soiled with the droppings of the pepper bark. At the little wooden railing which fenced petitioners from the Promised Land sat a brash kid with his feet on the rail. He was usually called Mervyn Le Roy, and insisted on greeting persons by their first names instead of addressing the daughters of studio executives properly as "Miss de Mille." In the wooden wall were wickers labeled CASTING DIRECTOR, and CASHIER. People lined up in front of them at appropriate times, but the daughters of executives swept through, snubbing Mervyn Le Roy [who would go on to be one of Hollywood's most prolific producers/directors, with *Little Women*, *Mr. Roberts*, and *Gypsy* among his seventy-plus films].

Crossing the hall, one came right out into the open air again. There, in a great rectangle of wooden shacks, carpenter shops, dressing rooms and such, were broad, low wooden platforms, the stages, open to the weather, and protected from the skies only by lawn awnings of white muslin called diffusers that pulled back and forth on guide wires. To a certain extent the sunlight could be regulated by the manipulation of these canvases. The rain could not be. When it poured the scenery got sopping and stood dripping and drenched under tarpaulins. The worn boards of the stage collected pools, and shooting was suspended. The first glass-covered stage was not erected until we had been there a year and was the exhibition piece of the company. All the shops went up in a fine blaze one Tuesday afternoon and were prudently rebuilt of cement. There being no walls of any kind around the sets, any studio member who wanted to could stop and watch and invite family and friends to join. Mary Pickford was the first actress to insist on privacy and was regarded as antisocial as well as temperamental and self-indulgent for doing so, but she was too expensive ($10,000 per week) to be gainsaid. Where the neighbors' houses over-looked the back lot the neighbors' kids and their friends formed a regular gallery whenever there was anything worth their attention.

Direction was largely improvisation, and acting consisted mainly of following, without showing irritation or fluster, signals shouted through a megaphone. To supply the rhythm which set dialogue or timed pan-tomime might have furnished and which everyone instinctively felt was needed, a couple of musicians stood by. They played anything they liked, appropriate or not, and they played without cease, through hammering, sawing, dragging, calling, banging, whispering and sobbing. In moments of intense passion, the violinist generally moved in close to the scene of operations like a good anesthetist, carefully feeding the efforts of the ear-nest young woman who was attempting to pull emotional significance out of thin air. She was given no build-up, no springboard of audience excite-ment, no pattern even—just told to pump out raw emotion under a blazing sky while she watched the yelling director or the chicken hawks overhead circling down from the hills and back.

The stories were generally settled in a day or two of conference. A list of sets and props was handed to the carpenters, a list of costumes to the dressmakers. The location man was told to hunt up a good place in the San Fernando Valley for a massacre. The camera man loaded his box, and they were ready to begin. It was my father who, coming from the tradition of a literate theater, suggested that it might be useful to write out in detail beforehand what they planned doing. He wrote complete little synopses for Cecil. Then he asked a writer friend, Margaret Turnbull, to come west to help him. The two of them wrote synopses sitting at desks in a small wooden house with screen doors on the lot. Pop got the studio painter to make him a sign which he hung on the doorknob, SCENARIO DEPARTMENT. And this was the first time these words appeared in Hollywood.

If there was no loitering, a feature full-length (five-reel) film could be shot in two weeks; with one week for preparation and one week for editing and cutting, a picture could be finished for the first running in about four weeks. The runnings or first showings occurred on Wednesday and Saturday nights. Every employee had the privilege of attending with his family. Everyone told the director what he thought of the work and offered his suggestions for improvement. Everyone was proud at the prospect of success, everyone saddened by a failure. New inventions were the boast of all, the first large close-up, for instance, or the daring sequence of a man leaving one house and arriving at another, omitting the intervening explanatory scene of his walking down the street.

* * * *

In those early days the citizens of Hollywood were openly contemptuous of the infant industry. Every now and then the comfortable maggot domesticity of Hollywood Boulevard was interrupted by a moving-picture unit, which arbitrarily roped off a section of sidewalk and made use of whatever portion of the town suited their story needs while the citizenry gaped in good-natured disdain or raw curiosity. A carload of Keystone cops would debouch in the leading thoroughfare, beat their victims on the head with cotton clubs, and effect a departure before the authentic constabulary of the town were aware of what happened. The townsfolk were amused but not surprised, since nothing the "movies" did surprised them. Picturesque, irresponsible people of precarious ways and bizarre tastes, they were considered no social threat as long as they were kept in their place. And they had a place; movies were not invited to join the better Los Angeles clubs. The contempt of the real estate operator for the movie was without blemish; it was his one perfect characteristic.

The citizens went to the picture theater about twice a week. They went to church on Sundays. They took drives to Beverly Hills to see the nurseries where poinsettias grew naturally in the ground. There were no art galleries. The theaters were way off in Los Angeles. There was one public library, and a Woman's Club which imported visiting lecturers. And that was all culturally. The citizens spent long parts of the afternoons moving the sprinkler from one section of the lawn to another. They gossiped. They rode about. The whole town seemed to drowse between its orange and avocado gardens, under its trolley wires and telegraph poles, under its raucous signboards, under its hills.

Behind this street of sultry, social make-believe and inflamed ambition, behind this tiny empire-building, the hills rose suddenly, untamed, pre-Spanish, coarse with desert weed and wild tearing sagebrush, riven with flood, blind with dust storm, formed and burnt in an endless sun, and hard and promising that the future was as unknown and terrible as the past, that there was enough strength and brutal promise in the land to stir the earth underfoot until the windows rattled and the people knelt in their little stucco churches and conversed urgently with God. And over all stretched the bare sky, the original sky, the peeled and exposed sky, blind and endless. ...

Once, years later when I was grown and far away, someone placed a sprig of sagebrush under my nose. I burst into tears.

While Agnes de Mille distained the lack of culture in Southern California, she fell in love with dancing after seeing Los Angeles performances by the great Russian ballerina Anna Pavlova and Ruth St. Denis, an innovator in modern dance. De Mille attended the Hollywood School for Girls and was allowed to take ballet lessons, but her father did not believe in dance as a career and sent her to UCLA, where she graduated cum laude with a degree in English. When her parents divorced in 1927, de Mille returned to New York with her mother and sister. Always strong willed, Agnes had her way in the end, becoming a charter member of what would become the American Ballet Theater and making her mark as a choreographer (and lead dancer) in 1943 with the distinctly American ballet Rodeo, *with a score by Aaron Copland.* Rodeo *led Rodgers and Hammerstein to ask de Mille to create the groundbreaking dance sequences for their musical* Oklahoma! *She went on win further acclaim for her choreography on Broadway and in films such as* Carousel, Brigadoon, *and* Gentlemen Prefer Blondes.

Agnes de Mille died in New York City on October 7, 1993, at the age of eighty-eight.

King Vidor 1915

King Vidor was born on February 8, 1894, and was raised in Galveston, Texas, where his father was a lumberman. Vidor's fascination with film was seeded at the age of fifteen when he saw French director Georges Méliès's A Trip to the Moon. *Soon after, the teenage Vidor was hired for the summer as a ticket taker and projectionist at Galveston's first movie theater, working ten hour days for $3.50 a week. With a homemade camera, he started filming local events, such as car races and aerial shows for newsreels. In 1915, Vidor married the twenty-year-old Houston beauty Florence Arto, and together they drove to California in a Ford that he had bought on time with an eighty-dollar down payment.*

Five miles along the California coastline north of Santa Monica was a fabulous place called Inceville. It was named after its owner and originator, Thomas H. Ince. It consisted of a profusion of open stages and false fronts of Western settings so familiar in films of that day. One could look in any direction and see Indian braves biting the dust as their horses were shot out from under them, or United States cavalry racing to the rescue of a besieged wagon train. One might also behold a betrayed fisherman's daughter dragged lifeless from the surf by her revengeful brothers, since the topography of Inceville also included the scrub hills of the Santa Monica mountains and the rocky coast line and beaches of the Pacific Ocean.

In the business section of Santa Monica were the Western Studios of the Vitagraph Company of America, whose main studios and headquarters were in Brooklyn, New York. They consisted of a one-story corrugated-iron building and, in the lot behind, a couple of open stages. ...

* * * *

106

Several summers before reaching California I had visited a famous West Texas health resort with two friends. There I met a beautiful young girl named Corinne Griffith.

Half a year later Corinne had written asking me if I knew anyone in Hollywood to whom I could give her a letter of introduction. I racked my brain, because I wanted to be of help in getting Corinne started in pictures. Finally I remembered a distant cousin who had married a stage comedian and was now in Santa Monica. This was all I needed for a letter of introduction for Corinne. She had presented the letter to my cousin-in-law, who had taken her to the director-general (a big title in those days) of Vitagraph. He had been immediately impressed with her rare beauty and guaranteed her two days' work a week at five dollars a day. If she worked more than two days, she would be paid five dollars a day.

Florence and I rang the doorbell of Corinne's Santa Monica apartment, and the two Texas beauties met for the first time. Corinne later introduced Florence to the head of Vitagraph, who then promoted Corinne to a three-day guarantee and moved Florence into the two-day spot.

With ten dollars coming in with certainty each week, we rented a one-room apartment with kitchenette on the ocean front not too far from the studio. I was to write stories, which I would try to sell to the Inceville or Vitagraph Studios. In addition I would continue to photograph freelance newsreel and travelogue scenes and fill in with any sort of studio work I could scare up.

I wrote fifty-two motion-picture scenarios of assorted lengths before I sold one. A sale was finally made to the Vitagraph Company for thirty dollars because of a month-long California rainstorm; I had luckily written a script that could be shot completely in the rain. It was aptly titled, *When It Rains It Pours!*. It kept the studio from paying unearned salaries for the long wet month. I also did work as an extra in courtroom audiences and French Revolution mob scenes. For this I was paid a dollar and a half per day and lunch at the studio commissary.

I never regretted these days, and always utilized them to study the directors at work. I had directed the little Texas films and I knew I was going to direct again. I kept my eyes and ears open and tried to absorb all that I could about the details and workings of a successful studio.

When the rapidly expanding Vitagraph Company outgrew their hundred-foot lot and moved to Hollywood, we went along with them. Corinne

King and Florence
Vidor. (Courtesy
of AMPAS)

was elevated to the status of a star and Florence was moved up to the fifteen-dollar-per-week guarantee vacated by Corinne.

As operations at Inceville began mushrooming, Thomas H. Ince bought and built an impressive array of studio buildings on a site in the new town of Culver City. These two migrations ended the career of Santa Monica as a motion-picture production center.

David Wark Griffith, at the top of his career, was the undisputed leader in the business of producing and directing motion pictures. *The Birth of a Nation* was having long runs throughout the country. "D.W." was the master that every young director watched, studied, and imitated.

* * * *

My first home in Hollywood was in a boardinghouse just around the corner from Griffith's amazing *Intolerance* set. *The Birth of a Nation* had cost less than a hundred thousand dollars to produce; Griffith had taken the enormous profits from this film and spent over a hundred thousand dollars to build a single set for his new spectacle, *Intolerance*. The setting was a reproduction of a Babylonian square surrounded by palaces and walls projecting upward to great heights. On top of these were runways wide enough for chariots drawn by four horses abreast to race along and space for hundreds of extras to participate in thrilling scenes.

Griffith had to employ a captive balloon to raise the camera high enough to encompass the full magnitude of the scene. The set itself occupied a square city block and was surrounded by a high canvas fence. It was located across the street from the studio proper and guarded by a corps of watchmen. I managed to make friends with the head watchman and was allowed to spend several Sundays examining the detail of the set's construction. When actual filming was in progress, I spent many profitable hours watching the great D.W. at work. ...

* * * *

I made the rounds of the studios looking for work. I wasn't particular what department of movie-making I landed in as long as I got to work inside a studio. I would sit for hours at the casting offices waiting for a chance at an acting job, then move on to the production office and make application as an assistant director, or property man, and, being refused, go to the camera department to apply as a cameraman or assistant cameraman.

In these pre-guild and pre-union days, the applicant was perfectly free in his quest.

Finally I landed a job at Universal. I was employed as company clerk at twelve dollars per week. My duties, unlike the familiar script clerk of today, were to keep the accounts of the individual unit to which I was attached. I was given twenty-five dollars cash for location expenses. Fancying myself as a creative artist, it had never occurred to me to ask for this bookkeeping chore. However, I was grateful for the opportunity to learn about costs and to familiarize myself with the workings of a production unit.

I spent two dollars and forty cents a week on streetcar and bus fare getting from my home in Hollywood to the Universal studio in the San Fernando Valley. The remaining nine dollars and sixty cents, coupled with Florence's ten dollars per week from Vitagraph, managed to pay our bills and left enough for a weekly dinner in Los Angeles, followed by an evening in a movie theater.

Some weeks at Universal there would be as many as thirty-five to fifty directors on the payroll. Men who had never been inside a studio were given directing assignments on pure bluff. They wouldn't have the slightest notion of what a camera could do. Some of these ne'er-do-wells would turn out several pictures before being discovered; by the time busy executives got around to viewing their initial efforts, they would be well into their third film. This gave rise to the criticism, "The picture is so bad that they have to make retakes in order to keep it on the shelf."

A director would finish a film late one afternoon, go to his office, and while wiping the sweat from his brow send an assistant over to the scenario department. On the wall was a rack of pigeonholes bearing directors' names and containing scenarios assigned by a director-general or some higher-up. The assistant would carry the scenario back to the weary director who would put it in his pocket and take it home overnight.

The following morning the casting office would notify him what members of the stock company were going to play the various parts; the location department would send instructions as to what exterior settings he would use; a cameraman would arrive from the camera department and the picture would be under way, the majority of films being short ones. Some of the men in charge knew more about assembly-line methods than what constituted first-class entertainment. This was the sausage-factory method of making films; thankfully its career was of short duration.

Universal was the first studio to offer public tours, at a cost of 25 cents, which included a box lunch. (Collection of Patt Morrison)

The towering set of Griffith's *Intolerance*. (Courtesy of MOMA)

All the stages were open and of great length. Sets were all lined up adjoining each other. On both sides of the stage were wide suspended runways that accommodated hundreds of daily visitors. A circus spieler was employed to escort the visitors through the studio and even during the filming of highly emotional scenes the sonorous voice of the professional guide resounded throughout the set and merged with the tinny raspiness of the portable organ employed to keep the actors in the proper mood. The visitors were charged twenty-five cents per head and the studio realized hundreds of dollars per day out of this annoying by-product.

After working at Universal Pictures, King Vidor began directing films for Goldwyn and Metro. By the time Metro Goldwyn Mayer was founded in 1924, Vidor was one of their more experienced directors, and his The Big Parade *the following year was a huge success and made John Gilbert a star. Vidor went on to be nominated for Academy Awards for* The Crowd *(1929),* Hallelujah *(1930),* The Champ *(1931),* The Citadel *(1938), and* War and Peace *(1957), yet never won. He was awarded an honorary Oscar for "incomparable achievements as a cinematic creator and innovator" in 1979.*

King and Florence divorced in 1924, and he married the actress Eleanor Boardman in 1926 and Elizabeth Hill in 1937. He had three daughters, and when he retired to Paso Robles, California, he continued to teach. He also spent his latter years investigating the 1922 unsolved murder of director William Desmond Taylor; Sidney Kirkpatrick used Vidor's research as the basis for the 1982 book Cast of Killers. *Throughout his life, Vidor maintained some of his earliest friendships with, among others, Adela Rogers St. Johns and Colleen Moore.*

King Vidor died in Paso Robles on November 1, 1982, at the age of eighty-eight.

DeWolf Hopper 1915

W illiam DeWolf Hopper was born on March 30, 1858, in New York City, the son of John Hopper and Rosalie DeWolf. His father died when he was five and, as an only child, "Wolfie" described his mother as "loving me not wisely but too well," as his explanation for why he was a self-proclaimed "spoiled brat." As a result of a case of typhoid fever at fifteen, Hopper lost all his hair and meticulously wore a hairpiece for the rest of his life. His mother gave him the best of everything, including a Harvard education, but as his wife Hedda explained, "he went in the front door and then straight out the back," giving up his planned legal career for the theater. He appeared on a variety of stages, but it was in 1890, when he recited the poem "Casey at the Bat" that he found lasting fame. Over the next thirty years he reportedly performed it ten thousand times (and he can still be seen on YouTube). His voice, more than his acting, seems to have been his most compelling quality, which makes it all the more confounding that he was lured to Hollywood in 1915 to make a silent film—at the age of fifty-seven.

I was playing in Gilbert and Sullivan repertoire at the Forty-eighth Street Theater in the late spring of 1915 when [Harry] Aitken[1] offered me a picture contract for one year at eighty-three thousand dollars. I had not taken the movies very seriously, but I took the eighty-three thousand and an early train for Hollywood. All my life I have had the merriest of dispositions, but I was unequal to laughing eighty-three thousand dollars off.

I was not, as I recall it, met at the Los Angeles station by an admiring and grateful crowd of fellow film actors and actresses who pelted me with roses. The men and women of the California film colony who had been laboring at twenty-five to one hundred and fifty dollars a week viewed this descent in force of the one thousand dollars-a-week high hats of Broadway with a jaundiced eye. They had toiled and sweated long in the vineyards

113

DeWolf Hopper in costume and wearing his perennial hairpiece.
(Courtesy of AMPAS)

and now that the grapes were ripe, we fair-haired boys and girls of the legitimate were to eat the fruit; eat it patronizingly with slightly curled lips.

They had their revenge shortly, but not many of them remained to enjoy it, for the mortality rate of the screen always has been appalling. Of the great names of the film world in 1915, actors, actresses, directors, those who survive undiminished may be counted upon the fingers of the careless sawmill hand. In the short interval others have shot up from the obscurity of extras and bits to blaze briefly and fade swiftly, gone with the cross-word puzzle, mah jongg and last year's favorite fox-trot tune. The lords and ladies of Hollywood of 1925, with an exception here and there, then were hangers-on on the fringes of the studios, school children or mere units in the census statistics....

* * * *

My first picture was *Don Quixote*. As I studied Cervantes' story, which I had not read until then, I fell captive to that mad, lean knight, as have all who ever read him, and forgot all my actor's disdain for the films. No boy or girl newly raised to stardom ever began his first picture with greater zest than I. I thought I saw before me an opportunity to recreate an immortal character of fiction in a fashion impossible to my own stage. But my new enthusiasm wilted progressively, once the camera began to grind.

The actor in the films is the creature of the director. The director is an important factor in the speaking stage, more so than the spectator often realizes, but in the pictures he dwarfs the players. They are puppets dancing at the ends of strings to his piping, seldom knowing anything of the sequence of the story they are enacting and little of its sense; theirs not to reason why, theirs but to clown or cry when and as a megaphoned voice instructs them to. No more initiative is expected or desired of them than of a squad of soldiers being drilled by a top sergeant in the manual of arms.

Perhaps if *Don Quixote* had fallen under the direction of D. W. Griffith it might have been a mark to date from in pictures, but Griffith's heart and more of his time, as far as I could observe, were going into his spectacle *Intolerance*, which he was producing on his own. He did write and direct *The Lamb*, Douglas Fairbanks' first picture, and I have been told that when the film was finished he said to the actor, "You'd better take your monkey shines to Sennett; they're more in his line."

No film is shot in the sequence in which it is shown on the screen. All the scenes falling on one location are taken in any order that the director sees fit, until that set, or location, is disposed of. The final fifty feet of a photoplay may have been among the first to be shot.

Our first set was a stable built in the studio. For five hours of a hot California day I rolled in the straw of the stable, which I shared with every sand flea and ant in California, clowning low comedy, much of it written, not by Cervantes but by a scenarist; stopping only to swab the perspiration that drenched me and doing that only because beads of sweat on the face photographed as pockmarks, when the director announced, "Now, Mr. Hopper, we will have the death scene."

It appeared that the stable set had to be removed to make way for another and that my death throes were down in the continuity for the stable.

I protested. "I want this death to signify something more than decomposition," I said bitterly. "It is symbolical. At least let me know why I die."

Not even the director, it developed, knew this at the stage of the proceedings.

"My dear sir!" I balked. "You might just as well ask me to be nauseated now and give me the emetic three weeks later."

But died I did, then and there. Cervantes saw fit to kill his hero of brain fever, but Hollywood's he-men all die with their boots on, and it was down in the scenario that I was to be shot. So I fell mortally wounded, why or by whom I had not then the remotest idea, and contorted my face and limbs this way and that way as the megaphone told me to do, for all the world like a fat woman on her bedroom floor taking her daily dozen to the voice of a phonograph record. I did sneak in a little dying of my own, and—may I say it?—it was pretty good; also as realistic as my cinema collapse, which was to come.

We were twelve weeks on *Don Quixote*. The film ran seven reels in its final form. Its only success was in Latin America, where the story was more familiar to picture audiences than in English-speaking lands.

* * * *

The worst ordeal of the pictures, I found, was the getting up in the working world and being on the lot in make-up by nine o'clock. Photography is all but independent of sunshine now, but it was not then. It was the high percentage of sunshine in Southern California, of course, that located the industry there to begin with. Actorlike, I had been accustomed all my adult life to going to bed with the arrival of the milkman and getting up about one o'clock in the afternoon. The workday world returns home at five o'clock and gives the evening to recreations. The actor does not finish work until his audience is ready for bed. He then eats, and enjoys his leisure. He might, you may suggest, be in bed himself by midnight and up by eight, with the forenoon free, but the leisure comes after work, not before, as all night workers know.

A lesser nuisance of picture routine is the necessity, when on location away from the studio, of appearing in public in costume and make-up. It is such a commonplace that the native does not bat an eye; would not, in fact, turn a head to see Lady Godiva ride by *au naturel* on her milk-white palfrey, but it gives the tourist something to write home about. I never ceased to feel like a cage of monkeys. My make-up for *Quixote* was a ghastly thing, suggesting a death mask. It registered naturally in the camera but I was an apparition to the eye. We were on location in Santa Barbara on one occasion and I had, as usual, made up in my room after an early breakfast. My room was on the fourth floor of the Hotel Potter. As I descended in the elevator the car stopped at the third floor to admit two elderly women, voyageurs from Prides Crossing, Massachusetts. The interior of the elevator was dim and they did not see me until they were crossing the threshold. When they did they screamed as if they had encountered the devil himself, and fled down the corridor.

DeWolf Hopper had traveled to Hollywood with his fifth wife, Elda (soon to change her name to Hedda), and their infant son, DeWolf Jr., who had been born in New York in January of that year, facts the reader would never learn from the above excerpt. These omissions may explain the number of Hopper's marriages—and then there is the fact that no less a Lothario than John Barrymore claimed that if he and Hopper "saw a girl at the same time, I learned to sadly bow out." Hedda followed her predecessors and divorced Hopper in 1922. By that time he was making a thousand dollars a week, but usually spent more than that on himself, remembering to pay alimony and child support only when there was nothing left.

DeWolf Hopper, by then on his sixth wife, died in Kansas City, Missouri, on September 23, 1935, at the age of seventy-seven.

[1]Harry Aitken, along with his brother, Roy, had financed *The Birth of a Nation* and then formed Triangle Film Company, briefly uniting D. W. Griffith, Mack Sennett, and Thomas Ince.

Hedda Hopper 1915

H*edda Hopper was born Elda Furry, one of nine children, on May 2, 1885, outside of Altoona, Pennsylvania. Her father, John, a butcher, took off for Alaska to hunt gold when Hedda was in the eighth grade, and she had to leave school to help with the family. When her father returned several years later, with nothing to show for his time away, Hedda resented him. She went to Philadelphia for what appears to be several years (exactly how long is hard to pin down, due to her habit of changing her age and altering her biography accordingly) before arriving in New York at twenty-two. She found work on the stage, primarily in the chorus, and first met DeWolf Hopper when they appeared in the same play in 1908. After divorcing his fourth wife, fifty-five-year-old DeWolf married the twenty-eight-year-old Elda on May 8, 1913.*

What follows are Hedda's remembrances of the same trip to Hollywood that her husband described in the preceding chapter.

Doug Fairbanks' first wife, Beth, found a home for us and engaged a Japanese couple to run it. The Fairbankses also had a Japanese couple, so when either of us entertained we pooled servants. And such service! Doug, dispensing with a chauffeur, drove his own car. It was several years before he started to make real money.

Twice a week we dined at the Fairbankses' modest house on Franklin Avenue or they at ours. A welcome guest was William S. Hart, who became so well known on the screen as a Western star that few remembered how good an actor he was on the stage when he and William Farnum starred in *Ben-Hur*. ...

* * * *

Geraldine Farrar came straight from the Metropolitan Opera and made a colossal impression. She played Joan of Arc for Cecil DeMille. She was madly in love with Lou Tellegen, who had made stage love to Sarah Bernhardt. A romantic figure, he gobbled up all the sweets of life and love, then literally cut short his days with a pair of shears—a suicide.

DeMille rented a house for Geraldine not far from ours. When she lifted her voice in song, every person within a quarter of a mile flung open the windows to listen.

Lou Tellegen was making a picture at that time. If Geraldine finished her day's work ahead of him, she'd find out where he was and walk to the farthest end of the lot to be near him, sit quietly like a modest extra girl until he'd done his scenes, then they'd go home together.

The first time I met Sam Goldwyn—he was Sam Goldfish then and married to Jesse Lasky's sister—we sat together on an outdoor stage to watch his partner Cecil DeMille burn Geraldine at the stake. I still think it was a better picture than Ingrid Bergman's Joan, but I could be prejudiced.

During that year I saw many pictures being made. I wanted to learn about them. Wolfie had insisted when I married him that I give up my career. He thought life owed him one wife who'd stay home while he did the acting for the family.

Nevertheless I watched closely. I saw D. W. Griffith put finishing touches on *Intolerance*, with eighty girls dressed as angels fluttering on wires thirty feet above the stage. A third of them became airsick before they could be lowered to terra firma. I'd seen plenty of actresses up in the air, but that was the first time I'd seen thirty of them flutter on wires.

In making scenes, Griffith worked directly from the Bible. He was meticulous about the effect he wanted for the Crucifixion of Christ and waited for foggy days. There were no fog-making machines then.

I remember Griffith, overtired by long hours of trying for perfection, ordering a break and calling for hot tea. The actors who portrayed Christ and the two thieves had been on their crosses four hours without a rest.

"Lower Christ too," said Griffith.

"What about my brothers who play the thieves?" said an actor.

"Lower the thieves too. Get tea for the whole company."

* * * *

Our first Christmas in Hollywood was unlike any we'd ever known before. Being troupers, we were used to snow on the ground and zero weather. We missed Broadway.

Hedda Hopper in *Battle of Hearts*. (Courtesy of Cari Beauchamp)

Our son Bill was eleven months old, but neither his father nor I got to see him on that day. He had a cold and his nurse—Wolfie called her the dragon—declared we'd give him germs. She overlooked the fact that we were perfectly well. But some of Wolfie's old cronies came to call, among them Douglas Fairbanks, William S. Hart and William Crane.

It was a lovely day, but there were no presents from Wolfie. He made a great deal of money and would lend or give a wad to any broken-down actor who told him a sob story, but he never got in the habit of spending it on his wives, except in the form of alimony. I always thought if he'd bought more roses and fewer automobiles, he wouldn't have had so many divorces.

However, the day was not without festivity. In the afternoon we went up the hill to Bill Farnum's house. There we found the greatest mixture of people you ever saw. Stars, bit players, cowboys, businessmen, old-timers, eastern visitors. Bill was a fine host; you didn't have to be important for him to feed you. "They're all people," he would say happily. He gave with both hands. There were plenty of leeches within arm's reach, but Bill neither knew nor cared. That day a turkey-and-ham parade passed across his dinner table. Bill carved and served and called, in his great mellow voice, for more.

While we were in Hollywood that year my parents visited us...Things were all right between Dad and me by then. Some time before I had written him a frightening letter, pointing out all his shortcomings as a father, including his dash to the Klondike, leaving his wife and family with nothing to support them but a stack of uncollected bills. The letter cleared the air between us. In turn, my father had graciously forgotten about his threat to horsewhip the man who had married his daughter. He was free to lap up Hollywood, which he did. At one time I thought he wanted to be an actor. He had certain qualifications, including no money and total lack of responsibility.

I did all the tourist things with Mother and Dad—took them to Catalina Island, hired a fishing boat—and Mother caught a thirty-five-pound albacore. Dad, his ego blasted, kept saying, "Mother, are you sure this is the one you caught?" I didn't let him get away with it. I never let him get away with anything. Sometimes, in the still of the night, I'd wonder if I wasn't too hard on him. Now that I'm older, I'm certain I was.

* * * *

Bowing to Wolfe's wishes, I turned down several picture offers during our year in Hollywood—one from the great D. W. Griffith himself—but when our friend William Farnum pleaded that he couldn't find a leading lady for his next picture, my lord and master changed his mind and gave permission.

That's how I got into my first film, *Battle of Hearts* [written by Frances Marion]. For me it was starting at the top. Farnum was William Fox's brightest, highest-paid star. His salary then was six thousand dollars a week; I got one hundred.

I had visions of fluttering my eyelashes, languishing in a scented boudoir, and indulging in passionate love scenes with the handsome hero in my screen debut. But no! *Battle of Hearts* wasn't a picture; it was an obstacle course.

Playing a fisherman's daughter, I wore a faded blue skirt or pair of Pa's pants, a man's turtleneck sweater, hip boots, and a stocking cap. The whole outfit was gussied up with oilskins and sou'wester to match.

In my first scene I drove a yoke of oxen along the beach at Catalina Island and gathered driftwood for our cookstove. We waited on Catalina Island for our principal prop, an ancient threemasted schooner bought in San Francisco, which was being sailed down the coast by two men. We prepared for scenes on the ship at Catalina; then it was to be taken to Santa Cruz Island and wrecked there. But a terrific storm blew up and our schooner never made port. Parts of the vessel were found; the men, never.

The fisherman Bill engaged for the film thought this an ill omen. We, being actors, never believed those seastory superstitions and went right ahead.

We moved from Catalina to Santa Cruz. That crossing from Santa Barbara is rougher than the English Channel, and our ship was overloaded. On anchoring we transferred from our large ship to rowboats in order to land on rocks. The first boatload, with Farnum, two male members of the cast, two movie cameras, and a couple of guns, didn't make it. The boat capsized and they went down in eighty feet of water. It's a wonder they ever got out alive, for they were wearing lumber jackets and heavy boots.

The second boat was more successful. Our director's wife, Mrs. Oscar Apfel, a few authentic fisherman, and I were in that one. Mrs. Apfel and I climbed a long hill to the camp and made for the cook tent. Someone remembered to bring a bottle of whisky along; we uncorked it, and when the wet and maddened star and his dripping friends hove in sight, we let 'em have it right from the bottle.

It was the cook's day off and he was in Santa Barbara, so Mrs. Apfel and I cooked supper—eggs and bacon for all hands. Finishing that feast, our star went to his tent. After helping with the dishes, I looked in to see if Mr. Farnum needed anything. There he was, sitting up in his bunk reading *Julius Caesar* by the light of a lantern. He said it quieted his nerves.

Mrs. Apfel and I, occupying a tent, slept in two army cots with blankets that dogs had fleaed up during many winters. The first night I woke up with a start to find field mice playing hide-and-seek over my body. They were hunting for the soap, left uncovered at the head of my bed. They got the soap and me at the same time.

Since our threemaster was lost, we had to build a wreck; but before we could tow it to the location selected, it wrecked itself on the other rocks. Bill gave up then, and we started shooting with half the deck under water.

I was terrified of deep water. My dear sister Dora had taken care of that. When I was young she elected to teach me to swim in the Juniata River. With my middle draped over a plank, she held onto my rear end. Somebody tripped her, she fell on top of me, and we went to the bottom. She got herself out; I came up gulping. I'm an expert swimmer today, as long as one foot's on the bottom. In deep water I'm as much good as a bluebird in a goldfish bowl.

When I told this to Farnum he hired three deepsea divers from Catalina to come along and protect me. He assured me there was no danger. Oscar Apfel stood on an improvised railing to direct a scene in which I was to dive off the ship. He said, "Now when I say, 'Camera!' you count three, then dive. I'll save you." Oscar yelled, "Camera!" the railing broke, he fell backward into the Pacific and came up with a baby octopus around his arm.

That killed any plans he had for me to dive overboard. Nevertheless I did have to hang onto a stout piece of driftwood, supposedly in mid-Pacific, and wave one arm while screaming for help. Hidden out of camera range under my log was a husky diver. He stayed by me till the bitter end. That picture nearly ended me; I lost thirty-five pounds.

Watching kids today who have everything done for them—doubles for danger, every sort of device to make them look good without any risk to themselves—I marvel that any silent star ever survived to tell about it.

When I saw *Don Quixote* on the screen I knew Wolfie would never have

Catalina Island was often used for location shooting. (Collection of Allison Burnett)

success in pictures. He was too old, and this medium too young for him.

When his year's contract was up and it was time for him to return to New York, he insisted on motoring. It would be difficult to bundle son Bill, his nurse Nannie, and me into a new car for a crosscountry ride. Besides, at that time there was an epidemic of some contagious disease and it was dangerous for children to travel. Wolfie decided that Bill, Nannie, and I should stay in California until the epidemic abated and join him later at the Algonquin.

He broke travel records tearing through the country, held court with theater owners and automobile men wherever he stopped, and had the time of his life.

Elda Furry claimed that she visited a numerologist to change her name because her husband was always confusing hers with those of his first four wives: Edna, Ida, Ella, and Nella. Whatever the rationale, she became Hedda Hopper in 1919 and moved her husband and son out of hotels and to New York's Long Island in a failed attempt at a normal family life. She filed for divorce in 1922 and the following year returned to Hollywood, but instead of having a house with staff, this time she checked into a small room at the Hollywood Hotel and looked for work. With the help of friends such as Frances Marion, Hedda found jobs acting. Putting her son in expensive boarding schools, she lived cheaply and was never financially secure until DeWolf Hopper's death in 1935; Hedda had taken out an insurance policy on his life fifteen years earlier and had continued to make the payments. By that time she had tried real estate, modeling, selling cosmetics, and a variety of other occupations to support herself and her son.

It wasn't until 1937, at the age of fifty-three, that Hopper was signed by the Los Angeles Times Syndicate to write a regular column on Hollywood. Louella Parsons had been the undisputed queen of tattle for fifteen years and had seen competitors come and go, but Hedda gave her a run for her money, supported by the studios who liked having two women to play off against each other. Hopper, always a prim conservative, became more right-wing with age, befriending the likes of J. Edgar Hoover, trumpeting the work of the House Un-American Activities Committee, and criticizing anyone in the Hollywood community who she thought was "pink." Her son, Bill, was often estranged from his mother, but eventually made his peace with her. He was a good-looking, six-foot-four actor who became known to television audiences of the 1950s and '60s as the detective Paul Drake on Perry Mason. Hedda Hopper loved the power her column brought her and worked until her death in Los Angeles on February 1, 1966, at the age of eighty.

Evelyn Scott 1916

E velyn Flebbe, born in Brookline, Massachusetts, on January 20, 1911, was
the daughter of George Flebbe and the writer Beulah Marie Dix. Beulah,
a graduate of Radcliffe, wrote several plays and as a result became friends with
Beatrice de Mille, the mother of Cecil and William. Beatrice had represented
authors and playwrights in New York, but after joining her sons in California,
she began writing scenarios for films. She encouraged Beulah to come west, stress-
ing the opportunities for writers. Beulah wasn't convinced, but Beatrice was a
strong personality and very persuasive. So, in the summer of 1916, when Beulah
was thirty-nine and Evelyn five, they came to California to test the waters

We arrived on July 2, 1916—wonderful weather, just as advertised. Neither
we nor it were newsworthy. Otherwise, the *Los Angeles Times* of that date
was as full of news as a pterodactyl egg of meat.

In France, the Battle of the Somme had begun to rage.

In Chesapeake Bay, a German submarine was lurking, on reliable report.

In Washington, D.C., President Wilson was exchanging notes with
Mexican President Carranza. Wilson's notes, the *Times* seemed to think,
were pretty mild. A cartoon portrayed him as a stenographer typing away,
while Uncle Sam, in battle dress, glared at him. The caption was "The girl
he left behind."

In Los Angeles, the Mexican crisis was occasioning some agitation for a
Home Guard (the National Guard had been posted to the Border) in case of
an uprising by some of the Mexican-background local population. In addition, there was the problem of a longshoremen's strike down at the port,
but it had not prevented two thousand pleasure seekers from taking boats
to offshore Catalina Island on the day before. For those who didn't wish to
go to sea, Thomas Ince was sponsoring a benefit rodeo, at the beach.

Inside Los Angeles, entertainment ranged from Anna Pavlova dancing her renowned *Dying Swan* to Charlie Chaplin on the screen in *The Fireman*, or Dustin Farnum in *The Lightning Conductor*, with Hunter's Posing Dogs live, on-stage.

A rose—the world's loveliest, of course—had just been christened for Los Angeles, though that week not everything about the city had been roses. Eight divorce suits were filed; in a single day, motorcars had snuffed out two among some half a million lives. To be fair, though, not only motorcars had accidents. Up in Oakland, an explosion damaged the smoking car of a train, just as it pulled in. Someone's luggage had concealed a bomb!

Nothing like that threatened us. Our only hazard on arriving at the station was climbing down the Pullman steps. Mother and I both had short legs, she by constitution, I by age. We were oval-shaped. Otherwise we didn't look alike. Mother's hair was brown. Mine was red, as a result of her earnest prayers. Her nose was long; mine was snub. She was beginning to wonder if she should have prayed more about that. We got off the train at Pasadena, not Los Angeles a few miles farther on, because our hostess wished to take us out to Hollywood by "the pretty way," not the ugly one from the main depot.

She was waiting underneath a palm tree. She had hair that looked like hammered silver, and seemed pretty old. Almost everybody that I met seemed old. Mother hadn't married till past thirty. I already knew that our hostess had two children Mother's age, William and Cecil. Her name was Beatrice de Mille and we were to call her Bibi.

After her hair, I noticed her black eyes, tinged with gold, which were like the strongest coffee coming to a boil. She wore a trailing dress, beads, combs, a scarf, and, for driving, a green veil. She had brought a car borrowed from her son Cecil, since her own wasn't large enough for us and the hand luggage needed on a five-day trip. A chauffeur stowed us in, and we were swung away from the station, which, architecturally, with its tiles and arches, was a cousin of the nearby Green Hotel.

As we drove across a bridge which had no water underneath it, Bibi and Mother talked about "the boys," William and Cecil, who had come to Southern California to make movies. Bibi had followed them and then invited Mother, whom she knew In The Theatre in New York, to pay her a visit. Bibi had been the New York agent for some of Mother's plays.

Back in Boston, Mother had despised the movies. Nickelodeons! They were trashy, in a class with comic strips. She had come West to see the country and a friend, but she was courteous, of course, and if this friend could truly be engrossed in films—Bibi, it seemed, was even writing motion-picture plays—then there had to be a little more to them than flash-and-smash.

I don't suppose I listened. I was nearly stupefied—ten more miles of view! A golf course was only a stretch of "back East" green. Bibi bought some grapefruit from a roadside stand. The price seemed a happy shock to Mother.

Then we were in Hollywood, and Bibi had us driven along Hollywood Boulevard because we would do our errands there, not because it was a streak of light and glamour right across the vision of the world. She took us also past the Lasky Studio, where she and "the boys" worked. It was silvery grey and, like her, it had a veil, a green haze of pepper trees.

Halfway up a hill, we came to Bibi's house. It was a bungalow, not the little and white kind, but big and brown, two stories, with a roof line that sagged, looking Japanese. It sat on a high foundation that enclosed a basement with a furnace which would spare us Southern California's first bitter

The Pasadena train station, where many visitors to Los Angeles disembarked. (Collection of Patt Morrison)

disappointment: why, it's cold at night—outside you need a coat and inside you need heat!

Fifteen steps led to a porch under ivy, ivy with rounded leaves, not the cornered kind we had at home. Suddenly I missed my home, the wet smell of the woods, the lady's-slippers you might find (but never pick) while walking to our cousins' farm, Pullaway (my rocking horse), and my father, who had had to stay in his bookstore selling books.

I missed home less, once I was inside Bibi's house. There was a blue rug, different from any others I had seen—Chinese—lots of benches, shelves, and even a desk, all built in, of auburn wood, an incense burner shaped like a volcano, puffing pleasant-smelling smoke, and an "altar rail" around the fireplace. This proved to be the perfect place for me to sit, though it was meant for grown-up feet.

Back across the porch you could see the hills. Lion-colored hills, my mother said, and then corrected, cougar-colored hills, as better suited to the West. On the skyline just across from us ran Vine Street, to the Boulevard and to Bibi's (and the boys') studio.

Bibi called us into the dining room. This was a good room, too. It had a cabinet, carved and inlaid with niches and drawers and the minutest bridge. It had a sideboard ornamented with a bronze lady on a bronze horse. In spite of her unlikely clothes and the falcon on her wrist, I took her to be Bibi, flanked by William and Cecil, also in bronze, as her guards. There was also a table with a mirror in the center and a circle of flower vases clasped by crystal chains.

Most wonderful of all, if you stepped on a panel in the floor, a door slid wide. Sesame! What magic might not lie beyond?

In warm fact, nothing but the kitchen. The panel was a device to help a maid with trays. But I didn't stay awake for facts. Bibi took us to our downstairs bedroom and I fell asleep while Mother was wondering if she could smell the ocean as well as incense oil, and sage and oranges in the glowing air. Tomorrow, I dreamed, if I stamped hard and said Sesame!, I would walk through a sliding door into all the treasures of a California Ali Baba's cave.

Good weather x scenic splendor + distance = Southern California, and no Southern Californian of even recent status failed to take advantage of all three. We were planning to stay with Bibi three or four weeks, but she wasn't wasting any of it.

Next morning, in the gleaming heat, we went over what Mother termed a mountain pass but was just a foothill notch into the San Fernando Valley and the Duchy of Lorraine. I had a picture book about the life of Joan of Arc, so I knew Lorraine was where that brave heroine had lived. Out in the Valley, Cecil DeMille was shooting scenes for a movie about Joan of Arc....

After leaving Cahuenga Pass on the historic road used by the Mission Fathers in the early days, we descended to the flats and passed a little brood of buildings hatched out among weeds. Universal City, Bibi told us, another studio. Every studio seemed to be completely separate. Universal, Lasky, Ince, or Fine Arts people kept apart, to some extent because of long hours and long distances, but also because the intense competition of a new business, where a small fortune might be won and a large one lost, required constant invention and encouraged secrecy.

Aunt Constance warned us to tell no one what the subject of her husband's present picture was. When word had got round the year before that he was making *Carmen*, someone else rushed through a version of the story on the theory that the public would buy tickets to whichever came out first. Cecil DeMille wasn't yet a name that on its own could guarantee a long line at the box office.

In the flats it was very hot. What air there was seemed clogged with groves of oranges and peaches, plus a billboard or two. There was even a mirage—what looked like a shallow puddle—shining on the surface of the road, always a few feet beyond the car. When we got to Domremy, Joan of Arc's village, we found a well, but it too was a sham, and a dreadful disappointment to a thirsty child.

Mother was in ecstasy. What a sham! Used to the one-sidedness of sets for the stage, she was entranced by the almost perfect "stone" and half-timbered cottages facing on the village square. The buildings had at least three sides, for the camera would view them from more angles than could any theatre audience. They were built against the hills in such a way that only trees would be in view—no cactus, which is not common to Lorraine.

Trained pigeons fluttered round the village belfry. There was a baby—not so trained. It cried. There were dogs and chickens and pigs. On a platform commanding people, animals, France, and, to my mind, all of history, stood Cecil DeMille. I looked up at him and made my "knicks," a half-curtsy which soon, luckily, succumbed to the crudeness of the West.

Uncle Cecil DeMille had a brisk, controlled face, a bright smile, and Bibi's eyes. He was wearing khaki and puttees. I already wished we had puttees. The California brush, bristling round except inside the village square, stabbed where it didn't slash. Foxtails poked into my socks and between my shoelaces. I felt full of pins, but this was no time to complain; the flight of villagers from the invaders was going to begin.

Joan the Woman was part modern, as were all of Uncle Cecil's pictures then. Historic grandeur got confined to flashbacks. In this case the flashback overwhelmed the modern story, displaying most of the life of Joan of Arc as envisioned by a World War I soldier, Wallace Reid, who decided in the trenches that he had fought with her in that other war.

Wallace Reid, then considered the handsomest young actor on the screen, didn't take part in the flight from Domremy. Geraldine Farrar was in the thick of it, as Joan. She was handsome, too. She had fine features, a proud carriage, and black hair. She was one of the leading opera singers of the day, and already had had movie success, starring in Uncle Cecil's *Carmen*, her most famous opera role, though of course in the picture not a sound came from her mouth. …

Bibi pointed out this doubly-shining star for me. Geraldine Farrar was wearing a black bodice and a brown skirt like any other female villager, but once you recognized her you saw no one else. Just as in one of Mother's favorite quotations, "where the MacGregor sat was always head of the table," so where Farrar set foot was center stage. In the drawings I had seen of Joan of Arc, the heroine was sandy haired, slender, with a fearless look, and very young. Brunette Geraldine Farrar was not exactly slender or quite young. Fearless? We should see.

When the scene began, the noise dropped off—not, of course, because the camera could hear, but because the actors needed to. There were a hundred or so, a throng for those days, waiting for directions. The cameras—two, I think—began to turn. The alarming enemy (Burgundians), in metal helmets and chain mail, brawled down the slope. The pigeons wheeled. The villagers began to run, carrying whatever could be snatched from their cottages. Mother had observed already, with a dramatist's envy, the variety of splendid props—coffers, basins, tankards, coverlets.

In the forefront of the action, a comfortably stout actress, Lillian Leighton, swept up a piglet and a goose. As she headed down the village street, there was trouble with the little pig. It squirmed and shrieked, enough to risk disrupting the scene and drowning out commands. All at once Farrar was at her side, seized the pig, smacked it, and tucked it underneath her arm, where it remained in apparently shocked silence as she went on with the flight. The scene ended as rehearsed; it was a good "take."

Mother had fallen silent as the pig. Not because Farrar, the diva, had been so quick-witted and so deft, but because Farrar, the Boston Irishwoman, hadn't hesitated, despite hoary anti-Irish jokes, to be capable about a pig. This Joan, too, was fearless.

In the car on our way home we hardly spoke. I itched from foxtails, but my spirit soared, with Farrar and the little pig. Mother's mind must have turned more to Uncle Cecil, for she wrote her mother in England that night, *I have more respect for the motion picture world than I ever thought to have, but as yet I see no chance in it for the author.*

Generations of writers, frenzied at what movies would do to their stories, would agree.

Evelyn and her mother lived with Beatrice de Mille for several years, and Beulah worked regularly for DeMille and a variety of studios. Her husband, George, eventually joined them and went into the real estate business. After Paramount did not renew Beulah's contract in 1924, she worked for Fox, Warner Bros., and Universal, writing several Sherlock Holmes *films. She wrote* Sunny Side Up *for Fox and* Their Own Desire *for M-G-M, as well as twenty novels. Beulah died at the age of ninety-four on September 25, 1970, at the Motion Picture Country House in Woodland Hills, California. Evelyn married the film editor David Scott and followed her mother into the business, working for over twenty years as a story analyst for M-G-M. She left the studio in 1973 to devote herself to writing full time and died in Ventura, California, on November 24, 1983, at the age of seventy-two.*

Gloria Swanson 1916

T he only child of Army officer Joseph Swanson and his wife, Addie, Gloria
  May Josephine Swanson was born in Chicago on March 27, 1899. She
spent much of her childhood on military bases in San Juan, Puerto Rico, and
Key West, Florida. On one of the annual trips Gloria made with her mother to
Chicago, she went with her aunt on a tour of the Essanay movie studio. Dressed to
the nines in clothes handmade by her mother, fifteen-year-old Gloria was immediately recruited as an extra and soon was playing larger roles. She had planned
on being a singer, but when acting turned into a steady position at $13.50 a week,
Gloria willingly left school, and she and Addie stayed in Chicago. Playing opposite
much older men, such as Edmund Lowe, Wallace Beery, Frances X. Bushman, and
Charlie Chaplin, Swanson taught herself to cry on cue and became friendly with
one of Essanay's staff writers, Louella O. Parsons. She was enjoying the work, her
independence, and the studio's communal atmosphere, when her mother announced
they were leaving Chicago to join Joseph in the Philippines. Gloria shared the
news with Wallace Beery, who had been transferred to Essanay's studio at Niles
in Northern California because of improprieties with underage girls in Chicago.
Swanson wrote that she hoped to see him when they stopped in Los Angeles.

On the train west, Addie confided to her daughter that she wasn't sure she
wanted to be married anymore, and perhaps they should stay in Los Angeles.

Wallace Beery, tanned and handsome, was at the station to meet us. He
was spiffily dressed and on his best behavior. He couldn't have been more
charming, and I could see that Mother liked him from the start. He said
he had driven down from Niles Canyon the night before and had found a
little place for us to stay in which he hoped would be all right.

"How far is Niles Canyon from here?" I asked.

"An eight-hour drive, but it's beautiful country."

Gloria Swanson, seventeen, and Wallace Berry, thirty. Hardly the picture of a happy couple. (Courtesy of Cari Beauchamp)

"Eight hours! I would never have written if I'd known it was that far away, Mr. Beery."

"Wally," he corrected me. "Wally to both of you. You got that? It was nothing. I have a brother living here, and besides, I use any excuse to get away from Niles. That's like the Klondike up there."

He had a new, open motorcar, with large carriage lamps on the sides and a heavy leather belt over the hood, in which he drove us around for a look at Los Angeles. There was not much to see. The city seemed to be composed entirely of factories, empty lots, gas stations, telephone wires, drugstores, open markets, and barns. Here and there cows ate weeds beside rickety houses. Wally said most of the beautiful homes were off the main drag or up in the hills. When we started seeing signs that read FOR RENT: DOGS AND ACTORS NOT WANTED, Wally laughed and said, "This is it. This is Hollywood. Look at some of these freaks. No wonder homeowners won't put them up. They'll do anything to attract attention to themselves and get into movies."

The men, women, children, and animals all looked absurd. I had never seen such weird costumes—loud suits, ruffled dresses, fur jackets, cowboy boots, and crazy hats. On every finger and ear, it seemed, jewelry flashed in the afternoon sun. "Fake, all of it," Wally said with affection. "They're desperate. Everyone wants to get into pictures. They don't realize it's all in the faces and the physiques. The stars don't dress like gypsies. These birds won't either, once they get jobs. My brother Noah is an actor here in Hollywood, and he doesn't dress up like some crazy pirate. He loves the place. When I finish this series of pictures I'm making in Niles, I'm coming down here too. It's the place, no question. Noah and I are looking for a house here so we can move our folks out from Kansas City."

The apartment he'd found for us was on Cahuenga Boulevard, a tree-lined street right in Hollywood, in a two-story house painted a hideous green. The apartment itself was fine, two nice rooms on the second floor, with furniture that wasn't too bad and a cute little balcony. Wally hauled in our bags and waited while we scrubbed off the train dirt. Later in a restaurant, he kept us in hysterics all evening with his stories about making films in Niles and with his imitation of Broncho Billy. He said it was the boondocks up there—no bathrooms, squeaky iron beds, bare light bulbs instead of lamps. He couldn't wait to come down and get started in Hollywood once his contract with Essanay ran out. If people in Hollywood still felt he was too ugly to play anything but villains in pictures, he would go back to New York and work on the stage.

"Who says you're ugly?" I asked.

"Do you really want to know?" he said, and laughed as he counted off every producer and director in Hollywood, starting with D. W. Griffith and ending up with Mack Sennett.

"Do you know Mack Sennett?"

"I've met him long enough to hear him say no, and I do a wonderful impression of him. Why?"

I told him Mr. Babile at Essanay in Chicago had written me a letter to Mr. Sennett, but I hadn't really planned on going to see him because Mother and I didn't know when we'd be leaving for Manila.

He said he couldn't believe his ears. He was appalled that I didn't know that Keystone was *the* studio or that Mack Sennett was a genius. "You act as if you don't care anything at all about pictures."

"I don't."

"Addie," he said to my mother, "Babile is no fool." Then he said to me, "Look, Gloria, do yourself a favor. Take your little letter in your little purse and get out to Mack Sennett as fast as your little legs will carry you. You can always go to Manila."

I could see that this was a new Wallace Beery. He wasn't such a playboy anymore, or such a show-off. He had clearly learned his lesson. Maybe the scandal in Chicago had done him good in the end. He seemed serious and ambitious, and he looked marvelous with his California tan. I was being perfectly honest when I said I'd love to see him on his next trip down. And he was being as firm as a father when he said, "You go out and see Sennett, you hear?"

The following Monday I got on a streetcar and took the long ride to the Keystone studio in Edendale. Remembering what Wally had said about the desperate gypsies of Hollywood, I wore the most dignified, elegant outfit I owned, and I had spent a full hour on my hair and face. The building was a large, sprawling shed with slanting glass roofs, topped by a big printed sign that said MACK SENNETT STUDIOS. When I entered the tiny office, which stood beside the shed, it was absolutely mobbed with people trying to see producers. There was no place to sit or stand. I tried to explain to several people that I had a letter of introduction, but they looked at me as if I were crazy. I was on the verge of leaving when someone called out my name.

"Gloria Swanson, what are you doing in California?" The speaker was a pale, thin man, and I couldn't place him or think of his name until he laughed. It was Frank Hayes from Key West, who after seven years still remembered my face, and my name. He and [his wife] Venice had moved out west for the climate and he was working at Keystone. I told him why Mother and I were in Los Angeles and what I'd done since I'd seen him in Florida. We exchanged addresses and I invited him over to Cahuenga Boulevard to see us.

"Hampton!" he called to a strange-looking man hurrying past. "This young lady has a letter to Mr. Sennett."

The other man sized me up and said, "She doesn't need a letter. What a crazy day." Then he said to me, "I'm Hampton Del Ruth. Come with me." He grabbed me by the hand and dragged me down a corridor to an office with Mr. Sennett's name on it. Mr. Sennett was not there. So Mr. Del Ruth dragged me outside to a back lot. "Wait right here," he said. "I see him." A few minutes later he came back with a man of about thirty in shirtsleeves and suspenders. "What about her?" he asked the man.

I smiled sweetly, but Mr. Sennett didn't say a word. He raised the brim of his hat an inch, chewed on his cigar, spat out the juice on the ground,

Gloria Swanson when she worked for
Mack Sennett. (Courtesy of MOMA)

and studied me as though I were a pony at a county fair. "The clothes are
terrible," he said. Then he came up close and said, "And that make-up is
a joke." I was absolutely furious and at the same time stung with embarrassment. As he walked away, he called back over his shoulder to Mr. Del
Ruth, "Have her call on Thursday."

"You hear that?" Mr. Del Ruth said.

"I heard it," I said.

"So call Thursday."

"Thank you," I said icily.

When I got home I told Mother that the Hayeses were in California
and that Frank would call us sometime soon. I also told her I had seen Mr.
Sennett—I could hardly say I'd met him—and that he had been terribly
rude.

"Well, then, that's that," she said, her bad faith in movie people firmly
restored.

I decided not to call on Thursday. Instead Mother and I washed our hair and sat on the balcony to dry it.

On Friday morning a man in a chauffeur's uniform rang our bell. "Miss Swanson, please."

"I'm Miss Swanson."

"Mr. Sennett has sent his car for you."

I said there must be some mistake.

"Are you Gloria Swanson from Chicago?"

"Yes."

"Then there's no mistake. Hurry please, they're waiting for you."

I was totally bewildered. No one had ever been ruder to me than Mack Sennett, but nobody had ever sent a car for me before, either. I took a look at myself in the mirror. My hair was a mess, but after what he'd said the other day, I thought, what difference did it all make? My eyes didn't look too bad.

"I'm sure I'll be right back, Mother. Shall I invite the Hayeses to dinner if I see Frank?"

"Yes. How about Sunday?" she called.

The chauffeur drove me to a bungalow across the street from the Keystone offices. Before he could open the door for me, a man ran out to shake my hand and introduced himself as Charley Parrott. He took me inside, where a group of men began to clap and cheer as soon as they saw me. A cute young boy ran up to shake hands with me. He said he was Bobby Vernon. He was a little runt of a thing, just my size. He pulled me into the middle of the room and stood there with me while everyone stared at us and nodded. Then Bobby introduced me to the director, Clarence Badger. Everyone in the room was talking excitedly. Bobby was terribly nice. He explained to me how Mr. Sennett had signed him the week before to be the lead in a new light romantic comedy company. Once Bobby was set for it, everyone had started looking for the right girl. Because Bobby was so tiny, it had to be someone very short. Hundreds of girls had shown up who were either too tall or too old for Bobby. Then on Monday Mr. Sennett had told Mr. Badger he had found the perfect girl; there was no need to look any further. When I didn't show up on Thursday, Mr. Sennett had had a fit. He almost fired everyone in the office because no one had my address. No one even knew my name. There was such a commotion that Frank Hayes finally heard about it and told Mr. Sennett who I was: Gloria

Swanson from Chicago. Then Mr. Sennett's chauffeur had to drive Frank to his house for my address. It had been a day of hysterics, which was why they were all so pleased to see me.

I told Bobby Mr. Sennett had caused all the commotion himself by being so rude.

"He isn't rude. He's just shy," Bobby said. "Besides, once he was sure what you would be like without a lot of make-up, what was there to say?"

"What was wrong with my make-up?"

"It made you look thirty, Mr. Sennett said. We're both supposed to look and act like lovable fifteen in this comedy. How old are you, really?"

"Sixteen."

"Well, act fifteen," Bobby Vernon said, "and so will I."

So that was it. At Essanay, with my hair up and smoking endless cigarettes, I'd been playing grown-up, well-dressed society ladies, and I had thought that that was what acting in pictures was all about. Now here was Mr. Sennett saying there were plenty of thirty-year-olds around to do that. He was demanding what for me was probably the hardest thing in the world: that I throw away the fancy clothes and wipe off the make-up and *act my age.* Bobby was the cute little boy next door, and Mr. Sennett had looked through all the eye liner and veiling and picked me to be his cute little girl. The earth had shifted under my feet again.

The Sennett system of making pictures, strange though it was after Essanay, was actually fun. For the first time, I enjoyed making movies. The California system was nothing but surprises. You never knew what the person next to you was going to do. Stunt men and gagmen and comics were all jabbering constantly and struggling to get their ideas accepted. As soon as someone thought of something he would jump to his feet and act it out. "Look," he'd say, "what if Bobby starts to dance close and Gloria backs off?" Then someone else would say, "Wait! What if *Gloria* started to dance close and *Bobby* backs off?" Then, without fail, everyone would start roaring a different version, and the set would turn into a shouting match with the director as the referee. "Let's try it again So-and-so's way," he would say. Then Bobby would grab me and we'd act out the version the director liked best.

I felt funny at first, being the only girl, but Bobby was a wonderful actor and treated me just as if we were going steady. He would ask me to dance and I would accept and we would do a few steps without any music. Then everyone would clap in unison and Bobby would spring a few ridiculous steps on me. I would begin to loosen up and follow him no matter how silly what he was doing was. Eventually I even forgot I was tongue-tied and suggested some ideas of my own. Mr. Badger said they were fine and left them in. When a gagman suggested something else, Mr. Badger said, "No, I like it Gloria's way." I was suddenly part of a family.

At Essanay we had spent most of our time changing clothes and waiting in the basement until our turn came. Then the director would tell us exactly where to walk and what to do, only he ever saw the script and knew what the scene you were doing had to do with anything else. But at Mr. Sennett's we made up our own stories as we went along. We got to know each other and to know how everyone in the company would react in a given situation. After a few hours of trying out different ideas and settling on the ones we liked, we would pile in a car and drive off to the location. There the cameraman would watch our rehearsal and then, when the light was right, would shoot the scene.

I never had time to worry about make-up or costumes. Every time I tried to look at myself in a mirror, all the men would kid me and tell me I looked perfect just as I was. They didn't care at Keystone if every hair was in place or whether the lights would ruin my mascara. Rather, as soon as the sun came out, it was like a four-alarm fire to race to the location and shoot. Then, as soon as it clouded over, back we would race to the bungalow to work out more routines. It was a wonderful way to earn a living.

When the picture was finished, Mr. Sennett screened it and had Mr. Badger call us all together so that he could pronounce his verdict. Mack Sennett, everyone knew, was not an easy man to please and he never gushed, so we were all very nervous when he entered the room. He said he hadn't liked all of the picture, that in fact some of it would have to be done over, but—and he paused—that if audiences didn't find it fresh and funny, they were crazy. He complimented Clarence Badger and said all he mainly wanted to do was to guarantee our group that we would go right on making pictures for Keystone.

We were ecstatic. Mr. Badger took me aside and told me Mack Sennett had thought I was terrific—the perfect match for Bobby. The studio was preparing a contract for me, and Mr. Badger said I should let him know if it was not satisfactory. In the meantime, my salary would be $100 a week. I could hardly believe my huge ears. That was $86.75 more a week than Essanay had paid me to start. Maybe pictures weren't so bad, after all.

Wallace Beery was soon driving down to Los Angeles almost every weekend to visit, and on her seventeenth birthday, Gloria Swanson married the thirty-year-old actor in Pasadena, with her mother as their only witness. Before long, Beery joined Swanson at Keystone, where he started spending her paycheck as well as his own, often on other women. Gloria claimed he raped her on their wedding night, and when she became pregnant, he gave her a potion that caused an abortion. Needless to say, the marriage was short-lived, and she left Keystone to make films with Cecil B. DeMille in Culver City. By 1919, the First World War was over, the Jazz Age was about to begin, and Swanson and DeMille (along with his screenwriter Jeanie Macpherson) caught the wave of changing mores in films that DeMille's brother, William, dubbed "sex à la mode." Clothed in some of the most fabulous lace, furs, and jewelry ever seen on the screen, Swanson inspired a generation of newly liberated females. Halfway through their six-film collaboration, her name began to be billed above DeMille's.

Barely five feet tall, with a large head, brown hair, huge sapphire-blue eyes, and a dazzling smile, Swanson was not a conventional beauty, yet during the 1920s she was the reigning Queen of the Silent Screen, and the first actress to be offered a million dollars a year. She turned down Paramount and joined United Artists to be her own producer, a mistake financially, as was her four-year professional and personal partnership with mogul Joseph P. Kennedy [father of President John F. Kennedy]. Swanson's life would eventually include five more husbands and three children (two daughters by different husbands and an adopted son). When she couldn't find work in front of the camera, she became a clothes designer, a painter, a sculptress, owner of a cosmetics firm, and an actress on Broadway and in summer stock.

After living an off-camera life that rivaled any film plot, she returned to stardom a second time in 1950 with her Oscar-nominated performance as the iconic Norma Desmond in Sunset Boulevard. *She often claimed she was nothing like Norma because she did not live in the past, although during the last few years of her life Swanson, like Desmond, became obsessed with a much younger man. Gloria was an early advocate of organic food and macrobiotic diets and appeared on television in shows such as* Burke's Law, The Carol Burnett Show, *and* The Beverly Hillbillies. *Her final big-screen role was in* Airport 1975. *Gloria Swanson died in New York City on April 4, 1983, after a brief illness, at the age of eighty-four.*

Colleen Moore 1916

C olleen Moore was born Kathleen Morrison in Port Huron, Michigan, on August 19, 1900. Her father was an engineer whose work took the family to Atlanta and then Tampa, Florida. Moore often said she had a normal, middle-class upbringing, but at an early age, she developed a passion for acting. Unlike the screen stars who came before her, such as Gloria Swanson and Mary Pickford, who had no path to follow, Moore read all the latest fan magazines, pasted articles about her idols in scrapbooks, and even saved pages for her own clippings, which she was confident would come. She knew what she wanted.

As I look back on it now I wonder at my audacity in dreaming that I could become a movie star. The vogue for beauty in those days was a tiny, well-rounded, blue-eyed girl with long blond curls—Mary Pickford—or a wee, doll-like, brown-eyed brunette also with curls—Marguerite Clark. I was a skinny kid with a turned-up nose and dark red hair worn in pigtails, and I didn't have blue eyes or brown eyes either. I had one of each.

But ignorance is bliss, and since we never see ourselves as others see us, my dream of becoming a movie star wasn't the least disturbed by such mundane matters as what I looked like.

* * * *

After Mother hung up the phone, she explained what had happened. My Uncle Walter, as editor of one of the Hearst newspapers, had a certain amount of influence in Chicago, and he'd been able to get first D. W. Griffith's *The Birth of a Nation* and then his *Intolerance* past the censors. When Mr. Griffith asked Uncle Walter what he could do to repay him, my blessed brainwashed Aunt Lib spoke right up. "We have a niece—"

Mr. Griffith groaned. "Not a niece!"

Also blessed—and also brainwashed—Uncle Walter nodded. "I'm afraid so."

My brother Cleeve, when he heard that, piped up, "She's a payoff!"

I stared at him, feeling like a deflated balloon. Cleeve was right. Hollywood wasn't sending for me. I was being sent to Hollywood—not because anybody out there thought I was any good, but simply to pay off a favor.

I stayed deflated for maybe a minute. How did I care how I got there? What mattered was I was finally going.

The night before we [Colleen, her mother, and her grandmother] left for Hollywood, Uncle Walter took us to the College Inn to celebrate. Aunt Lib told me it was a nightclub. When I asked her what that meant, Uncle Walter said, "It's a place where they don't have lunch." Then he raised his champagne glass and said, "Here's to Colleen Moore, the newest Griffith discovery and a future movie star."

I started looking around, wondering who Colleen Moore was.

Uncle Walter beamed at me. "That's you, baby."

My own name, he explained, was too long to fit on a movie marquee. Twelve letters was the limit. And since I was going to be seeing my name up in lights one of these days, a suitable name had to be found.

Uncle Walter had taken the problem to his archrival and sometime friend Teddy Beck, editor of the Chicago *Tribune*. Over a beer in a friendly neighborhood tavern they decided the time had come for introducing an Irish actress to the movies. There was a lot of good publicity in it.

They felt very creative and had another beer.

Morrison, they decided, sounded too Scotch. Why not chop it off and make Moore out of it? You couldn't get any more Irish than that. Feeling very proud of themselves, they ordered another beer.

Kathleen, while Irish, as indeed half of me was, definitely would not do because of the famous serial queen, Kathleen Williams. Something really original was needed.

They had another beer while they went over all the Irish names they could think of. Two beers later they were slapping each other on the back and ready to order drinks all around. They'd come up with Colleen, a Gaelic word of endearment meaning little girl.

Uncle Walter beamed at me again. "Now nobody can say you're not my child. I've given you a new name."

Colleen Moore. (Courtesy of Cari Beauchamp)

The last car on the California Limited from which porters would toss seeds that grew into ribbons of flowers alongside the tracks. (Collection of Patt Morrison)

"And I," Aunt Lib said, "gave her a career."

They glared at each other, then burst out laughing.

I laughed with them. It felt peculiar getting an entirely new name at the age of fifteen, but then everything I was doing now was new. Besides, hadn't Mary Pickford been born Gladys Smith? I began to feel quite professional.

The next day as we boarded the Santa Fe *Chief*, Uncle Walter handed me a letter. When the train pulled out, I opened it and read it.

"Dear baby," it said, *"Hollywood, where you will now be living, is inhabited by a race of people called Press Agents. The studios pay them a lot of money to think up stories about the players under contract and to persuade editors like me to print their stories. So the moral of this letter is, never believe one damned word you ever read about yourself."*

Uncle Walter knew what he was talking about. While I was reading his letter, Mother was reading the newspaper he'd handed her. In it was his own story—sent out on all the news wires—about how I became a motion picture actress.

According to the newspaper, I had been visiting Uncle Walter and Aunt Lib in Chicago that summer when D. W. Griffith came to their house one night for dinner. As a hoax I put on the maid's uniform and started serving. Mr. Griffith took one look at me and said, "Mrs. Howey, you've just lost a maid, and I've gained a new movie star." Then they revealed to him that I wasn't the maid, I was their niece.

As young and unsophisticated as I was, I shuddered as I read the story. Even today I wonder how a topflight editor like Uncle Walter could have concocted anything so corny.

Yet I know. Uncle Walter was so proud of "his child" that he couldn't bear to have anyone know I was a payoff, that neither acting ability nor looks had had anything to do with my becoming a "find."

The irony of it is that Uncle Walter not only wrote that absurd story, he told it so often that—against his own advice—he finally came to believe it himself.

The trip to California took three days and three nights….When we came out of the desert into California, I ran out to the observation platform to stare at the snowcapped mountains, the green orange groves, the palm trees, and the brilliant sky. I knew this was my land. This was where I belonged.

Mrs. Brown, a sort of studio chaperone, met us at the station in Los Angeles and took us to a small bungalow she had rented for us on Fountain Avenue, about a half block from the Griffith Studio.

Walking to the corner, I could see the crumbling city of Babylon—the huge, two-city-block set used in *Intolerance*—still standing. It was something to feast your eyes on.

The studio itself was a letdown. It was a large three-story barnlike structure made of clapboard and painted dark green, and attached to it in a very makeshift manner were many small buildings. It looked to me as if when they needed more room they just got together some old boards and added on another shack. I don't know what I expected—a marble palace, maybe—but it seemed incredible to me that all the great Griffith films had been made in that ramshackle place.

In front of the studio was a cement court, with groups of people sitting around, some in makeup, some not. After I was taken inside the studio to meet Mr. Griffith's manager, Mrs. Brown brought me back to the courtyard and over to a group of girls about my age to introduce me to them.

I recognized only one of them—Bessie Love. I'd seen pictures of her in *Photoplay*, with captions saying she was a star of tomorrow. But they were all so pretty and seemed so assured, I felt shy.

The names of the other girls were Mildred Harris, Winifred Westover, Carmel Myers, and Pauline Stark.

Pauline said to me right off the bat, "Are you going to the studio school? You have to go to school till you're sixteen, you know. It's the law."

"I'm going to have a tutor," I blurted out—and felt like a snob. But I didn't know what else to do except tell the truth.

They didn't take offense. They just said it was too bad, because the studio school was lots of fun.

Carmel said, "Have you met the Gishes?"

Mildred said, "I *adore* the Gishes, especially Lillian."

Winifred said, "Do you think it's true what they say about Lillian and Mr. Griffith—that he's madly in love with her?"

Bessie said, "Why wouldn't he be? She's the nicest person there is in the movies."

Pauline sighed. "Maybe they're secretly married."

I didn't say anything. How could I? It was all news to me, though my movie magazines had hinted that Mr. Griffith was in love with Lillian Gish.

Dorothy Gish was great, one of the girls said, and always full of funny remarks. Constance Talmadge, said another, was Dorothy's best friend. Bobby Harron, another put in, was in love with Dorothy, but she only looked on him as a brother.

Chat, chat, chat, on they went, talking about everyone at the studio. It was just like reading the fan magazines, only better. This was practically straight from the horse's mouth.

I loved it—until one of them turned to me and said, "Did Mr. Griffith really discover you?"

I may not have known what else to do except tell the truth when they asked me about going to the studio school, but I did this time. I was afraid if they found out I was a payoff, they'd blab it all over Hollywood, and I'd be out of the movies before I was even in them. I couldn't bring myself to repeat Uncle Walter's story. I just said Mr. Griffith saw me in Chicago, had a test made at Essanay, and gave me a contract.

Years later I found out that Carmel Myers was a payoff, too. Her father, a rabbi, was an authority on ancient history, whom Mr. Griffith had used as a consultant on *Intolerance*. He took no pay, only a contract for Carmel.

Mildred Harris' mother, the head of wardrobe, was such an expert on costumes she was rewarded with a contract for her daughter. Winifred Westover's father was a newspaper man who'd done favors for Griffith.

We were all payoffs except Bessie Love and Pauline Stark. And none of us wanted to admit it.

Before they could ask me any more questions, Mrs. Brown rescued me. She took me inside the big barn to meet Chet Withey, a Griffith director, saying, "This is Colleen Moore, the new girl Mr. Griffith sent out from Chicago."

He looked me over—kindly, if critically—and said, "She'll do. She can play the city girl with Mildred and Bobby."

I wondered if Mildred was the girl I'd just met and if Bobby was the Robert Harron I'd seen in pictures.

"Be here, made up, at nine in the morning," he added. "We're going out by the Soldiers' Home to shoot exteriors."

I couldn't believe it. I'd only been in Hollywood six hours, and I was already in the movies.

Afterward Mrs. Brown told me yes, it was Mildred Harris, and yes, it was Robert Harron, adding that for me to have a part in a picture with him was a lucky break for me. He was a big star.

She took me upstairs to a balcony that ran the length of the studio, its back wall one long row of doors. I was to share a dressing room with Mildred Harris, she said as she opened one of the doors to a cubbyhole of a room.

I looked on the door to see if there was a star there. There wasn't even a name.

Just then a vivacious blond teenager came rushing out of another cubbyhole, her arms stacked with clothes. "Here," she said to a cleaning woman, "you can have all my clothes—the good ones, too. My sister Norma just married a millionaire—Joseph M. Schenck—so I'm getting everything new—from the skin out."

I knew who she was even before Mrs. Brown introduced me to her—Constance Talmadge, who'd just been made a star because of her performance as the Wild Girl in Griffith's *Intolerance*. Star or not, millionaire brother-in-law or not, I couldn't imagine anyone giving away all the clothes she owned.

The half block back to our rented bungalow seemed a mile, I had so much to tell Mother and Grandma. Especially about Lillian Gish and Mr. Griffith.

When I did tell them that, Mother said, "I think if I were you, I'd say no more about this. Gossip is a dreadful vice. What goes on between Mr. Griffith and Miss Gish is their own affair, not yours and not the other girls'."

I was properly squelched, but I decided anyhow I'd take a good long look at them if I ever saw them together, just to see what I could see. I thought it was terribly romantic.

When Mother said she'd found a tutor for me, I told her I didn't need one, there was a school at the studio. But she said no, my lessons were to be sent to me from my convent school so that when I came home after my six months in Hollywood I'd be right up with my class.

It made sense to my mother. She didn't know, because I didn't tell her, that I wasn't ever going home. I couldn't.

In Barrie's play *Peter Pan*, the directions for locating that place of enchanting make-believe, the Never Never Land, were very explicit—"second to the right and then straight on till morning." And it was easy to get there. All you had to do was believe—and "think lovely, wonderful thoughts."

Explicit and easy and impossible to find, the Never Land.

Or so it seemed to me.

For years I had believed, if not in the Never Land of Peter Pan, in the Never Land of Hollywood. Had believed, had thought lovely, wonderful thoughts, and for all that my Never Land was a continent away, it might as well have been second to the right and then straight on till morning.

Until now. Now at last I had found it. I was right here in it, this place of enchanting make-believe. And I was going to stay here and become a star.

How could I possibly go home?

I was home.

Colleen Moore's "Uncle Walter" was Walter Howey, the legendary Chicago newspaper editor who was the inspiration for Walter Burns, the fast-talking, conniving editor in Ben Hecht and Charles MacArthur's The Front Page. *Once in Hollywood, Colleen quickly built an impressive body of work and, with her bobbed hair and carefree spirit, came to personify the Jazz Age in the 1923 film* Flaming Youth. *She was soon earning ten thousand dollars a week and was declared the top female star of 1927 by the* Exhibitors Herald. *She made the transition to talking films and worked continuously through her final screen appearance as Hester Prynne in the 1934 version of* The Scarlet Letter. *However, unhappy with the roles she was being offered, Moore walked away.*

From childhood she had collected and decorated dollhouses, and in the 1920s, her engineer father and studio craftsmen had built her a spectacular dollhouse castle, made to exact scale with exquisite fabrics and accoutrements, including electric lights. In the middle of the Depression, Moore was inspired to help children's charities and spent over a year traveling the country with "The Doll House," raising over six hundred thousand dollars. She had two short marriages before wedding the Chicago stockbroker Homer Hargrave, a widower with two children, in 1936; they stayed together until his death in 1964. By all accounts, Moore was as happy in her private life as she had been working in films. She also wrote two books in addition to her autobiography: Colleen Moore's Doll House *(1945) and* How Women Can Make Money in the Stock Market *(1960). She eventually retired to Paso Robles, California, near her long-time friend King Vidor. Colleen Moore died in Paso Robles on January 25, 1988, at the age of eighty-eight.*

Myrna Loy 1918

*yrna Loy was born Myrna Adele Williams in Helena, Montana, on
August 2, 1905. Her father, David, was the youngest man at the time
ever elected to the Montana state legislature; her mother, Della, was a trained
musician who had lived in California as a child. Myrna took dance classes and
performed in local theater, but her life changed dramatically in 1918. That year,
her family was stricken by the Spanish influenza pandemic that killed over fifty
million people worldwide. Myrna, her brother, and mother survived, but her
father, who had helped nurse the rest of the family back to health, died.*

Mother loved Montana, but she didn't love those winters. After my father
died, she contemplated returning to California. Her Ocean Park friend Viva
McLaughlin had moved to Culver City. "Well, if you come," she wrote,
"why not come to Culver City?" So we did. We moved to California, and,
of course, I thought it was fabulous—it always is when you come upon it.

We bought a house on Delmas Terrace in Culver City, a hamlet between
Hollywood and the Pacific Ocean. In our garden there were little orange
trees, a peach tree, and an apricot tree that bore fruit. Trellises arched
over the driveway laden with roses four or five times bigger than the wild
ones in Montana. We kept a goat out in the back. My brother had a touch
of TB, and goat's milk was prescribed. The TB didn't last very long; it
disappeared—apparently the goat's milk worked.

When we first arrived, I taught Sunday school at the Presbyterian
church. One day I missed the answer to some Biblical question from Mr.
O'Connell, the minister. He breathed fire and brimstone all over me. I
never went back. Mother worried afterward that he might see me dancing
between the two tall palm trees in the front yard. I staged dance recitals
there with Jean Vandyke, a girl from Mississippi whose brother was in the

movies, and Lou MacFarlane, my Ocean Park cohort. We wore makeshift Grecian tunics and did Ruth St. Denis poses like *The Water Lily* all over the front lawn.

MetroGoldwynMayer was in Culver City; I mean, later on—at that time it was just Goldwyn. There were quite a few studios there. Thomas H. Ince's resembled a Southern mansion—they even had a liveried black butler receiving authorized visitors at the door. Hal Roach had his studio there for years. There may have been other little flybynight places, but those were the principal studios. You weren't allowed anywhere near them unless you had official business, but we would climb over the fence into the Goldwyn back lot. We'd take pictures of one another doing dances on top of the fence and striking poses on the standing sets. We had great plans. I was going to be Ruth St. Denis with the studio and dance company, and Lou would write the plays for us to choreograph. Even as a kid, she made up the stories that we furtively played out together on the Goldwyn back lot. I would return there later under very different circumstances.

My mother put me in the Westlake School for Girls in Los Angeles. That had been decided in Helena, because some people she knew, rich brewers named Kessler, were sending their two daughters. She chose that very exclusive school not for its exclusivity—Mother was in no way ever a snob—but for its promise of an atmosphere that would foster my artistic pursuits. She didn't have a lot of money. My father's legacy would have sufficed in Montana, perhaps, but not in California, not with Mother's tastes. To supplement her income, she gave private music lessons and helped in a friend's dress shop. She used to get clothes for me there. Although far from the richest girl at Westlake, I was certainly the best dressed.

I commuted on the Venice Short Line, which went from Western Avenue all the way to the beach. We had wonderful streetcars—I wish we had them now. I would get off on Western Avenue, walk a few blocks to Westmoreland, and there was Westlake. My experience there began agreeably with an adored language teacher and a special music teacher, who came in to give me piano lessons. I could also dance at their May Festival. Privately, I studied ballet in downtown Los Angeles at Mme. Matilda's École de Choréographie Classicet. I loved those afternoons in town. After class, I would go to the public library, take out an armful of classics, and devour them on the Venice Short Line going home.

Mme. Matilda, a former star ballerina at La Scala, adhered to traditional

Myrna Loy practicing her poses for her appearance at the Egyptian Theatre. (Courtesy of AMPAS)

Downtown Culver City. (Courtesy of Cari Beauchamp)

European methods, teaching all the positions, all in French, swatting you if you moved incorrectly. She revealed my tragedy as far as ballet is concerned: I couldn't dance on my toes. They were too long. You really should have short toes, rather stubby, but mine were just hopeless. "Never, never will you dance on those toes!" Madame decreed. But lessons were an enriching experience, a base for everything that I did later.

Classes met on the top floor of the Majestic Building, in a sort of ballroom surrounded by big windows. One day during class, the whole room suddenly shook and the building swayed. I stood stockstill—stopped—which is often my reaction to such things. Others ran helterskelter, trying frantically to go down in the elevators, which had stopped. But Madame had been in the San Francisco earthquake. She stood in the doorway, where there's likely to be a steel girder to grab if the walls go. The walls didn't go. The center hit in Long Beach, I believe, so Los Angeles escaped severe damage. It was quite a jolt, though, my first earthquake. When I finally made it home, my two wonderful palm trees in the front yard were uprooted. There were aftershocks all night long in Culver City. They went on and on. I peered out the window, just repeating, "Oh, my God, this will never end …"

* * * *

During my second year at Westlake, the ladies in charge, the Misses Vance and Delaguna, called me into the office. "We understand that you are taking dance lessons downtown," they began rather accusingly.

"Yes, of course," I answered. "Haven't I been dancing at your festivals?"

"Oh, yes…yes…of course." They were struggling with this thing, you see. "Well, what do you plan to do with it?"

"I plan to do it as a professional," I told them. "I plan to be a dancer, a great dancer."

"*Well!* Well, this is terrible!" They were horrified. What went on afterwards escapes me, except the realization, as young as I was, that this was an *attitude* toward the theater. In those days, you see, such schools were just set up to make "ladies" out of us. Well, I'd learned all that at home—table manners, all those things. I didn't have to learn them at school.

We not only mingled with artistic people at home, but we had season tickets to the Philharmonic Auditorium, where Mr. Behymer brought great actors and concert artists. I saw Duse. I heard Chaliapin, Gigli, GalliCurci, even Paderewski. I saw Pavlova there when I was a young girl. She did *The Dying Swan*—not *Swan Lake*, but a special piece that Fokine, I believe, choreographed. She's been hit by an arrow—as I remember, they had little spatters of blood on the feathers—and she dies. Her death was the most touching and beautiful thing I had ever seen. I've watched others do it over the years and wondered, What's wrong? Something is missing. What did she do? Then I realized what it was: the heartbeat. Pavlova indicated the heartbeat with a hand over her breast, a slight but terribly touching gesture. It beat a little bit slower and a little bit slower until she died.

So, you see, this Westlake attitude stunned me. I didn't ask, "What am I supposed to do?" of those two ladies. I just said, "Thank you very much," and walked out of the office.

I went home and repeated the whole encounter to my mother. "This is awful," I told her. "I don't want to go there anymore." And she said, "Yes, it is awful, and you don't have to go there."

I switched from Westlake to Venice High School, toward the beach from us. Ironically, its level of cultural activity surpassed that of Westlake. Concerts were brought down from Los Angeles, and notable people from every creative field came to meet with us. My English teacher, W. H. Head—"Old Pop Head," we called him—taught us never to use a flat "a" or too broad an "a" but something in between. That remains one of my great lessons. Although my grandparents came from Wales and Scotland, none of their children affected British accents. Nor did they affect this socalled "Western twang"—much of that is put on. They spoke good English. Pop Head reaffirmed that. He also elected that I should play Ophelia in the senior class play—*if* the senior already cast broke her leg. The senior didn't break her leg, but it gave me a great opportunity to study Shakespeare. (I was touched and honored thirty years later when Venice High named its annual speech and drama awards "Myrnas," after me.)

Venice High had a great art teacher, Harry Fielding Winebreiner, so I began sculpting. Actually, I wasn't very good, not good enough to go on with it, but something rather special came out of it. The administration decided to decorate the fountain in a large lily pond in front of the school. Mr. Winebreiner, commissioned to create an appropriate sculpture group, chose a typically symbolic motif of that period: a girl reading a book, a young male athlete, and, towering above them, a figure symbolizing youthful aspiration. He chose me as the model for "Aspiration."

The ambitious statue, arms extended, head uplifted, required hours of rigid posing. He draped my body with wet cloth and gauze to get the flowing effect of the draperies. When it was finally finished, a local promoter, Bert Lennon, who later fathered the Lennon sisters, worked it into the city's Memorial Day pageant. A plaster cast of the statue and I were hauled aboard the U.S.S. *Nevada* anchored a half mile off Venice. Swathed in drapery beside my plaster likeness, I came to life on deck under the direction of Thomas H. Ince, no less, Culver City's pioneer filmmaker. They expected me to strew flowers from the prow of the battleship during the rest of the ceremony. Lord! The whole thing was a mess as far as I was concerned, but it attracted a lot of favorable comment. ...

During my time at Venice High, I taught dancing at the Ritter School of Expression in Culver City. My pupils were tiny tots—babies, practically—who didn't do much dancing, but we did manage to teach them something. My salary, forty dollars a month, went directly from Mrs. Ritter to my mother. I also filled in for a friend as a splicer at the Hal Roach Studio. The film had already been cut, and all I did was put the pieces into a machine and pull a lever to splice them. I don't remember the picture—there was a dog in it, I think. My paycheck was more memorable, because it was the first paid directly to me. It seemed like a lot of money, something like eighteen dollars for the week.

I continued dance and music lessons, becoming obsessed with the idea of dancing, if not on my toes, then in the modern styles of St. Denis and Duncan. I filled notebooks with lists titled "Emotional Qualities to be Expressed in Terpsichorean Form" and "Literary Characters to be Interpreted in Dance." I listed favorite poets and composers—Rupert Brooke, Rachmaninoff, Rabindranath Tagore—adapting them for recitals at the Ebell Club and other cultural groups, getting Lou MacFarlane and Betty Black to cut classes and perform with me. When I think of what I did! I don't know how I ever did it, but that whole time, that time of my life, was very good...

I left school at the age of eighteen. I had to. Not being able to graduate was a big tragedy at the time, but money was running low and I had to work, that's all. Nobody said, "Myrna, go to work!" I suppose it was that sense of responsibility instilled by my father. I don't mean to play the martyr—the chance to get on with my dancing probably delighted me.

I went down to some hall in Los Angeles to audition for Fanchon and

Marco. They were a dance team, sister and brother, who became very successful doing prologues for national theater circuits. They hired me for thirtyfive dollars a week, darn good money in those days. It certainly helped the coffers at home.

The Egyptian was a movie house but a very elegant one, every bit as beautiful as the Chinese that Sid Grauman built later. Grauman, the first person to really exhibit movies with style, had created this live prologue concept. His prologues were famous, and he was already something of a Hollywood legend. I didn't know him when I worked there. He was a god; everybody important is a god when you're starting out.

I started at the Egyptian in the prologue for DeMille's first *Ten Commandments*. Fanchon and Marco were marvelous dancers and hard taskmasters. Everything had to be very strict, according to form. The dance was supposed to be Egyptian to complement the picture's Biblical sequences, so we rehearsed all those square movements associated with ancient Egypt. We wore little pants and sort of Egyptian halters and head-dresses. It was very interesting and apparently quite beautiful, I was told.

No terrible trauma comes to mind surrounding my professional debut. We must all have been very scared but for some reason I don't remember. Mother came to see me, of course, and thought it was all right. She didn't think it was great; it wasn't—it couldn't compare to the kind of dance she was accustomed to—but she approved of my participation in every aspect of the arts, because she was a great fan herself.

Myrna Loy soon found work in front of the camera, but was usually cast as an exotic beauty with little to do but look exotic. She played beautiful slaves in several films, including Michael Curtiz's Noah's Ark *in 1928, and looked beguiling for a variety of studios before being signed in the early 1930s by M-G-M. It wasn't until 1934, when she was cast as Nora Charles opposite William Powell in* The Thin Man, *that her self-deprecating yet confident comedy style was allowed to shine. In the process, she redefined the role of wife as a witty, sexy partner in the five* Thin Man *films that followed. Myrna was also teamed with Cary Grant (*Mr. Blandings Builds His Dream House *and* The Bachelor and the Bobby-Soxer) *and Clark Gable (*Manhattan Melodrama, Test Pilot *and* Wife vs. Secretary) *and starred as Fredric March's faithful and loving wife in* The Best Years of Our Lives. *(Married and divorced four times, Loy quipped that she was a much more successful wife on screen than off.) While she continued* *to be a regular screen presence through the midfifties and made over one hundred films, Loy gave more of her time to civic affairs and politics. She campaigned actively for Adlai Stevenson, John F. Kennedy, Lyndon Johnson, and Eugene McCarthy. She was passionate in her opposition to the Vietnam War and her support for civil rights, fighting for decades against housing discrimination. She was the first Hollywood star to serve on a committee of the United Nations, becoming a member of the U.S. commission for UNESCO. Her final public appearance came in 1991 when, after never having been nominated, she accepted an honorary Academy Award. Myrna died in New York on December 14, 1993, at the age of eighty-eight.*

Budd Schulberg 1918

Born Seymour Wilson Schulberg in New York City on March 27, 1914, Budd was the son of film producer and studio executive B. P. Schulberg and his wife, Adeline "Ad" Jaffe. Budd was a young boy the first time he came to California.

Now I was beginning to hear about Hollywood for the first time. We were going to take a long, long train ride all the way across the country to a beautiful place on the opposite side. There it was warm with sunshine even in the winter time and all kinds of tropical fruit grew in abundance, oranges and grapefruit and figs and dates. It was a place where the air was clear and the climate so healthy that thousands of people traveled there every year just to enjoy the sun, the pastoral landscape, and the rejuvenating breezes. Little [sister] Sonya would stay home with Wilma [the children's adored nurse and companion] while I accompanied my parents on the four-and-a-half-day Pullman journey. It was to be a great adventure for all of us, since my father, despite his high position at Famous Players, had never been farther west than Chicago, and Ad's travels had been restricted to Middletown, Atlantic City, and Far Rockaway.

"All...aaaaaaaaaaboard!" My father handed me up the steps of the platform onto the crack *20th Century Limited* and into the waiting arms of a man in a white jacket with a big black face and a lot of smiling teeth. "Welcome aboard, young man. Are you goin' tuh Chicago?"

"N-n-no, I'm going to H-h-h-h..." I wasn't trying to give Hollywood the old ha-ha. It simply came out that way. Still smiling, the porter led us and the Abramses down the long windowed corridor to our drawing rooms.

A few minutes later we heard the sound of the Pullman doors slamming shut, the engine whistle calling us to attention, and then with a gentle lurch we were rolling forward through the dark tunnel to an unknown place called Chicago.

The Schulbergs and the Abramses had three drawing rooms—one for my parents, one for Uncle Hiram and his wife, and a third for their tall thirteen-year-old daughter and me....

* * * *

After we left the East, the landscape changed dramatically. From the splendid balcony large enough for two rows of seats at the rear of the observation car, Miss Abrams and I could watch Midwestern America streaming backward as the great *Chief* sped determinedly westward. Then on to the hot, dry, unexpected Southwest, as exciting to my parents as it was to me.

A man was racing his horse alongside the train. A man with a big hat and a rope wound round the saddle: a cowboy, an honest-to-God cowboy, not Max Aronson pretending to be Broncho Billy but a cowhand who looked after cows and steers and bulls and didn't aim his gun at you, didn't go around looking for the bad guys in the black hats, but was just out there in the dust and the grime working the range for a living. A true-to-life cowboy such as Daddy's movies and Uncle Hiram's movies and C. B. DeMille's movies would never show, because all work and no gunplay doesn't make jack, as my father would have said.

I watched my first real cowboy disappear into the dust of the sagebrush and the cactus. We were in rugged Western country now, crossing New Mexico. It was so hot and dusty that we could no longer sit on the observation platform, 110 in the shade, with no shade in sight for what looked like five hundred miles. We fought off the heat of the Southwest by pulling sheets from the berths, wetting them with what passed for cool water in the pull-down sink, and then draping them across the drawing-room windows: air conditioning, vintage 1918...Who would travel today, in an unairconditioned train through heat that blistered the land? Unthinkable. We lived the unthinkable, just as the pioneers who preceded us loaded their families and their spare worldly goods into covered wagons, crossed a continent without roads, climbed and descended hostile mountains, ran out of food and water, starved and drank a handful of sand for their final toast to whatever god drove them westward....

15063. Spring Street, Showing Hotel Alexandria, Los Angeles, California.

The Alexandria Hotel. (Collection of Patt Morrison)

The Beverly Hills Hotel under construction. (Collection of Allison Burnett)

Those were pioneers, and so were we, the Schulbergs and the Abramses, even though we traveled strictly first class.

And although the Santa Fe *Chief* was proud of its cuisine, the confident B.P. in all his 26-year-old affluence had made arrangements with the dining-car captain to take on special supplies at each great terminal where its local product was prized: choice beef in Kansas City and freshly caught brook trout in Colorado…With what marvelous ease did the son of the dollar-a-day sandwich man take to his newfound luxury. With the grace of a Jay Gatz he identified himself to the captain as soon as we were comfortably installed in our drawing rooms, but not in the brash, money-flashing, grammar-smashing way of the immigrant moguls among whom he moved. No, the young man from Rivington Street who had already forgotten the sound of Yiddish, having exchanged it for the language of Dickens, Galsworthy, and Shaw, knew to the manner born how to express his desires subtly to the traveling maître d', how to suggest the handsome bribe that would be forthcoming for extra favors without so much as a whisper of that vulgar commodity called money. "It's all arranged," he said to my mother, "we'll have brook trout for dinner at seven o'clock." ...

* * * *

In the movies, you always knew when William S. Hart was headin' into Injun country because suddenly, as the wagon train went by down in the valley, there would be a close shot of feathered headgear rising menacingly from behind a rock on the mountainside. Then a fierce bronze face (a painted Caucasian) would signal to a group of fellow-savages waiting behind him, their deadly bows and arrows at their sides. On our wagon train, the *Santa Fe*, the arrival of the Redskins was also announced by bows and arrows, but they were not weapons but souvenirs, hung along the window rails of our Pullman car, along with a generous spread of Indian blankets and silver necklaces. They had been put on at some mysterious stop before we were awake, the work of Hopis, Zunis, and Navajos, subdued long ago. Now they were working for Fred Harvey, who held the restaurant concession for the *Santa Fe* and also had a corner on the souvenir market.

It was because of Fred Harvey, we learned, that our train lingered an extra half hour in Albuquerque. It was there in the awful but somehow exciting heat of the New Mexican depot and trading post that I saw my first Indians. My small blue eyes were looking into their large brown ones because I was on my feet and they were squatting on the ground, leaning against the outside walls of the station facing the tracks. Silently they held up their wooden souvenirs, feeble miniatures of the weapons with which they had hoped to fight off the white man's guns a few generations earlier. The Indian wars were over now, though some of the older men squatting with the women and the doe-eyed children must have remembered the last of the lost battles. Now they were here on their ragged posteriors at Fred Harvey's

Albuquerqueland, hoping to sell a few limp trinkets to the palefaces whose pocket-money jingled louder than Navajo drums and Hopi tambourines.

* * * *

The last morning, the fourth day out from New York City, began with a sense of exhilaration. Any minute now we'd be crossing the border into California. In 1918, the name still had a magical ring.

Finally leaving the desert behind, we entered the land of the orange groves. More orange trees than any Easterner had ever seen, miles and more miles of them, each one decorated like a Christmas tree with great orange bulbs. From the observation car Miss Abrams and I could smell them and almost taste them. Indeed for lunch we did taste them: oranges sliced thinly, scalloped, sprinkled with powered sugar and decorated with a maraschino cherry, served as a special dish.

San Bernardino. We were in the land of Spanish names that spoke to us of a time when California was a country of Spanish land grants that stretched for twenty miles from fence to fence, and of Spanish missions, San Juan Capistrano, San Diego, and Santa Barbara. The Yankee gold-rushers had moved in on the Spanish and the Mexicans, and had taken over the city we would soon be reaching, Los Angeles, the city of the angels. The orange trees were behind us at last, but we were passing vineyards, passing a dried-up creek that was grandly described as the Los Angeles River, and then we all had our noses to the windows as we approached the low-lying nondescript skyline of northeast Los Angeles, rolling to a stop at an odd-looking red-brick Moorish-style station. With a grand flourish the smiling porter brushed us off in what was not so much a cleansing as a ceremony of arrival. The sun was beating down, not as intensely as in Needles near the Arizona border but hot enough to inform us that we had come to a lush and exotic land.

Our luggage piled onto baggage trucks, we were driven through a small Far Western city of undistinguished four- and five-story buildings. We passed the Spanish Plaza. Olvera Street, all that was left of the original village of the *conquistadores* and their Indian peons. A real Mexican church. And then just as suddenly as we had come upon it we left it behind. We were crossing Main Street, not the derelict alley for winos it would be half a century later but the main thoroughfare of downtown L.A., narrow, crowded with autos and people and streetcars clanging.

Our proud procession of Schulbergs and Abramses drove to the grandest hotel in town, the Alexandria. Standing there in all its glory at Fifth and Spring Streets, it was named for the great Mediterranean port founded by Alexander the Great. Many miles to the west was our Venice, with canals that were said to rival Italy's own, and halfway between, a Greek theater, open to the starlit skies and scooped out of a Santa Monica mountainside to suggest a theater in Athens, though the dramas performed were more apt to be pious morality plays than the works of Euripides and Aristophanes.

Into the lobby of the Alexandria we marched. How vast and grand it seemed, with marble pillars, and its fabulous million-dollar rug, so named not for its cost, though it seemed opulently Persian to our Eastern feet, but because it was there that Mack Sennett and Charlie Chaplin, Louie-come-lately Mayer and his star Anita Stewart, Joe Schenck with his stars the Talmadge sisters, Mabel Normand, D. W. Griffith, William Desmond Taylor—geniuses, con men, cloak-and-suiters become overnight movie moguls—cooked up their million-dollar deals. From that crowded, overly ornate lobby sprang the new spirit of the new industry being born before our eyes.

The lobby was also full of unknown girls showing off their faces and their figures in hopes of being discovered. And in those simpler, silent days, girls with striking faces *could* be discovered on the spot. Along with Geraldine Farrar and Mary Garden from grand opera there were a host of hopefuls from all the little towns across the country, waiting for Mack Sennett to put them into fetching one-piece bathing suits. The doors of the Alexandria lobby were not marked Ladies and Gentlemen but Obscurity and Fame. ...

The Alexandria! Until the business moved uptown to the larger and grander Hotel Ambassador in the early Twenties, it was the capital of fil-mania. The whole damned industry was there together in one big hotel. You could get laid, you could become a star, you could start a new movie company, and you could go broke, all in that same place the same afternoon.

I'm not sure whether it was because of these nefarious goings-on in the lobby and the bar and the upper floors of the Alexandria, or because it started to rain, that my mother decided to remove me from its hectic atmosphere. I remember that the rain bucketed down; the land of eternal sunshine began to look like a Griffith production of the Great Flood. I sat by the window staring at the sheet of water and crying. I had been promised a trip to the mountains. But here I was in downtown Los Angeles, with no park to play in, not even a balcony, surrounded by a lot of noisy, frantic, laughing people. Their names meant nothing to me. "I w-w-want to s-see the m-m-mountings," I cried. "Mom, you and D-d-daddy promised me I could see the sun sh-sh-shine on the mountings."

One reason Ad had made up her mind to take me away from the lurid Alexandria, away to something finer, was that she was hating Los Angeles herself, the phonies and the fourflushers who passed themselves off as producers and directors, the little whores ("hoors," she called them) who knew only one way to become actresses. The phonies and the fourflushers and the wheeler-dealers are there to this very day, in their Cardin suits, their dark locks looped over their foreheads, their eyes roving and their minds spinning. But in those days it was a little easier because everything was new and everyone was an overnight wonder. Who knew Triangle Pictures from Quadrangle Pictures, or World from World-Wide? Who knew if you were talking to the junk man who hadn't even sold his broken-down wagon, or to the mastermind of the next big merger between Metro and Goldwyn (the Goldwyn Company that the peripatetic loner Sam had already abandoned to form a still-newer Samuel Goldwyn Company)?

Everything was in flux the day we walked into the Alexandria lobby, the old standbys like Essanay and Vitagraph on their way down, fly-by-nights like Peralta and Jewel just passing through, the big independents like Famous Players-Lasky and Universal very much holding their own, and a whole new cluster of companies signing one or two stars and one or two top directors and beginning to claw their way up.

I wish I'd been old enough to understand more of what I saw, but I heard it all in due time, from my parents and their friends who were dealing in the lobby in the late Teens. So I feel as if I was there for the famous fisticuffs—one of filmdom's many such unscheduled events—between Charlie Chaplin, the Little Tramp with a penchant for Lolitas, and Louie Mayer, the ex-junkman and not yet the polished rajah, super-showman, super-hypocrite, arch-conservative of my high school days. Chaplin had just suffered a tempestuous divorce from Mildred Harris, the wife he had taken (under rather hurried circumstances) when she was sixteen, and was feuding with L.B., who was just getting his first movie company together. Needing every star name he could attract, Mayer was billing Mildred as "Mrs. Charlie Chaplin," which sent Charlie into a fury.

Encountering Chaplin in the Alexandria dining room, the pugnacious L.B. challenged him to step outside onto that million-dollar rug, and is said by my mother and father, who happened to have ringside seats, to have flattened the highest-paid actor in the world. L.B. must have felt he had no choice. Anita Stewart was his only star. Marshall [Mickey] Neilan was his name director, but Mickey often would not even tolerate the eager boss's presence on his set. If L.B. was going to survive he needed every break he could get, and if they weren't coming his way he simply had to make them himself, and damn the consequences, damn Charlie Chaplin, screw the world! The Alexandria days were desperate times. Those were the days from hunger, when what you lacked in credentials and assets you made up in bluff and *chutzpah*.

Eager to expose me to the tropical countryside of southern California, Ad hired a car and driver and we went what seemed a very great distance, from Sunset Boulevard as it wound through small-town Los Angeles on its way west, through sparsely settled Hollywood with its little movie studios, white bungalows, and stucco bungalow courts. We paused at Sunset and Vine, and stared at the spreading Famous Players-Lasky studio, where DeMille was remaking *The Squaw Man*, which had established him as a director five years before. Even though they'd lost Mary Pickford, the studio was still going full blast. They had Gloria Swanson, whom C.B. was transforming from a background bathing beauty to a foreground sophisticated siren in naughty pictures like *Don't Change Your Husband* and *Male and Female*. The former one-barn studio was now devouring all the open country around it.

But of course we couldn't stop in to visit, not with B.P. on the outs with [Paramount founder Adolph] Zukor and ready to start a rival company. No, we kept right on driving into Beverly Hills, way out in the country then, a lone house here and there on the flatlands, and back up on the hillocks at the foot of the Santa Monica Mountains a few mansions of the stars, modeled on Spanish haciendas, surrounded by acres of terraced gardens and groves.

The landmark on Sunset Boulevard in Beverly Hills, toward which we were slowly motoring, was the enormous pink stucco Beverly Hills Hotel. When we first came to the Beverly Hills Hotel, it was an isolated resort hotel filled with wealthy old couples from the East, the white gentile aristocracy wintering in the sun of the Far West as now they winter in Palm Beach or the Bahamas. White-haired ladies rocked on the front portico. Oriental servants in uniform performed their duties with quiet bows. Everything was hushed and genteel. The gardens outside the hotel offered an exotic zoo, with plume birds from Florida and South America, and many different kinds of monkeys.

No talk of movies here. Chances are my mother and I would never have been admitted to this elite clientele if they had known my father's calling. For although the Great War had broken down some of the resistance to the movie people, "No movies" was still a sign to be found in many a boardinghouse window on the quiet streets of Hollywood. The gentle old ladies who came to the Beverly Hills Hotel to escape the bitter Eastern winters and to enjoy the purest of air and the clearest of skies would have turned up their noses at the sight of Fanny Ward or Lila Lee. They might stare at a face so perfectly formed that it would be blown up to the full size of a silver screen and still betray no blemish, but there would still be that turn-away voice of disdain, "She's a movie!"

The Schulbergs returned to New York for a few years, and B.P. started his own company, Preferred Pictures. Preferred went bankrupt in 1925, and the family moved back to California when B.P. became head of production for Paramount.

Budd Schulberg grew up in Hollywood watching his father's career rise and fall and rise again. He also felt the increasing tension in his parents' marriage because of, among other things, B.P.'s affairs with the actresses Clara Bow and Sylvia Sidney. Budd's mother, Ad, was a powerhouse in her own right and became a top agent. Schulberg went to Dartmouth, traveled to Russia one summer with his friend Maurice Rapf, graduated in 1936, returned to Hollywood to become a screenwriter, and in the midst of the Depression, joined the Communist Party. All this gave Budd a clear-eyed if cynical view of Hollywood, evidenced by his first novel, What Makes Sammy Run?, *which was published in 1941. Schulberg told the story that Louis B. Mayer was so offended by the book that he told B. P. Schulberg that Budd should be deported. B.P. responded: "To where? Catalina Island?"*

During World War II, Budd worked with John Ford on films for the War Department and, while preparing evidence for the Nuremberg trials, was ordered to arrest the German filmmaker Leni Riefenstahl and bring her to Nuremberg. Schulberg, who stuttered his entire life, became a prolific writer of novels, short stories, and screenplays, including On the Waterfront *(for which he won an*

Academy Award for best screenplay in 1954), A Face in the Crowd, *and* The Harder They Fall. *He had left the Communist Party after only a few years and later named names to the House Un-American Activities Committee, but in old age concluded that "the attacks against real and imagined Communists in the United States were a greater threat to the country than the Communist Party itself." He was also active in civil rights and mentored African-American writers during the last thirty years of his life. He claimed always to be fighting for the little guy, one way or another. Budd Schulberg died in Westhampton, New York, on August 5, 2009, at the age of ninety-five.*

Lenore Coffee 1919

L enore Coffee was born in San Francisco on July 13, 1896. From a young
age, she was taken regularly to plays, operas, and the ballet. She wanted to
be an actress, but her father did not approve; instead, she started writing, while
adding movies to her list of cultural obsessions. Lenore said silent films were "like
being taken by the hand and led into a dream world of tranquil, flowing movement." Her parents divorced, and Coffee was hired as a writer for a San Francisco
advertising company, living with her mother in a hotel near Lenore's office.

One day when I walked home by an unfamiliar way I was about to pass a
cigar-stand when something on a magazine rack caught my eye. It was a
large, thick magazine with a shiny orange-red cover and, lettered in black,
were the words THE MOTION PICTURE EXHIBITORS' HERALD,
January 1919.

I had no idea what an "exhibitor" was (it meant a cinema-owner), but I
did know a trade paper when I saw one; so I bought it and it opened up a
new world to me—an inside look into the fabulous realm of the "movies." I
went through it, page by page, gleaning bits of information, news and gossip. Then, almost at the back, was the announcement that Clara Kimball
Young was in desperate need of a story. It gave the address of The Garson
Studio, Glendale Boulevard, Edendale, Los Angeles.

My heart really leapt and I felt I must find an idea to turn into a story
for Clara Kimball Young! She was a most beautiful woman with dark hair
coiled low on her neck, great, lustrous dark eyes and a very emotional yet
sweet personality; not lacking in strength, either. I thought back over the
films I had seen her in and tried to think of a new role—something she
had not done before—and I couldn't remember ever seeing her in a picture
with a child. But I didn't want her married, for I wanted a love story. So

my next idea was that she should meet a man who had no wife, but did have a child. From that small seed the story grew; and that is precisely the way I work today. Find just one small idea, or the germ of an idea, and build a story round it.

It was called *The Better Wife*. On 8 January I sent it to the Garson Studio and on 22 January I had a letter saying they would buy the story for one hundred dollars. I was tremendously excited, even though it was an absurd sum, which I didn't know then.

At least I had the wit to telegraph my acceptance (for I knew telegrams were a matter of record) saying, "Offer accepted provided I am given proper screen recognition." I got the cheque, and I got the screen recognition, and my career began.

In March I read in the paper that Harry Garson was in San Francisco to conclude the selling of a new film he had made called *The Unpardonable Sin*. I knew I must see Mr. Garson, so on Saturday afternoon I went to the St. Francis Hotel and asked for him. The clerk looked at a box which was full of long envelopes and said, "His key is here so he's not in the hotel." I made up my mind that I would sit with my eyes riveted on that box for I knew that the man he gave those envelopes to would be Harry Garson. Three hours later, in walked a large, handsome man with almost white hair, olive skin and golden-brown eyes; as I had anticipated, the clerk handed him all the large envelopes. I was up from my chair in a matter of seconds and practically skidded across the large lobby to say, "Are you Mr. Garson? I'm Lenore Coffee." He gave me a startled look. "Are you the girl who wrote that story for Miss Young?"

When I said "Yes" he asked, "Where did you learn how to write for the movies? Do you realize that everything you wrote could be photographed? Of course, the story wasn't long enough and we had to add incidents, but everything you wrote was a fine scene. How did you learn how to write in this form?"

I told him how much I liked pictures and how often I went to them, and that I supposed I had absorbed the form unconsciously. We had sat down by this time and he said, "You know, this is a mammoth industry and it's going to be bigger than anybody ever imagined. But you won't learn how to write for it by staying here in San Francisco; you'd better come down to Hollywood."

Fifteen minutes later I walked out of the St. Francis Hotel in a daze of

The Cocoanut Grove. (Collection of Patt Morrison)

William Fox Studios, with a large glass-roofed studio to let in light. (Collection of Allison Burnett)

happiness. I had a year's contract at fifty dollars a week to come to Hollywood and learn all about the movies! I was to arrive on the 5th of May.

So I was on my way to Hollywood. Truly, the lark was singing at my gate. But not for long, for as we left the station to take a cab to our hotel the first sight which met our eyes was a huge billboard announcing FAREWELL BALL FOR CLARA KIMBALL YOUNG. It was dated 4 May—the night before!

My mother was all for going straight back to San Francisco, but I knew that the fact that I had written a story which had actually been made into a film which was soon to be released and with my name on it was bound to give me some sort of entrée. I remembered a banker friend of my father's and said I would telephone him when the banks opened at ten o'clock. This I did and explained my situation. First he said that both Miss Young and Mr. Garson had left that morning for New York, but added that there would be no great difficulties. "After all, I am doing some financing for Louis B. Mayer who is using the old Lois Weber studios. I'll pick you up around eleven o'clock and I can introduce you to him."

I persuaded my mother to unpack and while I waited in the lobby for my father's friend I became conscious of the very flat speech of the people around me. And the types were countrified: they didn't seem to belong in a city....From the very beginning San Francisco had a real society, with a capital "S," and Los Angeles, if they thought of it at all, was regarded as a "hick town."

My father's friend turned up on time—a nice, middle-aged family man with children. After the usual comments on how much I had grown up since he last saw me and how surprising it was that I had actually sold an original story to the movies, he said: "First, I am going to call at Fox studios to see Jack Kerrigan." Jack Kerrigan was billed as J. Warren Kerrigan and was the most important of the big, handsome Western stars. I had never met a film star before and was very excited about it. The dressing-rooms at the studio were like cabins all in a row, the doors opening out, and when we arrived at Kerrigan's he was standing in the doorway with a rather bemused expression on his face looking at a parcel that had been sent to him by an old lady fan. It was two sets of pyjamas; one in pink, embroidered with blue forget-me-nots, and the other in blue with pink forget-me-nots—some of them in the most unlikely places. He was extremely pleasant and agreeable and was later to become a great star in *The Covered Wagon*.

As Jack Kerrigan and I left we passed one of the stages; I was stopped short when I heard a man shouting, "Cover up your navels, girls! I don't want to see any navels showing."

My friend saw my stunned look and said, "They're shooting an oriental picture, Turkish, I think. Would you like to have a look?" Well, indeed I did like and we went on to the set, which was a harem guarded by huge ebony slaves. Seated cross-legged in a row were eight or ten very pretty girls in filmy Turkish trousers and modest tops with a tiny bit of midriff showing. They were pulling up the waistbands of the trousers, but every time they did a rhythmic waving of the arms to the wailing music of an oriental flute, the trousers would slip and the forbidden navels would come winking out. Suddenly the director called over the prop man. I couldn't hear what was said but in a matter of seconds I saw something being handed out to each one of the girls. Soon I saw that they were all working their jaws like mad. Chewing gum, I thought. And I was right, for a moment later they plugged the wads of gum into their navels, clamped the trouser bands firmly over them, and the scene went on. I was fascinated by this example of ingenuity, as I was to be hundreds upon hundreds of times.

From there we went down to the old Lois Weber studio on Melrose Avenue. Lois Weber was one of the first women directors of films, which she also wrote and produced. Her studio was a rambling, shingled bungalow with a stage behind it. All stages were pretty elementary at this period, with white cloth and silvered boards to act as reflectors. They depended largely on the constant sunlight of Los Angeles.

Louis B. Mayer had been an exhibitor near Boston and his first great success was either showing a film entitled *From the Manger to the Cross*, made in the Holy Land, or a film of *The Passion Play* as performed at Oberammergau. The records are not clear about this. But after his success, Mayer sold his interest in the movie-house and, with the money, came to Los Angeles to start a moving picture company. He had two female stars, one of whom was Mildred Harris, then married to Charles Chaplin and awaiting the birth of their first child. The other was Anita Stewart.

My father's friend introduced me as a girl who had already written and sold an original story which had been made and was soon to be released, and this made a great impression, as I knew it would. He went on to explain how I had come down under a verbal contract with Harry Garson for a year but when I arrived Mr. Garson and Clara Kimball Young had vanished. Mr. Mayer said he couldn't afford to pay me fifty dollars a week but would pay me thirty and see what I could do. First of all I was to read all the material he was considering and then go in and tell the stories to his stars and convince them that they should make the films. My mother felt that a drop from fifty to thirty dollars was not worth staying in Hollywood for, but I thought differently. I remember saying dramatically, "My destiny is here."

The first thing I was given to read was a novel called *The Fighting Shepherdess*, which Mr. Mayer fancied for Anita Stewart. She was a delightful girl with pretty brown eyes, and was very amiable and much amused by the intensity with which I told the story. She agreed to do it, which of course was a little victory for me. Meanwhile, Mildred Harris had her baby, a boy, but it lived only a very short time and her marriage to Chaplin ended soon after.

Part of Mr. Mayer's programme was Marshall "Mickey" Nielan's production of *In Old Kentucky* from a famous play. He had sent his assistant to Kentucky to select locations and I remember so well the telegram which came back saying, "There's nothing in Kentucky that looks like Kentucky. Better shoot in California."

I had put in eight weeks at this job, when suddenly I got a telephone call from Harry Garson. He had come back to California and he said, "Where are you? I've got eight weeks' back salary for you—four hundred dollars. You'd better get over here quickly and collect it." ...

I reported to the Garson studio with my year's contract in full effect and was handed all my back salary, so the money I had made with Mr. Mayer was extra, but I had yet to meet Clara Kimball Young. On my second day I heard a sort of tremor run through the front office and looking out I saw a beautiful Pierce Arrow town car with a liveried chauffeur and two red Chow dogs seated beside him. As the chauffeur stepped round to open the car door, a middle-aged woman with blond hair, "Aunt Eva," stepped out carrying a jewel case, and after her stepped Clara.

She was unlike anything I had imagined; she was much smaller than she appeared in pictures. I moved away from the window quickly as I saw she was coming in and Harry Garson said, "Clara, this is Lenore Coffee, the girl I brought down from San Francisco. She wrote *The Better Wife* for you." Clara gave me a long, cool look and then a quick smile. "It was a fine story," she said. Then she turned to Harry and said, "You know, Harry,

I think you were right—she looks like a bright girl." She came towards me with her hand outstretched and said, "I hope you'll be happy with us." From that moment on she was a mountain of kindness to me.

The Garson Studio was only two blocks away from the Mack Sennett Studios and the Keystone Cops would go roaring up and down the street while we were playing delicate or passionate love scenes, and no one paid the slightest attention. I soon realized that it was my great good fortune to be in a very small, one-company studio because anything I would take on meant a saving on salaries. Ostensibly I was brought down to learn how to write but as I apparently knew a little about that already, Mr. Garson suggested that I would learn more about the actual making of pictures if I had a certain responsibility. At that time the titles of "continuity secretary" or "script girl" did not exist; but he suggested that I make notes during the shooting so that I would feel that I was part of the production. I ended not only doing that but by reading all the fan mail, all the submitted original stories, making cutting notes, writing titles—all this was magnificent training which I could never have had in a larger studio.

In 1919 Hollywood was a village. Hollywood Boulevard could have been any Main Street in America. The heat was a clear desert heat. The sky, a strong, deep blue and the mountains like cardboard cut-outs—you could hardly believe they had any backs to them. Behind those mountains was the San Fernando Valley, as yet unexploited, save for Universal Pictures having built Universal City with its own Post Office. On the corner of Hollywood Boulevard and Vine Street was a very large and beautiful orange grove, and one street down was the Lasky studio with its front lined by a row of lovely pepper trees. Pepper trees have a special beauty of their own—the trailing branches of the weeping willow without their melancholy. But, alas, the berries exude a juice which dripped and damaged the tops of automobiles. So, in order to save a few cars, whole rows of these trees were chopped down!

There were only two small movie-houses, the Iris and the Hollywood. Between them was the Public Library, a modest, thickly vine-clad building with a good assortment of books. Across the street, a bit farther up, was the Jesuit church, so smothered in vines that when the windows were open they clambered into the church as if, as one pious worshipper said, "They wanted to hear the sermon."

And there was Gower Street with its corner drugstore, called "Gower

Gulch," for it was the hang-out for what we called "drugstore cowboys" in Western gear, ready at any moment to jump on a horse or a bus, wherever a few dollars might be made. On warm evenings—and this meant for eight or nine months of the year—one could walk up and down Hollywood Boulevard and in the course of almost every block meet people with whom one would stop and chat. And people of many nationalities, for accents didn't matter in silent films. All were happy to play bit parts, even extras— and former enemies became friends and associates. You can't share box lunches on location without a certain camaraderie springing up. With the European market opening up, these people were in great demand. There were also some English with a sprinkling of Welsh and Irish.

I wish I could make the picture, the "feel" of Hollywood at this time as vivid to you as it still is to me. It was like a carnival; or the way one feels when the circus is coming to town, only the circus was always there. Actors walked about in heavy grease-paint make-up, and out-of-work actors did precisely the same thing, hoping to create the impression that they, too, were employed. Their shirts, whether day or dress, were always tinted blue, pink or yellow because of the reflection which white gave in those days of a limited lighting technique. They called this "halation." And the birth of dark glasses came about as a guard against the Klieg lights which, if carelessly looked into, could scorch the eyeballs.

Then there was the marvelous custom of shooting at night during the very hot weather. We would begin at eight o'clock in the evening and continue until four o'clock in the morning without a stop. Coffee was kept hot on an electric plate and there were trays of sandwiches. There was a kind of magic about those nights. They were done only with principals and all went on so quietly. There was a relaxed atmosphere and a sense of intimacy with the medium in which we were working. I think I felt closer to the moving picture industry during those nights than at any other time. And it was such fun to come back to Hollywood Boulevard and eat ham and eggs and greasy fried potatoes at John's all-night restaurant, and roll into bed at five o'clock in the morning.

Actually, there wasn't another restaurant opened in Hollywood until Frank's in 1921, later called Musso Frank's and still there. But, around this same time, a man from the East took one look at Hollywood Boulevard and said to himself, "What this place needs is a good New York style delicatessen, featuring German and Jewish food." He found an empty store across from the Hollywood Hotel and in no time at all the Gotham opened featuring chopped chicken livers, blintzes, Swiss cheese, frankfurters, often called "hot dogs," and the big, thick knackwurst, over-grown frankfurters. It flourished from its very first day.

Hollywood Boulevard was a villagey street. There was a large market which served superb breakfasts at a counter. Great beakers of fresh orange juice, ham and eggs, bacon and eggs, French toast, waffles, and that delight of American men, pancakes with maple syrup. It was packed with movie people, for calls to work were early.

With only one proper hotel, rooms in private houses were at a premium. After being promised the first vacancy at the Hollywood Hotel, I found one close to the Boulevard. My mother had fled northwards. She detested southern California and during all the years I lived there, made only short visits. Across the hall from my room was a very pleasant and friendly young woman, Anne Bauchens, who was a cutter for the great Cecil B. DeMille, whose film *Male and Female*, had just been released. Of course, the very name of DeMille was music to my ears and I listened avidly to any bits about him and his productions she might tell me. I even had fantasy dreams that, through Annie, I'd actually meet him. But it was to be six years before this happened, and when it did it was to make an enormous difference to my life. A milestone which looked a mile high. And was.

At the corner of Hollywood Boulevard and Highland Avenue was the famous Hollywood Hotel, where you were always certain to find friends, for actors are gregarious people. The hotel itself was inviting, surrounded by a large veranda with rows of rocking-chairs where one could sit and watch the movie world go by. It really was a glorified theatrical boarding-house, with large, ragged gardens at the back, but an excellent tennis court. And no matter at what hour one came in, night or day, there would always be someone sitting either on the veranda or in the lounge with whom one could have a chat. Actually, it was the nerve centre of the town, as well as its grape-vine.

And it was to this hotel that Samuel Goldwyn brought his group of "Eminent Authors," which he had created. It was a brilliant idea, even though few of them adapted themselves to the tricky business of writing film scripts; but it lent dignity to this fast-growing industry, and Goldwyn was the first to do it. When I moved into the hotel in 1920, I was stunned to see, *en masse*, such celebrities as Rex Beach, Rupert Hughes (uncle of

Howard Hughes), Sir Gilbert Parker, Edward Knobloch, and even the great Somerset Maugham himself.

Elinor Glyn, or Madam Glyn as she preferred to be called, was not with this group but arrived at about the same time, looking, as someone said, just like the Chalk Cliffs of Dover. She made a big impact on Hollywood, one of her first pronouncements being, after one look at Clara Bow, "That girl has IT!" Thereafter, Clara Bow became the "IT" girl. And "IT" became a synonym for sex-appeal.

Of course Elinor Glyn was the author of a novel [*Three Weeks*] which had become an enormous success, so she very quickly made herself a part of the Hollywood scene and her presence led to all manner of rhymed, bawdy references, the most popular being:

Would you care to sin
Like Elinor Glyn
On a tiger skin
Or would you prefer
To err
On some other fur?

Sir Gilbert Parker had asked Madam Glyn, along with others of whom I was one, to come up to his room for drinks. He became quite amorous and made an attempt to take her in his arms. With magnificent hauteur, she held out her hand. "You may kiss my hand. All emotion begins at the wrist."

I was quite impressed by this, but later on found that there was a contrasting side to Madam. When she was having her first book filmed she was very much in evidence and I actually saw her bring a dark, brick-like blush to the face of a very tough casting director. They were discussing the type of young men, some twelve or fifteen, to form the Palace Guard. She discussed the physique she wished in great detail, adding: "You must remember they are going to wear those silk, skin-clinging tights, so make certain they are the correct size. There is nothing so obscene as a man's legs in wrinkled tights." She gave a shudder. Then, just as the casting director was about to turn away, she said in a firm loud voice: "And no jock-straps." The casting director stopped dead in his tracks. He'd never had such an order before and certainly not from a woman. He stammered: "But you said the tights were to be skin-clinging." Madam Glyn, with perfect sang-froid, replied: "Of course. That is why there are to be no jock-straps. I do not believe in inter-fering with Nature." It was said that on the days of these tests the Gotham reported a lamentable shortage of knackwursts!

* * * *

With Malibu just a stretch of anonymous beach and Palm Springs not yet ready to shake off the dust of the desert to emerge as a great resort, all the social life of the people in the movie business centered in Hollywood. A very lively social life it was, but very "small townish," very close-knit, almost parochial. The same people did the same things at all the same places at the same time.

For example: there was a district named Vernon, outside the city limits of Los Angeles and thus free of its jurisdiction. So boxing, spoken of as "the fights," was permitted. It was quite the thing to go there in semi-dress; black tie for the men, a dinner dress for the women. The pattern was, din-ner in down-town Los Angeles at Marcel's, then on to Vernon. After the fights small parties gathered at private houses so drinks could be had.

Another very popular entertainment on Sunday evenings, regularly observed, was to dine at Victor Hugo's before going on to the Orpheum to see the vaudeville show, which changed weekly. The house would be packed with movie people, all of whom knew each other and, in many instances, some of the performers.

Every important play or musical from New York went on tour, across all those 3,000 miles which lay between the East and West coasts. The Mason Opera House was always booked to the rafters well in advance. And when the D'Oyly Carte company came the English contingent turned out in full force.

I must not leave out the wonderful old Philharmonic Auditorium in down-town Los Angeles, built as early as 1906 by the Temple Baptist Church. There we heard operas, symphony orchestras from all parts of America, concert singers, violinists and pianists. It was there I heard the then famous Vladimir de Pachmann play. He was the greatest living expo-nent of Chopin. By this time in his life he had become quite dotty and his so-called companion, actually his keeper, was always lurking in the wings. Often he would pause after playing a particularly brilliant passage, clap-ping his hands and crying out, "Bravo! De Pachmann! Bravo!"

It was there that I saw Eleonora Duse in her performance of Ibsen's

Ghosts. She was to die only a few months later in smoky, sooty Pittsburgh, far removed from the sun of her native Italy. And I saw Anna Pavlova dance *The Death of the Swan,* so beautiful that it almost hurt to breathe.

Besides the theatres there was a very good repertory company at the Morosco Theatre where many excellent plays were put on, especially those which were not coming out on tour from New York.

There was a great deal of party-giving—not the later, much publicized and frequently exaggerated "wild" parties, but rather villagey affairs where you were sent amusing, hand-written invitations with place cards to match, both with personal touches or teasing jokes; and everyone contributed to the evening's entertainment.

There were no Beach Clubs in these early days; public beaches were used and the one at Crystal Pier became the favorite for the movie folk. There was, also at the beach, the Ship Café—an actual ship tied up at the pier, the interior unchanged. And on Ocean Boulevard was the Sunset Inn, the "hang-out" for Fatty Arbuckle and his crowd. But neither was patronized by what one would call the "top drawer" of Hollywood. Midway between Hollywood and Los Angeles, the Cocoanut Grove opened in 1921 and was, and still is, a very popular dining and dancing spot.

Lenore Coffee spent the next forty years in Hollywood as a much-in-demand "fixer-upper," as she called doctoring other people's scripts; she also wrote her own original screenplays and adapted plays and novels into films. She is credited with writing eighty-five silent films, of which only a few survive. She worked for Goldwyn, Mayer, Thalberg, and DeMille over the years and, in 1924, married the English novelist and director William Cowen. She was twice nominated for the Academy Award for Best Adapted Screenplay for Street of Chance *in 1930 and* Four Daughters, *which she wrote with Julius J. Epstein, in 1938. That same year she moved to Warner Bros., where she stayed for over a decade. She had two children, and in 1959, the family moved to England where she wrote her autobiography,* Storyline. *She summed up her time in Hollywood by saying: "They pick your brains, break your heart, ruin your digestion—and what do you get for it? Nothing but a lousy fortune." Coffee returned to California in 1981 to live at the Motion Picture Home in Woodland Hills, where she died on July 2, 1984, at the age of eighty-seven.*

Alice Guy 1919

Alice Ida Antoinette Guy, born outside Paris on July 1, 1873, was not only the first woman director; she was one of the very first directors, period. She was the fifth child of an arranged marriage between a young convent girl and a book publisher ten years her senior. Alice was sent to boarding schools, but after her father died and her older sisters married, she had to leave school to support her mother. Trained as a typist, Alice worked for Leon Gaumont, a manufacturer of photographic equipment, and in 1885 they attended the Paris screening of the Lumière brothers' short film Workers Leaving the Factory. Guy convinced Gaumont that he should let her make films with his cameras, in addition to her office duties; he agreed and in 1887 Guy, a teenager, became head of Gaumont's new film production business. Over the next ten years she directed over one thousand short films. In 1907, she married the photographer Herbert Blaché, and when Gaumont sent him to New York City, Guy quit her job to go along. After giving birth to a daughter, Guy created her own studio, Solax, in 1910. She hired many people who would go on to help build the infant film industry, including the future directors Lois Weber and her husband, Phillips Smalley. Solax was initially successful, but got caught up in the Edison Trust battles, and the war in Europe played havoc with the distribution of their films. Guy had given birth to a son in 1912, and several years later, both her children caught the measles, so she moved to the healthier climate of North Carolina to nurse them. When she returned, Blaché, who had stayed to run the studio, had taken up with one of his actresses. He announced he was moving to Hollywood and that the studio was being rented out to other directors, so Guy took a job writing and directing the film Tarnished Reputations at two thousand dollars a week for six weeks. During the shoot, however, she and many others caught the Spanish influenza, which had become a pandemic in 1918.

That influenza was truly terrible. Five members of my company were infected, four died.

My husband, passing through New York, came to see me. I believe my sad look moved him. He asked me to rejoin him as soon as I could. Six weeks later, with my children I took the road for California.

We made the New York–Chicago trip by night. When we arrived in Chicago where we had to pass a few hours waiting to change trains, it was deep night and the glow of the smelters made it look like a real inferno. The journey went on, banal enough, with stops to take on water, through prairies of sagebrush. A cowboy undertook to race the train. Then we stopped on a Navajo Indian reservation. People brought fragile pottery and copper necklaces for sale alongside the train. "You have time to visit the village," said the conductor.

In their huts the Indians beat the copper to make plates and drinking vessels. The women card wool and weave handsome blankets and carpets, famous everywhere in the United States. Women carry their babies on their hips, sometimes they seat them on two branches attached at an angle, pulled gently by a little horse.

The village of Albuquerque is frequented by many artists. The Navajo are proud, sad and handsome. Scattered on the surrounding hills one can see a few isolated tents.

It was night when our train entered the great Colorado desert. Another fairyland! We stayed until morning with our brows pressed to the windows. There was sand, great slabs of stone, giant cactus bearing flowers and fruits, enormous stars that seemed to hang within reach, and on the corners of the blocks of stone, doubtless wet with dew, miniscule rainbows. The howl of coyotes was like an orchestra.

My husband met us in Los Angeles and led us to Hollywood. He had rented an apartment in a pleasant hotel on Sunset Boulevard, at the foot of a hill planted all the way to its summit with a Japanese garden. The hotel itself had a fine garden of exotic trees where sometimes a flight of little parakeets would settle. There I saw and smelled a skunk for the first time.

I found most of the actors there whom I had known. Sunset Boulevard was very lively. Actors strolled casually, still in costume, shopping for a meal, a drink, cigarettes. Soon I also was recognized and welcomed.

Hollywood was not all beautiful gardens. Oil was still important and the derricks rose everywhere. Hundreds of workers were employed in

Alice Guy. (Courtesy of MOMA)

Oil wells cover Los Angeles County's Signal Hill. (Collection of Allison Burnett)

drilling. Many houses were lighted and heated by natural gas.

In the naphtha wells were found the heads of tigers with elephant tusks. I have seen strange little red crabs drawn out of the wells, perfect copies of a Japanese mask. There was much to interest a scientist.

Hollywood smelled of eucalyptus or of petrol, according to the direction of the wind. The studios were built as far as possible from the derricks.

Hollywood Hotel was quite gay. There was a ball at least once a week, often cut short by an act improvised by one of the tenants: Jim Corbett ("Gentleman Jim") organizing a fight with Milton Sills.

I was not particularly gay and I often took refuge in the billiard room. My two children adored that and even my baby, crawling on top of the pool-table, tried to manipulate a billiard cue heavier than he was.

I wanted very much to go down to Mexico. But unfortunately, I was the victim of a hold-up, my car was terribly wrecked and my daughter hurt. The tragedy would have been complete if a group of five automobiles had not arrived at the spot and set the gangsters to flight. A doctor was among the rescuers. He bandaged my daughter and we continued on to the next town where she could be cared for. I had to abandon my car to the insurance people and we took the train back to Los Angeles. Two weeks later I went back alone to retrieve my automobile and returned by the ledge-like road between the Pacific Ocean and Sierra Madre. It would need a long chapter to describe the beauties of that route…

Herbert Blaché directed *The Brat* [1919] and *Stronger Than Death* [1920] with Nazimova. I had become his assistant, rather, but with very long intermissions.

New religions were constantly coming to light: theosophy, new science, Christian Science. I visited the centers, was taken by the abundant literature and was finally invited by the Christian Scientists to visit and discuss the scenario for a propaganda film. On the agreed-upon day, I went to the rendezvous and was given a few pamphlets which I read. I was shocked to see the way in which they treated the Christian religion; its priests were charged with all the sins of Israel.

I said, "I understand that you value your faith, but is it truly necessary to drag others in the mud in order to witness that faith?" There…the priestess cut me short.

"Ah!" said she. "Are you Catholic? Useless to go any further, you cannot work for us."

Tired of hotel life and for private reasons also I had decided to rent a little bungalow. Nazimova, who had become attached to my children, came often to visit us. She herself had a very agreeable house on Sunset Boulevard where we were often invited to tea. While my children played in the garden she questioned me about French literature and music. I did my best to inform, happy that someone loved my country. For her I hummed the "Chansons Tristes" of Duparc, which she adored.

During one of these visits we learned that the Prohibition Act, voted by Congress in 1919, was to be applied after a delay of eight days. Nazimova seized the telephone and invited all her friends to come next day for a cocktail. We attended, Herbert and I, and were very gay when we started homeward after midnight.

In Venice, a fashionable beach not far from Hollywood, an old rotting hull of a boat lay on the beach. An intelligent restaurateur transformed it into a bar, restaurant, ballroom especially reserved for movie people. There we decided to pass the last night of legal libation. By dawn I was, I think, the only one to have stayed sober...not by virtue, but by taste. I detest alcohol, apart from an occasional cocktail.

One anecdote, among a hundred: A couple struck with love ran to waken the "coroner" (justice of the peace), signed all the necessary papers, found a minister somewhere who blessed them. Waking next morning, their wits recovered, they recalled that they had been married already, and had no other recourse but to run to Reno to get divorced. The law doesn't joke about bigamy.

Those were the great days of moonshine stills, whisky glasses disguised as milk glasses; adulterated alcohol that caused all sort of damage, smugglers, gangsters. The State soon found that the cure was worse than the disease.

It was now that I received a letter from my lawyer and one from [Joseph] Borries [of the U.S. Amusement Company] asking me to make at least one visit to Fort Lee [New Jersey]. I found kind, faithful Borries at his post, happy to see me but very changed.

"Ah, Madame," he told me, "Come back. Defend yourself. They'll leave you nothing but the eyes to weep."

He told me how M.S., the bank representative, stole all the interesting furniture (we had some very good things bought at auction; among others, two beautiful Elizabethan chairs that many decorators had borrowed to copy, a whole set of Empire furniture, etc.).

"Mr. Blaché has lost interest in everything," he told me. "He has refused a rental which was modest enough but which would have allowed you to pay the taxes. The two little companies to whom he sublet the photographic studios have both had fires and the insurance company flatly refuses to pay for the damage."

In short, everything went from bad to worse.

It was then that a producer made me a rather preposterous proposal.

"Put fifty thousand dollars in the business and we'll give you the direction of *Tarzan of the Apes.*"

At the thought of guiding the acrobatics of that colossal ape-man my blood froze. Happily it was out of the question: I didn't have fifty thousand dollars.

America, they say, always takes back everything she gives you. Completely discouraged I resolved to return to France with my children.

Unlike all the other protagonists in this book who came to Los Angeles at the beginning of their film careers, Alice Guy arrived after she had soared to the top of her profession and was facing failure and depression. In 1922, Solax was officially no more, and she and Hebert Blaché divorced. She returned to France with her children, where she looked with little success for work in the film industry. She did not have copies of any of her films and, desperate to prove what she could do, she made a fruitless trip to America in 1927 to find the films she had made there. By the late 1930s, Guy was living with her daughter Simone in Paris and depending upon her for support. Simone worked for American embassies in Europe, and Alice moved with her; they lived for several years in Switzerland and then Washington, DC. Guy was in her seventies when she was recognized for her accomplishments and contributions to film. She started giving lectures, which inspired her to write her memoirs. In 1955, she was awarded the Légion d'honneur by the French government and honored by the Cinémathèque Française two years later. Alice and Simone moved to Mahwah, New Jersey, in 1965, where Alice Guy died in a nursing home on March 24, 1968, at the age of ninety-four.

Winfrid Kay Thackrey 1921

W *infrid Kay Knudtson was born on May 15, 1899, in Bismarck, North Dakota, and raised on a ranch. A short, attractive brunette, she was a Midwesterner through and through, yet like so many young women in the early twenties, the Jazz Age, movies, and women's newly won right to vote sparked her imagination.*

A job as a script clerk had not been my dream when I came to Hollywood in 1921—far from it. The name had all the romance of an overworked clerk filing reports in some dismal office day after day after day. Definitely not a career woven of dreams. But I can think of no place on earth where dreams can change more drastically, for better or for worse, than in Hollywood.

I came here from a cattle ranch in North Dakota, via St. John's Academy of Fine Arts and the Art Institute of Chicago. I was educated as an interior decorator, and I was firmly convinced that Hollywood really needed me. Motion picture sets in 1921 were abominable. They desperately needed help, and who could be more helpful than someone with my background?

But Hollywood wanted nothing to do with me. It was impossible even to get *in* to a motion picture studio. A girl has to eat, so I tried various decorators. There were few, and I was solidly rebuffed.

Barker Brothers, to whom I applied in final desperation, employed a personnel manager of great charm. He was a rotund little man with a cigar stuffed between rotund lips. He listened for perhaps half a moment, then leaned back in his swivel chair, crossed his fat knees with difficulty, and pontificated: "We don't employ women decorators."

I had heard this so many, many times. "Why not?" I asked, trying not to sound as angry as I felt.

"Well, ya see ..." He paused for another leisured puff at his cigar. It was a small, bare room, with no open windows, choked with smoke. "A woman decorator ..." he shook his head as if unable to imagine such an absurdity, and a smile curled the corners of his wet lips. "Well, ya see—here at Barker Brothers we're in business to make money—"

I sprang to my feet. "How strikingly individual!" I blazed. "I never heard of anyone in business to make money." My voice had begun to quaver like an amateur singer trying to hit high C. "You! You can go to Hell!" I ran out the door, slamming it hard, rejected the elevator for the stairs, spilling tears as I went. I'd leave California and never come back—go to Koyukuk, Timbuktu, Cucamonga, or...or—but nothing of the kind was possible. The coins in my purse wouldn't buy a bus ticket to Burbank.

Stumbling down the stairs, the sole of one slipper flapping free, I was alone with my tears. I wore no makeup so there was no streaking of rouge and mascara, but my nose dripped and my chin drizzled. Rummaging in my jacket pocket produced nothing in the way of a handkerchief. Somewhat inelegantly, I wiped my cheeks, chin and nose on the starched ruffle of my pettiskirt. Taking a long breath, my shoulders squared, my head came up, and I swung open the door to the first floor. I settled my felt turban firmly, walked two blocks to Grand Avenue and J. W. Robinson's, where I found a job in their drapery department selling curtain fabrics over the counter and by the bolt.

When I worked in Minneapolis at Weber-Werness Studios, Decorators, or at Styer Studio, Decorators, in Chicago, there hadn't been a *bolt* of fabric in their stockrooms, only sample lengths from eastern wholesalers, swatches of fabrics, sketches of elegant furniture. Robinson's had none of this. But it was a job. I was given a small salary and commission. Now I could pay my streetcar fare to 103rd Street, where my friends, Ferne and Les Brockway, gave me their couch, dinner, and breakfast for two dollars a day.

Eventually the head of the drapery department let me order a few sample lengths of upholstery and drapery fabrics, and gave me the occasional use of a company car that I might drive to the home of a prospective customer. The freedom of a car was fabulous. I ran it all over town and began to know the streets.

Vine Street ran up a hill to end abruptly in an orange grove. Santa Monica Boulevard ran toward the ocean, but ended in a streetcar barn in Sherman. Beverly Hills was almost nonexistent. Robertson Boulevard and

Building a "set" at the Metro Studios, Hollywood.

Building a set at Metro Studios. (Collection of Patt Morrison)

Famous Players-Lasky Studios, with offices on the left and glass-covered stages on the right. (Courtesy of MOMA)

La Cienega? Not even a glint in anybody's eye; and Pruss Drive ended in a muddy bog long before it reached Culver City. When I had the car I could be depended on to be gone all day, sometimes bringing back an order to Robinson's. That kept me in favor—and in gasoline.

But motion pictures were always my dream. There were few studios; I tried them all repeatedly. Warners on Sunset Boulevard, Fox on Western Avenue, Metro Pictures in Hollywood, Fairbanks Studio, Famous Players Lasky, and Universal Studios. Lasky got most of my attention. It was closer to Robinson's, easier to reach in my lunch hour. Here, too, nothing! Nobody wanted to see me. No, there were no jobs for *set dressers*, as I found decorators were called at motion picture studios.

On a boiling hot day in August of 1922 I began my daily pilgrimage to that studio's front entrance window.

"No, Mr. Little is not in."

I persisted. The young man sighed and called back to one more in authority. "Miss Nuisance is here again to see Tommy Little."

My name was Knudtson, anglicized to "Nuteson." It was NOT Nuisance. I knew he was trying to be funny, but I corrected him anyway. He laughed good naturedly, adding: "Anyway, Tom Little is still in the East," and, "No, we have no information as to when he'll return." With that he turned away. So did I. I was mad! I didn't believe him. I had put myself through three art-school years, some of it by working as a secretary half-days, and knew the "not in" routine like I knew the holes in my shoes, and I was sick of being Miss Nuisance.

A high board fence completely surrounded and enclosed Lasky Studio. There HAD to be another gate somewhere. Not all *trucks* came in the front gate. Or did they? I decided to walk around and see.

I had walked six or seven blocks when a big load of lumber standing beside a wide, closed gate attracted my attention. The driver climbed down from the truck, slowly walked toward the gate, and hooked his hand onto the other side—a spring perhaps, or a latch. The gate shuddered and sprang away from the post. The driver followed. Finally, my lucky day! I ran behind the truck when his back was turned. He pulled the truck through. I followed, knowing he would close the gate and lock it again. Moving forward when he moved back, running in front of the truck while he fumbled to relock the gate, I ran a few feet, did not look back, then slowed to a walk.

Not far away a company was breaking for lunch; I quickly joined the crowd. Everyone was in costume. The village was Bavarian. That much I knew. My sagacity ended there. They broke up into small groups, laughing, visiting. Two men were walking down the dusty road. Neither was in costume. I caught up with them.

"I beg your pardon, but could you perhaps direct me to the office of Tom Little? I seem to have missed a building or two, made a few wrong turns."

"Lost your road map, eh?" one man asked affably. "I don't know this studio too well myself, what about you, Jimmy?"

The man addressed had lost his waistline some time ago, but he still wore it belted to the last notch. A slouch cap dropped over his right eye as if it were a beret, an unlighted pipe was in his hand, and his arms were bare to the elbow. His blue, short-sleeved shirt was scalloped with sweat beneath each arm, and his pants probably had been white when the day began.

"Hell, I almost live here," Jimmy growled. "Yeah, I know where Little hangs out but it may not be easy to tell you how to get there from here." They both stopped for a moment while Jimmy knit his brows, began pointing directions, stopped and sighed. "It's easier to take you there," he decided. "I've got to see him anyway 'bout that damn beer garden tomorrow."

While we walked we talked. I admitted I was looking for a job.

"What as? One of Little's prop boys?"

"No. A decorator."

He laughed. "You're a kid." He glanced at me sideways, pushed his pipe into his mouth and lit it. "You could be all of seventeen. You look like a kid and there's a lot of responsibility—"

"I've studied art and decoration for three years and worked as a decorator in Minneapolis and Chicago—" I was getting mad again.

"All right, all right," he interrupted. "I believe you. But you still look like a kid."

I wondered why he kept saying I was a kid. True, my hair was in braids, but they were not pigtail braids hanging down my back like a schoolgirl. They were heavy brown braids piled one on top of the other across the center of my head. I always wore earrings and today a dab of lipstick. What's so kidlike about that? My snub nose was freckled in abundance, but I knew many adults with freckles; and as for clothes…my one dress-up outfit. Black crepe accordion-pleated skirt, a plain white blouse, a black jacket covered with wriggling white soutache braid—dry cleaned when I could afford it. I glanced at my shoes. I'd forgotten them. Plain old Mary Jane black patent-leather, low heels, a single strap across my instep. They must be the culprits. I'd bought them in the children's department—cheaper than in adults'—toes now scuffed, holes spreading on the soles.

"God knows if Tommy will find a job for you, but if you are what you say you are, we could use you," he was saying. "Tommy is a great guy, but he's right out of props—'decorating' pretty much means paperhanging in his book."

"Well, I know decoration," I said, somewhat mollified. "I've studied period furniture and antiques and fabrics—"

"I said I believe you. Now cool down! I'll be glad to introduce you, and you can give Tom your own credentials."

He did, and I did.

It was at least three months later that I learned, to my dismay, that my benefactor was the famous motion-picture director James Cruze. I had seen many of his pictures, and I was later to see *The Covered Wagon* at least three times, but I had never seen a photograph of him. (I now have a photograph of him hanging in my home. It was taken nearly fifteen years later. There are three men in golf clothes: my husband, Eugene Thackrey, Maxwell Anderson, and James Cruze. The photograph was taken before I really knew any of them. So much for the very long arm of coincidence.)

I spent the afternoon with Tom Little, a tall, angular man, excessively thin, slow, smiling, with the look of an incredulous cowboy. He wanted to know all about me, but what he wanted to know most was what I knew. He had just returned from the East Coast with several carloads of furniture, which they had been unloading into the property department for several days. Tom had bought blindly at auctions and antique houses. He knew his purchases could be used in dressing sets for Lasky Studio, but he hadn't the vaguest idea whether the furniture was Grand Rapids, Spanish Mediterranean, or Rocky Mountain Rococo, and he really wanted to know. He couldn't have found a more willing and eager "authority" than I.

Tommy lifted muslin covers from a fabulous mahogany banquet table, its many carved chairs stashed in a long row. "I bought these at auction— Old English, they said, and I thought they might lend a touch of class to

Queen Elizabeth, scheduled for spring shooting."

"Stunning," I said, "but not for Queen Elizabeth. She died a hundred years before Chippendale began designing furniture."

"It's real Chippendale then?" he asked anxiously.

"Very fine and very authentic Chinese Chippendale." I ran my hand over the smooth mahogany curve, while I tried to remember my exams. "The classic Queen Anne cabriole leg with its claw and ball foot came in around 1735, the splat back was universally used—the back often elaborately carved. Chippendale and his son borrowed and combined their own designs with the French, particularly Louis XV, and later the Chinese. There were many fine cabinetmakers in the mid-seventeen hundreds; in England, the Adams Brothers, Sheraton, Hepplewhite—"

"What about Americans? Anything that was strictly our own?"

"Most of ours were simple pieces designed for more recent wealth, much of that was elegant, though—like the lyre-back Duncan Phyfe—"

He lifted another muslin cover, smiling expectantly, "Like this?"

"Like that!" I exclaimed. "You really scored!" Closely examining a drawer in a table, I found squared rusting nails in ill-fitting holes. "Not just reproductions. Antiques!"

Anyway, they were nice, and so was Tommy Little.

Around four o'clock he bought us cups of coffee at a small lunchroom on the lot, and we leveled. There was no job for me, but he would keep his ears open.

Amazingly enough, he did. I had gone back to Robinson's happily unaware that this kind of promise rarely reached fruition. Perhaps that is why I wasn't surprised, only delighted, and excited beyond belief, when I had a phone call from him several days later telling me to "go over to Warner Bros., find the stage where Jack Conway is shooting *Lucretia Lombard*. Their sets are lousy and Conway needs help."

The prospect of a real motion-picture job frightened me out of my wits. I had never been on a set before; had never seen a motion picture being filmed. I knew nothing about the decoration of a set. A house obviously was quite a different matter, but *how* different I could only imagine with foreboding.

"You won't have any trouble," Tom reassured. "If you get into hot water just tell'm you've only dressed sets at Triangle in New York."

"New York!"

"Yeah, they do things different there. They won't know as much as you do anyway, so hold on to your hat. Lemme know how you come out. And give my regards to Jack Conway. He's the director, an old friend. I told him I'd send you." He hung up. I worried all night.

After reading part of the script the following morning, I worried more. I had not seen a script before and incredible as it may seem today when scripts are read and studied in colleges all over the world, it was totally puzzling to me. What did it mean? LONG SHOT. CLOSE UP. AKELEY SHOT. FADE IN.

Warner Bros. was located on Sunset Boulevard in those days. The studio was white pillared with the façade of an old Southern mansion. There were two or three stages, many offices, and a large room they called the property department. I found my way to the studio and introduced myself to Eddie Sutherland, assistant director on *Lucretia Lombard*. They were not shooting at that moment so he showed me the next set they would be using.

"We'll move in here tomorrow night, rehearse, and shoot the following day," Eddie said. "So dress the set, finish it probably by late afternoon tomorrow."

The set was an oak wainscoted hall in a Jacobean mansion. A magnificent spiral staircase swept up to a second floor. To my astonishment there was no second floor! It was being constructed on another part of the stage. Actors would climb the stairs and hide out of sight until the camera stopped turning, and action would pick up on another day on the other set. I didn't even know the story was strictly modern, with an old mansion simply as background. I thought the actors would dress in the period costumes of the Jacobean mansion. Had there been time that first morning to read the full script it may have helped, but probably not. I was too confused to think beyond the first floor and the immediate problem of walls, drapery, rugs, furniture.

There were no rental stores in Hollywood or Los Angeles. Without color in film, pieces were not so easily recognizable and the same old furnishings could be used over and over again. New items were rarely purchased.

Eddie introduced me to André, a charming elderly French gentleman. He was Warner's "art department."

"Anything you need André will find," Eddie said. "He'll sign a requisition for anything you need to buy and, of course, hold down the purchases." Then he went back to the company filming the stage.

André got me a car and I went to Robinson's because I knew what they had and time was short. I bought two sample lengths of tête-de-nègre hand-blocked linen with a large garland of flowers centered in the fifty-inch length. I would use this for draw curtains and for a formal lambrequin at a large French window beside the stairs.

André shook his head. His hair was as white and scrambled as a tuft of white angora yarn, rarely combed, never trimmed. His paint-splattered smock established him in my eyes as an artist. I could trust him. He had been in the United States for many years, but he still retained his delightful French accent. "Roses are so beautiful but is too much dark color, and cornflower is too dark color blue and green leaves—" He shook his head again. "All dark color will photograph black. Is a waste. But not to worry. I fix."

And fix he did. He had long draw curtains made that night of brown burlap, much less expensive than linen, then copied the garlands using light, bright pastel chalks. The result was lovely. I hope I kissed his fuzzy white head. I wanted to.

I also wanted a landscape wallpaper to climb the wall beside the spiral staircase. "Ça, c'est beau. Très Français," he said appreciatively, but nothing like this could be found in Hollywood, especially in a day. This marvelous little man spent several hours that night sketching a landscape in watercolor, highlighting it in pastel chalks, green weeping-willow trees shadowed in light purpling grays, distant snow-crested mountains with a small stream cascading over rocks into a canyon at the foot of the stairs. I was ecstatic, and when he let me rent the biggest, most beautiful Oriental blue-and-gold rug that Robinson's had in their rug department, I knew that God had smiled on me. I probably went to Mass twice the following Sunday.

Jack Conway was pleased with the room, so was Irene Rich, the star. But when Conway said, "The center of the room looks a little naked. Perhaps we could play something in the foreground." I fled to my white-haired friend André.

"What does he mean, 'play something'? A musical instrument? And foreground? What foreground? Where?" This, too, was resolved without my ignorance showing.

"All we have in props is a Louis XIV chaise longue," I said, quoting André.

"Don't be a showoff," Conway said and smiled. "A *chaise longue*, she says. Bring in the settee and perhaps a shawl or a scarf, something that Irene could have casually dropped on her way upstairs."

"But a chaise longue belongs in a lady's dressing room or bedroom, not sitting in the middle of the floor in a hall," I argued, with André. He shrugged, "*Qu'importe.*"

So we brought in the chaise longue and stood its back to the camera. The upholstery color bothered me—a bilious green—but again I was told, "It will photograph light gray; don't worry about it."

A few days later I faced another bewildering problem in a corner of a bedroom. That's all there was—just a corner. It was beautiful young Norma Shearer's bedroom. She arrived late, breathless, happy. She had been out dancing the night before at the Cocoanut Grove; it was one of her first dates with handsome young producer Irving Thalberg. Kenneth Hawks, second assistant, Millie (Lewis) Milestone, and their dates had been in the same party. While they laughed and talked, I placed a dressing table with its full-length mirror against one wall. Norma was to enter and go immediately to the mirror. The cameraman knew that half the stage would show in the mirror if the dressing table remained against that flat wall, so he moved the dressing table into the corner. Now Miss Shearer would be seen in profile instead of full face in the mirror.

After the first rehearsal she turned to the cameraman, an old friend, smiling radiantly. "Thank you for changing the angle—my nose is so much better in profile."

He bowed slightly, "A most beautiful nose at any angle," he said. But as Millie Milestone passed me, he whispered, "She's as cross-eyed as Ben Turpin."

The picture went well and so I decided to find myself a room in the neighborhood of the studio. The friends with whom I lived, Les and Ferne Brockway, had introduced me to a man who worked with Les at the Bank of America. "A man must have three pluses before my pulse quickens," I told Ferne. "Tall, of course, a great dancer, and he has to drive a car." Their friend was shorter than I. His stiff black hair, brushed straight up in the pompadour of GI days, made him seem taller, but I was not impressed. Still—he *did* have a car, so some compromise was worthy of consideration under the circumstances.

Over a weekend we canvassed the Vine Street, Sunset, Hollywood, and

Melrose areas. I could not afford an apartment or a furnished flat, only a room. Many homes wore a ROOM FOR RENT sign pinned to their front porches. A yellow frame bungalow on Carlton Way wore one that said:

ROOM FOR RENT
No Actors
No Jews
No Kids or Pets

Even so, believe it or not, something about the place seemed attractive.

A plump, elderly woman fidgeted around in a Mother Hubbard dress while watering the lawn and pretending not to notice our car pulling up at the curb. I was determined to get off on the right foot. "My job is in movies," I admitted. "I'm not an actor and I'm not Jewish, but I am Catholic, which may be worse. I am not married and have no children or pets."

She leaned down to turn off the hose, sizing me up from under beetle brows, her heavy red hand brushing straggling ash-blonde hair back from her sweaty forehead. She took her time. When she straightened she had made up her mind.

"Live and let live, I always say. Some actors is all right and some Jews and Catholics is all right. I got a Jew right now, livin' in the other room I rent. He's Paul Kohner, a German Jew fella."

The room was so small I could hardly turn around in it, hot as the afternoon sun, but clean and the bed comfortable. I would not be there long anyway. My youngest brother, Frederic, had said he would come up from San Diego when he graduated from high school and we'd rent an apartment so we could cook.

My job did not worry me. When *Lucretia Lombard* finished, I had been asked to complete decoration on a second picture. It was called *The Marriage Circle*, again starring Monte Blue, with Creighton Hale and King Vidor's beautiful young Texas wife, Florence Vidor. It was the story of a young physician and his wife, and of his best friend (Hale), who was also a physician and also in love with the young wife. The first set was in the living room of their apartment in (then) modern Vienna. There were windows and a fireplace with a mantel.

At Canal & Chaffin, Decorators, on Wilshire Boulevard, I found several small, bronze figurines standing on rose quartz pedestals, and a handsome silver candelabra. I would use the candelabra at one side of the mantel and the figures in a group at the other side. On that first morning of shooting,

I met director Ernst Lubitsch for the first time; a squat, paunchy man of determined stride, black hair slicked down on a somewhat flattened head, short neck, and a cigar like a nervous toy torpedo that flipped from one side of his mouth to the other as he talked. His accent was heavily German, and when he laughed I expected the rumble of a bear; it came out as a giggle. He strode quickly to the living room mantel. I waited with bated breath for high praise from the great man. He picked up the candelabra from the mantelpiece, swept the figurines into his pudgy arms, and gave them back to me. Then he picked up a stunning Lalique lamp from an end table and gave that back to me, too

"You don't like them? I thought they were so right for modern Vienna—and so beautiful—"

"*Too* beautiful. I photograph *people*. I want audience should see *people*, give *people* all attention, not look at pretty objets-d'art do-dabs—is distraction. Nicht gut."

Of course he was right; I had now learned an important lesson.

Winfrid Kay Thackrey was determined to stay in the film business. She went in and out of the steno pool and worked off and on as a script supervisor and director's assistant through the 1960s, often with Gregory La Cava on films such as Bed of Roses, Stage Door, *and* My Man Godfrey. *In the process, she met and worked with many of the greats, including Irving Thalberg, George Kaufman, Robert Wise, and William Wyler. For several years, Kay served as Norma Shearer's private secretary. In the late 1930s, she married the newspaper writer Gene Thackrey, who was credited with writing four screenplays as well as serving as the technical advisor on* Gabriel Over the White House *and* Washington Merry-Go-Round. *Kay's delightful book,* Member of the Crew, *is one of those rare accounts of Hollywood as told by someone looking up from the bottom. She retired to San Rafael in Northern California to be near her son, Sean, and died in Los Angeles on October 1, 2002, at the age of 103.*

Sam Jaffe 1922

S am Jaffe (not to be confused with the actor of the same name) was born in New York City on May 21, 1901, the son of Russian immigrants. He left high school after his freshman year to work full time at the New York offices of Paramount Pictures, where his brother-in-law, B. P. Schulberg, was the general manager. Jaffe started as a messenger boy, moved up to shipping clerk, and then worked as a film salesman. When Schulberg returned from a stint in Los Angeles to form his own company, Preferred Pictures, Jaffe joined him.

B. P. Schulberg's company was called Preferred Pictures, and they were making movies in Los Angeles, silent pictures of course, with Katherine MacDonald, their star. She was called "The American Beauty." The posters would have a picture of Katherine MacDonald and an American Beauty Rose.

Schulberg was in New York, and I was working for him in the contract department. We had a contract with First National, which distributed pictures. First National was made up of various important exhibitors who had formed a company of their own. Instead of buying pictures from other companies, they were distributors and exhibitors at the same time.

Anyway, one day I talked to Schulberg and said, "This job that I have is a very clerical job, and it requires no initiative. Anybody can do it." Finally I said, "Look Ben, I'd like to go out to the coast. I don't know what to do, I don't know how to get there, but I'll take any kind of a job." He was very dear to me, almost like a father. He said, "Yes, go ahead." I said, "All right, you write to Fineman." Bernie Fineman was the man who was running the studio.

And so I came out here. This was the big event of my life. I bought a steamer trunk and packed, and told my parents I was going. They didn't understand the film business; it was something very strange, something from outer space to them. When I arrived, I moved into a little cheap hotel above a restaurant on Olive Street. That was the center of town because Beverly Hills was the country. In fact, beyond the Beverly Hills Hotel *was* country. It was all dirt roads to the beach. When I got married, my wife used to say, "I'm going into the village," which was Beverly Hills. It was a little village with some stores, a lot of empty space.

Anyway, I came out and got settled in this little hotel room. It was very, very inexpensive. The bathroom and the toilet facilities were down the hall. I placed all my personal things in this trunk, and when I'd go off to work I would lock it so there was nothing anybody could take.

I drove out to the studio, which was in an old car barn. It was on Pico and Georgia Street. It consisted of an open stage; one office on the side of the stage was the producer's. The other side was the office for the studio manager. In the back was some space to store props and our reflectors and equipment of that kind, and the chairs for the stars. We had also a small carpenter shop. It was very small, and the whole thing was one block square. We made one picture at a time. We only had one stage.

I first went to the studio and met B. P. Fineman, Bernie Fineman. I've always had a grievance with him because he kept me waiting. I remember so well, I was sitting on a bench and I heard laughter. I thought, "Well, this can't be a serious meeting and he is keeping me waiting."

Fineman had a friend, who later Schulberg engaged, named Bennie Zeidman, B. F. Zeidman. He was, later on, a publicity man for Douglas Fairbanks, Sr., and subsequently Schulberg, at Paramount, gave Fineman and Zeidman jobs. While it showed that Schulberg didn't forget his friends, I think that his kindness didn't help his career. Instead of engaging people who were not capable and competent, he should have gone out and engaged people that had the ability to be producers. But Schulberg himself did so much of the creation of the picture—he helped write them, he helped produce them, so he really carried these men.

* * * *

When I first started the job, I didn't know what it was all about. I'd never worked on the stage. I remember this very elderly, burly man who wore leather puttees. His hands were gnarled and calloused. He was the property man. They didn't pay him the whole year round; they engaged people for pictures, like the cameraman, the assistant director, and so on. I'll never forget, one day he was nailing down a rug, and I picked up a heavy chair. As I was going past him, he got up and bumped his head badly. He cursed me, chased me with a hammer, and said, "You son of a bitch!" He ran after me and I was scared to death. I ran into one of the shops and locked the door. I said, "Look, forgive me, I'm sorry. It wasn't my fault." He just happened to raise his head at the wrong time.

At that time, we would shoot interiors on an open stage with just sunlight. We used reflectors, like you use on location, to reflect the light. We didn't use any electricity or lights to shoot the interiors. I remember one incident where there was a tablecloth that fluttered in the wind, which of course would have been strange to see. We put something on the tablecloth so it wouldn't flutter.

There was a director, an assistant director, a property man, and a few other people standing around. In those days we didn't have any union, so I could pick up a light or a chair or a rug or anything. Today, everything is unionized, the electricians can only pick up the lights and the property man can only pick up the director's chair. It's all unionized. Nobody touches anything. But in those days, I cleaned off the set. I carried in furniture. Whatever was needed, everybody jumped in and did it.

We started the same hour, nine o'clock. In those days, we worked overtime. I mean there was *no* overtime! In those days we laid out a picture and it took two weeks. That meant working Saturdays and Sundays, and nobody complained. There was no extra money. Actually, there were times when we would start at nine, break for lunch, break for dinner at six o'clock, and then work until maybe ten, twelve o'clock. The actors were falling off their feet. They'd come in barely able to stand up, but we had a schedule, and money was tight. It *really* meant that we would run out of funds if we didn't do that. So, good or bad, we had to press the schedule and finish.

* * * *

Bernie Fineman never came out on the set, so there was no contact. The company knew there was a producer, but he never came out on the set. I don't know when he talked to the director, maybe in his office, but never on the set. I thought it was strange. I also found that at times Katherine MacDonald would show up late, come at ten o'clock. Of course it wasn't that serious because we would just work that much later. But I got the feeling that it was disorganized.

The studio manager never came out. He was a gray-haired man named Jim Hum. So there were these two men, on both sides of the stage, with no contact with the company. That's one of the reasons, when the picture I was working on was finished, I went back to my little room and got pencil and paper and wrote this report to Schulberg, suggesting that he come out and replace Bernie.

I wrote that Schulberg had all the creative ability, that he was a writer, a newspaperman, and that sitting in New York concerned with distribution was something that his partner could be doing.

Schulberg had said to me before I left New York, "There's a very famous lawyer by the name of Edwin Loeb. If you have any problems out there, go see this man Loeb." It was a very constructive thought on Schulberg's part.

I called Mr. Loeb, whose office was downtown, and said, "I'm Sam Jaffe. I'm Schulberg's brother-in-law, and I've written a report. I'd like to come and see you about it." He was very, very dear, warm, and friendly. He said, "Sure, come on over, kid." I remember he addressed me as kid. I was twenty-one.

It was a famous law firm: Loeb, Walker and Loeb. I came into Mr. Loeb's office and handed him this pencil-written report, telling Schulberg that I thought the company was badly run, that he should come out, discharge Fineman, and take over.

Mr. Loeb read this report and was very impressed. He was a wonderful man, very short, very nervous, bald, always touching his scalp. I remember him saying, "How were you able to see all these things?" I said, "Well, Mr. Loeb, it was all in front of me, the whole operation. It was very obvious to see. I saw how things were being done, and I realized that Schulberg was making a big mistake by not coming out and actually making the pictures."

Schulberg took my advice, and came out with my sister and the family... and rented a house on Lorraine Boulevard, I think. He came to the studio and went into Fineman's office. I remember we weren't shooting; the stage was clean and empty. There was nobody around except Fineman and the studio manager. He went in to tell Fineman that he had come out to take over. I waited breathlessly to see what happened, and they came out and sort of had their arms around each other. It was very friendly. I was surprised. Schulberg told him that he was going to be the active producer and he was dispensing with Bernie's services. I think he paid Fineman some extra money, I don't know.

They bid each other goodbye, and Schulberg said, "Well now, what do you want to do?" I said, "I want to be the studio manager."

I felt I could do it. It was simple. I knew what Hum was doing. He was never on the set, so I didn't see any particular activity. Whatever he was doing I felt sure I could do. I remember that Schulberg was very amused, saying, "Do you think you can do it?" I said, "Well, Ben, I won't let you down. I can do it. You can do your job, I'll do mine." He said, "Go in and tell Hum that you're going to take over the job." I was kind of taken aback but I said, "Fine."

I walked in, very hesitant and embarrassed. Hum was writing. He was a handsome man with gray hair. He looked up and said, "What can I do for you, Sam?" I swallowed twice. I didn't know how to get started. I said, "Well, you know, Mr. Hum, you know that Schulberg has taken over, and he's now going to be the producer. He wants me to be the studio manager."

He looked up, startled. I'll never forget. Good-humored, he smiled. He got up, took his hat and said, "Good luck to you," and shook hands, and that was the end. I never saw him again. He walked out of the office, and I took over.

I felt my way around. When you say "studio manager" it's nothing. It's a little stage with two offices and a couple of shops. In those days, we had to rent the rugs, furniture and drapes and the whole thing, and it meant getting people ready. All the works of the company unfolded in front of me, so I saw what was happening. We'd engage a drapery man, a group of carpenters to build sets, and painters. I knew all that, I could do that. So, that was it. That was the beginning of my career as a studio manager.

Preferred Pictures was one of the dozens of small production companies that in the mid and late 1920s fell victim to mergers or bankruptcies; and in 1925, both Schulberg (as a producer) and Jaffe (as his production manager) moved to Paramount. Jaffe was soon production manager for the studio and worked with directors such as Ernst Lubitsch, Josef von Sternberg, and Rouben Mamoulian; and executives such as Jesse Lasky and Walter Wanger. In the late twenties, Jaffe supervised the construction of Paramount's sound stages, but by 1932, the company was in receivership because of the Depression; Schulberg was fired and Jaffe resigned, moving over to RKO and then Columbia. In late 1934, Jaffe became an agent, joining his sister, Ad Schulberg, and Charlie Feldman at the Schulberg-Feldman agency. After only a few months, he struck out on his own and built the Jaffe Agency, representing actors such as Peter Lorre, Jennifer Jones, Humphrey Bogart, Joan Bennett, and Fredric March. Jaffe merged again with Feldman, before leaving the agency business in 1961. He went on to produce several films, including Born Free *in 1966. Sam Jaffe died in Los Angeles on January 10, 2000, at the age of ninety-eight.*

Will Hays 1922

W illiam Harrison Hays was born November 5, 1879, in Sullivan, Indiana. Trained as a lawyer, he was an astute and clever politician; by 1918, he was the chairman of the National Republican Party, masterminding the Republican takeover of Congress, the same Congress that would refuse to ratify the Versailles Treaty and leave President Wilson's League of Nations dead on arrival. Under the slogan "Back to Normalcy," Hays raised millions of dollars for the party's 1920 nominee, Warren Harding, and when Harding and his running mate, Calvin Coolidge, won in a landslide, Hays was rewarded with the cabinet post of Postmaster General. Hays, a little man with large ears and a mild-looking visage, would be referred to as "General" for the rest of his life. Hays might have stayed a Washington power broker for years, but when Fatty Arbuckle was arrested in San Francisco in 1921 for allegedly causing the death of a young ingénue, the studio chiefs panicked. Between the postwar jingoism that was bubbling throughout the country and the Arbuckle scandal, they feared a backlash against Hollywood's Jewish moguls and a call for censorship, which would threaten all they had built. Adolph Zukor of Paramount, who released Arbuckle's films, and Joe Schenck, who produced them, joined together in the fall of 1921 with William Fox and half a dozen other studio heads and asked Hays to become the "czar of the movies," as head of the newly created Motion Picture Producers and Distributors Association (today simplified to the Motion Picture Association of America or MPAA).

Hays had plenty of skeletons in his closest, including acting as an intermediary for Big Oil in what later became the Teapot Dome scandal, but his outspoken opposition to sending "obscene" material through the mail as Postmaster General gave him a squeaky-clean image. Just as baseball had sought a neutral third party in Judge Kenesaw Mountain Landis to save the game's reputation after the Black Sox scandal of 1919, the studio heads sought a similar savior in Will Hays. He

*accepted the hundred-thousand-dollar-a-year position in January of 1922, and
even though Arbuckle was found not guilty a few weeks later, Hays knew what the
studio heads expected of him: he banned Arbuckle from the screen for life. After
spending several months establishing his New York office, Hays headed to the belly
of the beast, Hollywood.*

I had been president of MPPDA for four months...But now, with headquarters firmly established, plans mapped, and allies gained, I wanted to meet our front-line soldiers—the writers, directors, cameramen, actors, and actresses—who really made the pictures. These folks were the backbone of the industry, and without their understanding and support I knew that all of our fine resolutions "to achieve and maintain the highest possible moral and artistic standards" would be as sounding brass and tinkling cymbals.

I realized that there was only one place where any evil in motion picture production might be eliminated and its great and good advantages retained, and that was on the set, at the time and place the pictures were actually shot.

Finally, I was naturally curious. I trust I was never too much impressed by glamour. Had I been so, I would have been far too naïve to have been of any use. Nevertheless, I had a human hankering to see at first hand the remarkable land of Make-Believe of which I had, four months previously, been elected Wizard.

Before I left New York, confidential friends who had recently returned from the West Coast told me that studio sentiment, like all Gaul, was divided into three parts: those who were enthusiastic, those willing to withhold judgment, and those who regarded the whole idea of hiring me, or anyone like me, as a tom-fool scheme born in the brains of their panic-stricken employers. It must be remembered that our organization was a producers association, not an employees' guild. The distasteful appellation of "czar" had given some of the folks out there the notion that I was going to poke about the sets like a room inspector in a military school. By far the majority of actors and actresses were fine people whose lives, both private and professional, were above reproach. They were quite properly wondering whether to regard my advent as an expression of cordiality—which it was—or as an indignity.

Arriving on the *California Limited* late on Sunday afternoon, July 23, our party left the train at Pasadena, to be greeted by Jesse L. Lasky, Joseph M.

From left to right, Irving Thalberg, Louis B. Mayer, and Will Hays. (Courtesy of MOMA)

Schenck, and Abraham Lehr, and taken to Mr. Lasky's home at Hillside and La Brea Avenue for tea. Afterward I was asked by an interviewer if I felt nervous as I alighted from the train to begin this new adventure. I replied that our party included my boyhood chum Max Puett, Jim Connery, Maurice McKenzie, Fred Beetson, and Joe O'Neill. I am sure that had I gotten stage fright these good friends would have seen me through. As it happened, however, I was far too engrossed in our problems and in the work that lay ahead of us. It may be that Hoosiers do not faze easily, or perhaps I felt a sort of pre-kickoff elation.

In 1922, Hollywood proper was chiefly a residential district with spacious grounds and gracious homes, and I am sure that if some of the earlier inhabitants who have passed on or moved elsewhere were to return to Hollywood Boulevard and Vine Street today they would feel like Rip Van Winkle coming back to Times Square. And most of the studios were still centered there. Jesse Lasky's "lot" was a block south of the now famous Hollywood and Vine corner, standing on a site that had been an orange grove not many years before. The term "Hollywood" has gradually become a geographical misnomer, so far as the location of the motion picture industry is concerned. It is, of course, a section of Los Angeles, as Harlem or Greenwich Village is a section of New York.

The Ambassador Hotel on Wilshire Boulevard. (Collection of Patt Morrison)

* * * *

I was going to disappoint those who expected me to behave like a house detective. At my first press conference that evening, I declared that threats of censorship would be removed only when its causes were removed, and that removing those causes was part of my job.

In the next five days I was to meet so many people and to see so many new faces that my memories of the tour are somewhat kaleidoscopic. The two chief impressions I formed were of the vastness of the enterprise and the earnestness of all those participating in it.

As to the earnestness of the stars, production heads, and employees, I felt sure that if all the stories of Hollywood debauchery had been true there would have been no time to make motion pictures. I found "motion pictures" to be almost a monomania with motion picture folk, almost to the exclusion of other interests. I had been warned in advance that directors and actors especially were given to "talking shop." This was all right with me; I had not come to Hollywood to talk about the price of eggs. But I quickly realized that few people in our country were as diligent or as interested in their profession as the film folk.

Every day of the week was crowded, the ride on the whirligig beginning Monday morning. We left Max's home shortly after eight o'clock, traveling downtown in a motorcade of a dozen automobiles preceded by motorcycles with their sirens screaming. The streets were decorated with bunting and flags and big signs reading WELCOME WILL HAYS! In the caravan were Jesse Lasky, Abraham Lehr, Irving Thalberg, Hal Roach, Thomas H. Ince, Charles Christie, Joseph Schenck, and others. Although the day was hot, Mayor George E. Cryer and a number of city officials were standing in the sun outside the Chamber of Commerce Building (the old location at Second Street and Broadway) and extended to me a welcome which, although it lasted only a few minutes, was so genuine and sincere that for once I was at a loss for words. Then we began our flying visits to a number of studios, starting with Fox, whose great lot now situated between Beverly Hills and Westwood had not yet been built. Mr. Fox and his able lieutenant, Sol Wurtzel, were presiding over the studio now used as an annex. Not for a moment did I forget that I had come to Hollywood to learn. And I had quite a faculty of tutors; somebody humorously estimated that it consisted of twelve general managers, thirteen attorneys, twenty-six director generals, and the Los Angeles Chamber of Commerce!

I addressed a group at all the studios that day and the next. Despite the skepticism of some, it was a day of making new friends. At the Ince Studio I met [the writer and uncle of Howard] Rupert Hughes for the first time. He jumped on the running board of my automobile and introduced himself just as we were swinging into the circular driveway in front of the colonial mansion that was the main building of the lot. I told him that we had a mutual friend, Ralph Hayes, in Washington, who had asked me to say hello for him. Then Rupert bent over and whispered in my ear:

"I'm supposed to deliver a eulogy about you. What do you know that's any good about yourself?"

"Not a thing!" I replied.

That was the beginning of a continuing and very warm friendship. I recall how Rupert broke down the barriers of constraint when introducing me to the crowd by pointing to me, speaking as if none of them had ever heard of me until this moment, and telling them who I was and what I hoped to do. This started everyone laughing and got the group in a receptive mood.

Another friend I made that day is Cecil B. DeMille. It was he who introduced me at the Lasky lot. In all, I made five speeches that morning to the personnel of as many studios. I remember that at Lasky's, ancestor of the present Paramount Studios, there was a small boy—not a child actor but a "water boy." In those days a few such youngsters were lucky enough to get jobs during their school vacations as errand boys for the stars and the director on the set, and one of their duties was to fetch water. I was warming up to my subject, telling the folks that I was not a dictator with a new broom but that we were all partners with similar responsibilities, all for one and one for all, share and share alike. At this point the small boy who was in the front row looking up at me, sang out:

"Does that mean you and me split salaries?"

I believe that I was the first to guffaw, and there was a tremendous roar of laughter. The interruption did my cause more good than harm, I think, and I feel this was largely due to the witty way in which DeMille handled the situation.

* * * *

I was guest of honor that day at a luncheon given by the Chamber of Commerce at the Hotel Alexandria in downtown Los Angeles. On the way

I was greeted by the band of Branch No. 24 of the National Association of Letter Carriers, an organization of which I am a proud life member. In my speech there I told them quite sincerely that I was approaching motion pictures not merely with the viewpoint of the men who had millions of dollars invested in the business, but with that of the parents who had millions of children interested in it. Nobody applauded that statement more heartily, or shook my hand more cordially when I had finished, than the motion picture executives at the table with me.

It had been a strenuous morning and I had been promised a quiet afternoon. I wonder now if that, too, was a prank, for the afternoon was devoted exclusively to a visit to the Douglas Fairbanks studio. I would hardly call an afternoon with that dynamic popular favorite, as he was in his heyday, quiet or restful. He was shooting *Robin Hood*, with Allan Dwan directing and Enid Bennett playing opposite him as Maid Marian. I climbed about the sets and saw everything. Although he was not to make *The Thief of Baghdad* for a year, he spoke to me earnestly of the project, of which he was already dreaming. I found Doug [Fairbanks] and Mary [Pickford] an extremely gracious host and hostess.

There was one experience on the Fairbanks lot I was fortunate enough to escape. Doug, a great practical joker, had an "electric chair" rigged up in the parlor of his bungalow on the lot. Visitors were always urged to sit in the chair, which appeared the most comfortable in the room, whereupon Doug would push a button and the visitor would get a shock. Since I had heard something about it, I managed to side-step the chair, despite Doug's earnest entreaties, and we had a good laugh when I finally admitted that I knew all about it.

That night it was my turn to see Doug get a bit of hazing, for he was one of a hundred candidates initiated into the Loyal Order of Moose. As a member of the Indianapolis lodge, I was invited to attend. Sidney Chaplin and his famous brother Charlie "went through" that night. The Moose is an order of loyal American principles. I do not know whether Charlie still belongs.

On the following day I visited Warner Brothers Studios at its old Hollywood location, the Christie Studios and Metro. The last-named was not yet Metro-Goldwyn-Mayer, and the lot was situated on Santa Monica Boulevard near Cahuenga.

At United Studios, I was a guest of Joe Schenck and his wife, Norma

Talmadge. Endeavoring, as one must occasionally in setting down memoirs, to pin-point exactly what happened on that particular day, I have had recourse to the back numbers of two newspapers. One states I had lunch with Mr. Schenck and Miss Talmadge in their private bungalow, the other that I had lunch with a thousand people; they were an exciting couple.

At any rate, Miss Talmadge was making a picture called *A Voice from the Minaret*, of which Mr. Schenck was the producer and Frank Lloyd the director. On the set, I found the actual operations of picture-making to be fascinating. This was my second day and I was beginning to feel like an old-timer. But a couple of days later I got my come-uppance at Metro, when I walked onto a set that was supposed to be the office of a rural justice of the peace. I was greatly impressed by its realism; it looked for all the world like a hundred such offices I had seen back home. I remembered having a telephone call to make, and I walked over to the wall and picked up the receiver while the folks on the set watched me, suppressing their smiles. The telephone, of course, was a "prop" and, after clicking the receiver several times and getting no response, I turned around and everybody burst out laughing.

At least I had not been sent, as many newcomers were, for the "key to the camera" or a "box of smiles."

Another incident proved to me that I was still a tenderfoot, although I hope that when it comes to a matter of sentiment I shall always remain one. Little Jackie Coogan was making one of his appealing "kid" pictures on the set next to Miss Talmadge. I believe the name of the picture was *Fiddle and I*, although the title may subsequently have been changed. E. Mason Hopper was directing, and producer Sol Lesser was present with Jack Coogan, Sr. As we entered the set the forlorn little figure of Jackie, with his wistful face and ragged clothes, was stealing from what was supposed to be his home and bidding a silent good-by to his sleeping grandparents because he realized that they were so poor that they could no longer support him. "The Kid" was a masterly little actor and he was putting his whole heart and soul into the touching farewell scene, blinking at the sleeping old couple and brushing the tears with his ragged little sleeve.

I broke down and started to cry myself. Then I remembered where I was and turned to hurry off the set. Joe Schenck grinned and called out, "Will! You forgot your hat!"

But I was not thinking about my hat. What the world needed—and I believe I said so at the time—was more human and heart-warming pictures like that. And if we got them, the agitation for censorship would become an unnecessary impertinence.

On that day I also visited the Robertson-Cole Studios, where RKO now stands, and there met Jane Novak, Carter DeHaven, and Ethel Clayton. Later I was introduced to Buster Keaton, Conway Tearle, Baby Peggy, Ruth Roland, Tom Mix (another of my son's boyhood heroes), Clyde Cook, and Marie Prevost. The same day, at Metro, I met Lon Chaney, the man with a thousand horrific faces, and his appearances were always masterpieces of his own and the make-up artist's skill. I asked him humorously which face he was wearing that afternoon.

"Just my everyday one, Mr. Hays," he grinned. The next evening I was happy to see Jackie Coogan, no longer wistful or in tatters, at the banquet which the studios gave at the Hotel Ambassador in my honor, or, as I prefer to think, in honor of the Association.

I have attended many testimonial dinners, and a few of them, if I may brag a little, were tendered to me. But I think there were never so many celebrities gathered in one dining room as on this brilliant occasion. I remember that crowds of curiosity seekers and fans gathered, hours ahead of time, on Wilshire Boulevard in front of the Ambassador and pressed up to the very doors, so that it was with difficulty that the traffic policemen were able to keep the approach to the hotel open.

These fans had not gathered to get a peek at me. There were in all some fifteen hundred people in the banquet room—this was a year before the famous Cocoanut Grove had opened—and just about all the stars in the industry were present, among hundreds of other prominent people.

Prior to the banquet, in an anteroom which at the time I thought must have been the size of Grand Central Station, there was a reception at which I was introduced to representatives of the Motion Picture Actors' Equity, the Los Angeles Film Exchange, the Board of Trade, the Screen Writers' Guild, Western Motion Picture Advertisers, Theatre Owners' Association, the Assistance League, Assistant Directors' Association, the Motion Picture Producers' Association, and perhaps a few others.

Following the reception, we entered the banquet room and took our places at the table …. As I looked over the gathering of fifteen hundred, I came nearer to feeling a touch of stage fright than ever before or since. To be quite frank, there was good reason. Many of these people were already on my side, but I knew that others had come as an act of civility, or for purely social reasons. Some of these, quite properly from their point of view, were indifferent to me and to my program. And some resented the idea of Will Hays, whose name they still confounded with the word "censorship."

Rupert Hughes kiddingly complimented the guests on how nicely they had behaved and how well they looked in their evening clothes, furnished (he professed to believe) by the Western Costume Company. Everybody laughed. Benignly he said he felt sure that they had made a good impression on the guest of honor. The guest of honor himself, looking at the people, wondered how many of them gave a continental what kind of impression they had made on him. What was more to the point was what sort of impression I would be able to make on them .... I told them of my disagreement with the whole principle of censorship and of my faith in the more manly and democratic process of *self-control* and *self-regulation*; but I said that such self-regulation had become a necessity, not only because of outside threats, but because the industry—the folks sitting before me— had become very important. They were important to their country, as trade no longer followed the flag, it now followed the films. If American pictures, shown everywhere, were to reflect credit on and not contempt of the American way of life, the ladies and gentlemen of Hollywood must henceforth regard themselves as ambassadors of Hollywood and of America. They had become important, too, I said, to the youth of our land, to the children who admired them, in some cases indiscriminately, even to the point of frank emulation. I had not come, I added, as one seeking to impose pressure, but in order to study the problem jointly with them.

I was gratified at the ovation. Jesse Lasky, mopping his brow, came over to me and shook my hand and told me he was proud of me. That was the greatest accolade of all.

* * * *

Thursday, the day following the banquet, was almost as busy as the preceding ones. At the Hal Roach Studio, I remember, we were taken on a set and seated near an arena to watch a performing lion being photographed. He was a big devil with a great black mane, and evidently a temperamental artist in his own right, for after a few moments he suddenly bounded to the top of a platform and then leaped over the screening that separated us from the arena. For the second time that week I left a set hurriedly, without bothering about my hat.

That night I was again the guest of honor, this time at a dinner of the Chamber of Commerce at the Los Angeles Women's Club .... By now my week at the "front" was speeding to its close. On Friday I had lunch at the Little Club with Elmer Harris, Arch Reeve, Fran Lloyd, Maurice Campbell, Frank E. Woods, and others.

* * * *

On the same day, I met with a large group of writers, directors, publicists, and advertising men—I think about one hundred and fifty in all. It was an especially favorable occasion, for this was the most articulate section of the industry. I sometimes think that writers, even more than actors, are individualists; while their external conduct is more repressed, their attitude is more apt to be cynical. Hence at this, as at every other opportunity, I emphasized the fact that I carried no arbitrary power and was in no sense a dictator. Speaking to the directors, I appealed to their ingenuity and artistic pride, hinting that it takes vastly more artistry to be interesting while observing decent limits than when being risqué. I told them, for example, that instead of seeing how far they could get an actress to lift her skirt and still stay within the law they might try seeing how low she could leave her skirts and still maintain audience interest. They laughed heartily and got the point. It was a very candid group; but somehow that made them easier to convince.

The week ended in a blaze of glory with a mammoth all-industry rally at the Hollywood Bowl. The great outdoor amphitheatre, built in the hills above Hollywood and now nationally famous, was at that time just a huge excavation with a temporary stage; the granite tiers had not yet been installed. I am told that on Saturday afternoon, at the time of the rally there were fifty thousand people present, and from where I sat on the rostrum I could see that the place was not only jammed to overflowing but that crowds had taken positions of vantage on the surrounding hillsides. It was gratifying, too, to see that a large block of seats—I think about four hundred—had been reserved for the postal workers of the Los Angeles area.

The committee on arrangements included William S. Hart, chairman, Irving Thalberg, Mike Levee, B. F. Rosenberg, Glenn Harper, Jesse Lasky, Frank Woods, Sol Lesser, Bert Lytell, Joseph W. Engel, and John McCormick. Thanks to these gentlemen, everything went like clockwork.

All the studios shut down at noon, and the personnel of each marched in a body to the great Bowl, many of the players in the costumes of the productions they were currently making. It was a riot of color, yet it all blended into a harmonious pattern on that glorious, cloudless summer day.

The gates of the Bowl were thrown open at half-past two, although in obedience to the decree of the committee I did not arrive until later. At the appointed hour I was escorted from Max Pruett's home by a police detail, which preceded my car. At Hollywood Boulevard and Cahuenga Pass I joined the "big shots" and, as we turned off the boulevard to Highland Avenue, the American Legion band met us and marched ahead of us to the Bowl. Crowds lined the sidewalks, and everywhere I looked cameras were clicking.

The Legion band retired as we reached the gates of the Bowl, and my old friends—the band of Branch No. 24 of the National Association of Letter Carriers—played as I was escorted to the platform. There were more bands that day! Sid Grauman had his own theatre orchestra there and also a number of variety acts to entertain the folks prior to calling the rally to order.

The first thing I was asked to do was call the roll of the studios. The response was most impressive. An interesting feature of the proceedings was the greeting broadcast to the rally by radio station KHJ and picked up by a radio car furnished by Harry Chandler of the Los Angeles *Times*. That was new and hot stuff in those days, and the *Times* reported that it was the first time such a radio stunt had ever taken place.

I did not make the only speech that afternoon, but I was determined to make the speech of my life. It was my opportunity to address the public and the industry jointly—with nearly the whole personnel of the industry there. We live in a critical age, and reading of the unanimity of the occasion, it may occur to some that there was a certain amount of "management pressure" involved. Well, if on the Great Day of Judgment we learn that this was partly true, I for one do not care. I was not a candidate seeking office—I already had the office—and this was their business as much as mine.

Hitherto I had spoken to individuals or to selected groups. I had spoken mainly to the "elite." This time I had before me the entire fellowship of the "university," practically the whole population of filmdom.

Jesse Lasky was chairman of the historic occasion. I was introduced, however, by Dr. Allen Shore, president of the Hollywood (not Los Angeles) Chamber of Commerce, for this was Hollywood's day.

It was my day too. Tears came to my eyes as, spontaneously, the people of Hollywood rose and cheered. And while it took another ten years to evolve the Production Code which is now practically constitutional in the industry, the wedge had been driven. It was the first step to be judged not by its length but the direction it took. The folks of Hollywood bought the goods.

Will Hays seems to have taken his hero's welcome in Hollywood as his due, and for a man who said he had "come to learn," he appears to have done most of the talking. However, he was the lobbyist the industry thought it needed. He did manage to postpone codified censorship until 1934, when, due to overwhelming pressure from women's organizations and the Catholic National Legion of Decency, the Production Code was formally adopted. To maintain the power of his own office, Hays hired the Legion's zealous and anti-Semitic spokesman, Joseph Breen, to enforce the Code. Liberty *magazine would write in 1936 that Breen's appointment gave him "more influence in standardizing world thinking than Mussolini, Hitler, or Stalin." Questions were raised as to whether or not Hays had negotiated himself into a position where, according to* Film Weekly, *he was a "mere Hindenburg" with Breen as, "the new Hitler of Hollywood."*

Will Hays held on to his high-paying job until shortly after the end of the Second World War. He died where he was born, in Sullivan, Indiana, on March 7, 1954, at the age of seventy-four.

Norma Shearer 1923

E dith Norma Shearer was born on August 10, 1902, in Montreal. The young- est of three children of Edith and Andrew Shearer, Norma was born with a cast in her left eye that made her look cross-eyed, but she always had ambition, personality, and determination. In early 1920, Norma's mother had grown tired of Montreal and her husband's business failures; she left him and her eighteen-year- old son, Douglas, and took Norma and her older sister, Athole, to New York, where she was determined to see seventeen-year-old Norma become a star. They lived together in one room with a bathroom down the hall, and Edith found work in a department store while the girls worked as movie extras. D. W. Griffith turned down Norma for a role in a film and the great Flo Ziegfeld informed her that, with her figure, fat legs, and her cloudy eye, she would never be a success on the stage. But she persevered, continuing to find work as a model and extra, before being cast as a featured player in The Stealers, a Robertson-Cole film shot in New York.

Hollywood—that land of fantasy and dreams that I had never been able to reach, mysteriously referred to as "the coast." For three years it had evaded me and now for some strange reason I had not only one offer but three, one after the other from three different companies in California. I thought somebody must be playing a joke on me out there!

First Universal wanted to know if I was available and possibly interested in coming to California? Interested? Available? I'd been available for the last three years! Then I received an offer from Pathé—they were expand- ing from newsreels into making serials—thrillers. It seemed they were looking for someone to develop as a new serial queen. Serial queen!! I was delirious at the prospect!! I had always imagined myself making breathless escapes from the villain, hanging by my teeth over a rushing river, like Pearl White in "The Perils of Pauline."

Irving Thalberg and Norma Shearer. (Courtesy of Jimmy Bangley)

While they were discussing contract and what name they should give me—Norma Noble was suggested—my wise agent, Mr. Small, decided I should wait for the third offer which might be coming from the Louis B. Mayer Company any moment. He said that this would be the best, to sit tight. He suggested if they called me from the other offices, to say my mother was ill and that I couldn't come down to sign the contract for a few days.

So I held on in an agony of suspense afraid I would lose out—afraid those golden opportunities that I had waited three years for might slip right through my fingers.

I didn't know that all this time somebody out there had been watching me in those awful pictures in which I had been playing—that somebody out there seemed to believe in my future.

A few dreams later a train was carrying me, my mother and our grey trunk, full of hope—to Hollywood. I had signed a contract with the Louis B. Mayer Company for five years with options to be exercised every six months if they liked me, and if they didn't—a four week guarantee and a return trip ticket to New York. As I lay in my berth at night and watched the scenery slip by in the moonlight I wondered just how long it would be before I saw it again—on my way back.

It was five days before we fell out of those upper berths in the land of palm trees and sunshine. No one met us of course except a taxi driver. He said he'd better take us to Hollywood—he thought we should live there instead of Los Angeles if we were going to be movie stars. He said the Hollywood Hotel would be the place for us, that they all went there.

We thought that would be lovely, too, until we saw the taxi meter going up. Nine dollars later we were sure he was taking us back to New York via Sunset Boulevard. But we arrived at last at the Hollywood Hotel and it looked wonderful to us. Our Mecca. Allah be praised!

The next morning we telephoned the Louis B. Mayer studio and announced our arrival. We found to our surprise that it was way over at the other side of town up North Broadway on Mission Road next to the Selig Zoo. This sounded ominous but away we went in another taxi, back to Los Angeles again.

We were sitting in the reception room waiting to see whomever we were supposed to see, when a very polite and modest young office boy came through a small swinging gate which he held open for us as he smiled quietly and said nothing. In we went and he followed us opening another door down the hall where we found ourselves obviously in Mr. Mayer's office, very large and luxurious.

To our amusement the young man went around the big desk and sat down behind it. I thought he'd better get up out of that chair before someone came in! Then he started pressing buttons on that big shiny desk and I thought, now he's playing games—he'd better stop fooling around or Mr. Mayer will come in and fire him! He looked so handsome I didn't want that to happen!

Just then Mr. Mayer did come in and the young man stood up calmly and introduced us to him. Then two other gentlemen came in, directors called Mr. Stahl and Mr. Niblo—famous names vaguely familiar, who bowed and shook hands with us graciously and went out again.

We realized this young man who so kindly greeted us couldn't be the office boy and we soon found out he was Mr. Irving Thalberg, Hollywood's Wonder Boy. I began to suspect also that he was running Mr. Mayer's studio with his permission. I didn't know he was going to run my life too and from now on I was going to spend it trying to live up to his expectations.

I should have known—or perhaps I did—as soon as I looked at those dark brown eyes, they were so wise. They looked as if they knew everything that had ever happened, or was ever going to happen, which made them sad. They looked as if they could see way into the future and were enjoying a very private little joke which made him smile—a very gentle smile that made him kind.

And when we left the studio Mother said, "Did you see those eyes?" And I said, "I should say I did—what eyes!" Then she said strangely, "Would you marry him?" And I said, "Only if he asked me." But he didn't—I knew he wouldn't. At least not for a long, long time.

I also knew I had just seen the most beautiful face on a young man I would ever see—and that he was a Jew. Perhaps that was why he was so beautiful.

* * * *

Of course, Norma Shearer did marry Irving Thalberg, but not until September of 1927, four and a half long years after first meeting him. In 1924, Thalberg became head of production for Metro-Goldwyn-Mayer, the studio created by the merger of Metro and Mayer's company on the Goldwyn lot in Culver City.

While Thalberg went out with a variety of young women, most notably Carl Laemmle's daughter, Rosabelle, and the actress Constance Talmadge, Shearer joked about being his "spare tire," the only woman willing to put up with his last-minute cancellations and obsession with work. She managed to have a fling or two as well, most notably with the director Victor Fleming. Once Shearer and Thalberg were married, Norma also had to agree that Thalberg's mother ruled their roost, planning the meals, parties, and just about everything else. Shearer concentrated on her career and Thalberg oversaw it. She starred in such M-G-M hits as The Last of Mrs. Cheyney, Their Own Desire, *and* The Divorcee, *for which she won the Academy Award for Best Actress in 1931. She easily made the transition to sound films, and her brother, Douglas, an engineer in Canada, joined her in Hollywood, where Thalberg entrusted him with supervising M-G-M's newly created sound department. (Douglas Shearer's name is in the credits of over nine hundred M-G-M films made between 1928 and 1955, and he won seven Oscars in the process.) Norma's sister, Athole, married the director Howard Hawks in 1928.*

Norma Shearer went on to win acclaim for her performances in Let Us Be Gay, A Free Soul, *and* The Barretts of Wimpole Street, *but two other actresses were not so pleased by Shearer's success: Joan Crawford and Marion Davies. Crawford believed her career suffered because the best roles went to Mrs. Irving Thalberg. Davies, the mistress of media titan William Randolph Hearst, left M-G-M in 1934 because of Hearst's displeasure with, among other things, Marion not being given the role of Elizabeth Barrett Browning in* The Barretts of Wimpole Street.

Irving Thalberg had been born a "blue baby," was stricken with rheumatic fever in his midteens, and had what was considered a weak heart, but it was pneumonia that killed him in September, 1936. Norma was left to raise their two children, six-year-old Irving Jr. and one-year-old Katherine. Shearer took off several months to mourn before going ahead with Romeo and Juliet, *which Thalberg had been planning for her at the time of his death. She made several more films, including* Idiot's Delight *and* The Women, *proving her comedic talents, and had several well-publicized relationships, including one with George Raft. She left filmmaking for good in 1942 and married a Sun Valley ski instructor, Martin Arrougé, who was a dozen years her junior. Skeptics were many, but Arrougé signed a prenuptial agreement, and he and Shearer stayed married until her death in Woodland Hills, California, on June 12, 1983, at the age of eighty.*

Mary Astor 1923

L ucille Vasconcellos Langhanke was born on May 3, 1906, in Quincy, Illinois, and dubbed "Rusty" by her parents because of her auburn hair. At the age of twelve, she mailed her photograph to the publishers of Motion Picture Magazine and was chosen as one of their "Fame and Fortune" winners, until the magazine's editors realized she was underage. Her father took this as a sign that someday his beautiful daughter could support him in the manner to which he wished to become accustomed; two years later, he moved the family to New York City, where Famous Players-Lasky put Lucille under contract and changed her name to Mary Astor.

"You are so goddamned beautiful you make me feel faint!" a famous collector of beauty whispered into my ear during a test for a picture called *Beau Brummel.*

I was a very young seventeen, a veteran of three years' work in movies having made six feature-length films and about a half dozen two-reelers and had become, I thought, very blasé about the glamour of it all, partially, I suppose, because I had played nothing but adult roles. I was too tall and too serious-faced to be cast as a child or an exuberant adolescent. I had worked with some of the top stars, Richard Barthelmess and Dorothy Gish (and with a newcomer named William Powell). I had a bowing acquaintance with other stars who had sets on the same stage. In silents there were always two or three companies using the same stages. In New York they were converted lofts or garages, except for Famous Players-Lasky, with whom I was again under contract. In Hollywood the F.P.-L. studio was a rambling green-painted barnlike building on Vine Street shaded by pepper trees.

I came out to Hollywood in April of 1923, and worked with Jack Holt,

Agnes Ayres and Thomas Meighan, among others, and almost every day I saw Pola Negri and Gloria Swanson who were in the midst of a feud about cats: One wanted them fed and taken care of, the other wanted them Out! Out! Nita Naldi would shock the tourists by smoking a cigarette in a foot-long holder and wearing a Japanese kimono, which she would adjust elaborately, revealing that she had nothing on underneath and a very voluptuous body indeed. There would be little gasps, and the set would soon be cleared of visitors who would carry home a juicy story of immoral actresses.

As far as acting was concerned, I simply did what I was told to do. This I was good at. For too many years I had searched for cues as to my father's disposition and desires. And this ability called forth praise of "How beautifully she takes direction!" You bet I did! In silents the direction went on during the action; after the camera turned, I'd hear, "Now look at him, Mary—that's it—you can't believe it! Tears come to your eyes—reach out and touch his arm—gently, gently." The more experienced actors would refuse anything but the minimum of offstage cueing, like perhaps, "You hear the door slam—" but I wouldn't have been able to carry a whole scene without help. Not because I'd forget what we had done in rehearsal, but because I was afraid I'd do it wrong. You see, I was "stupid"—I really thought I was—and that was the role I played in life. It was very safe.

When Paramount loaned me to Warner Brothers to play in *Beau Brummel* with John Barrymore, I was called for an afternoon of making just a short test, just some film in a costume approximating one I would wear in the picture, mainly for the producers to see how Mr. Barrymore and I would look together on the screen. The Warner Brothers' new studio was an impressive white building on Sunset Boulevard and only a few blocks from the apartment on Hollywood Boulevard where we were living temporarily. Our home base was still New York, and the studios at Astoria on Long Island.

Mother and I walked to the studio that hot afternoon in September, and I was carefully drilled on what I was to say to Mr. Barrymore when I met him. I was half sick with anxiety and nervousness in anticipation of being in the presence of this great man. I had seen him on the stage with his brother Lionel in *The Jest*. And of course in the movie *Dr. Jekyll and Mr. Hyde*, and I had read every word about him I could find in the movie magazines.

Mary Astor and John Barrymore in *Beau Brummel*. (Courtesy of AMPAS)

Mother said, "Now Rusty, you say to him, right after you shake hands, you smile and say, 'I can't tell you, Mr. Barrymore, how pleased I am that I'm going to work with you. I feel it is a great honor, and I shall do my very best to please you.' You hear me, Lucille? Are you listening!"

"Mm-hm."

After putting on some makeup and fixing my hair and putting on an Empire-style gown from the Western Costume Company, which didn't fit very well, I went downstairs to the main stage, Mother following at my heels. There were no other sets standing, just a flat and some lights over in a corner and a skeleton crew for the test. I walked the long dark mile over to the little set and met Harry Beaumont, the director, who took me over to a white-wigged gentleman in a red Hussar jacket and modern gray slacks—evidently it was to be only close-ups—and Mr. Beaumont introduced me to Mr. Barrymore. He took my hand and said with a nice grin, "How do you do, Miss Astor, I've been looking forward to this. I saw your picture in one of those horrible movie magazines when I was coming out here on the train and—"

Harry interrupted with, "And this is her mother, Mrs. Langhanke."

"Mrs.—ah—Langhanke?" he asked, pronouncing the name very well, and Mother nodded happily. "May I call you Mrs. Astor? It would be so much easier."

"Of course, Mr. Barrymore. I can't tell you how pleased we are that we're going to work with you. We feel it is a great honor and we'll do our very best to please you."

The well-known eyebrows went up.

"We?" He gave the small word the full force of his sarcasm. He paused long enough to let her fluster and say, "Well, I mean of course," and said, "Yes, of course," and took me by the elbow and walked me into the light.

Metaphorically it was the beginning of a very important light, for in the next three years he would teach me that I was a person, that I was somebody in my own right and not just a "goddam trained seal." Like D. W. Griffith, Barrymore had spotted the similarity of my father to a walking cash register, but unlike D.W., he did something about it. It was the beginning of respect for the business of acting, of learning that it was a craft that was never completely learned. Most important, he taught me that there was a world other than that which was run by Otto Langhanke. There were books, all kinds of books, besides those containing the poetry of Goethe and Heine; there were other kinds of music than Wagner and Beethoven and Bach—a lilting song from a musical comedy was not necessarily trash—and there was laughter and kindness and fun. It wasn't necessary always to approach the world with a clenched fist of determination or a bowed head of submission. It was a major beginning, then, but it was also the beginning of trouble, love, disappointment.

At the moment though I had a festival feeling—as though banners were snapping in the wind and sunlight. The charm of Mr. B. was the real thing, and the first time I had encountered it in anyone. He had magic and magnetism. Such charm is rare; when it is cultivated, it fades in and out, with inadequate power like a flickering light bulb. But when it is real, it seems to be steadily nourished in vitality—by an energy of spirit perhaps. It is secure with self-knowledge; he knows who he is, he has no need to boast or to be modest, no need to seek attention, or to reject it.

Now I was the recipient of this charm, and I felt expanded and at ease. For he made me feel that there was only one person in the world—me.

* * * *

From offstage where the camera was still running, Beaumont said, "Just take her in your arms a minute, Mr. Barrymore. Let's see your faces close—" He drew me to him saying, "Get your face downstage—they want to see you." He touched my cheek with his finger and I leaned my head onto his shoulder. He tightened his grip, and said, "You're so beautiful—" and Harry Beaumont said, "Now let's see the profiles again." We parted and he was smiling, "It's quite true—you have fantastic beauty," and to forestall any adolescent squirming under compliments, he went on quickly, "Raise your chin a little—remember you are a lady-in-waiting to the queen, and as such," he stepped back and cocked a knee in a courtier's bow, "dear Lady Margery, I give you my homage." Bowing over my hand, he kissed it gently. "Isn't that enough, Harry? It's hot as hell in here. Come on," to me, "let's get out of these lights."

The star system was in full flower at this time and all the nuances were reflected on the set. The star and his leading lady (or a feminine star and her leading man) had all the best of it. Like a king and queen they were above reproach. They were not called from their dressing rooms until everyone else was present. The director would line up the shot with the cameraman, rehearse the "lesser actors" sketchily; if there were extras, they would have been given an earlier call, instructed as to where they should be, or should go or do—whatever.

A director, a star and the lead had canvas chairs with their names on them, and no one dared to sit down in those chairs. The property man would have them ready for us when we came off the set, side by side, and a little apart from the common herd. And no one would be so familiar as to draw up a chair and make conversation. Even poor little "Mrs. Astor," if she wanted to speak to me, would beckon from afar. I'm sure she hated it.

Mr. Barrymore was of the theater rather than the movies and so the etiquette was adhered to most strictly. He was addressed as *Mister* Barrymore and I as *Miss* Astor. The lesser lights, even those who had played leading roles but were taking smaller parts because of the importance of this picture, were first-named: Irene Rich, Carmel Myers, even older distinguished actors such as Alec Francis, Clarissa Selwynne, Willard Louis. There were canvas chairs for them too, of course, but no names on the back and they got them themselves.

The picture was filmed at any easy pace, no production schedule, no pressure from the front office. If we had been working hard on a difficult scene, we'd be given a rest.

The routine of making a silent was similar to that of today as far as the actors and directors were concerned. A scene was blocked out, rehearsed and shot. The difference was in the techniques. Except for a special scene that could not be taken again—a battle scene, a car falling over a cliff—there was only one camera, and that was mounted on a tripod and hand-run with a crank. If you said the words, "a thousand and one," neither fast nor slowly, you had the rhythm of one turn of the crank for normal speed. The camera could be speeded up or slowed, but the projector ran at a constant speed. If the camera was cranked faster than the projector, the action would be slowed down in projection; if the camera was slowed up, the action would be speeded up. This was the only trick the camera could perform.

Another big technical difference was the lighting. Film negative was slow and so the lights had to be powerful. "Luggin' iron," was how the electrician described his job, for all the lights were mounted on iron pedestals and they were heavy and cumbersome. Overhead as general illumination were the banks of Cooper-Hewitts, which gave out a pale, sickening greenish-blue color. They were our original neons. Most of the other lights around the camera on the floor were carbon arcs; the smaller ones with two arcs in a reflecting box were called Klieg lights. A glass slide and a "silk" protected us from the Kliegs to some extent, but all of us at one time or another became afflicted with what was called "Klieg eyes," a very painful damage similar to snow blindness. There were carbon-arc spotlights up high, and to light the backgrounds there were the great brutes of sun arcs which hissed and crackled and whined. "Inkys"—incandescents—were to replace all these; some were already used in close-ups, but they were not strong enough for general lighting.

The heat was unbelievable, sapping our strength. So occasionally they'd cut the master switch, leaving a couple of work lights on, and we'd sit around in the cool gloom and talk or make jokes, or take a walk and have a Coke. This was quite customary. In those days, no one was expected to stand the pressure that became part of the making of movies later on.

Young Mary Astor did have an affair with the thirty-something John Barrymore, fresh from his success as Hamlet on Broadway. Their affair lasted almost three years but was over by the time the two were paired again in Don Juan *in 1926, one of the first films that included sound, predating* The Jazz Singer *by a year. Astor had no trouble making the transition to talkies, and proved her wide range by playing the prim wife in* Red Dust *(1932), the manipulative Brigid O'Shaughnessy in* The Maltese Falcon *(1941), and the comedic princess in* The Palm Beach Story *(1942).*

Astor's second husband threw Mary into the media spotlight in 1936 when, during a custody battle over their child, he made public her personal diary, which graphically detailed her affair with the playwright George Kaufman. ("When George lays down his glasses, he is quite a different man.") However, the scandal didn't impact her career, and she won an Academy Award for Best Supporting Actress for The Great Lie *in 1941. After M-G-M continued to cast her as the mother in films such as* Meet Me in St. Louis *(1944) and* Little Women *(1949), she left the studio. Astor appeared occasionally in films and on television through the fifties and early sixties. She was married four times and wrote five novels in addition to two memoirs:* My Story *and* A Life on Film. *Mary Astor died at the Motion Picture Country Home in Woodland Hills, California, on September 25, 1987, at the age of eighty-one.*

Louella Parsons 1925

L ouella Rose Oettinger *was born on August 6, 1881, in Freeport, Illinois.
She was working part time at the Dixon, Illinois,* Evening Telegraph
*when she met and married reporter John Parsons in October of 1905. Their
daughter, Harriet, was born the following August, and Louella divorced John
shortly thereafter. By 1912, Louella was a screenwriter for Essanay studio in
Chicago, and three years later she published* How to Write for the Movies, *a
book that was advertised in fan magazines and gave her the credibility to get her
own column at the* Chicago Herald. *Always ambitious, Parsons moved to New
York in 1918, where she wrote about movies for the* Morning Telegraph. *Film
production was moving to California, yet most of the company chiefs remained
in New York, so Parsons quickly carved out a niche for herself, befriending and
interviewing stars when they came to town. It was her effusive praise for Marion
Davies—and questions about how much Davies's paramour William Randolph
Hearst was spending to promote her—that caught the attention of the press baron.
Davies introduced Parsons to Hearst, and in 1923 he hired her to write for his
newspapers. The Hollywood legend, that Parsons got her job for life after witness-
ing Hearst accidentally shoot producer Thomas Ince on board the Hearst yacht off
Catalina, is intriguing, but spurious—Parsons did not come to California for the
first time until a year after Ince's death.*

It was in the days of Prohibition, the old Montmartre Café, the Cocoanut
Grove, the Charleston, and the Black Bottom, that I came to Hollywood
the first time. Bands were playing "Yes, Sir, That's My Baby." The girls
were wearing kneelength evening gowns and big bows on highheeled slip-
pers, Clara Bow was the biggest boxoffice star. Now we call those times
"the good old days."

The social barriers had relaxed a little. It had become smart for the local

Louella Parsons. (Courtesy of AMPAS)

socialites to include an actor in a dinner party now and then if only for the quaintness of the thing.

Tom Mix was entertaining Los Angeles in more ways than one around his fabulous diningroom table, elaborately equipped with a fountain that sprayed water alternately blue, pink, green, and red.

Lilyan Tashman eccentrically tied a blue satin ribbon on the first white piano Hollywood had ever seen—and thereby earned a reputation for great chic.

Ona Brown, then the wife of director Clarence Brown, was a movie social leader. Bedecked in diamonds like a plate of armor up her arms and across a heart of more glittering gold than her jewels, Ona would preside over Clarence's dinner table, loudly remembering former and more affluent loves in her life.

Clara Bow, a lonely little thing, played poker in the kitchen with her cook, her maid, and her secretary.

John Gilbert landed in jail on a charge of disturbing the peace after Greta Garbo got as far as the courthouse—and then refused to marry him.

Bess Meredith's house on Crescent Drive (Bess, Frances Marion, and Jeanie Macpherson were the foremost scenarists of the day) was the mecca for the foreign writers, actors, and directors who were just beginning to filter into Hollywood.

Gloria Swanson had electrified the fan world by taking time off to have a baby at the height of her glamorous, coiffured career. A Negro hairdresser named Hattie, who whipped up Gloria's hairdos, could have written her own figure at any studio in town.

Norma Talmadge and Joseph Schenck had bought the Cudahy mansion on Hollywood Boulevard—a sprawling, white, terraced estate that had already been labeled a jinx after Cudahy committed suicide there.

The beauties of Hollywood were the sloeeyed Dolores Del Rio, the wideeyed Madge Bellamy, the wistful May McAvoy, the goldenhaired Marion Davies, the aloof Corinne Griffith, the fullblown Billie Dove, the lovable, exotic Bebe Daniels, one of the closest female friends I have ever had.

Not yet had Hollywood chopped down its shady pepper trees along the Boulevard—and not yet was the sight of an orange tree in the heart of "town" a rarity—when I arrived in the capital of the movies to make my home with my cousin, Margaret Ettinger, who had married Harry Maynard and was faring well as a press agent of the glittering darlings of the cinema.

Margaret had a small house out in the less hectic district of Hollywood and a small son, Gordon Maynard. It is a tossup whether Gordon or I caused more havoc in her small, brownshingled domicile.

I had always had a gift for creating a great deal of confusion in otherwise normal lives. I don't just live in a house. I live all over it—and notes for my column are just as likely to be located on the kitchen stove as is the coffee pot.

It was fortunate that Margaret and I were both busy women. Otherwise our joint domicile might have developed a case of too much personality under one roof. Instead, we had an enormous amount of fun in a wholly unorthodox household. We kept no particular hours, coming in from our jobs at outlandish times. We ate when we felt like it, talked half the nights away, gossiped endlessly about the merrygoround of the town in which we were professional onlookers, and generally had the time of our lives. Harriet would come out and join us on her vacations from school, and if ever the phrase "a good time was had by all" applied to any group of relatives it applied to us.

Movie studios had become increasingly more important, more imposing. In Culver City sprawled the famous Metro-Goldwyn-Mayer lot, and the colonial mansion that first housed Tom Ince, then Cecil B. DeMille and the studio where Hal Roach and his "Our Gang" kids made pictures.

The old Universal farm was now a city in more than name. Paramount occupied an acre in the heart of Hollywood. The Warners had erected an edifice that looked like one of the Houses of Morgan on Sunset Boulevard where Marie Prevost and Monte Blue made sophisticated comedies for Ernst Lubitsch.

But above everything rose the royal shoulders of Mary Pickford and Douglas Fairbanks, regal and untouchable in their enshrined palace as the Sweethearts of the World. Mary and Doug had merged their business interests as well as their real love story and made pictures within a stone's throw of one another on the old United Artists lot.

Pickfair was the palace of Hollywood and Mary and Doug its Queen and King. At least once a week I dined with them—an honor that, in those days, was comparable to a weekly bid to Buckingham Palace.

Early in the development of Beverly Hills, with the Pickfair Estate at upper center. (Collection of Allison Burnett)

The studio built by Thomas Ince to resemble Washington's Mount Vernon was taken over by Cecil B. DeMille, Pathé, and then David O. Selznick, who used it as his logo. It is still in operation today. (Courtesy of Cari Beauchamp)

There was the "Fairbanks" crowd, consisting of Charlie Chaplin, gay and amusing and not taking himself too seriously at that time, John Barrymore, Tom Geraghty—and last, but far from least, Elinor Glyn.

What a woman was Elinor! Redheaded, greeneyed, definitely regal in bearing and far more intelligent than her literary classic, *Three Weeks*, would indicate, Elinor was—without being fully aware of it—the life of the party.

She had a great trick of fixing her narrow, green eyes on one and saying elegantly, "Let's see—you remind me of an animal—is it a buffalo or water spaniel?"

Elinor, herself, was definitely a tigress. She worked at it. She never permitted the picture of the queen of the jungle to leave your mind in her presence if she could help it. It was la Glyn who decided that Mary Pickford was a fawn, Marion Davies a dove, and Clara Bow an "It" girl. Elinor said that Clara was the only woman she had ever met who had "It." The only male with "It" who had come under her ken was Rex, the King of Wild Horses! Ella Williams, known to all Marion Davies' friends as Bill, and I used to amuse ourselves guessing what animal Madame Glyn would call certain stars she had not yet named. Bill had been with Marion for many, many years and is one of her most loyal friends and one of my best friends.

At first I was afraid I was going to be terribly homesick for New York in this strange town of Hollywood. And then I began to love it.

If Louella Parsons had resisted relocating to California because she was afraid of being just another Hollywood reporter, she soon realized that she was in a league of her own. Her syndication gave her a wide reach, Hearst's distribution deal with M-G-M gave her special status with that studio, and no other reporter had her privileged access to the many guests Hearst hosted in Beverly Hills and at his estate near San Simeon (most called it Hearst Castle, he called it "the ranch"). While Parsons visited New York often, Los Angeles soon became home. She was generally a booster of Hollywood and its movies, but she loved her scoops; her 1933 announcement that Mary Pickford and Douglas Fairbanks were separating made the front page of papers around the world. Parsons remained unchallenged until Hedda Hopper became a columnist for the Los Angeles Times Syndicate in 1937. Studios welcomed the competition, and Louella and Hedda's legendary feud lasted the rest of their lives. Parsons continued to write until 1965 and died on December 9, 1972, in Santa Monica, California, at the age of ninety-one.

Valeria Belletti 1925

V aleria Belletti was born in New Jersey on October 11, 1898, the only child of Italian immigrants. Her father left them and returned to Italy after a few years, and Valeria and her mother lived together until her mother's death in 1923. By that time, Valeria had been working for several years as the secretary to New York patent attorney and founder of the New York Theatre Guild Lawrence Langner. In 1924, Belletti and her best friend, Irma Prina, decided to take a summer trip to California; the two young women traveled the state, flew in an airplane, and stayed with various family friends. Prina returned home in September as planned, but Belletti had fallen in love with Los Angeles and decided to stay. She lodged at the YWCA before meeting some women with whom she shared an apartment. She found work with a "nature and drugless" doctor before being hired, through a letter of introduction from Lawrence Langner, as a temporary secretary for prominent entertainment lawyer Joseph P. Loeb of Loeb, Walker and Loeb. Belletti had been in Los Angeles for only a few months when she wrote Prina the following letter, written on Samuel Goldwyn Company stationery.

Feb 19, 1925

Dear Irma,

I just had to write to you to tell you of my good fortune. I'm in the movies—of course, not an actress. I'm private and social secretary to Mr. Samuel Goldwyn. Can you imagine it! The odds were about 50 to 1 against me, but through Mr. Loeb's influence, the position was given to me. So far as I can see, it's the sort of job that I've always dreamed about, but that I never, by any stretch of imagination, hoped to get.

As Mr. Goldwyn's secretary, I come in contact with every phase of the movie industry; looking for new material; keeping in touch with the producers in New York; reading new books; turning over possible material to the scenario writer who happens to be Frances Marion; hiring actors and actresses, directors, camera men; keeping in touch with the art director, publicity man, the projection and cutting rooms and ever so many other things. Everything is so new and interesting that I just love to work. Of course, I am not busy just now, because Mr. Goldwyn is in Europe and we've just finished a picture called *His Supreme Moment* with Ronald Colman and we don't start another production until the first of May, which will be *Stella Dallas*. We're only starting to look for a cast suitable for the characters of the play and things won't be ready for actual shooting until May. I'm working in Hollywood of course, and it's too bad you can't come out to the coast now, because I could get you in the studios to see everything.

I met Mr. George Fitzmaurice today. He does all our society pictures. I also met Ronald Colman who is a very charming young man. Have you seen him in pictures yet? His latest was *A Thief in Paradise*.

I wish you could see the studios inside. They are a town in themselves. We have named streets and different shops, such as barber shops, beauty parlors and cafes. Yesterday I didn't have much to do, so I walked around the lot and watched different pictures being taken. Did you know that a regular three piece string orchestra is on each set in order to produce the necessary emotions in the stars? I enjoyed listening to the music more than watching the acting.

Mr. Lehr, who is the general manager, told me that as Mr. Goldwyn's secretary I would have to look very smart and dress well. He told me that if I needed any money for this purpose he would be glad to give it to me and pay him back when I could. Mr. Loeb told me the same thing. Really, it is astounding how free people are with their money here. He gave me the afternoon off to do whatever shopping I needed to do and I certainly did go to it. I bought so much that I feel as if I'm a different person entirely. For once in my life I bought real stylish clothes and they do make a difference. Of course, I have to keep my hair marcelled, but in view of the salary I am being paid, I can easily do it.

My salary to start with is $40.00 a week and when we go in production on May 1st, my salary will be $50 because I'll be much busier. The girl who had my job was getting $65 and she had been with Mr. Goldwyn only 9 months. She left because she was ordered to go away for a long rest cure due to a lung infection.

Valeria Belletti enjoys the beach.
(Courtesy of Margery Baragona)

I'm just reading a book called *Ann's an Idiot*. It's not one of the very latest, but it is fairly modern. That's part of my job, but as I've been reading for about an hour, I thought I'd quit a while to write you this letter because on account of it being a rainy day, there's little going on and the general manager has left for the day.

I don't know how long my job will last—it all depends on whether or not Mr. Goldwyn likes me. I'm told that he is very temperamental and rather difficult to get along with. However, I'm rather accustomed to temperamental people so that will be nothing new to me. Even if I do get fired when he gets back, I will have enjoyed my short stay and will have gotten a slight knowledge of the movie industry.

I have become very friendly with a Miss Manee who is Mr. Maurice Tourneur's secretary and reader. She is very intellectual and has read so much that I feel positively stupid in her presence. However, she seems to like me because she keeps inviting me to lunch with her.

By the way, I wish you'd see the little cafe we eat in. It is so picturesque.

You see people (mostly men) in all kinds of make up and costumes and of course there are no outsiders at all. Just movie folks. It is surprising how few girls there are on a studio lot. I just can't seem to get used to all the men. None of them are very interesting; and most of them are just types that I couldn't possibly make an effort to be friendly with. I did meet one chap who seemed awfully nice—he was Dr. Gardner's chauffeur. As I was leaving the studio yesterday afternoon, a car came out of the gate and stopped and this fellow asked me if I was going to Los Angeles; I said I was so he invited me ride with him, which of course I accepted. The car he was driving was a new Rolls Royce and believe me I felt big driving though Los Angeles in it. I hope I meet him again.

I'm still living with Florence and Nancy in our Bungalow. We have rented a piano and we have some real nice times at home. Florence brings over some of the men teachers in her school and Nancy has some of her boyfriends come over. When they come they always bring some good stuff to drink and we make cocktails and dance or play bridge. The boys are really nice fellows, that is, good morally, so that you need not worry that I have left the straight and narrow. We all go out together and we've been to a number of real wild bohemian cafes in Hollywood. It's fun watching and I'm also gaining quite some experience in the way of mankind.

I'm feeling perfectly splendid and am all enthused and pepped up. You have no idea how glad I am I left New York. Now I realize what a rut I was in when I was home. Here I've been meeting all kinds of interesting people and although I miss Mr. Langner and all my friends in Jersey, I feel that I'm enjoying life more here. Another thing, I don't know whether it is the sunshine or just what it is, but I feel much more carefree and lighthearted. After all, I believe it is one's duty to seek and if possible find happiness and that is my aim.

Give my regards to your folks and let me hear from you real soon.

Love, Valeria

Valeria Belletti stayed on with Sam Goldwyn, by then an independent producer, for several years and worked with him on many pictures, including films starring Ronald Colman and Vilma Bánky. Belletti had a series of beaus, including one who wanted to be an actor. She pointed him out to Goldwyn's screenwriter Frances Marion, who was impressed enough with his tall, chiseled good looks to write a part for him in The Winning of Barbara Worth. *Filming took him to Nevada for over a month, and when the movie was released, Gary Cooper was such a standout that he immediately was signed by Paramount, where he soon became the boyfriend of Clara Bow. Soon after, Belletti left Goldwyn to go to Italy to find her father. By the time she arrived, she learned he had died several months earlier. She returned to Los Angeles and went to work for Cecil B. DeMille at Pathé in Culver City until early 1929. Finding a husband was the theme of many of her letters to Irma (Valeria wrote more than seventy over six years) and in 1928, she married the man who asked her, Tony Baragona, a chiropractic student, who went on to set up his own practice in Santa Barbara, where the couple lived with their son, Tony Jr., and where Valeria died in 1959, at the age of sixty-one.*

Ben Hecht 1926

B en Hecht, the son of Russian Jewish immigrants, was born in New York on February 28, 1894. His father, Joseph, was a garment worker, and when Ben was six, the family, which now included an infant brother, moved to Racine, Wisconsin. His father manufactured women's clothes there, and his mother, Sarah, ran their store, Paris Fashions. Ben was a voracious reader and, after a short stint at the University of Wisconsin, moved to his aunt and uncle's home in Chicago in 1910. He hoped to find work as a writer but was hired by the Chicago Daily Journal as a photographer; within four years he was their star reporter. He wrote fast and with flair, and claimed that he "haunted streets, whorehouses, police stations, courtrooms, theater stages, jails, saloons, slums, madhouses, fires, murders, riots, banquet halls, and bookshops." He also met and befriended Charles MacArthur, a fellow reporter who would become his writing partner (and who was the brother of John D. MacArthur, the insurance executive who created the MacArthur Foundation and the MacArthur "Genius Awards"). In 1915, Hecht married Marie Armstrong, the Journal's only female reporter, and had a daughter. The following year, he jumped to the Chicago Daily News when they offered to send the couple to Berlin to cover the First World War.

In 1918, Hecht met and fell in love with Rose Caylor, a reporter for the Daily News, but Marie would not agree to a divorce. Ben left reporting to start his own literary magazine, lost his money, and then went to New York with Rose, writing four novels, none of which sold well. After giving Marie what money he had, they divorced, and Ben and Rose married in 1925. Desperate for money, he received a telegram from his friend Herman Mankiewicz in Hollywood: "Millions are to be grabbed out here and your only competition is idiots." How could he resist? Leaving Rose in New York, Hecht headed to California for what he thought would be a few weeks of work, living with his friend Charlie MacArthur on an avocado ranch. Hecht kept Rose updated on his activities through a constant stream of letters.

My Dearest One,

I just talked to you—your sweet sleepy voice, my darling, still rings in my ears—as far away as heaven. Never have I missed you so. This first day in Hollywood has been like a year in Siberia.

About my first day. Last night [director Lewis] Milestone, the 2 Selznicks [producer David O. and agent Myron] & 6 or 7 other people came to our place. David got very nasty toward Charlie—around midnight. Charlie had been drinking & was undressed, going to bed. David called him lots of Selznicky names—why, God knows—he too was drunk—(his wife [Irene Mayer Selznick] was along). Charlie acted coy & fuzzy for 25 minutes under this tongue lashing. Then he took a crack at David. They fought for ten minutes—Charlie handling him superbly. Then David bit Charlie's arm—badly—so Charlie with his new set of false teeth sunk them into David in 7 places, so David looked like he had been ripped by a buzz saw. Then Myron the gladiator jumped Charlie. I tried to pull him off but it wasn't necessary. Our friend Angus almost tore his head off with 2 right smashes to the jaw and then for good measure bit his initials into Myron's arm. After all this carnage, during which Charlie looked like a dozen murderers but remained particularly calm and concentrated. You would have loved seeing him—after the carnage Charlie fell sound asleep & woke up this morning with a few rather ugly swellings on his face. It was certainly a queer welcome to this town.

Your lover Bennie

Darling,

Sunday morning—I feel miraculous. I think only in terms of my departure and such thoughts roost on my spirit like a flock of paradise birds. Goldwyn is frothing like a maniac for me to stay another two or three weeks. I have refused. I am leaving here Monday—a week from tomorrow. I've taken another job. [Howard] Hughes offered me ten grand for a week's work on *Scarface*. I'm doing it as homework when I'm not with Goldwyn. Also we'll have some more changes this week from another story I've done while here—(I think). The [Ronald] Colman movie has been received so far with hosannas. Hughes is out of his mind with delight over my first day's work on *Scarface*. Says it is more than four authors did for him in two months. [Howard] Hawks, the director, a charming gent, and a hero aviator, is pleased. Home in a week, or counting the ride, 10 days from this

Ben Hecht, with Charles MacArthur at the typewriter. (Courtesy of AMPAS)

minute. Home, Rosie, and a resumption of human existence that will seem like a miracle.

Ma, Pa, and Pete [Ben's younger brother] were here in the hacienda yesterday afternoon. Gilbert (Jack) was also here, doing his usual jumping Jack antics. He made love to Ma who giggled like a child with a hair ribbon being rumpled. She is afraid it'll get in the papers she said this morning. I sent the folks home at five yesterday and went with Charlie, Jack, and Johnny to Gilbert's beach home in Malibu—a toy house like a New England sea captain's place—a toy house and a toy man facing the rain and wind of the Pacific—and it rained a thousand storms last night too. Gilbert got drunk as usual. And a fifth gentleman named Dick Hyland came in—a former all American halfback and a tough edition of Rudy Vallee in a white sweatshirt—very handsome and American. The five of us drank—the boys yelping for women—no women being within a day's ride, so they could yelp loud and long with no uncomfortable results. We drank, me sticking to gin, and sang and hollered and drowned out the ocean storm—the halfback grew sentimental, then wild, and Gilbert's heart started breaking because the phonograph was playing some song or other, and Charlie began to bellow like a stallion, poor boy, and Johnny stood swaying like Clifton Webb in "Moanin' Low." All the while the sea roared in the front yard and the storm beat a thousand drums on this toy house.

A magnificent character to write is Gilbert—as unreal, flash-in-the-pan emotions, flash-in-the-pan wit, flash-in-the-pan satyr as has never been put on to paper—a barking Pomeranian—a Japanese lantern—a sputtering candle in a lot of glowing tissue paper. He passed out at 10:30.

* * * *

Tonight I go to dinner with Hawks. I like him. He is one of the few half humans—to whom movies are a pleasant sideline, a thing to be done as work, not to be lived as a career. My health is superb. My spirit is strong. I have money. I gave Ma some hundreds. I have power, luck, everything—and YOU. I got YOU, Holy Jesus. These weeks—socially remembered—seem like something I passed on a boat among Samoans or some other unintelligible and mysterious tribe of manikins. Everybody I've met is nice but flapping in the wind, unrooted, empty, straining and a thousand times more tossed up for grabs than New Yorkers. The home life is invisible. All exiles. All with memories growing thin, desire thinning out, waiting for yesterday to come back. Goodbye my darling. [Art director Herman] Rosse is at the door. Fat, greyer, sadder, more confused and very touchingly shy.

Ben

Darling Rosie,

Aches, neck, back, eyes, heart—oh, so tired. The folks are playing cards. Me, too tired to join. I sit and look at them & think of you. Uncle Harris—his sourspoken, frightened, amateur tyrant wife sneers (as you once wrote) and sighs. I hear the Goldwyn Bonanza is waiting for me at home. It is quite exciting. I turned suddenly, to poor slicker Sam's horror, into a leading lady—suddenly called him names, told him to stick all his bonanzas where they belong—that I was sick of being promised stick-candy tomorrow if I ate up all my spinach—and carried on so Leland [Hayward, agent and producer] grew pale. I said that I didn't want any more Colman money either; I didn't care if Sam blackballed me in Hollywood—that I was going home and not to bother me anymore. I hated movies anyway, etcetera…So Sam got on the phone and whined, but I told him I wasn't out here for love or to get in right with him—that so far he had not kept his word and that life was a wistful pursuit of cobwebs. All this made me supremely happy. I never really enjoy myself unless I am causing mucho trouble, I guess.

Now I feel like a happy child again. Butter wouldn't melt in my mouth, and tomorrow when I read the jokes to Sam I will feel terribly sorry for all the worry I gave him. He stood to lose 150 grand if I walked out, so he must be pretty nervous still to think how hysterical I am—so I giggle & will sleep nice tonight unless you come to me with your mama's hand and start spanking me as you did last night. I woke with a sore behind, honest, and a pair of wet pajamas but such a delicious memory of your shining sadist's eyes and stern compressed lips that I felt it was a fuck well lost. Oh how tired I am. From writing 100 pages of dialogue & continuity in 4 days—rewritten as well—12 hours a day without stopping—all I feel is numbness and a buzzing. And I remember my Rosie, my Owner, and sigh, close eyes, dream a minute, kiss your knees, your thighs, while something in me murmurs mama, sweet one, sweet Rosie—and I feel a phantom of sweetness as if this moment too were a dream like last night. I have no news except the tale of labor already recited. Please forgive me for my jealousy letters. I couldn't help writing them. I got frightened. Now I'm not frightened anymore. I know you love me. It overwhelms me. We will be Happy Happy.

I hate to stop writing you now. I can see you reading these aimless words hoping for something vivid. It's me, mama, yawning on a bed beside you—me half asleep, me wanting my behind rubbed, falling asleep pressed against you, legs entwined. Write me more of your sins—I thrilled for an hour after reading the last—adored—Rosie, Good night

Bennie

Love from ALL, they yell.

Darling One,

I hate to write you this. I've been up since 5 a.m. brooding. But the movie has hit a dozen snags. Charlie and I have worked like fiends, and it's not done yet. It'll be done in 10 days, and I'll leave. I couldn't stay out here any longer. I feel less and less alive without you. As for writing the play's third act, not unless you came out could I do it. I am all out of inspiration, verve, etcetera. *Monkey Business* looks like a sure sale—for at least 25 grand so we can build the [garden] wall soon.

The flowers here—roses and geraniums—bloom all year the gardener tells me. He gets tired of looking at them. They are like things painted perpetually on the air. No drama of conception, birth or adolescence for these blooms. My tennis is getting marvelous. We use the court and pool daily. Every day two or three or four gents come over in the afternoon to play and swim—no dames—and we go into the pool naked—thus revealing the most fantastic varieties of cocks I've ever seen in print or out—general effect being of a sausage display ranging from pig sausage to bolognas. It's quite humorous and reduces the male to some sort of appendage-swinging fauna of sheerly comical design...

I am going to a party Saturday night at Mank's [Herman Mankiewicz] house—for me—we dress. I haven't gone to hardly any of the shindigs. They are more boring than anything I've ever encountered. They positively appall one socially. I've never seen nor heard so intense torture as a room full of movie people all bombinating movies at each other—all those toy celebrities. I can't get over them—they're like a pack of cultured

Harland Dixons—cultured as he was—but without his charm or personality—just his theories all spouting at once. [Harland Dixon was a noted dancer and choreographer.]

My sweet, I feel better since writing you. I'll write again tomorrow with more news. Love me. Be happy and strong and don't worry. I'm true to you as if I were a papoose on your sweet back, where I belong.

Bennie

Ben Hecht was Hollywood's H. L. Mencken: a cynical, brilliant critic and satirist of its people and culture. While claiming to hate Hollywood, Hecht kept coming back, but not before making a name for himself on Broadway with the play The Front Page, *cowritten with MacArthur. Including* His Girl Friday, The Front Page *would go on to be filmed four times.*

Hecht won the first Oscar for screenwriting for Underworld *(1927), was nominated four more times—for* Viva Villa! *(1934),* Wuthering Heights *(1939),* Angels Over Broadway *(1940), and* Notorious *(1947)—and won another for* The Scoundrel *(1935), cowritten with MacArthur. Hecht also became one of Hollywood's first "script doctors," and was paid small fortunes for quick rewrites of dozens of scripts, almost always uncredited; David O. Selznick paid Hecht ten thousand dollars for his work on* Gone with the Wind.

During World War II, Hecht was one of the earliest and loudest voices of concern over the fate of European Jews. Ben and Rose had a daughter and they stayed married until his death in New York City on April 18, 1964, at the age of seventy.

Sergei Bertensson 1926

S ergei Bertensson was born in Russia in 1885; his father was a doctor and his mother was the daughter of an historian. Their home was a veritable salon, and Sergei worked for the Ministry of the Imperial Court after graduating from St. Petersburg University with a degree in the history of Russian theater and literature. In 1919, he joined the Moscow Art Theatre as codirector of the Musical Studio with Vladimir Ivanovich Nemirovich-Danchenko, a renowned novelist and playwright, who had founded Moscow Art with Konstantin Stanislavsky. In 1925, Bertensson and Nemirovich-Danchenko toured the United States with the Musical Studio, but after a falling-out with Stanislavsky, Nemirovich-Danchenko decided to accept an offer from Joe Schenck, the head of United Artists, for a yearlong contract to write and direct whatever he wanted. Bertensson went to Hollywood with Nemirovich-Danchenko as his assistant and translator; what follow are Bertensson's diary entries for their first week in Los Angeles.

25 September

In the afternoon we approached Los Angeles. A half hour before our final destination, at Pasadena Station, a representative of United Artists joined us on the train, greeted us, and asked Vladimir Ivanovich, his wife and son, and myself to move to the saloon carriage where the delegation would come to pick us up.

At 2:00 p.m. we arrived at Los Angeles. Immediately a whole bunch of delegates led by the mayor entered the carriage. Every delegate wore a ribbon with an inscription in gold: "Welcome Danchenko." They brought all of us to the platform where a boys' band played a comical reception on mouth organs, and some girls in Egyptian costumes gave out oranges from huge baskets. Then the mayor delivered a speech and presented Vladimir

247

Ivanovich with a golden (cardboard) key to the city. The delegates, among whom there were representatives of the city administration, the press, cinema, theaters, and clubs, all wanted to shake hands with us, to give us flowers and fruit. An enormous crowd of people was standing on the platform; the boys' band was playing some kind of march. Innumerable shots for newspapers and the cinema were taken. But the most comical thing was that in the heat of the celebration, the United Artists representative took me aside and divulged, "We know that Mr. Danchenko is a great celebrity, and we have been given an order to arrange a proper reception for him, but we do not know who in fact he is." In the brief space of time that we had, I tried to satisfy his healthy curiosity, but I noticed that my interlocutor did not have any idea what I was talking about. Escorted by policemen on motorcycles that stopped the entire traffic with the roar of sirens, we were rushed by car to Hollywood. We checked into the wonderful Hollywood Plaza Hotel. The hotel management had sent flowers to our rooms and immediately directed reporters for interviews.

26 September

The newspapers published reports about our arrival and portraits of Vladimir Ivanovich. Starting from 11:00 a.m., accompanied by the head of the financial department of United Artists, we were searching for villas for ourselves. We found two wonderful houses within two minutes walk of each other. These villas are located in the gardens and are perfectly equipped for comfortable and pleasant living.

At 5:00 we went to the Pacific Ocean by car. This trip took forty-five minutes of fast driving to complete. Wonderful places, a splendid boulevard with palm trees, below—bathing huts, cafes, small dachas, hotels, restaurants, a huge place like "Luna-park" with different attractions, a whole palace in Oriental style. In the darkness, all of this was flooded with electric lights, and even the contours of the buildings were shining, seen very clearly against the background of the dark sky.

27 September

Our visit to the United Artists studio. An immense yard, a part of which is occupied by set units and various installations for the shooting of movies such as a big ship, a train, houses, streets, etc. These pavilions are very spacious and provide room for lots of separate pieces of set, built of genuine materials and in real size. Close to the pavilions, the wardrobe, the greenroom, and the marketing department are attached. In other detached houses there are the set workshop, the sculpture workshop, the department for the cutting of film, two halls for the working preview of movies, many other production divisions, and the management's office.

As Schenck himself was absent, his deputy—Considine—received us. Despite the fact that he was only thirty-two, he is burdened with great responsibilities. Because of that, he has an air of pleasant and calm self-confidence. Hastily he tried to get some advice from Vladimir Ivanovich concerning the shooting of *Resurrection* by Tolstoy, but Vladimir Ivanovich refused to advise him. He motivated his refusal as follows: "For a Russian *Resurrection* is such a great work that it cannot be treated superficially. But if I focus my attention on it properly, it will go to my head. And I cannot do that now. However, to give you a few words of advice is impossible, because this may be picked up by reporters, and newspapers, especially Russian, will immediately announce that Nemirovich-Danchenko is making a film of *Resurrection*."

Considine ordered his employees to admit us to any shooting at the studio, to show us all the affiliate workshops and old movies, which we might find interesting. We visited the marketing department. This is a whole institution with lots of people on the staff. We made the acquaintance of the head of design, set designer Mansis. [Bertensson is almost certainly referring to art director William Cameron Menzies.]

He is a young man. In fact, he is the creator of all the set, props, and costumes for all the productions, and that inevitably makes his work banal and stereotyped. But here his work is highly appreciated, and he is considered a great talent. All the works on set are carried out in relief (building, molding) and are exceptionally realistic.

We visited one of the pavilions. This is a colossal building, sort of a shed, where shootings of many separate scenes and pieces could be carried our simultaneously. The shooting of the movie *François Villon: Vagabond Poet* starring John Barrymore is in progress. [The film was released under the title *The Beloved Rogue*.] Barrymore takes part in this movie not only as the principal actor but also as a codirector and coscriptwriter. At the moment when we arrived, the shooting of one of the folk scenes in the inn was taking place—a drunken debauch of tramps, prostitutes, etc. We witnessed the moment when they were drinking wine, throwing fruit at

A premiere at Grauman's Egyptian Theatre. (Collection of Allison Burnett)

each other, and one of the tramps, in drunken excitement, was whirling some girl above his head. All that was done in a banal but quite brave way. The director of the movie, Alan Crosland, greeted us in a very courteous way and allowed us to watch. All the work he was doing with the actors virtually amounted to the accurate reproduction of the script. It turned out that, except for the principal actors, no one was familiar with the play, neither with his or her own part. The director, during the shooting, would shout into a megaphone to every person saying what he or she should do. When he was doing that, he was absolutely calm, neither making use of his temperament nor letting his imagination fly away with him. He gave the impression that any mediocre director in Russia would seem more artistic in comparison to him. It is very hard to believe that this very director staged *Don Juan* with John Barrymore—the movie in which there is something interesting.

28–29 September

We continue watching the shooting of the same movie. There have not been any enjoyable or at least interesting moments so far. Vladimir Ivanovich is in a muddle about what could be done here. We should either admit that everything—scripts, staging and performing methods— is completely wrong and must be eliminated, or we should slowly start training people, unspoilt by clichés, people with whom we could prepare something, according to an absolutely new method.

In the studio we saw two old movies. One of them—*The Eternal Flame* with [Joseph Schenck's wife] Norma Talmadge—is a tasteless melodrama. It bursts upon the eye that the actors are not able to wear eighteenth-century French costumes. The other movie—*Her Sister from Paris* with Constance Talmadge—is a light, merry, modern life comedy. We got a dreary impression of both screenings.

30 September

We continue watching the same shooting. Several scenes were staged in our presence, but none of them could dissipate that dreary impression. Vladimir Ivanovich said, "It is possible to do something only by starting to stage a movie of your own. But, apparently, I would have to find a Russian assistant with English language, someone like Bulgakov, who could fulfill my tasks with the actors."

Again we saw the Talmadge sisters in two of their old movies. Both of the actresses are undoubtedly not bad, but the movies themselves are silly and vulgar.

In the evening we were taken to the best movie theater in Hollywood, the so-called Egyptian Theatre, whose director is [Sid] Grauman.

It is called Egyptian because the auditorium was made in the Egyptian style. The theater is big, with a seating capacity of 1,800, and is designed with crude luxury, although it is very comfortable. Unusually for American habits, it has no balcony. In front of the entrance there is a splendid yard, covered with marble. When you enter the yard, on a pedestal you see a figure that at a glance could be taken for a mannequin, but in fact this is an actor made up and dressed in Venetian clothes who stays there to attract audiences with pantomime and marionette-like gestures. His gestures are so perfect that everybody is under the complete illusion that he is a clockwork toy.

In the center of the yard on an easel they have installed a portrait of Vladimir Ivanovich with an inscription WELCOME DANCHENKO.

At the entrance we were met by a representative of the theater's management who gave each of us a present—a wooden box of cigars and Egyptian cigarettes—and showed us to our seats, the best in the auditorium. At that moment on the screen they were already showing different views and moments of our arrival at Los Angeles. Then the program preceding the screening of the movie started. A big symphony orchestra played a potpourri from *Carmen*, and a divertissement called *A Night in Venice* was presented. During some thirty to forty minutes we were listening to some very decent singing from soloists and choir; there were also dance numbers performed both by soloists and by corps de ballet. Clowns, whistlers, acrobats, and a mandolin player were involved as well. The rhythm of the show was splendid, and it gave the impression of a production in a European music hall, although not stretched for the whole evening but concentrated into a half an hour.

After that a big movie with Barrymore—*Don Juan*—was shown. Vladimir Ivanovich had seen this movie before, in New York; at that time he liked it in general, and now his impression became even stronger. During the interval we were invited to the office of the theater's director Grauman, who was very curious about Vladimir Ivanovich's opinion of the film, the divertissement, and the way the theater was arranged. Vladimir Ivanovich sincerely praised everything.

Douglas Fairbanks and John Barrymore. (Courtesy of AMPAS)

1 October

Today we eventually met Barrymore during the shooting of one of his scenes. When he learned why Vladimir Ivanovich had come here, he sounded extraordinarily glad. "I hope you understand—this is wonderful, this is grandiose!" said he. "As if a god from Olympus has descended to Hollywood. We need you so much—you can teach us so many things! When I learnt you were Nemirovich-Danchenko, my first thought was that you were not that very person, the real Nemirovich-Danchenko, but maybe his brother. I just could not believe it!"

He was literally in somewhat of an ecstasy, and, being moved by emotions, he kissed Vladimir Ivanovich's hand, to the great confusion of the latter. As for me, I actually restored my acquaintance of Barrymore because

I had met him before—at the backstage of the Moscow Art Theatre, during the theater's first visit to America. He immediately recalled our meeting after *The Three Sisters.*

In accordance with Barrymore's request, we joined him and went to watch the screening of the scenes filmed today. Together with the director, two assistants, and the director of photography, he was choosing the best moments. Vladimir Ivanovich did not like anything in particular except certain scenes with Barrymore. Without doubt, everything he does contrasts sharply with the work of his colleagues. One could feel the sincerity and experience of an outstanding actor and, from time to time, some kind of inspiration. However, to our disappointment, many good and important moments played by Barrymore either were shown in the background and often could scarcely be discerned or were overshadowed by the irrelevant and untalented contributions of his partners.

On the same day we watched the new Douglas Fairbanks film *The Black Pirate.* The whole film is made up of Fairbanks' favorite tricks and has nothing in it with regard to inner content.

The scenes, taking place on a big sailing ship, are staged quite well. The ship itself, the sea—all those look very beautiful and real. Who can imagine my surprise when in the yard of the studio I saw that very ship in its real size standing in a very large pool without water? It turned out that the pool would be filled with water, and it would replace the sea.

After *Black Pirate* we watched one of the recent movies of Mary Pickford—*Little Annie Rooney.* This is an ordinary, sentimental story from New York life, but Pickford animates it with her sincere and touching performance. Vladimir Ivanovich considers her an undoubtedly gifted and very attractive actress.

After an unsatisfying, frustrating, and bemusing year, Sergei Bertensson and Vladimir Ivanovich Nemirovich-Danchenko returned to Russia. Nemirovich-Danchenko and Stanislavsky reconciled and took up separate roles at what was now called the Dramatic Studio and the Art Theatre School. Nemirovich-Danchenko died on April 25, 1943. Discouraged with the Soviet government's increasing influence over the theater, Bertensson eventually returned to Hollywood, where he wrote books and tried his hand at screenwriting. He died in 1962.

Robert Parrish 1926

R obert Parrish was born in Columbus, Georgia, on January 4, 1916. He was a movie-mad boy of ten who was taking full advantage of his hometown's three movie theaters when he moved to Los Angeles with his parents, brother, and two sisters.

Nineteen twenty-six was a vintage year—the heart of the Roaring Twenties. The songs I remember from our Victor records were "All Alone," "Pretty Baby," "Always," and "California Here I Come." Calvin Coolidge was trying on Indian headdresses. It was the year of the first Dempsey-Tunney fight.

It was also the year the Coca-Cola Company transferred my father from Columbus, Georgia, to Hollywood, California...We moved into a five-room duplex bungalow in the heart of Hollywood. A bedroom for my mother and father, a bedroom for the two girls and a bedroom for me and my brother.

I was enrolled in the fifth grade at Santa Monica Boulevard School, less than a mile from twenty-three film studios. It usually took ten minutes to walk from my house to school—unless I used a short cut through the Paramount and F.B.O (later RKO) back lots, under the fence to the adjacent Hollywood Cemetery, a dash across four acres of marble slabs, headstones, and dead flowers, then through a secret hole in the surrounding high cedar hedge, across Van Ness Avenue and, panting, through the school gates as the bell rang. That way, I could make it in just under four minutes...

* * * *

Charlie Chaplin's casting director came right into our schoolroom. He asked who would like to work in a movie called *City Lights* and about half

Young Charlie Chaplin.
(Collection of Allison Burnett)

The Chaplin Studio on La Brea Avenue. (Collection of Patt Morrison)

of us raised our hands, mostly girls. Then he asked how many could shoot peas through a peashooter, and the girls' hands went down. The casting director selected me and Austin Jewell and told the teacher to send our parents in to see him at the Chaplin Studio on North La Brea Avenue. Luckily, my father was out of town so I went that afternoon with my mother. My father would not have approved. He was never interested in anything to do with the movies.

The casting director explained that I would have to go to the California Department of Child Welfare in downtown Los Angeles, have a medical examination, and if found sound of mind and body and up on my school-work, I would be given a work permit. When that was done, I was to come back tomorrow and meet the director.

"D. W. Griffith," I thought. "Who else?" I would actually meet my hero, the man who told everybody what to do, the man with the big megaphone who told Douglas Fairbanks how to slide down the sail, told Tom Mix's horse, Tony, how to paw the ground when counting, told the Our Gang kids how to be naughty and Lillian Gish how to be sad.

My mother and I got on the Pacific Electric streetcar at La Brea and Santa Monica Boulevard. I was thinking about Griffith when she said, "Robert, you must do exactly as Mr. Chaplin says tomorrow." I said I would, but I knew Mr. Griffith would have the final word. Through his megaphone.

The next day, we went to the casting office at 7:00 A.M. My mother checked me in, showed the assistant casting director my temporary work permit, and told him she would leave me with him because she had to go home and get her other children off to school. I was given an extra's voucher and told to wait in the outer office.

After being alone for about fifteen minutes, I was joined by Austin Jewell. He had worked in some movies before and already had a permit. He promptly told me the names of the movies, the stars, directors, and how much he had been paid: "*Quality Street*, starring Marion Davies; director, Sidney Franklin; three dollars. *Casey at the Bat*, starring Wallace Beery; director, Monty Brice; three-fifty and a box lunch. (We made that one at Wrigley Field.) *Sparrows*, starring Mary Pickford; director, William Beaudine; five dollars."

As he gave me his list of credits, I noticed that he kept saying the word "director" but he never said "D. W. Griffith." After he didn't say "D. W.

Griffith" about ten times, I wrote him off as a fake who had never worked in any movies. He didn't even know who the director was.

It turned out that I didn't either. When the assistant director came and took us out to the back lot where *City Lights* was being shot, I saw fifty or sixty people hanging around doing different things. A man was powdering another man's face and another man was powdering a very pretty lady's face. A man in overalls had a flat board about four feet square with the silver paper pasted on one side of it. He was aiming it at the sun and reflecting the sun's rays onto Charlie Chaplin.

A man with a megaphone yelled, "Quiet!" which seemed like a dumb thing to yell because nobody was talking and the only sound I could hear was the soft pat-pat-pat of the powder puff on the beautiful lady's face. The man stopped patting and the man with the megaphone yelled "Quiet!" again. I kept my eye on him because I figured when he took the megaphone away from his face I would finally see D. W. Griffith.

The assistant director with us whispered, "Quiet now boys. They're ready to shoot." Austin Jewell and I whispered, "Yes, sir" in unison. The man with the megaphone turned it in our direction and yelled "Quiet!" at the top of his voice. I wondered if D. W. Griffith ever did anything but yell for people to be quiet when they were already quiet. I waited for him to yell at Charlie Chaplin and tell him how to twirl his cane or skid around the corner on one foot or wiggle his mustache or something. Instead, Charlie walked over to him, took the megaphone out of his hand, and said in a very soft voice, "If you are through yelling, we'll make that shot."

The megaphone man didn't look like D. W. Griffith at all. He didn't look like much of anything except a man being gently criticized by his boss. He said, "Yes, sir." Then he turned to the cameraman and said, "Roll the camera." Chaplin went back to his position on the street corner, the man beside the camera said, "Running," then, "Speed." The megaphone man said, "Start your background action!" Some people with powdered faces started to walk around in the background. Charlie Chaplin said, "Action, Virginia," and the beautiful lady with the powered face walked toward Charlie, holding her hands out like a blind person. She touched Charlie. He jumped, tipped his hat, twirled his cane, and smiled at her. She didn't react. She just stared ahead, out at the traffic which was rushing by in front of her.

There were about ten cars. They would drive by, turn around in a circle outside of camera range, and drive back in the opposite direction. The extras in the background did the same thing. After Charlie had twirled and tipped and smiled a few times, he held his hand up toward the camera and said, "Cut." The megaphone man yelled, "Cut!" and everything stopped.

I told Austin Jewell that I thought the director always carried the megaphone and told everyone what to do. I also told him that D. W. Griffith directed every movie. Austin thought this was an interesting idea, so he passed it along to the assistant director. The assistant director laughed and told the cameraman. The story finally got to Chaplin and he came over and asked where I had learned this bit of information. I said my mother had told me and he said that on this picture they were making an exception and that Mr. Griffith was letting him direct it. He took the giant megaphone from the assistant director and pantomimed a movie director at work. He pretended to yell through it, first through the small end, then the big end. He put it on the ground and leaned his elbow on it, thinking. He sat on it, crossed his legs, took off his derby, scratched his head and thought some more, then he stood up, got the megaphone stuck on his foot, and limped around.

Everyone stopped work and watched the act, all laughing hysterically. When Chaplin had finished, he gave the megaphone back to the assistant director and told him to get the cars and extras ready for another "take." While this was being done, Chaplin explained that what my mother had probably told me was that D. W. Griffith was a great director, but he couldn't possibly direct every movie made. He also said that yelling through the megaphone wasn't always the best way to get people to do what you wanted them to do—that it was usually better to speak quietly or not at all. He said he found it best to show people rather than tell them. He then went on to explain that Austin Jewell and I were to be newsboys and we were supposed to shoot peas through a peashooter at him while he was helping the beautiful blind girl, Virginia Cherrill, across the street. Then, sometime later in the picture, when the tramp (Charlie) was released from jail, the girl (Virginia) would have recovered her sight and she would ignore the poor tramp (Chaplin always referred to the tramp in the third person). He said he would tip his hat and offer to guide her across the street. While he was doing this, I was to sneak up behind him and grab his cane. When he turned to recover the cane two men would grab him and try to pull him away. I was to hold on to the cane as long as

I could. He asked if I could do this. I said yes and offered to show him. He said, "No. I'll show you when the time comes." He told us to go with the second assistant director to wardrobe and make-up, and he would show us our parts when we came back. He then went back to the set to repeat the scene he had just done. The megaphone man yelled, "Quiet!" As we tip-toed away, I took one last look over my shoulder for D. W. Griffith. I didn't see him. I never did.

Robert Parrish continued working as an actor through the late 1930s, often uncredited; he took great pride in his professionalism and the financial contribution his work made to his family, particularly after his parents divorced. It was during filming of The Informer, *in which Parrish had a small role, that director John Ford became a mentor and encouraged him to become a film editor. Parrish apprenticed under Ford, worked on a series of documentaries, and went on to win an Academy Award for editing* Body and Soul *in 1947; he was nominated two years later for* All the King's Men.

In the early 1950s, Parrish transitioned to directing, working primarily in Europe. For twenty years he lived in London and Klosters, Switzerland, near his longtime friends Irwin Shaw and Salka Viertel. Parrish and his wife, Kathleen, whom he had married in 1942 and with whom he had a son and a daughter, returned to America in 1980. Parrish also wrote two delightful autobiographies, Growing Up in Hollywood *and* Hollywood Doesn't Live Here Anymore. *One of the many tales he told was about Charlie Chaplin, thirty-five years after making* City Lights, *telling Parrish that "he never forgot me telling him that D. W. Griffith directed every movie."*

Robert Parrish died on December 4, 1995, in Sag Harbor, New York, at the age of seventy-nine.

Maurice Rapf 1928

M aurice Rapf was born in New York City on May 19, 1914. His father,
*Harry Rapf, was managing vaudeville acts when Warner Bros. brought
him to Hollywood in 1921. Harry was at the side of Louis B. Mayer and Irving
Thalberg at the founding of M-G-M in 1924 but never received the public
acclaim in which the other two men basked. Harry was the one behind the scenes,
"discovering" talent such as Lucille LeSueur, aka Joan Crawford, with whom he
had a long affair. His son, Maurice, went to public schools near the family home
in Windsor Square, close to downtown Los Angeles. One of his fondest memories
was when his family moved to the beach for the summer, when he was fourteen.*

During the course of his career, my father, like other movie moguls, had
various summer homes. The first one I remember was on the oceanfront in
Santa Monica within walking distance of L. B. Mayer's, Irving Thalberg's
and Jack Warner's homes. The twelve- or fourteen-room house we rented
was actually on property owned by William Randolph Hearst. It was a
guest house for the huge hotel-like establishment, complete with Olympic-
size swimming pool, that he had built for his lady-love, the actress Marion
Davies.

I know that we rented the Davies-Hearst guest house for the summer
of 1928 because that was the year when I got my first driver's license (at
age fourteen in California in those days) and, shortly, thereafter, my first
automobile. Thomas, our chauffeur, taught me how to drive in my parents'
Cadillac limousine, which, without synchro-mesh transmission, was not
an easy car for shifting gears. Since it was about three feet longer than the
average car, parking was no cinch, either. Once I could manage the limo,
taking the driving test in my father's Buick coupé was a snap. And, with
license in the offing and after much wheedling on my part, my parents

promised me a car of my own for my fourteenth birthday. I had assured them I could find something fairly cheap, probably for less than a hundred dollars, and I started reading the classified ads and making a tour of the used car lots.

Believe it or not, there were many cars advertised for less than one hundred dollars in those days, including venerable Ford Model T's that would require my learning new skills in order to shift gears with a foot pedal. Ford no longer manufactured the Model A with the gas tank in front of the windshield. Well, I found a car; I think it was a 1924 Dodge, sometimes called a "Dodgé," as if it were French, and I took my father to see it one Saturday afternoon. He took one look and shook his head. "I can't let you drive that heap," he said. "It's dangerous. How much would a new car cost?"

So I went to the local Ford and Chevrolet dealers and found that it was possible to buy a new Chevrolet roadster for four hundred and seventy-five dollars. It was actually a bit more than that because the quoted price didn't include a spare wheel with a tire. You picked your brand in those days—Goodrich, Firestone, Goodyear, or Kelly-Springfield (the latter had a wonderful print ad that featured a small boy in long johns with a tire over his shoulder and the caption "Time to Retire"). The spare tire added about twenty-five dollars to the cost. Later, you would buy an automatic windshield wiper, wind wings, and a fancy ornament that included a thermometer to replace the prosaic radiator cap on the front of the hood. So much for that first vehicle, which I drove with pride from the beachfront of Santa Monica to L.A. High School for several weeks from mid-May to the end of June and during summer vacation.

Our rented beach house was so spacious that we were invaded by family visitors from the East. My mother was always big on relatives, and my father and grandmother threw out the welcome mat for anyone who came from Denver, where they had spent the last years of the nineteenth century. That summer, I remember visits from a large contingent of New York Uhlfelders (my mother's family, including my grandparents, a few uncles and cousins), Herbie Stein and Blanche Preeman from Denver, and the Newmans, former Denver residents now operating theaters in Seattle. The Newmans' daughter Vi became the first wife of Pandro Berman, later a noted movie producer.

That Fourth of July, my friend Budd Schulberg and I pooled our

Marion Davies's beach house at Santa Monica. (Collection of Allison Burnett)

Malibu Colony. (Collection of Patt Morrison)

resources to buy fireworks in Culver City, where their sale was legal, and we worked out a program and set up chairs for our parents and friends to watch our display on the Santa Monica beachfront as soon as it got dark. We had begun with a modest overture of a few sparklers and roman candles when suddenly we heard a loud bang in the sky and, in a moment, we could see explosives form a huge American flag. And there, down on the beach, in front of the Davies estate, was a cannon that had catapulted this elaborate fireworks display into the sky. And that was just the beginning. Every fifteen seconds or so, another monster display burst in the sky above our heads. The puny sky rockets we had prepared, the pinwheels and flaming fountains, would have to wait for another occasion. All eyes were obviously on the Hearst-Davies fountain of lights down the beach. As Budd said, "Davies shooting off *her* stuff made *our* stuff look sick."

In 1929, my parents actually built a second home in the Malibu beach colony—an area that then was and still is a haven for people in the entertainment industry. The Malibu land was owned in 1929 by the scion of a pioneer California family, Mrs. Rindge, who refused to sell. But she needed money after the stock market crash, so at the end of the 1920s she decided to lease the beachfront land in thirty-foot parcels on a ten-year basis, at a dollar a front foot, to those who chose to build on it and were willing to take the risk that she might not renew the leases at the end of ten years. (This accounts for the fact that to this day so many of the houses in the Malibu colony nearly abut each other and are built, for the most part, on narrow lots at right angles to the ocean.)

My parents built a twelve-room house on their thirty feet and then leased another ten feet to the north which made that side of the house more open than most of the others. Rosabelle, the daughter of Carl Laemmle, president and founder of Universal, built on the lot directly south of us. She had once been engaged to Irving Thalberg, who jilted her to marry Norma Shearer, causing her to be known as "Poor Rosabelle." But Poor Rosabelle rebounded quickly, married a nice chap named Stanley Bergerman (later to become a successful agent), and then built their beach house so close to ours that we could touch hands if we reached out of our respective bedroom windows.

Some of the happiest years of my life were spent at Malibu. My father, an avid fisherman, chartered a fishing boat almost every Saturday during the summers and would take off from the Malibu pier with his cronies

(Leon Schlesinger of Looney Tunes and Bill Koenig, general manager of Universal, were habitués) to catch barracuda, yellowtail, and the staple of the kelp bed area, calico bass, some of which ran as large as five pounds.

My close friend Budd Schulberg, son of B. P. Schulberg, then the production chief at Paramount (whose family had built on ninety feet of Mrs. Rindge's land), usually went along on these fishing trips. He and I earned our right of passage by cleaning everyone's fish, then taking what the fishermen didn't want to distribute to our adult movie friends along the Malibu beach—such people as the directors Herbert Brenon, Frank Capra, Bob Leonard, and Tod Browning; the actors Neil Hamilton, Maureen O'Sullivan, Ruth Chatterton, and Ralph Forbes; and various producers, writers, and agents. Our rewards might be delicious milkshakes at the Brenons' living room soda fountain or a sail with O'Sullivan's boyfriend and later husband, John Farrow. It was fun.

On Sundays, most Malibu residents had open houses, which is to say that there were a few invited guests and many more who knew they would not be turned away. (The Schulbergs had a tennis court that was a special attraction.) After a while, my mother began to dread these Sunday invasions, but it was my grandmother who supervised the preparation of the food—her pot roast (made from the brisket) and potato pancakes achieving considerable fame and often attracting too many guests.

I was always puzzled by the fact that the "movie-crowd" often left the temperate Los Angeles area on weekends, despite the fact that they lived suburban lives with tennis courts, swimming pools, and easy access to the beach—especially after the founding of the Malibu colony, which had been preceded by the popularity of the ocean front in Santa Monica. But there were frequent weekend jaunts—to Palm Springs, to the Coronado Beach Hotel, to Agua Caliente during its short period of existence, to Arrowhead Springs, to Big Bear, to Santa Barbara, even as far north as to Carmel and Monterey. (Bear in mind that in the 1920s and early 1930s, Las Vegas, though it already had legalized gambling, was a rough and tumble frontier town, used by Hollywood folk primarily for quick marriages and divorces.) I suppose that since most movie people were transplanted easterners, they were accustomed to escaping from the workplace to the countryside. And those weekend jaunts were usually taken by groups of intimate friends— mostly movie people, to be sure, but crossing studio lines.

After a short stint at Stanford, Maurice Rapf joined his friend Budd Schulberg at Dartmouth and, while still in college, they spent a summer together in the Soviet Union. After graduating in 1935, Rapf returned to Hollywood, joined the Screen Writers Guild, and cowrote They Gave Him a Gun *for Spencer Tracy, Disney's* The Song of the South, *and, with Schulberg,* Winter Carnival. *Both he and Schulberg were briefly members of the Communist Party, and when Rapf was blacklisted in 1947, he moved his family to Vermont where he continued to write as well as produce and direct documentary films. Rapf was always passionate about his politics and stopped speaking to Schulberg for a dozen years after Budd named names for HUAC (a list that did not include Rapf's, although several other "witnesses" did name him as a Communist). Rapf, who was married to Louise Seidel for fifty-six years and had three children, began teaching film at Dartmouth in 1967 and five years later became its director of film studies. Rapf and Schulberg renewed their friendship when they both had sons at Dartmouth. In 1998, the Writers Guild gave Rapf cowriting credit on the 1954 Columbia film* The Detective. *Rapf died at the age of eighty-eight on April 15, 2003, in Hanover, New Hampshire.*

Salka Viertel 1928

S alka Steuermann was born on June 15, 1889, in Sambor, in what was then a part of Poland that belonged to Austria-Hungary. She was given a good education, but her passion was the theater. When the attractive redhead was in her early twenties she was accepted into director Max Reinhardt's company in Berlin, where she met the Viennese stage director Berthold Viertel. The couple married in April of 1918, and moved to Dresden where Salka gave birth to their sons Hans and Peter. For the next several years, Berthold and Salka lived in Germany and worked throughout Europe. Salka managed to run the household and to act after the birth of another son, Thomas, in 1925, but by this time Berthold had tired of directing plays and running a theater. His dream was to write, and when Fox Pictures, at the urging of German director F. W. Murnau, offered him a three-year contract to write and direct movies in Hollywood, he jumped at the chance. Salka, already concerned about the growing militarism in Germany, was more than happy go with him to America, temporarily leaving the boys with relatives until she and Berthold were settled in Los Angeles.

We were told that the interest of the American audiences in silent films had declined and people lined up for long stretches in front of the Warner Brothers Theater, where an announcement of the *Jazz Singer* blazed from the marquee. Commonplace and of a sticky sentimentality, it had a tremendous impact on the audience. Berthold wondered what influence the "Talkies" would have on his contract. For a stage director and a writer, the "Talkies" could offer greater possibilities than the silent film, although Murnau looked with horror upon them. To compare the *Jazz Singer* with *Sunrise* or with King Vidor's *The Crowd* was sheer blasphemy. *The Crowd* was a fine motion picture about man's frightening beehive existence in big cities. The *Jazz Singer* had in our eyes nothing to recommend it except Al Jolson in blackface.

We tried to pack as many impressions of New York as possible into the few weeks we spent there, but Murnau's impatient telephone calls forced us to leave. A wonderful, fast train took us West. Everything was fabulously exciting and we reported it to our boys, our parents and friends on train stationery with the head of an Indian Chief on it.

We loved our Negro porter and the waiters in the dining car; we were delighted by our drawing room compartment, fascinated by the landscape. New Mexico and Arizona, with the gorgeous reds and browns and the splurge of purple and ochre in the fantastic rock formations, awed us with their beauty. The train was cutting through the desert...The sky was higher and the nights very clear and starry, the weird Joshua trees, the pale sagebrush...All day long we stared spellbound through our window, imploring the porter to wipe it clean of dust. He did it reluctantly, contemptuously repeating, "Desert, it's nothing but desert ..."

I was learning by heart the names of the places we were passing: Peabody, Joliet, Independence, Topeka, Amarillo, Santa Fe and Emporia (which I thought must be a good city because in German *empor* means "upward").

Then, on the fifth day, when we woke up we saw endless orange groves. The sweet smell of orange blossoms pervaded our compartment. We were in California. In Pasadena, Herman Bing, Berthold's new secretary, and an unavoidable publicity man waited for us with a big, black chauffeur-driven automobile.

I expected California to be all sunshine and flowers but we found Los Angeles cold and overcast, with the sun, against which we had been so emphatically warned, invisible. While we were driving along Sunset Boulevard I noticed that there were no sidewalks in front of the uniform, clapboard houses and bungalows. An extraordinary fantasy was displayed in roof styling: some roofs were like mushrooms, many imitated Irish thatch and the shape of others was inspired by Hansel and Gretel's gingerbread house. Ice cream was sold in the gaping mouth of a huge frog, or inside a rabbit; a restaurant was called "The Brown Derby" and looked like one. The buses we passed offered SERVICE WITH A SMILE, and during our whole ride Berthold was busy writing in his notebook the slogans on stores, buildings and billboards:

"Hillside Homes of Happiness—your servants will enjoy working as you will enjoy living in an Outpost Home."

"Toilet seats shaped to conform to nature's laws."

"How easy it is to shave when you control hydrolysis."

"Less hair in the comb, more hair on your head."

"Don't fool yourself! Halitosis makes you unpopular."

"Teeth may shine like tinted pearls, still pyorrhea attacks four out of five."

To avoid the downtown traffic, our chauffeur did not drive through the city, which on the first fleeting glimpse was uninviting and ugly. JESUS SAVES, read a sign, towering over a large building, and Mr. Bing explained that this was Aimée Semple McPherson's Temple. We had never heard of Aimée Semple McPherson and wanted to know who she was. Our companions perked up and eagerly told us the gossip, and much of it appeared to be true, about the lady preacher. Aimée had brought romance and glamor to religion, joy to the poor, and her Temple rivaled the Roxy in showmanship. It sounded fascinating and we were determined to attend her services as soon as possible.

Our suite at the Roosevelt was almost identical with the one in our New York hotel, and just as overheated. There was a big bouquet of red roses for me and a case of whisky for Berthold, this time in the bathtub. The roses were from Murnau, the whisky a welcome from the studio.

"They must think we are alcoholics," I said to Bing.

He sighed: "In our profession one needs a drink rather often." I offered him one immediately.

After we were installed in our rooms he said good-bye, asking Berthold to call whenever he needed him and saying that he would report our arrival to Mr. Murnau. In the car I had already noticed that when he mentioned Murnau he seemed to be terrified by his grandeur. It did not fail to irritate Berthold.

The telephone rang and I answered. It was Murnau, happy that we had arrived at last. I thanked him for the roses and said that Berthold was taking a shower and would call later.

"Just tell him I don't need him today. I am shooting tests," said Murnau. "Only wanted to say hello."

Berthold was furious when I gave him the message. Murnau's "I don't need him" was sheer Prussian arrogance. Although I explained that Murnau did not sound overbearing, the jarring note was a prelude to the many clashes in their odd friendship.

The German journalist Arnold Hoellriegel, who was also staying in

The Roosevelt Hotel, In Hollywood, California.

The Roosevelt Hotel on Hollywood Boulevard. (Collection of Patt Morrison)

the Roosevelt, wanted us to have lunch with him. Coming downstairs we heard a cacophony of shrill voices as if from an enormous, excited poultry yard. The lobby was packed with women of whom the youngest could not have been less than seventy. About a hundred of them tottered around on high heels, in bright, flowered-chiffon dresses, orchid or gardenia corsages pinned to their bosoms. We wanted to know the purpose of the gathering but were told only that the ladies were Republicans. Hoellriegel's traveling companion and photographer, Max Goldschmidt, was not permitted to take pictures. After lunch Hoellriegel suggested that we take a look at the studios, but I pleaded that we drive first to the ocean.

The afternoon was gray and chilly, a mist hanging over Santa Monica. We drove along Pico Boulevard, a long, straight highway leading to the ocean. Again we saw shabby bungalows, occasional palm trees, gasoline stations, nurseries, markets and endless "lots for sale." Then the highway rose to a hilltop and we could see a bright, silvery glimmer, which changed into a wide strip of an iridescent, mother-of-pearl hue. We passed a lovely cemetery shaded by trees, like those in the "old country." It was called Woodland. Turning right we stopped in front of a rambling hotel

surrounded by an old, beautiful garden with enormous gum trees, sycamores and cypresses.

Having crossed the street and the well-kept lawn of an esplanade, shaded
by eucalyptus trees and tall palms, we found ourselves on the rim of a cliff.
Below was a highway, with automobiles flitting by; beach houses and clubs
turned their backs to the road and the glassed-in front porches faced the
ocean. To our right was the little bay of Santa Monica Canyon, surrounded
by hills covered with shrubs, trees, and scattered houses. On our left was a
pier, whose wooden pillars reached far out into the ocean. We drove to its
entrance. A gaudy, yellow building, with a tower-like superstructure har-
bored a merry-go-round. It had the most magnificent fierce horses, carved
in wood and painted by a real artist. They looked like the steeds on the
monuments of great generals. The loud orchestrion was playing old-fash-
ioned music. At each end of the long pier were fishmarkets, between them
ice cream stalls and little shops renting fishing rods and selling bait, dusty
abalone shells, starfish, coral beads and chewing gum, and a shack where a
Filipino lady in a sequined costume was telling fortunes. Men and women
in sunbleached jeans, and of all ages, were fishing from the pier. Boats were
tied up below and one could go sailing outside the little bay. Everything
was so lovely and peaceful: the people on the pier and the merry-go-round
and the swaying boats. I begged Berthold to let us live in Santa Monica.

When Berthold mentioned this in the studio, people were horrified:
Santa Monica! Everybody who lived there became rheumatic, had chronic
bronchitis and gout. "Then why would all the rich people have houses
there?" I argued. I was told that those houses were air-conditioned and
sound-proofed; their owners had the means to protect themselves from
ocean air and the pounding surf. Only Herman Bing's objection made
some sense: living in Santa Monica, Berthold would have to get up half an
hour earlier to be on time at the studio. My vision of the mad daily rush
made me resign myself to a house in Hollywood.

Emil and Gussy Jannings gave a party for us. Emil, a lusty character-
actor, had the gross and expansive sense of humor one calls "Rabelaisian."
His wife Gussy, blond and very chic, had once been a cabaret singer, a
well-known *diseuse*, and had become a stoical, imperturbable, though
sharp-tongued consort. Invited with us were Conrad Veidt, lanky and
handsome, and short cigar-smoking Ernst Lubitsch, now a celebrated
film maker, but who had not changed since our *Judith* days.[1] Both had

uninteresting pretty wives. A successful German director, Ludwig Berger, was also there. Paramount had signed him because of his European fame, but they did not know what to do with him. Max Reinhardt appeared after dinner with young Raimund von Hofmannsthal, son of the Austrian poet. He said that he had fallen in love with California, which Jannings, who hardly knew it, detested.

All those who had been some time in Hollywood seemed starved for new faces and, as I soon discovered, irritated with the old.

The Jannings lived in a grand-style Hollywood mansion, which they rented from the millionaire Josef Schenck, one of "filmdom's pioneers." Situated in the center of Hollywood Boulevard, it had a large garden, swimming pool, tennis court, and a huge living room with a multitude of lamps. The diversity of lamps and especially the extraordinary shapes of the lampshades, struck me as a specialty of Hollywood interiors.

Throughout the evening the main topic of conversation was the catastrophic impact of the talking films upon the careers of foreign stars, until the exuberant entrance of the precocious "Mann children," Erika and Klaus [children of the renowned novelist Thomas Mann], brightened the atmosphere. They had just arrived in Hollywood on their journey around the world. Very young and attractive, they were refreshingly irreverent and adventurous. They brought with them the atmosphere of Berlin's night life which electrified the party. It was very late when we left with them, discussing the evening on our way back to the hotel. Berthold was fascinated by Janning's impersonation of "Jannings in real life," an amalgamation of his monstrous egotism with roles he had played: Harpagon, Henry VIII, with glimpses of the good-natured, straightforward *Deutscher Michel*. We agreed that it was a great performance; that Conny Veidt was most handsome and a darling; Lubitsch inscrutable but worth knowing better; and Ludwig Berger's fate a warning to European directors.

I had rented the least expensive house I could find. It was on Fairfax Avenue, near the hills of Laurel Canyon, unpretentious but pleasant.

As soon as we moved in I asked Bing to help me choose a car and teach me how to drive. Half an hour later we returned in a Buick. Berthold was doubtful that a good car could be bought so quickly. I sat behind the wheel, death-defying Bing next to me. Nonchalantly I released the brakes, shifted into first gear and drove around the block. At least one of our problems was solved.

Had Berthold had any sense of direction, had he been less absent-minded and more interested in mechanical things, and had he been able to remember the difference between the brake and the accelerator, he also would have learned to drive. Under the circumstances, it was lucky that he stalled the car as soon as he touched the gearshift. After smashing a bumper and tearing off two fenders, he conceded defeat and De Witt Fuller joined our household as chauffeur. Bing could now devote himself entirely to typing, translating Berthold's script and giving him English lessons. We also engaged Emma, a Negro housekeeper, although Jannings threatened never to have a meal in our house. Now we were set, and certain that we would stay for a while in America.

* * * *

We were settling down. A German-American teacher prepared Hans and Peter for school. I went shopping, had my English lesson and wrote endless letters. On weekends I drove the children to the beach or to the Santa Monica Pier and my beloved merry-go-round.

The Fox executives began to invite us to parties at which the ritual separation of the sexes brought me in closer contact with their ladies. To do them justice, they were often much nicer than their husbands, and more intelligent. I liked the warm-hearted Marion Wurtzel, wife of Berthold's producer, the incredibly boorish Sol Wurtzel. She was born in Poland in a small Jewish community and used to invite me with other studio wives for lunch, always suggesting that we go shopping afterward. In no time she would spend three or four hundred dollars with the disarming explanation: "When I was a little girl I had to share one pair of shoes with my sister. Now I can afford things I don't need."

The Feyders [European director Jacques Feyder and his wife Françoise Rosay] arrived and were going through the stage when everything seemed *"très amusant"* and *"tordant."* But slowly the lunches and parties were getting me down. Françoise suggested that we play golf, but soon she also became convinced that golf did not answer all our needs. We were professional women and to survive in Hollywood we had to work.

* * * *

At last I got Berthold's consent to rent a beach house, "but only for the summer," and drove to Santa Monica.

At the corner of Seventh Street and San Vicente Boulevard, a road led down to the beach. It had rained in the morning and small white clouds hung above the ocean, which was covered with whitecaps. The breeze brought the scent of orange blossoms. On my left was a road winding uphill, on my right shacks and adobe huts and lots overgrown with weeds and geraniums. I faced a clapboard schoolhouse, small and rural, on which the roads seemed to converge. Children, mostly Mexicans, played on the slides and swings of the recreation ground. All this was peaceful and quiet: old sycamores and gnarled oaks, a swollen brook which rushed toward the ocean, dividing the road into two lanes, both leading to the Ocean Highway. I remembered having seen somewhere a billboard advertising a real estate office.

I found it next to "Inspiration Point," where Palisades Park ended and Ocean Avenue began to descend toward the canyon. A young man, tall and dark, introduced himself as Mr. Guercio and offered to show me several houses. One, suitable for a large family, was right below, though not directly on the beach.

We drove down a short, winding road overlooking the ocean, and stopped in front of a large, fenced-in house in the so-called English style. Two pine trees grew on each side of the entrance; next to them a magnolia spread its glossy leaves and enormous white blossoms. The fence was overgrown with honeysuckle, entangled with pink Portugal roses. The air was suffused with fragrance.

To get to the beach we had only to walk to the end of the street and descend the steps to a tunnel under the highway.

Mr. Guercio opened the front door and we went in. The first floor consisted of a very vast living room with a fireplace and a dining area. It had eight windows and a glass door which opened into the garden. A staircase between the dining area and living room led to the bedrooms; they also were spacious and had a view of the ocean. There were plenty of bathrooms and showers, and servants' quarters next to the garage. In the garden grew a pitasphorum tree and the inevitable hibiscus bushes, also an apricot and fig tree. At the far end an old incinerator tried to hide behind a lonely, bedraggled lilac bush. Mr. Guercio said that the lilac never bloomed, but this did not shatter my hope that one day it would, and it increased my desire to take the house. The rent was $900 for the three summer months but, if we wanted to take it for a whole year, it would be proportionately less. The house was in receivership, owned by a bank in Santa Monica. The bank was obviously responsible for the atrocious furniture, the armchairs and sofa covered with black velvet which faced the fireplace, and the shabby rattan garden chairs filling the rest of the room. The bedrooms were less offensive as they had only the essential things. From the windows one could see the ocean and the sharp profile of the hills on the other side of the canyon, and I could hear the waves pounding the shore.

I showed Berthold the house. He liked it, and in June, after Hans and Peter had finished school, we cut ourselves off from Hollywood and moved to 165 Mabery Road.

From their first days in Hollywood, the Viertels gravitated to the German émigrés already in California, and that bond grew stronger when the couple decided to stay indefinitely, in part because of the worsening political climate in Europe. Emil Jannings, however, left soon after being handed the first Academy Award for Best Actor—for two films: The Way of All Flesh *(1927) and* The Last Command *(1928). He returned to Berlin where he costarred in* The Blue Angel *for Josef von Sternberg, and acted in propaganda films for the Nazis.*

As Hitler's power increased, more German artists arrived in Los Angeles, often finding camaraderie and solace at 165 Mabery Road. Salka held a regular Sunday salon, but the house was usually filled with friends seven days a week. Bertolt Brecht and brothers Heinrich and Thomas Mann were regulars; the future director Fred Zinnemann, from Austria, was nineteen when he was hired as Berthold's secretary. Christopher Isherwood lived over the garage. Salka had known many of her visitors from the Max Reinhardt troupe in Europe and began a long-term affair with one, Max's son Gottfried.

Berthold Viertel was too iconoclastic to flourish in Hollywood; brilliant, but self-defeating, he turned to writing poetry and, for a while, Salka made enough to support them both. Of her many friends, Greta Garbo stood out for her fame and power, and when her first talkie, Anna Christie, *was filmed in both English and German, Salka played the role of Marthy, which was portrayed by Marie Dressler in the English version. Salka's acting career was limited because of her accent, so she turned to writing. She cowrote Garbo's* Queen Christina *(1933),* The Painted Veil *(1934),* Anna Karenina *(1935),* Conquest *(1937), and* Two-Faced Woman *(1941).*

Word spread of Salka's generosity, and letters from people asking for her help to leave Germany poured in. She turned to friends at M-G-M to vouch for artists trying to get visas and became the prime organizer behind the European Film Fund, created to rescue Jews and political writers. Some of her visitors, such as the Russian film director Sergei Eisenstein, caught the attention of the FBI. Salka was put on a watch list and was eventually blacklisted. Salka and Berthold divorced in 1947; he married again, returned to Europe in the late 1940s, and died in Vienna on September 24, 1953, at the age of sixty-eight.

By the early 1960s, Salka had little to hold her in California; her boys were grown and Gottfried Reinhardt had left her long before for a younger woman. Salka returned to Europe and settled in Klosters, Switzerland, where her son Peter and his wife, actress Deborah Kerr, lived six months out of the year. Salka spent time with her adored granddaughter and worked on her autobiography, which this generous woman with so many friends called The Kindness of Strangers. *In Klosters, she had a community that was reminiscent of Mabery Road; regular visitors included the novelist Irwin Shaw, David Niven, Garbo, the editor and director Robert Parrish, and Gore Vidal.*

Salka Viertel died in Klosters on October 20, 1978, at the age of eighty-nine.

[1] In Germany, Viertel and Lubitsch had both been in the 1913 Max Reinhart production of Christian Hebbel's play *Judith.*

Laurence Irving 1928

L aurence Irving was born in London on April 11, 1897. His parents, Harry and Dorothea, were both actors, as was his grandfather, Sir Henry Irving. Laurence was sent to school in South Dorset and attended Wellington College. He was seventeen when England entered the First World War and he trained as a pilot, but an infected throat gland required surgery, a long convalescence, and his departure from what would become the Royal Air Force. He studied art at several schools and in 1920 married Rosalind Woolner. Laurence worked as a book illustrator, painter, and theater set designer.

Irving's friend, playwright and screenwriter Eddie Knoblock, had worked with Douglas Fairbanks on several films, and when Fairbanks talked to him about his plans to make a movie from the book The Man in the Iron Mask, Knoblock suggested he look at Irving's set designs. When Fairbanks and Mary Pickford stopped in London during a European tour in May of 1928, Douglas cabled Irving and asked him to come to the Hyde Park Hotel and bring "examples of your work." At this point in their careers, Fairbanks and Pickford were huge international stars, mobbed everywhere they went, and unable to travel without security. Yet when a nervous Irving showed up at Fairbanks's hotel room, carrying as large a portfolio as he dared, he found the star in the bathtub. Fairbanks acted as if nothing could be more normal and within a few hours had charmed Irving into agreeing to come to America to design the sets for The Iron Mask. Leaving his wife and children in London, Irving met the Fairbankses in Naples and set sail with them. They stopped over in New York for a few days and Mary Pickford did the unthinkable: she had her famous golden curls cut off and emerged with a stylish bob.

When we boarded "The Indian Chief," the platform was thronged with reporters, photographers, and film fans swarming on their queen, Mary

Mary Pickford and Douglas Fairbanks mobbed by fans in London. (Courtesy of MOMA)

Fairbanks on the set of *The Iron Mask*. (Courtesy of AMPAS)

Pickford. These Chicagoans were the first to hear and to see that her fabulous curls had fallen to the scissors of a New York hairdresser and to learn, not without dismay, that the world's sweetheart had put her hair up. If the Pope had appeared in St. Peter's with a full-bottomed wig, his global flock would have been no less shocked. The crowd did not temper their curiosity as to the shorn lamb who dodged their speculations on her future with an inscrutable smile. Douglas, himself uncertain as to what her impulsive haircut portended, skillfully parried the imposition of importunate columnists. But Mary's pretty head, regardless of her coiffure, was well screwed on. As it turned out, she was a jump ahead of him and her fellow stars as our super-train, hooting like a wistful owl, began its 3000-mile haul westward. Now our party occupied the whole of one coach.

For the first two days and nights, I sweated it out in my luxurious oven, its walls hot to the touch, its unconditioned air murdering sleep. So, on the third, I welcomed Douglas's call shortly before dawn to take me to the observation car to view the foothills of the Rockies. Though their distant peaks were curtained with cloud, they were a welcome landfall after the oceanic horizons of the featureless plains. Nearing Albuquerque, while I breakfasted, I watched a wedding procession shuffling down the street of a forlorn Indian village towards a parched adobe church—a priest and his acolytes in sun-bleached vestments, the bride and bridegroom in their western Sunday best, a few disheveled redskin guests, and behind them two feathered braves letting off guns to keep the evil spirits at bay. The happy pair were having the best of both metaphysical worlds.

* * * *

At Pasadena Station a horde of liege men and women and loyal subjects welcomed their king and queen safely returned from a crusade to win the hearts of Europeans to the idolatry on which the inhabitants of its Ephesus—thousands of suntanned players, writers, craftsmen, technicians, and executors—depended for their fairy affluence. Doug handed me over to his eighteen-year-old son, "Junior." As the crown prince of Hollywood, he had a sophisticated poise beyond his years. He had, of course, hereditary right of entry into the film studio and had already made the most of it. ...

At the wheel of a powerful two-seater coupé, Junior, with an engaging detachment, concluded an informative and wryly humorous prologue of the motion-picture pageant in which I was to play a minor role. Of that drive I remember only the succession of gigantic roadside advertisements in dazzling white frames that made me feel as though I were being whisked through an exhibition of pictures painted by a prolific artist with impressive vulgarity. Never having visited Spain or Italy, the Mediterranean houses and pseudo-estancias struck me as original and picturesque and complementary to the brown, arid hills on which they were artfully perched by real estate dealers. All too soon we turned off Hollywood Boulevard, down a street overshadowed by a wall of buildings, and drove through steel gates, guarded apparently by a Texan philosopher and his Alsatian dog, into an enclave where soon I would have to justify the fabulous expense of my transportation thither.

In its centre stood three studios and the carpenter's shop, each like an outsize airplane hangar. On two sides these structures were enclosed by buildings that met at right angles made by Douglas's and Mary's headquarters, their purposes and uses contrary for all their contiguity. Douglas's dressing room, in effect a hall with an ever open door, led to a steam bath and a cold plunge. To Douglas, privacy was a deprivation. At all hours members of his court and visitors were welcome—at their own risk. For beside his dressing room table was an armchair into which the unwary, conscious of the privilege of his warm invitation to take a seat, sank in prospect of an intimate chat with their distinguished host, only to leap from it with a yelp of dismay as their posteriors tingled from an electric shock galvanized by a switch concealed under his dressing table. This hospitable snare, eagerly anticipated and relished by an audience delighting in practical jokes of any kind, betrayed, perhaps, his Teutonic ancestry, akin to the ponderous pranks played by Edward VII on his long-suffering courtiers.

In contrast Mary's bungalow had the cloistered calm of a nunnery where its Mother Superior welcomed only faithful friends and business associates in awe of her perspicacity. There Mary, when not herself filming, spun daily from the threads of her talent as an artist and femme d'affaires the web of financial security for herself and her dependent relatives. Having been the family breadwinner since she was five years old, industry and thrift had become as obsessive to her as her faith in Christian Science.

Beyond the studios was a vast open space, "the lot," which from a distance appeared to be the relics of a world fair exhibiting every style and period of architecture known to man—a jumble of facades of stone, marble tiles, and brick skillfully rendered in plaster on frameworks of timber and chicken wire. There were the recognizable backgrounds of long-remembered films preserved intact by the perpetual sunshine until they outlived useful adaptation and were demolished to make room for new productions. Though more substantial than stage settings, each was truncated to the limits of the camera's lines of sight, their jagged silhouettes reminding me of a shell-torn Belgian town.

* * * *

The first day in a film studio was spent in a whirlwind of introductions that stripped me of all memories but one—my presentation (for such in its regality it seemed) to David Wark Griffith who, in my esteem, had towered above his fellow United Artists. He was of smaller stature than I expected but his features were, like my grandfather's, those that would have distinguished a leader of any profession. He received me with polite gravity and accepted my homage as though it was his due. I was shocked to find this pioneer, whose inventive genius and passionate faith in the new medium had been the impetus on which the whole rickety edifice of Hollywood was based, was so little respected by the mandarins of the dynasty he had founded. Every foot of film threaded through the gates of its hundreds of cameras every day bore the imprint of his daring experiments …. So I found myself face to face with a dispirited visionary accepting his loss of aesthetic and financial independence and fulfilling his obligations to the corporation by remaking an early potboiler, *The Battle of the Sexes*, which he did not bother to endorse with his signature. Though I met him again, I was unable to unwind the bandages of his wounded egotism.

* * * *

Douglas and Mary invited me to stay with them at Pickfair until Maurice Leloir [the esteemed seventy-five-year-old French artist and set decorator] and Leon Barry [French actor and director who was to play Athos to Fairbanks's D'Artagnan] arrived from France when, perhaps, the three of us could live together in one of the pseudo-Spanish apartment houses on an estate known as Andalusia. When at the end of that long day we took our lighthearted departure from the studio, dusk was falling, and with it the carefree spirits of my hosts. I was surprised to see that the family Rolls

Royce was preceded and followed by less elegant vehicles full of armed guards; this was a necessary precaution, it was explained to me with some embarrassment, against gangsters who had threatened to kidnap Mary and hold her for ransom. A few hours later I was gazing from my bedroom window on the moonlit garden. A man was lurking in the shadows of the surrounding trees. Accidentally I brushed against the lavatory seat, which fell with a resounding clang on its pan. The man whipped round and, as quick on the draw as William S. Hart, weaved his revolver to and fro, ready to riddle the imagined intruder. Relieved to know he was a guard and not a bandit, I crept back to bed ashamed of having triggered off a false alarm but deeply impressed by the protection of the peacefully sleeping household. This was not the last time that the sinister undercurrent below the serene surface of Hollywood's public image intruded on, what Douglas so vehemently insisted, was the best of all possible worlds. In a way, I was glad to know that the West was still a bit wild.

Pickfair was an unpretentious house of no particular style, though certainly more English than Spanish—the sort of house a prosperous Edwardian actor-manager might have built on the river above Maidenhead. The interior decorator had evidently intended to furnish it in hotel-Adam style, but thanks to Douglas and Mary's liking for homey comfort, the rigours of the period had been alleviated. The big sitting room, open to the hall, had a large well-upholstered settee and deep armchairs. After dinner these were arranged to face the far wall, where a discreetly hidden screen was lowered on which the latest motion pictures were projected from a booth concealed in the staircase. To watch these while my hosts made running commentaries on them and on occasion, for the screen reached the floor, the substantial Chaplin joined the shadowy performers to make uproarious and well-deserved fun of the banalities of directors and players, was an education in the pitfalls of making motion pictures which all too easily could lapse into bathos.

If Pickfair was Hollywood's Palais Royale and the mecca of distinguished visitors or ambitious film folk, its sovereigns' court was remarkable for its modesty and constancy. Douglas spent his brief weekends with a trinity of old cronies—Kenneth Davenport, Earl Brown, and Tom Geraghty. The first two were companions of his Broadway theatrical youth and the third an Irish newspaperman turned scriptwriter, with the double-barrelled wit of his twin nationality and flair for contriving the kind of practical jokes in which Douglas and Chaplin delighted ....

At the time of my appointment, Junior was ardently courting an up-and-coming film actress, Joan Crawford, who soon found herself in this genial company. The Texas peasant, as it were, beloved by the handsome prince had gained her footing in the studios by the unflagging exercise of her powerful personality in a milieu where even such beauty as hers was commonplace. In her continuing struggle for recognition she had little time to cultivate the domestic arts. Eager to win Mary's approval as a step-daughter-in-law, she brought to those Sunday gatherings a piece of needlework and, during lulls in our follies, stitched away demurely. As the weeks went by, her stitching seemed to make little progress so I suspected that, like Penelope, she unraveled this effective property to make it last through the run of her betrothal. Douglas, though at this stage he did not betray it, must have had misgivings at the prospect of a grand paternity incompatible with the youth and agility of his heroic impersonations.

I first set eyes on Chaplin literally in the flesh when we met in Douglas's steam bath. I introduced myself. Perhaps the honour in which he, as a boy actor in London, held my grandfather (he had attended his funeral in Westminster Abbey) commended me to him. This was another rich legacy I inherited from "the antique," for the objects of Charlie's reverence were few. The setting of our first meeting might have come from a play by George Bernard Shaw. Through clouds of vapour and in the infernal heat, he looked what he was—an imp in the train of Mephistopheles working subversively on the side of the angels. I soon found that we had more frivolous bonds and lively prejudices in common—the basis of an enduring friendship. He had scarcely begun to tell me of his recent visit to William Randolph Hearst's monumental folly in the hills of San Simeon than we were joined by Sam Goldwyn who, wrapped in a towel and with the nutcracker features of one of Leonardo's grotesques, might have been a subsidiary character from Raphael's *School of Athens*.

Not long before, Goldwyn had insinuated himself, sponsored no doubt by Joe Schenck, into the bosom of the United Artists. This was no mean achievement, for earlier in her career Mary had taught him an overdue lesson in good manners. Douglas and Charlie were by nature antipathetic to the hierarchy of the industry he represented. In fact, Goldwyn had done much to raise the level of its products. His flair for detecting and assembling talents resulted in some of the most entertaining and distinguished films of that period. His promotion was instinctive, for he had no cultural pretensions; his malapropisms (though they were often used as pegs for others to hang their wit on) are legendary. For all this I, and apparently his associates, did not find him agreeable company. He did not disguise a resentful arrogance toward the artists on whom his self-expression depended ....

Chattering away to Charlie, I was unaware of Goldwyn's eminence or of the mischief afoot for his discomfiture. Word had got around that though such excessive ablutions were not to his taste, he suspected that in the steam bath business confidences were exchanged in the sweat of his colleagues' brows and that, in his own interest, he should join the perspiring elite. This particular intrusion of commerce into what might be called a boiling of friends was not to be endured. Suddenly the light went out, the steam was turned full on, and the stygian suffocating darkness was rent with three tremendous explosions that set my eardrums ringing. When the lights went up, Goldwyn had vanished. Charlie, smiling inscrutably, seemed unperturbed. He had been, of course, party to the plot; his hand was on the steam valve, and one of Douglas's trainers had switched off the lights while another fired three blank cartridges from a revolver. Goldwyn rarely returned. The baths were safe for "thermocracy."

* * * *

When Maurice Leloir and Leon Barry arrived, we set up our ménage in Andalusia. We shared a large sitting room and the services of a matronly Madame Vinard, though no Trilby was forthcoming to be our model *mascotte*. Leloir appeared to be frail for the change in environment and strenuous work that lay ahead of us. Noting his bow legs and that he was evidently no horseman, I attributed them, thanks to my early indoctrination in infant maladies, to rickets. My diagnosis was confirmed when he told me that, during the commune of 1871, as he lay, a weakened and emaciated youth, in his garret room in Paris, a communist press-gang searching for recruits to man the barricades took one look at the recumbent skeletal figure, decided he was dead, pulled the sheet over his face, and left him in peace. Yet his strong white hair *en brosse* should have told me that his frailty was deceptive, for mentally and physically he proved to be as alert and vigorous as the best of us.

Leloir spoke only his native tongue, but so slowly and with such simplicity of phrase that, helped out by Barry's workaday stage-English, my halting French did not hinder our mutual understanding. He was an uncompromising Parisian, making no concessions during his first absence from his beloved city. He crossed the Atlantic in *La France*, and in Hollywood patronized only one restaurant known as Musso Frank's, which had some resemblance to French cuisine. I could not have had two more charming, courteous, and good-humoured companions to live with in such close intimacy for our long spell of exile.

* * * *

Such was the background to my working days and indeed to my waking hours, for soon I was totally committed to rekindling the splendor of *Le Roi Soleil* and to furnishing the daily adventures and misadventures of D'Artagnan and the Three Musketeers. Only those who have given months of their lives to making a motion picture can understand this prolonged absorption in a task that, however frivolous and ephemeral it may seem to wiseacres, depends for its success on the loyal and attentive cooperation of the humblest member of the unit engaged on it. The fact that Douglas was reinvesting a million of the dollars he had earned as an actor-producer in the art he served was, to one of my ancestry and upbringing, an imperative challenge to do the best I could for him.

After The Iron Mask *was completed, Fairbanks asked Laurence Irving to stay on in Hollywood. Irving said yes, on the condition that his family was brought over from England. Fairbanks agreed, and Irving went on to supervise the sets for* The Taming of the Shrew, *Fairbanks's first talkie, and the only film in which Fairbanks and Mary Pickford starred together. Irving witnessed the difficult transition from silent to talking films, and appreciated the opportunities and experiences Hollywood afforded him, but he missed England. Irving and his family returned there in the 1930s, and he became an acclaimed set designer for the stage. He served in the Intelligence Department of the Royal Air Force during World War II and later wrote a biography of his grandfather, Sir Henry Irving.*

Laurence Irving died in Kent, England, on October 23, 1988, at the age of ninety-one.

Maurice Leloir 1928

M aurice Leloir was born in Paris on November 1, 1851, to a family of successful artists. His mother, Héloïse Colin, was a watercolorist and his father, Jean-Baptiste Auguste, with whom he trained, specialized in historical paintings.

Maurice went on to become a celebrated painter, designer, illustrator, and social historian. His paintings illustrated books and he designed theater sets for Sarah Bernhardt. He was also recognized as an expert in historical costumes, which is why Douglas Fairbanks came calling at Leloir's Paris home.

Fairbanks had already brought on Laurence Irving to design the sets for The Iron Mask, the movie the actor was producing and slated to star in. Now, Fairbanks wanted to hire Leloir to be the studio's "artistic director," supervising the sets and costumes for historical accuracy. Fairbanks thought Leloir had been a friend of Alexandre Dumas, père, and had illustrated his novel The Man in the Iron Mask, on which the film was based. Leloir explained that, no, the book had been published before he was born and he had not known Dumas, although he had been a friend of his son.

Undisturbed by the correction, Fairbanks pleaded with Leloir to join him in Hollywood. At first the seventy-five-year-old Leloir, who had never been outside France, thought the idea absurd, but as Irving had been charmed in London, so Leloir was in Paris. He found Fairbanks to be "a devil of a man with his candid and merry eyes, his captivating smile, his air so good and energetic! In short, on the 20th of June, the Ile de France cast off from Le Havre and twelve days later, I was going to spend five months in Hollywood."

A voyage on the Ile de France is a wonderful cruise. The extravagant luxury of this ship would be a marvel even without the decorative paintings and the ultra-modern sculptures. One look at them, in spite of the stability of the boat, is capable of provoking sea sickness.

The trip across the country is less amusing. One has the time to admire the Hudson River, to view Lake Erie, and then stop in Chicago on Lake Michigan, which would be able to contain the whole of England. Everywhere we [Leloir was traveling with his nephew] were welcomed and entertained, pampered and guided by the representatives of United Artists.

From Chicago to Los Angeles, one could pass the four days in the Pullman coach more cheerfully if the landscapes were less monotonous. This eternal flat desert, uniform, without water, without vegetation, of a dirty grey color, rarely showed any life. Then in California came the beginning of greenery, the product of irrigation; and one is seized with admiration for those men who had the courage, the stubbornness to come here in the days of old, to these localities in wagons drawn by oxen or mules.

* * * *

Fairbanks had preceded us. He waited for us with his general staff of friends at Pasadena, the last station before Los Angeles. Pasadena seems to be a suburb of millionaires, and Douglas wanted me to make my entrance by this sumptuous road, just as at Paris we debark people of distinction at the Station of the Bois de Boulogne.

One is bewildered by the immensity of Los Angeles, which covers an entire region—really a city populous and crowded, which, like all the American cities, bristles with buildings of the New York style that resemble immense beehives. This city stretches on in a band of greenery over 30 to 40 kilometers as far as the Pacific Ocean. Its huge suburbs have names like Pasadena, Hollywood, Beverly Hills, Venice, Long Beach. From the port of San Pedro one can embark for Europe, going either via China or via Panama.

Hollywood itself has a center of luxury, a boulevard with big department stores, and a few large buildings. The homes in Hollywood, except on the boulevard, are not adjoining, but in some spots are widely scattered. Most of them look like the pretty little cardboard buildings for children. This aspect is not misleading, because it is really cardboard that is the foundation of construction as it is for the sets for the cinema. It does not last more than 10 years and then only thanks to the climate. One knocks down this castle of cards and one makes another, that is all.

These bungalows are, in general, composed of the ground floor, only topped sometimes by another floor, rarely by two. All modern comforts

Maurice Leloir reviews the ladies' costumes for *The Iron Mask* and approves their curtsies. (Courtesy of John Tibbetts)

are installed in them, bathrooms, electricity. The red tiles, the green roofs combined with the white or colored wall, create some gay notes in the greenery, oleanders, roses, banana trees, palms, mimosas and eucalyptus. They are always properly maintained against a background of lawns that are always green and copiously watered, to which one gives a "shave" in the morning with the lawn mover. The sidewalks are paved in cement and extend along the wide avenues or boulevards laid out in a clean checker board. As far as the eye can see, there are lines of ultra-fast autos, some busses or streetcars, and no pedestrians. Everyone, because of the spread of the town, is obliged to have his auto, from the millionaire to the workman and the domestic servant. A colored maid arrives in her car in the morning to do your housework.

There are almost as many streets, avenues, promenades and paths on Hollywood Boulevard as on our Parisian boulevards. When the shops close around 6:30, they leave their display windows well lit until late in the evening. After dinner you go for a walk along the Boulevard. Usually, when we come out of the French restaurant Musso and Frank, we walk along smoking our cigarettes and look at the shop windows.

Sometimes there would be an extraordinary excitement on the day of a movie premier. When a new film was announced for the Egyptian Theater, the Grauman's Chinese Theater or Warner Bros., it turned into a madness. Alongside the two sidewalks of Hollywood Boulevard from place to place the roaring electrical generators are stationed, setting in motion a host of revolving beacons that stand every 100 feet. Behind the city, the mountains are adorned with the same. The mob crowds in to see once again the stars and leading men and women in full evening dress spill out of their superb autos in front of the theater, bright with photographic and radio equipment. All is covered by the dome of a splendid starry sky. It's a land gay, stylish, neat and comfortable. Maybe a Frenchman would miss the Parisian streets, winding all askew and making the distances seem shorter. Even the occasional untidiness is picturesque!

Everything here is enormous, colossal. At Los Angeles the stadium for football is immense. Every Saturday the 80,000 seats are reserved in advance and those still in their homes remain glued to their radios during the game listening anxiously to the account of the different periods of the match and the final result.

In the mountains behind Hollywood there is held, in the summer, an extraordinary concert in the "Bowl," which is named because of the disposition of the surrounding mountains. It is located at the bottom of a depressed valley shaped as a bowl; and between three high hills there is built a stand, shaped like a half-moon, for the orchestra. From there to the top of the hill, planks form benches than can hold 25,000 spectators. At the hour ordered, 9 in the evening, all the lights are extinguished. Only the orchestra is lighted. Looking from above, the 150 musicians appear the size of ants. In the midst of an absolute silence, under the light of the moon, the excellent artists execute the works of which nothing is lost; the most delicate sounds of the violin or of the flute are equally heard from anywhere. Every Saturday evening thousands of autos, tramways and busses bring to this spot a multitude struggling to find places to sit.

When we think that this group of cities is the work of only a few years, the result of a gigantic effort of these chaps who have created all this out of the total desert, one is filled with admiration and respect.

In Hollywood, life is very comfortable. Certainly the beauty and mildness of the climate exert an influence on the residents. One lives here very free and without embarrassment. The heat apologizes for the appearance. Clothes and shoes are made of cloth; there is no waistcoat, and often not even a jacket. One goes to and fro, very comfortably, on the boulevard, in shirt-sleeves, the collar open, the head bare. Most Californians have the top of their heads as bronzed as their faces and their arms. I do not know how their scalps can withstand a sun which is sometimes over 90 degrees in the shade! It is a coquetry of the two sexes to be scorched by the rays of the sun. On Sundays at Long Beach at the edge of the Pacific, one sees a real ant hill of men and women, almost nude, stretched out flat on the sand and cooking all day under an implacable sun. Furthermore, however much it is considered as the utmost indecency to be seen in pajamas, it seems entirely natural that in an open car one travels the 20 miles separating Hollywood and the beach wearing at most just a tiny bathing suit. Here, in America, almost all the young women are pretty, and, thanks to sports, admirably built. It is not the artist who is going to complain!

Maurice Leloir's joie de vivre comes through on every page of his book, Five Months in Hollywood with Douglas Fairbanks. *If it reads like a wide-eyed love letter to America and Hollywood filmmaking, that was the author's intention: Leloir wrote it hoping to pierce the prejudices he believed many of his fellow French held against Americans.*

Leloir's works are in many international museums, including the Metropolitan Museum of Art in New York. The two thousand costumes he donated to the Musée Carnavalet in Paris formed the basis for their extensive collection. Maurice Leloir died in Paris on October 7, 1940, at the age of eighty-eight.

Ralph Winters 1928

R alph Winters was born in Toronto on June 17, 1909. His father, Sam,
was a Brooklyn-born tailor, barely earning enough to support his family.
They moved to Montreal and Philadelphia, where nine-year-old Ralph caught a
respiratory disease, and doctors recommended he be taken to a warm, dry climate.
Sam Winters's little tailor shop was not enough to keep the family on the East
Coast, so in 1918, they moved to San Bernardino, California, where Ralph's aunt
and uncle lived.

[Four years earlier] Marcus Loew, the owner of Metro Pictures, had
bought Goldwyn Pictures, creating Metro-Goldwyn Studios. Loew then
bought Louis B. Mayer Productions and hired Mayer to head the new
studio. Within a few weeks of the merger, Loew agreed to add Mayer's
surname to the title and—out of those mergers—a new film company was
born: Metro-Goldwyn-Mayer.

A wonderful alliteration that was to become famous.

Within two years of the merger, M-G-M was flowering. Its slogan was
"More Stars Than There Are in Heaven." It was true. Almost every big
star in the industry was eventually under contract to M-G-M: Norma
Shearer, Clark Gable, Greta Garbo, Robert Taylor, Elizabeth Taylor,
Spencer Tracy, James Stewart, Joan Crawford, July Garland, Robert
Montgomery, and many more.

At its height, M-G-M employed twenty-five hundred people and had a
weekly payroll of a million dollars. It had ninety writers under contract,
and so many directors they had to have their own building. Everything
that was necessary for the making of a movie, M-G-M had on its Culver
City lot; its own wardrobe department, filled with countless costumes of
every period, a construction department, a machine shop, a paint shop, a

carpentry shop, an art department, a casting department, a building half the size of an airplane hangar to hold props, and on and on.

* * * *

So how did the son of a poor Jewish tailor come into this great industry just a moment in time before *Metro-Goldwyn-Mayer* and the rest of the motion picture industry flowered?

My mother's uncle, Jake Levy, played pinochle with a guy by the name of Jerry Mayer, who happened to be the brother of Louis B. Mayer. Now these two guys—Jerry and Louie—also happened to be mad at one another. Jerry was opening a fancy tailoring shop on the second floor of some fancy building on Hollywood Boulevard. In spite of the anger that existed between the two brothers, Louie furnished the new tailoring shop with all the rococo furniture, props, and drapes from *The Merry Widow* picture. Uncle Jake got Jerry and my Dad together and Dad went to work for Jerry in the fancy tailoring shop. Everything was going along fine until the following Passover when Jerry and Louis were at a Seder together and made up. Jerry gave up the fancy tailoring shop and went to work at M-G-M. And bingo! Dad was brought to M-G-M to work in their wardrobe department. Lucky M-G-M!

Dad worked hand in glove with Adrian, the world-famous costume designer who was under contract to M-G-M, and who designed exclusively for all the stars, men and women. My father was always quiet, respectful, and capable, and everyone called him "Sammie." Everyone except Greta Garbo, who called him "Saum." At that time, Garbo was the most glamorous, mysterious, and aloof movie star of all filmdom and her name a household word around the world. Though Garbo guarded her privacy in the extreme, she was always relaxed and jovial when she came to the wardrobe for a fitting. In fact, Garbo was very fond of Dad and loved to banter with him.

Garbo would put on her costume in the privacy of her dressing room, then come out into the fitting room where Dad was waiting with his pins and needles. My father was a very shy guy, but a tailor has to use his hands when doing a fitting, and Dad could tell that she was naked under her costume. As he molded the cloth to her body, he would turn beet red. Then Garbo would tease him, asking in her very sultry voice, "What's the matter, Saum?"

* * * *

By the time I was eighteen, Dad could occasionally get me a job as an extra. I

MGM Studios. (Collection of Patt Morrison)

was an extra in *The Trail of '98*, a silent movie starring Dolores Del Rio and Ralph Forbes. I played a sailor in a picture called *Valencia* starring Mae Murray. It was worth playing hooky from high school; the pay was three bucks a day—not too shabby. Hey, you could get a lot of mileage out of three bucks in 1927. A guy could take his girl out to dinner on three bucks. I always gave my mother two dollars and kept a buck for spending money.

The following year, when I turned eighteen and was ready to graduate high school, my family could not afford to send me to college. The only way I could have attended college was to work my way through, and I didn't think I could get the best education that way. Besides, the picture business was already in my blood. By now, the Winters family was living in Culver City.

The wardrobe department where my dad worked was just across the studio street from the editorial department's building. On the other side of our building was a big stage. The path between our building and the stage was known as "cutting alley."

Dad decided that I should have a job in the editorial department on my way to being made the head of the studio. He acquainted himself with the head of editorial, Danny Gray, a tough little Irishman who hailed from New York and spoke Brooklynese—"film" was pronounced "fillum."

Danny was a short fellow with auburn hair and a rather large, crooked nose that was etched with hills and dales, but I was in complete awe of this imposing figure of a man. Dad made Danny a couple of suits and *voilà*, I had a job.

At first, the job was not at the studio but in the laboratory where the film was developed. The lab was Consolidated Film Industries on Melrose Avenue in Hollywood, and we lived in Culver City, ten miles away. My shift was from eight o'clock in the evening until four o'clock in the morning. Eight o'clock in the evening? Yep! It was scary. During the first week, I thumbed a ride to work and thumbed a ride home every evening. Then Dad bought a 1923 Chevy, with no top and a cone clutch for fifty bucks. He probably found it in some cave. Every time I let the clutch out, the car jumped about twenty feet. But it got me back and forth.

I was assigned to work in the drying room. Picture three long glass boxes, each about four feet in width, fifteen feet long, standing from ceiling to floor. The wet film enters the box through a slot at one end, goes over rollers, which carry the film through the box while hot air is blown through the box, and comes out the other end dry. It arrives on reels that hold a thousand feet, which is the industry standard. All three machines going at the same time. When the reel fills up, you better be there to break the film and catch the loose end coming out of the machine, and start a new reel. These three machines never stopped and they used to really keep me hopping. I felt like Charlie Chaplin working in the factory in *Modern Times*.

I got one day off a week. From my salary of eighteen dollars a week, I gave my mother fifteen and kept three. That job only lasted three months, thank goodness. I was laid off when work became slow due to the tax season. Every year, every piece of picture negative left in the state of California after March 15th was taxed. It was therefore incumbent on picture studios to ship all the negatives of unfinished and finished pictures out of the state by that date because the tax was quite heavy. On an ordinary run-of-the-mill movie that cost $500,000 to make, the tax could be as much as $25,000. (Later, much later, Governor Ronald Reagan abolished this tax. What a boon to the motion picture industry.)

I was hoping and praying to get a job at M-G-M, and in April 1928, Danny Gray hired me as an assistant editor at the studio. Hallelujah!

Now little Ralphie began to swim in the vast ocean that was M-G-M.

* * * *

I didn't know a sprocket hole on a piece of film from a hole in the ground, but I was getting twenty-five bucks a week. Hey, I was a king!

Best of all, I got to see my dad. Because film was flammable, I had to step out of the cutting room whenever I wanted to smoke. I would run over to the wardrobe department for a quick few minutes to chat with my father. I will cherish those wonderful moments forever.

On his first day at work, Ralphie was going to get his first major lesson, and I can honestly say that it burned into him like a doggie getting branded.

I was made the assistant editor on a silent picture entitled *Four Walls*, a prison story starring Joan Crawford and John Gilbert. My editor was Harry Reynolds, a wiry little guy with a sharp nose and a lean look. He had small, brown, flinty eyes and straight brown hair.

One of my jobs was to carry the film from the cutting room to the projection room and back to the cutting room. For some reason, film editors never carried film. This was an unwritten law—you know, like only seniors in high school could wear corduroy pants. It looked pretty funny to see some poor assistant editor staggering along with a load of film in his arms while the editor walked along beside him, empty-handed.

On the morning of that first day, we were showing the rushes, or "dailies" as they are called now, to the producer of the movie, a white-haired gentleman by the name of Harry Rapf. Mr. Rapf became upset because he thought Joan Crawford's gown was cut too low—too décolleté. In today's world, the picture would get a PG rating, but this was the era of Will Hays, the censor czar of moviedom, and censorship was very tough. Mr. Rapf wanted the scene retaken.

"Throw this stuff out," Rapf said. "It's no good."

Being Mr. Eager Beaver, I grabbed the two reels of film, ran out of the projection booth, and rushed back to the cutting room. Our cutting room was on the second floor of the cutting room building. Outside, at the end of a narrow balcony, was a giant, empty trash can into which I threw the film. At four o'clock in the afternoon, Harry Reynolds turned to me and said, "Take the rushes back to the projection room. Mr. Mayer is anxious to see them."

Louis B. Mayer, the head of the biggest movie studio in the world, wanted to see the rushes? Suddenly, I felt like a giant mass of Jell-O. "I threw them out like Mr. Rapf told us to do," I answered, my voice quivering.

My boss went white. "Find them!" he snarled.

I took off like a wounded deer. I clattered down the narrow balcony. I tore the lid off the ash can, which was about three-quarters full of all kinds of junk, and dove into the can headfirst. I dug through sawdust and other bits of trash to the very bottom, and there, thank God, were my dirty but precious rushes. I blew most of the dirt off, and triumphantly carried the two reels to the projection room.

Unbeknownst to me, positive film was never physically thrown away. Although a new print could be made from the negative, which was stored in a vault, every piece of positive film—good and bad—was kept in the cutting room until the picture was finished.

Harry Reynolds certainly should have killed me and I think he wanted to. He was a mean bastard and a hard taskmaster who kept me on edge constantly. He was always very tense and uptight. He was really tough. Later in my career, as I looked back, I realized that he was the hardest man I ever worked for. Maybe that was good.

Once he told me to find a piece of a scene that he needed. This piece came from the middle of a scene that had been put in and taken out of the picture a couple of times already. I hunted high and low through dozens of scenes. No luck. At the end of the day, he said, "When I come in tomorrow morning, I want to see that piece of film on my bench."

I stayed at the studio all night, going through every scrap of film in the cutting room. It was lost! Panic!! It was now 6 a.m. and time was running out on me.

Down to the negative vaults I raced to see Jerry, a woman with thick muscular arms and slicked-back, dark brown hair. She was a great lady and a good friend. Jerry was in charge of a small vault that took care of the negatives of all the movies during their first week of shooting before they went into their permanent places in the main negative vaults. Jerry located the negative of the scene, ran it over to the lab, and had a print made for me.

I placed the film, a whole new print of the scene Reynolds wanted, on his bench. Of course, when he came to work that morning, he figured out exactly what had happened. But he just looked at me and never said a word.

Sometimes, when the director overruled the editor, the assistant editor got caught in the middle. William Nigh, the director of *Four Walls*, walked into the cutting room one day when Reynolds was out. Nigh, a long, slim drink of water and a nice guy, wanted a change made in the picture. He asked me to make the cut, but I was scared to death. I wound the reel down to the place he was talking about and he made the cut. Cut? Hell, in the old days, the editor or the director took the film between thumb and forefinger and just snapped it. Only sissies used scissors. Sometimes the "snap" would rip through two or three frames of film. Then, when the film was spiced, those torn frames would be lost. Later, when sound came in, the film had to be cut very carefully. The picture and the soundtrack had to be kept to the same length in order to hold sync. In the *real* old days—when "moving pictures" first started—they never even made positive prints. They never had editors. They just cut the negative to what length they thought was correct and made release prints from the negative.

When Reynolds came back to the cutting room, he gave me hell for allowing Nigh to touch the film.

When you're on a movie lot, anything can happen. One day, while walking on the lot, I saw this gorgeous woman who seemed to be looking for something on the ground. It was Joan Crawford. Joan Crawford was the most beautiful woman I had ever laid eyes on. She had just become engaged to marry Douglas Fairbanks, Jr. I asked her if anything was the matter.

"I dropped the diamond ring Doug just gave me," she said. "And if I lose it, he'll kill me."

I fell to my knees like a plummet and helped her search for the ring until we found it. She thanked me profusely.

These were still the days of silent movies. After a picture was cut together, titles were written and spiced into the film. You could change a whole story using different titles. At M-G-M, there were a group of writers who worked with the directors and producers on the titles, which were essential to the picture.

On the day of a sneak preview, there was always a batch of new titles to be cut into the picture. These usually came from the lab late in the day because producers and title writers worked on new ideas up to the last moment before the preview deadline. The editor would put the new titles into the picture using paper clips, and then the reels would be turned over to the assistant editors who in turn would take out the paper clips and splice the title and picture together. In those days, splices were made by hand. The assistant editor scraped the emulsion off at the frame line with a razor blade, applied film cement to the scraped-off part and laid the next piece of film on the scraped-off film. It was pretty primitive. All the assistants to all the editors were called in to help splice these titles into the picture, and I was one of those called in to splice. Actually, the quality of an assistant was judged on how good his splices were and how fast he could make them.

One day, Louis B. Mayer called a meeting of the editorial department. Gee! It wasn't often that the big boss came around. We convened in the open space outside "cutting alley" in front of the Washington Street bathroom.

"We're going to make 'talkies,'" he announced to the thirty-five editors and assistants gathered before him.

This was an exciting proposition, but then he asked, "How are you going to cut them?"

Danny Gray got up and said, "Mr. Mayer, if you can shoot them, we can cut them." Danny had a lot of nerve, as no one in the entire editorial department had a clue as to how the job could be done. At the same time, we did our editing on a Moviola. A Moviola is a piece of machinery that you can view a piece of film through. Picture a shoe box that holds a shoe, size thirteen EEE, standing on end, slightly tilted forward with a magnifying glass at the top. Inside the box is a motor driven by a foot pedal, much like the one that would run a sewing machine. It would be small enough to sit on one's desk.

Now to make a sound Moviola: the silent Moviola was set on a little table the size of a typewriter stand. Next to the Moviola, they set a contraption that sound tracks run through. It was interlocked with the picture Moviola so they would run together and stay synchronized.

During this time we had the use of just one sound Moviola for the entire cutting department. I can still see the editors lined up waiting for their turns to use it. Meanwhile, the machine shop was working feverishly to convert the other silent Moviolas to sound. The whole department worked on the challenge every night for many weeks. Trial and error, trial and error. But the job finally did get done. All the major studios, including M-G-M, made their own sound equipment. Everything was bastardized. It took years before any kind of standard equipment was in use.

Ralph Winters went on to become a two-time Academy Award–winning editor, for King Solomon's Mines *(1950) and* Ben-Hur *(1959), for which the chariot race alone took three months to edit. He was also nominated for* Quo Vadis *(1951),*

Seven Brides for Seven Brothers *(1954),* The Great Race *(1965), and* Kotch *(1971). He is credited with editing over seventy films, covering every conceivable genre, ten of which were for the director Blake Edwards, including* The Pink Panther *(1963),* A Shot in the Dark *(1964), and* Victor Victoria *(1982). Winters was elected president of the Motion Picture Editors Guild in 1965 and 1966 and served on its board of directors for twenty years. He was also, according to those who worked with him, a genuinely nice guy. His final film credit was for* Cutthroat Island *in 1995.*

After almost seventy years in the business, Winters contrasted the time he started to that of when he left: "Your Mayers and your Laemmles and the old time directors grew up with film. And they loved film. Today they love money." Winters had five daughters with his wife Teddy, who died in 1985 after more than forty years of marriage. Winters remarried later in life and left ten grandchildren and four great-grandchildren when he died in Los Angeles on February 26, 2004, at the age of ninety-four.

Noël Coward 1929

Noël Peirce Coward was born on December 16, 1899, in Middlesex, England, into a lower-middle class family. By the age of twelve Noël was already on the stage, and by twenty-five he was an experienced actor and had seen a number of his plays produced. Several of them had been made into films in England by the time Coward visited Hollywood in 1929. Always a magnet for interesting, witty, and idiosyncratic people, Coward was a keen observer of his surroundings.

Looking back over my ten days in Hollywood made me gasp a bit and wish for a little neat brandy. I felt as though I had been whirled through all the side-shows of some gigantic Pleasure Park at breakneck speed. My spiritual legs were wobbly and my impressions confused. Blue-ridged cardboard mountains, painted skies, elaborate grottos peopled with familiar figures: animated figures that moved their arms and legs, got up and sat down, and spoke with remembered voices.

The houses I had visited became indistinguishable in my mind from the built interiors I had seen in the studios. I couldn't remember clearly whether the walls of Jack Gilbert's dining-room had actually risen to a conventional ceiling, or whether they had been sawn off half-way up to make room for scaffolding and spluttering blue arc-lamps.

I remembered an evening with Charlie Chaplin when at one point he played an accordion and at another a pipe-organ, and then suddenly became almost pathologically morose and discussed Sadism, Masochism, Shakespeare and the Infinite.

I remembered a motor drive along flat, straight boulevards with Gloria Swanson, during which we discussed, almost exclusively, dentistry.

I remembered, chaotically, a series of dinner parties, lunch parties, cocktail parties and even breakfast parties. I remembered also playing a

A young and dapper Noël Coward. (Copyright: NC Aventales AG)

game of tennis with Charlie MacArthur somewhere at two in the morning, with wire racquets, in a blaze of artificial moonlight, and watching him, immediately afterwards, plunge fully clothed into an illuminated swimming-pool.

I remembered [actress] Laura Hope Crews appearing unexpectedly from behind a fountain and whispering gently: "Don't be frightened, dear—this—*this*—is Hollywood!"

I had been received with the utmost kindness and hospitality, and I enjoyed every minute of it; it was only now, in quietness, that it seems unreal and inconclusive, as though it hadn't happened at all.

Noël Coward would make many more trips to California over the years, selling many of his plays to Hollywood, including Private Lives, Design for Living, *and* In Which We Serve, *for which he received a special Academy Award for "outstanding production achievement" and was nominated for Best Screenplay. A prolific playwright, songwriter, actor, and diarist, Coward was a fixture in London's West End and on Broadway for years. He was known for his wry, slightly detached humor, which could pierce convention with stiletto accuracy. Coward was knighted by Queen Elizabeth in 1970 and awarded a Tony in 1971 for his contribution to the theater. His unique combination of talents led his friend Lord Mountbatten to conclude: "There are probably greater painters than Noël, greater novelists...greater librettists, greater composers of music, greater singers, greater dancers, greater comedians, greater tragedians, greater stage producers, greater film directors, greater cabaret artists, greater TV stars. If there are, they are twelve different people. Only one man combined all twelve different labels— The Master. Noël Coward." Coward died in Port Maria, Jamaica, on March 26, 1973, at the age of seventy-three.*

Acknowledgments

When Bette Davis was asked if she had advice for young women who wanted to get to Hollywood, she took a drag on her cigarette and drolly responded, "Take Fountain." It remains a great suggestion: Fountain is a street that runs parallel to Sunset and Santa Monica, and Bette was right—it is almost always the fastest way to get to Hollywood Boulevard.

Stories like that make me smile and think about all the fabulous people who have traversed those same roads over the years. And I have often found that my favorite part of the hundreds of books I have read on film history, for work and pleasure, is the story of someone's arrival in Hollywood. There is an innocence, excitement, and sense of possibility that is infectious, and it reminds me that everyone, including the greats, struggled to find their place in the world.

So when Bob Wallace, with whom I serve on the PEN Center USA board of directors, approached me about doing a book for his publishing company, this anthology emerged (I am sure that more than a few glasses of wine were also involved). What started out as a project I thought would take a month or two ended up consuming much of the last year and a half, but in the process, Bob has become a great friend, raising the bar at every turn. Best of all, we have laughed a lot.

Many others played key roles in the making of this book. First and foremost was Sharon Cornelius. In October 2013, I was speaking at a Pepperdine University conference entitled "Women in Hollywood: 100 Years of Negotiating the System." It was inspiring, but the real joy came when my friend Tamara Martin introduced me to Sharon. She was an accomplished organizational-conflict coach, experienced in dealing with high-powered people, but was interested in expanding her knowledge of old Hollywood. When I told her I was in the middle of gathering speeches, oral histories, and portions of manuscripts for this book, she immediately volunteered to help. I assumed her contribution would last a few weeks, but Sharon is still with me and has proved invaluable, not just as a transcriber, but as an editor, sounding board, and most of all, great friend.

As the project started to gel, I reached out to old friends for ideas and assistance, and the response was overwhelming. Patt Morrison, the Emmy Award–winning broadcaster and columnist, offered her collection of historic postcards; and acclaimed novelist and filmmaker Allison Burnett lugged over half a dozen binders holding a small portion of his incredible collection of old Los Angeles photographs.

Much time and great care has been given to ascertain and locate rights holders for material in this book and we are particularly grateful for the assistance and generosity of the following people who played pivotal roles in helping us with clearances and permissions. For Frances Marion, Richard Thomson; for Harold Lloyd, Suzanne Lloyd; for Karl Brown, Kevin Brownlow and Julia Brownlow; for Raoul Walsh, Hank Kilgore; for Anita Loos, Mary Anita Loos and Angela Shanahan; for Gloria Swanson, Michelle Aman; for Colleen Moore, Judith Colemen; for Sam Jaffe, Judy Silber; for Mary Astor, Marylyn Roh; for Norma Shearer, Mark Vieira; for Ben Hecht, Kristine A. Somerville; for Maurice Leloir, John Tibbetts; for Robert Parrish, Kathleen Bottijiliso; and for Ralph Winters, Judy Hanaurer.

Budd Schulberg's excerpt is reprinted by permission of the Miriam Altshuler Literary Agency on behalf of Budd Schulberg, copyright 1981 by Budd Schulberg; Lillian Gish's by permission of Lillian Gish under license by CMG Worldwide, Inc.; Salka Viertel's by permission of Thomas J. Kuhnke on behalf of her estate; Henry King's by permission of the Directors Guild of America; and Noël Coward's by permission of Alan Brodie Representation Ltd. Agnes de Mille's excerpt is reprinted by permission of Harold Ober Associates Incorporated. Copyright 1951, 1952 and renewed 1979, 1980, by Agnes de Mille. *Dance to the Piper* is forthcoming from New York Review Books in November 2015.

Permission to use the material from Laurence Irving, Winfrid Kay Thackrey, Alice Guy Blaché, Sergei Bertensson, Ralph Winters, and Maurice Rapf has been granted by Scarecrow Press. In addition, for their assistance in facilitating these connections, we thank Genevieve Maxwell and Claire Lockhart of the Academy of Motion Pictures Arts and Sciences, Devin Snell and Kathy Garmezy of the Directors Guild, Jennifer Barbee of the Writers Guild as well as Tim Rooks, Larry Mirisch, Edmund R. Rosenkrantz, Brooke Anderson, Kate Brower, Keith Lawrence, and Samantha Barbas. If anyone has been inadvertently omitted or overlooked, acknowledgment will gladly be made in future printings.

One of the joys of living in Los Angeles is that I am near the Academy of Motion Picture Arts and Sciences' Margaret Herrick Library, which I was in and out of over a dozen times for this book. The breadth and depth of its collections are unrivaled, as is its experienced staff, including but hardly limited to Jenny Romero, Faye Thompson, Andrea Battiste, Jonathan Wahl, Matt Severson, and Linda Mehr.

When I had questions, I was helped as always by the generosity of other film historians. A minute detail in the life of Cecil B. DeMille or Norma Talmadge? Mark Vieira responded immediately. Exactly where was Hobart Bosworth filming? Marc Wannamaker knew the answer. Elsie Janis's mother's real name? Lee Morrow was there. A fact about Fatty Arbuckle? Joan Myers and Paul E. Gierucki came through. Others including Jane Bartholomew, Tracey Goessel, Patty Tobias, and all the Daughters of Naldi provided information and encouragement, as did my colleagues at the Mary Pickford Foundation, Elaina Archer and Sloan DeForest.

I am also grateful for and humbled by the support of Peter Jones, Clay Eide, Gail Slamon, Terry Christensen, Jeff Fang, Rosa Ramirez, Drew Foster, Suzanne Lloyd, Karen Johnson, Allan Ellenberger, Karen Shatzken, Henry Stotsenberg, Gary Shoffner, Jimmy Bangley, Bob Birchard, Maggie Renzi, Laura Bickford, Judy Balaban, Nancy Olson Livingston, Felicia Farr Lemmon, James Curtis, Michelle Fuetsch, and the late Kate Mantilini.

Also crucial was the always-generous Kevin Brownlow. Gene Hatcher, whom I first met through Kevin, is the world's expert on all things Ben-Hur, but he is also a meticulous editor, and his time, energy, and giving spirit were very much appreciated. Holly Palance read and reread and, best of all, listened a lot. Sincere thanks as well to copy editor Califia Suntree; Margot Frankel, who was so patient in helping select photos and designing the cover; and Eva Guralnick, who handled the interior design.

And my deep gratitude to my sons, whose unconditional love and support mean everything to me. Five books and almost twenty years ago, I wrote the following dedication to my then very young boys: "To Teo and Jake with the hope that they may know the joy of women as equal partners and the freedom that comes from learning from history." I am so happy for them that those words have come true. They are both in committed, equal partnerships with smart, accomplished women, and their involvement in the world around them inspires me daily.

Sources

Hobart Bosworth, from his lecture "The Development of Motion Pictures in Los Angeles", given on February 26, 1930, at the University of Southern California.

Mrs. D.W. Griffith (Linda Arvidson), from *When the Movies Were Young* (New York: E. P. Dutton, 1925).

Mary Pickford, from *Sunshine and Shadows* (New York: Doubleday, 1955).

Frances Marion, from *Off With Their Heads!* (New York: MacMillan, 1972).

Henry King, from *From Silents to 'Scope* (Los Angeles: Directors Guild of America, 1996).

Harold Lloyd, from *An American Comedy* (New York: Longmans, Green and Co., 1928).

Lillian Gish, from *The Movies, Mr. Griffith, and Me*, with Ann Pinchot (New Jersey: Prentice Hall, 1969).

Karl Brown, from *Adventures with D. W. Griffith*, edited by Kevin Brownlow (New York: Farrar, Straus and Giroux, 1973).

Lionel Barrymore, from *We Barrymores* (New York: Appleton-Century-Crofts, 1951).

Virgil Miller, from *Splinters from Hollywood Tripods: Memoirs of a Cameraman* (New York: Exposition Press, 1964).

Cecil B. DeMille, from *The Autobiography of Cecil B. DeMille* (New Jersey: Prentice Hall, 1959).

Raoul Walsh, from *Each Man in His Time: The Life Story of a Director* (New York: Farrar, Straus and Giroux, 1974).

Anita Loos, from *A Girl Like I* (New York: Viking Press, 1966).

Elsie Janis, from *So Far, So Good!* (New York: E. P. Dutton, 1932).

Marie Dressler, from *Life Story of an Ugly Duckling* (New York: Robert M. McBride & Company, 1924).

Agnes de Mille, from *Dance to the Piper* (Boston: Little Brown, 1951).

King Vidor, from *A Tree is a Tree* (Hollywood: Samuel French Trade, 1981).

DeWolf Hopper, from *Once A Clown, Always a Clown* (New York: Garden City Publishing Co., 1925).

Hedda Hopper, from *From Under My Hat* (New York: Doubleday, 1952).

Evelyn F. Scott, from *When Silents Were Golden* (New York: McGraw-Hill, 1972).

Gloria Swanson, from *Swanson on Swanson* (New York: Random House, 1980).

Colleen Moore, from *Silent Star* (New York: Doubleday, 1968).

Myrna Loy, from *Being and Becoming* (Knopf: New York, 1987).

Budd Schulberg, from *Moving Pictures: Memories of a Hollywood Prince* (New York: Stein and Day, 1981).

Lenore Coffee, from *Storyline: Recollections of a Hollywood Screenwriter* (London: Littlehampton Book Services, 1973).

Alice Guy Blaché, from *The Memoirs of Alice Guy Blaché*, edited by Anthony Slide, translated by Roberta and Simone Blaché (Lanham, Maryland: Scarecrow Press, 1996).

Winfrid Kay Thackrey, from *Member of the Crew* (Lanham, Maryland: Scarecrow Press, 2001).

Sam Jaffe, from his 1992 oral history for the Academy of Motion Picture Arts and Sciences, conducted by Barbara Hall.

W. H. Hays, from *The Memoirs of Will H. Hays* (New York: Doubleday, 1955).

Norma Shearer, from Mark A. Vieira's *Irving Thalberg: Boy Wonder to Producer Prince* (Berkeley, California: University of California Press, 2009).

Mary Astor, from *A Life on Film* (New York: Dell, 1967).

Louella O. Parsons, from *The Gay Illiterate* (New York: Doubleday, 1944).

Valeria Belletti, from *Adventures of a Hollywood Secretary: Her Private Letters from Inside the Studios of the 1920s,* edited and annotated by Cari Beauchamp (Berkeley, California: University of California Press, 2006).

Ben Hecht, from "Lost in Lotus Land: Ben Hecht's Hollywood Letters," which originally appeared in *The Missouri Review,* Volume 32, Number 3 (Fall 2009), as curated by Kristine Somerville and Speer Morgan.

Sergei Bertensson, from *In Hollywood with Nemirovich-Danchenko 1926-1927* (Lanham, Maryland: Scarecrow Press, 2004).

Robert Parrish, from *Growing Up in Hollywood* (New York: Harcourt Brace Jovanovich, 1976).

Maurice Rapf, from *Back Lot: Growing Up with the Movies* (Lanham, Maryland: Scarecrow, 1999).

Salka Viertel, from *The Kindness of Strangers* (New York: Holt Rinehart and Winston, 1969).

Laurence Irving, from *Designing for the Movies: The Memoirs of Laurence Irving* (Lanham, Maryland: Scarecrow, 2005).

Maurice Leloir, from *Five Months in Hollywood with Douglas Fairbanks,* originally published in France in 1929 and translated into English in John C. Tibbetts' and James M. Welsh's *Douglas Fairbanks and the American*

Century (Jackson, Mississippi: University Press of Mississippi, 2014).

Ralph Winters, from *Some Cutting Remarks* (Lanham, Maryland: Scarecrow, 2001).

Noël Coward, from *Present Indicative* (New York: Doubleday, 1937)

Index

"*f*" refers to picture

A

Academy Award
 Astor, Mary, 228
 Barrymore, Lionel Herbert, 60
 Coffee, Lenore, 179
 Coward, Noël Peirce, 302
 Dressler, Marie, 97
 Loy, Myrna, 157
 Miller, Virgil, 62
 Parrish, Robert, 260
 Pickford, Mary, 18
 Schulberg, Budd, 167
 Shearer, Norma, 221
 Winters, Ralph, 298
Academy of Motion Picture Arts and Sciences,
 18, 34
Adams, Constance, 64
Adams, Stella, 3, xf
Adventures with D. W. Griffith (Brown), 56
The Affairs of Anatol, 72
Aimée Semple McPherson's Temple, 269
Airport, 141
Aitken, Harry, 113, 117n1
Aitken, Roy, 117n1
Alexandria Hotel (Hollywood), 9, 41, 58f, 59, 67,
 160f, 163–65, 207f, 209
The Alfred Hitchcock Hour, 47
All the King's Men, 260
Altman, Robert, 47
American Ballet Theater, 104
American Expeditionary Forces, 92
American Film Institute, 39
"America's Sweetheart", 18
Anderson, Broncho Billy (Anderson, Gilbert M.),
 18n1, 135
Anderson, Maxwell, 191

Angels Over Broadway, 246
Anna Christie, 97
Anna Karenina, 275
Ann's an Idiot, 237
"The Anvil Chorus," 22
Aoki, Tsuru, 23
Apfel, Oscar, 64–65, 122–23
Arbuckle, Roscoe Conkling ("Fatty"), 179, 205
Armistice (November 1918), iv
Aronson, Max, 159
Arrougé, Martin, 221
Arto, Florence, 106–7, 108f, 109–10, 112
Assistance League, 212
Assistant Directors' Association, 212
Astor, Mary (Lucille Vasconcellos Langhanke)
 about, 222–28, 224f
 Academy Award, 228
 Barrymore, John, 223, 224f, 225–28
 Barthelmess, Richard, 222
 Beaumont, Harry, 225–26
 Famous Players-Lasky, 222
 Gish, Dorothy, 222
 Griffith, David Wark, 225
 Hollywood, 222
 Holt, Jack, 222
 Langhanke, Mrs., 223, 225
 A Life on Film, 228
 My Story, 228
 Warner Brothers, 223
Astor Theatre (New York), iv
Auguste, Jean-Baptiste, 286
Augustin Daly Company, 1
Ayres, Agnes, 222

B

Babile, Mr., 135
The Bachelor and Grant, 156
Back Pay, vi

Badger, Clarence, 138, 140
Balboa (Newport Beach), 35, 37f
Baldwin, Evelyn, 14
Balshofer, Fred, 6
Bánky, Vilma, 238
Baragona, Tony, 239
Barbary Coast, 79
Barker, Florence, 8
Barker Brothers, 186–87
The Barretts of Wimpole Street, 221
Barrymore, Ethel, 60
Barrymore, Jack, 89
 Janis, Elsie, 89
Barrymore, John
 about, 60, 234
 Astor, Mary, 223, 224f, 225–28
 Bertessson, Sergei, 249, 251–53, 253f, 254
Barrymore, Lionel Herbert
 about, 57–60, 74, 223
 Academy Award, 60
 Biograph Studios, 57
 Griffith, David Wark, 59–60
 Hollywood, 57–60
 Morosco, Oliver, 59
 Wilcox, Daeida, 57–59
 Wilcox, Horace Henderson, 57–59
Barthelmess, Richard, 33, 222
Bathalday Inn (Michigan), 29
The Battle at Elderbush Gulch, 49
Battle of Hearts, 120f, 122
Bauchens, Anne, 176
Bauman, Charles O., 95
Beach, Rex, 176
Beau Brummel, 223
Beaudine, William, 257
Beaumont, Harry, 225–26
Beck, Teddy, 143
Bed of Roses, 197
Beery, Wallace, 133–34, 134f, 136, 141, 257
Beetson, Fred, 207
Behymer, Mr., 153
Belasco, David, 15
Bell, Alphonzo, iii
Bellamy, Madge, 231
Belletti, Tony (Jr.), 239
Belletti, Valeria, 235–39, 237f
Belmont (San Diego), 35
The Beloved Rogue, 249
Ben-Hur, 118, 298
Bennett, Enid, 210
Bennett, Joan, 203
Benny, Jack, 80
Bergerman, Stanley, 264
Bergman, Ingrid, 119

Berman, Pandro, 262
Bernhardt, Sarah, iv, 119, 286
Bernstein, Isadore, 61–62
Bertessson, Sergei
 about, 247–54
 Barrymore, John, 249, 251–53, 253f, 254
 Crosland, Alan, 251
 Fairbanks, Douglas, 253f, 254
 Grauman, Sid, 250f, 252
 Hollywood, 248, 252–54
 Los Angeles, 247, 252
 Menzies, William Cameron, 249
 Moscow Art Theatre, 247, 254
 Nemirovich-Danchenko, Vladimir Ivanovich,
  247–49, 251–54
 Pickford, Mary, 254
 Schenck, Joseph, 247, 249, 251
 United Artists, 247–49, 250f, 251–53
The Best Years of Our Lives, 156
The Better Wife, 169, 173
Betty in Search of a Thrill, 91
The Beverly Hillbillies, 141
Beverly Hills
 de Mille, Agnes George, 104
 Enchanted Hill estate, vii
 Green Acres estate, 39
 Hays, Will, 208
 Jaffe, Sam, 199
 Pickfair estate, vii, 18, 232, 233f, 281–82
 Schulberg, Budd, 160, 165–66
 Thackrey, Winifred Kay, 187
Beverly Hills Hotel, 60, 160f, 165–66, 199
Biblical costumes, v, 85
biblical epics, 72
Biblical sequences, 156
The Big House, 28
The Big Parade, vi, 112
The Big Trail, 80
Bing, Herman, 268–69, 271–73
Biograph, A. B., 22
Biograph Company, 17
Biograph films, 14
"Biograph Special," 8
Biograph Studios (Los Angeles), 41–43, 42f
Biograph Studios (New York City)
 Barrymore, Lionel Herbert, 57
 Brown, Karl, 49
 Gish, Lillian, 40–42, 86
 Griffith, David Wark, i, 5, 13, 49
 Griffith, Mrs. D. W., 5–6, 8–9, 13–14
 Lloyd, Harold, 36
 Loos, Anita, 81–82, 84
 Pickford, Mary, 15–16, 18, 18n1
 Walsh, Raoul, 73–74, 80

Biograph troupe, i, 5–6, 9, 13
The Birth of a Nation, iv, 46, 80, 86, 109, 117n1, 142
Bison brand of pictures, 6
Bison Company, 3
Bitzer, Billy, 8, 12
Brown, Karl, 49, 50f, 52–56
Loos, Anita, 86
Blaché, Herbert, 180–81, 183, 185
Black, Betty, 155
Black Diamond Express, 8
The Black Pirate, 254
Black Sox scandal, 204
Blondeau tavern (Los Angeles), 36
Blue, Monte, 196, 232
The Blue Angel, 275
Bluebeard, 21
Board of Trade, 212
Boardman, Eleanor, 112
Body and Soul, 260
Bogart, Humphrey, 80, 203
Boggs, Francis, 2, 5–6
La Bohème (film), 47
Borries, Joseph, 184
Bosworth, Hobart, 1–4, 91–92, 305, xf
Bosworth's studio, 4, 27
Bow, Clara, 166, 177, 229, 231, 234, 239
Bower, John, 58
Bracken, Bert, 32–33
The Brat, 183
Brecht, Bertolt, 275
Breen, Joseph (Hitler of Hollywood), 216
Brenon, Herbert, 265
Brice, Monty, 257
Brigadoon, 104
Brockway, Les and Ferne, 187, 195
Broken Blossoms, 46
Brotherton, Joseph, 32
Brown, Clarence, 4, 231

Brown, Karl
about, 48–56, 50f
Adventures with D. W. Griffith, 56
Biograph Studios, 49
Bitzer, Billy, 49, 50f, 52–56
Famous Players-Lasky, 56
Griffith, David Wark, 49, 50f, 51–56
Hollywood, 48, 51–56
Kinemacolor, 48–49, 51
Leezer, Johnny, 54–55
Loos, Anita, 87
Wyckoff, Alvin, 54
Brown, Mrs., 147–48
Brown, Ona, 231

Brown, William and Lucille, 48, 51–52
Browning, Elizabeth Barrett, 221
Browning, Tod, 265
Brownlow, Kevin, iv–v, 56
Bruce, Kate, 8
Brunton-United Studio, vi
Burke, Billie, 59
Burke's Law, 141
Burns, L. L., 67–68
Burns, Walter, 149
Bush, Pauline, 62
Bushman, Frances X., 133
Butler, Daddy, 8

C
Cabanne, Christy, 73–75, 77, 80
Cagney, James, 80
Cahuenga Boulevard, 36, 58, 71, 135–36
Cahuenga Indians, 57
"California Here I Come," 254
California Historical Association, 58
California Limited (train), 7fig, 8, 144f, 205, ixf
Campbell, Maurice, 214
Canal & Chaffin, 196
Capra, Frank, 4, 265
Captains Courageous, 60
Carey, Harry, 60
Carmen, 130, 251–52
Carnegie Hall, 87
The Carol Burnett Show, 141
Carousel, 34, 104
Caruso, Enrico, 19
Casey at the Bat, 257
Cast of Killers (Kirkpatrick), 112
Catholic National Legion of Decency, 216
Caylor, Rose, 240
Cervantes, 115–16
Chamber of Commerce (Hollywood), 216
Chamber of Commerce (Los Angeles), 208–9, 214, 216
The Champ, 28, 112
Chandler, Harry, 215
Chaney, Lon (Sr.), 62, 212
Chaplin, Charlie
about, 18, 39, 127, 163, 234, 294
Coffee, Lenore, 172–73
Coward, Noël Peirce, 300
Dressler, Marie, 95–96
Loyal Order of Moose, 210
Parrish, Robert, 255, 256f, 257–60
Walsh, Raoul, 78–79
war bonds, iv, 96
Chaplin, Sidney, 210
Chaplin Studio (La Brea Avenue), 256f, 257

Charles, Nora, 156
Charlie Chan, 62
Chatsworth Park, 46
Chatterton, Ruth, 265
Cherrill, Virginia, 259
Chicago Herald, 229
Chinese Chippendale, 192
Chinese laundry (New York), 2
Chorus Equity Association of America, 96
Christian Science, 183, 280
Christie, Anna, 275
Christie Studios, 210
A Christmas Carol, 60
Cinémathèque Française, 185
circus spieler, 112
The Citadel, 112
City Lights, 255, 258, 260
City of the Queen of the Angels, 19. *See also* Los
    Angeles
Clark, Marguerite, 142
Clayton, Ethel, 212
Coca-Cola Company, 255
The Cocoanut Grove, 170f, 179, 195, 212, 229
Coffee, Lenore
    Academy Award, 179
    Bow, Clara, 177
    Chaplin, Charles, 172–73
    DeMille, Cecil B., 176, 179
    Epstein, Julius J., 179
    Garson, Harry, 169, 171–74
    Garson Studio, 168–69, 173–74
    Glyn, Elinor, 177–78
    Goldwyn, Samuel, 176, 179
    Harris, Mildred, 172–73
    Hollywood, 169, 171, 173–79
    Hollywood Boulevard, 174–76
    Kerrigan, Jack, 171–72
    Lois Weber studio, 172
    Mayer, Louis B., 171–73, 179, 206f
    Parker, Gilbert (Sir), 177
    Sennett, Mack, 174
    Stewart, Anita, 172–73
    vaudeville, 178
    Young, Clara Kimball, 168–69, 171–73
Colin, Héloïse, 286
Collins, James Finlay, 77–78
Colman, Ronald, 34, 236, 238, 241
Columbia film, 203, 266
Common Law, 29
Connery, Jim, 207
Conquest, 275
The Conscientious Citizens, 20
Consolidated Film Industries, 294
The Constipated Citizens, 20–21

Conway, Jack, 192–95
Coogan (Sr.), Jack, 211
Cook, Clyde, 212
Coolidge, Calvin, 204, 255
Cooper, Gary, 239
Cooper-Hewitts, 227
Copland, Aaron, 104
Coquette, 18
Corbett, Jim, 183
The Covered Wagon, 56, 171, 191
Coward, Noël Peirce, i, 300–302, 301f
Cowen, William, 179
Crawford, Joan, 221, 261, 283, 291, 295, 297
Crews, Laura Hope, 302
Crisp, Donald, 60, 74
Crosby, Jimmy, 2
Crosland, Alan, 251
The Crowd, vi, 112, 267
Crucifixion of Christ, 118
Cruze, James, 56, 191
Cryer, George E. (Mayor), 208
Crystal Pier, 179
Culver City
    about, vi, 109, 141, 189, 220
    Loy, Myrna, 150–51, 152f, 153, 155
    Metro-Goldwyn-Mayer, vi, 112, 151, 210,
        220, 232, 291–92
    Pathé, 39, 239
    Ritter School of Expression, 155
    Thomas Ince Studio, vi, 23, 209, 233f
    Winters, Ralph, 291, 293–94
Curtiz, Michael, 4, 156
Custer's Last Stand, 17
Cutthroat Island, 299

D
Dalton, Dorothy, 79
Daly, Augustin, 2
Daniels, Bebe, 231
D'Artagnan, 285
Davies, Marion
    about, vii, 28, 80, 221, 257
    Hearst, William Randolph, 261
    Parsons, Louella Rose, 229, 231, 234
    Santa Monica beach house, 261, 263f, 264
Davis, Bette, 47, 303
Davis, Mildred, 39
de Havilland, Olivia, 80
de Lappe, Wesley, 19
de Longpré, Paul, iii, 13
de Mille, Agnes George
    about, 98–105, 100f
    Beverly Hills, 104
de Mille, Cecil, 98–100, 102, 104

Hollywood, 99–105
Jesse L. Lasky Feature Play Co., 98–99
Lasky, Jesse, 98–99, 101–2
Le Roy, Mervyn, 102
Pickford, Mary, 103
Turnbull, Margaret, 104
de Mille, Anna George, 98–102, 105
de Mille, Beatrice (Bibi), 64, 126–31
de Mille, Cecil, 98–100, 102, 104, 126–27,
  129–32
de Mille, George, 132
de Mille, Henry, 64
de Mille, Margaret, 98, 100
de Mille, Mrs., 69, 71
de Mille, William, 64, 98, 126–27, 129, 141
de Pachmann, Vladimir, 178
de Portola, Gaspar (Governor), 57
Death Valley Days, 56
The Defenders, 47
DeGrasse, Joseph, 62
DeHaven, Carter, 212
Del Rio, Dolores, 231, 293
Del Ruth, Mr., 136–37
Delaguna, Miss, 153
DeMille, Cecil B.
  about, vi, 6, 9, 64–72, 79
  Adams, Constance, 64
  Apfel, Oscar, 64–65
  Belletti, Valeria, 239
  Coffee, Lenore, 176, 179
  father of the Hollywood film, 67
  Gelbfisz, Schmuel, 72n1
  Goldwin (Goldfish), Sam, 64, 68, 72
  Goldwyn Company, 72n1
  Hays, Will Harrison, 209
  Hollywood, 65, 66f, 67–71, 99
  Hollywood Boulevard, 67
  Hopper, Hedda, 118–19
  Jesse L. Lasky Feature Play Company, 64–65,
    66f, 68
  Lasky, Jesse, 64, 68, 72
  Pickford, Mary, 64, 72
  The Squaw Man (play), 64, 66f, 69–72
  Stray, Stella (bookkeeper), 68–69
  Swanson, Gloria, 72
  vaudeville, 64
  The Warrens of Virginia, 15
DeMille, Cecilia, 69, 71–72
DeMille, Constance, 72
DeMille, Richard, 72
DeMille, William, 72
Design for Living, 302
The Detective, 266
DeWolf, Rosalie, 113

DeWolf Jr., 117
Dillingham, Charles, 92
Dinner at Eight, 60, 97
Directors Guild, 34
The Divorcee, 221
Dix, Beulah Marie, 126–32
Dixon, Harland, 246
Don Juan, 228, 251–52
Don Quixote, 115–17, 123
Don't Change Your Husband, 72, 165
Dougherty, T. E., 81–82, 84–85
Douglas Fairbanks studio, 210
Dove, Billie, 231
D'Oyly Carte company, 178
Dr. Gardner's chauffeur, 238
Dr. Jekyll and Mr. Hyde, 223
Dressler, Marie (Leila Maria Koerber), iv,
  93–97, 94f
Drew, Maurice and Georgina, 57
Driscoll, Patty, 79
drugstore cowboys, 175
Duen, Christian, 58
Dumas, Alexandre, 286
Duse, Eleonora, 178–79
Dutch settlers of Manhattan, 1
Dwan, Allan, 210

E
Eastman Kodak, i
Edison, Thomas, i, iii
Edison Trust battles, 1
Edward VII, 280
Edwards, Blake, 299
Egyptian Theatre, vii, 152f, 250f, 252, 289
Eisenstein, Sergei, 276
Ellis Island, v
Emerson, John, 87–88
Enchanted Hill (Beverly Hills estate), vii
Engel, Joseph W., 214
Epstein, Julius J., 179
Essanay (S and A) film company, 18n1, 135,
  139–40, 164
Essanay movie studio, 133
Essanay studio (Chicago), 229
The Eternal Flame, 251
Ettinger, Margaret, 232
European Film Fund, 276
Everyman, 39
Exhibitors Herald, 149

F
A Face in the Crowd, 167
Fairbanks, Beth, 118
Fairbanks, Douglas

Bertessson, Sergei, 253f, 254
Dressler, Marie, 96
Hays, Will, 210
Hooper, DeWolf, 115
Hooper, Hedda, 118, 121
Irving, Laurence, 277, 278f, 279–85
Jaffe, Sam, 199
Janis, Elsie, 89, 92
Leloir, Maurice, 286–87, 290
Loos, Anita, 87
Parrish, Robert, 257
Parsons, Louella, 232, 234
Pickford, Mary, vii, 18, 28
Robin Hood, vii
Thackrey, Winifred Kay, 189
Walsh, Raoul, 80
war bonds, iv, 96
Winters, Ralph, 297
Fairbanks, Douglas (Jr.), 279, 283
Fairbanks Studio, 189, 210
The Falcon, 62
Famous Players, 79
Famous Players-Lasky Studios, 56, 164–65,
    188f, 189, 222. *See also* Lasky, Jesse L.
fan magazines, iv, vii, 142, 147, 229
Fanchon and Marco, 155–56
Farnum, Dustin, 71, 90, 127
Farnum, William (Bill), 32, 118, 121–23
Farrar, Geraldine, 118, 131–32, 163
Farrow, John, 265
FBO Pictures, vi
Feldman, Charlie, 203
Ferdinand, Archduke, v
Feyder, Jacques, 273
Fiddle and I, 211
The Fighting Shepherdess, 173
Fine Arts Studios, 74–75, 77, 130
Fineman, Bernie, 198–202
The Fireman, 127
First National, 198
Fiske, Minnie Maddern, 1
Fitzmaurice, George, 236
Five Months in Hollywood with Douglas Fairbanks
    (Leloir), 290
Flagstaff (Arizona), 64–65, 68
Flagstaff station, 65
Flebbe, George, 126
Fleming, Victor, 221
Flynn, Errol, 80
Fonda, Henry, 33
Forbes, Ralph, 265, 293
Ford, John, 4, 166, 260
Ford Model A, 262
Ford Model T, 262

Four Daughters, 179
Fox, William, 204
Fox Studios, 189, 267
La France, 285
Francis, Alec, 227
Franciscan friars, iii
François Villon: Vagabond Poet, 249
Frank Fay's Show, 92
Franklin, Sidney, 92, 257
Frederick, Faye Thomas, 59
A Free Soul, 60, 221
Frohman, Charles, 96
From the Manger to the Cross, 172
The Front Page, 149, 246
Fuller, De Witt, 273
Furry, Dora, 123
Furry, John, 118, 121

G
Gable, Clark, 80, 156, 291
Gabriel Over the White House, 197
Gandolfi, Al, 69
Ganthony, Richard, 96
Garbo, Greta, 97, 231, 275–76, 291
Garbutt, Frank, 89–92
Garden, Mary, 163
Gardner, Ava, 34
Gardner, Dr., 238
Garland, July, 291
Garson, Harry, 169, 171–74
Garson Studio, 168–69, 173–74
Gaumont, Leon, 180
Gaumont Company (Paris), iii, 180
Genthe, Arnold, 19
Gentlemen Prefer Blondes, 87–88, 104
George, Henry, 98
George V, King, 48–49
Geraghty, Tom, 234
Gigi, 88
Gilbert, Jack, 243, 300
Gilbert, John, 112, 231, 295
A Girl's Folly, v–vi
Gish, Dorothy
    about, 40, 42, 53
    Astor, Mary, 222
    Harron, Robert, 53
    Hollywood, 41–46
    Moore, Colleen, 147
    Walsh, Raoul, 74, 78
Gish, James, 40
Gish, Lillian, 45f
    Biograph Studios, 40–42, 86
    Griffith, David Wark, 40–44, 46
    King, Henry, 33

Marion, Frances, 46–47
Mayer, Louis B., 47
Parker, Dorothy, 146
Parrish, Robert, 257
Pickford, Mary, 40–41, 45f
Sennett, Mack, 41
Walsh, Raoul, 44, 74, 78, 86
Gish, Mary, 40–42
Glyn, Elinor (Madam Glyn), 177–78, 234
Goldschmidt, Max, 270
Goldwyn, Samuel (Goldfish)
  about, 33, 39, 64, 72, 98
  Belletti, Valeria, 235–39
  Coffee, Lenore, 176, 179
  Irving, Laurence, 283–84
Goldwyn Company, 72n1, 112, 164
Goldwyn Pictures, 291
Gone with the Wind, 246
The Good Little Devil, 41
Gore Brothers, 36
Gotham (eatery), 176, 178
Gower Gulch, 174–75
Grand Central Station, 212
Grand Hotel, 60
Grandon, Frank, 8
Grant, Cary, 156
Grauman, Sid
  about, vi–vii, 156, 215, 252
  Bertessson, Sergei, 250f, 252
  Chinese Theater, 289
  Egyptian Theatre, vii, 152f, 250f, 252, 289
  Loy, Myrna, 156, 215
Gray, Danny, 293–94, 298
"A Great Big Little Girl Like Me" (song), 93
The Great Lie, 228
The Great Race, 299
The Great Train Robbery, iv
Green Acres (estate of Harold Lloyd), vii
Green Acres estate (Beverly Hills), 39
Greenwich Village, 87
Griffith, Corinne, 107, 109, 231
Griffith, David Wark (Lawrence Griffith)
  about, i, iv, 50f
  Astor, Mary, 225
  Barrymore, Lionel, 59–60
  Biograph Studios, i, 5, 13, 49
  Brown, Karl, 49, 50f, 51–56
  Gish, Lillian, 40–44, 46
  Griffith, Mrs. D. W., 5, 11–14
  Hollywood, 74–80
  Hooper, DeWolf, 115, 117
  Hooper, Hedda, 119, 122
  Irving, Laurence, 281
  Loos, Anita, 82, 83f, 84–87

Marion, Frances, 22, 24–25
Moore, Colleen, 142–43, 145–46, 148
Parrish, Robert, 257–60
Pickford, Mary, 15–16, 18, 22
Schulberg, Budd, 163
Shearer, Norma, 217
Swanson, Gloria, 135
Vidor, King, 109, 111f
Walsh, Raoul, 74–75, 77, 80
Griffith, Mrs. D. W. (Linda Arvidson)
  about, 5–14
  Biograph Studios, 5–6, 8–9, 13–14
  Hollywood, 6, 7f, 13
  Sennett, Mack, 8, 20
Griffith films, 146
Griffith Studio, 146
Growing Up in Hollywood (Parrish), 260
Guercio, Mr., 274
Guy, Alice Ida Antoinette
  about, iii, 180–85, 182f
  Blaché, Herbert, 180–81, 183, 185
  Légion d'honneur, 185
  Los Angeles, 181, 182f, 183, 185
  Nazimova, 183–84
  Solax Studio, 180, 185
  Weber, Lois, 180
Guy, Simone, 185
Gypsy, 102

H
Hal Roach Studio, 155, 213
Hale, Creighton, 196
Hallelujah, 112
Hamilton, Helene, 29
Hamilton, Neil, 265
Hamlet, 228
Hammer, R. H., 8–9
The Hand That Rocks the Cradle, vi
Happy Birthday, 88
The Harder They Fall, 167
Harding, Warren, 204
Hargrave, Homer, 149
Harlow, Jean, 28
Harper, Glenn, 214
Harris, Elmer, 214
Harris, Mildred, 147, 164, 172–73
Harron, Robert (Bobby), 8, 12, 53, 147
Hart, Betty, 2
Hart, William S., 79, 118, 121, 161, 214
Harvey, Fred, 99, 161
Hattie, 231
Hawks, Howard, 221, 241
Hayakawa, Sessue, 23
Hayes, Frank, 136–38

Hayes, Helen, 88
Hayes, Ralph, 209
Hays, Will Harrison
    about, 204–16, 206f
    Beverly Hills, 208
    California Limited, 205, 207
    Christie, Charles, 208, 210
    DeMille, Cecil B., 209
    Fairbanks, Douglas, 210
    Hal Roach Studio, 213
    Hollywood, 207–8, 210, 213–16
    Hollywood Bowl, 214–15
    Hughes, Howard Rupert, 209, 213
    Ince, Thomas H., 208–9
    Lasky, Jesse L., 205, 207–9, 213–15
    Lehr, Abraham, 207–8
    Mayer, Louis B., 203f
    Metro, 210–12
    MPPDA president, 203
    National Republican Party, 204
    Pickford, Mary, 210
    Roach, Hal, 208, 213
    Schenck , Joseph M., 205, 207–8, 210–11
    Teapot Dome scandal, 204
    Thalberg, Irving, 206f, 208, 214
    Zukor, Adolph, 204
Hayward, Susan, 34
Hayworth, Rita, 80
Hearst, William Randolph
    about, vii, 9, 221, 229
    Davies, Marion, 261
    Irving, Laurence, 283
    Pickford, Mary, 9
Hearst Castle, 234
"Hearts and Flowers," 22
Hecht, Ben
    about, 149, 240–46, 242f
    Chicago Daily Journal, 240
    Goldwyn, Samuel, 241, 244
    MacArthur, Charlie, 240–41, 242f, 243, 245–46
    Mankiewicz, Herman, 240, 245
    Milestone, Lewis, 241
    Oscar, 246
    Selznick, David O., 246
Hecht, Joseph, 240
Hecht, Rosie, 240, 243–46
Hecht, Sarah, 240
Hedda Gabler, 1
Henderson, Dell, 8
Henderson, Mrs. Dell (Lee, Florence), 8
Her Sister from Paris, 251
Hicks, Eleanor, 8
Highland and Sunset, 0f

Hill, Elizabeth, 112
Hill, George, 4
His Girl Friday, 246
His Supreme Moment, 236
Hoellriegel, Arnold, 269–70
Hoffman House, 59
Hoffman's (eaterie), 10
Hollywood (Los Angeles), v, 6
    Astor, Mary, 222
    Barrymore, Lionel Herbert, 57–60
    Belletti, Valeria, 238
    Bertessson, Sergei, 248, 252–54
    Brown, Karl, 48, 51–56
    Coffee, Lenore, 169, 171, 173–79
    Coward, Noël Peirce, 300–302
    de Mille, Agnes George, 99–105
    DeMille, Cecil B., 65, 66f, 67–71, 99
    Dressler, Marie, 94, 97
    Gish, Dorothy, 41–46
    Griffith, David Wark, 74–80
    Griffith, Mrs. D. W., 6, 7f, 13
    Guy, Alice Ida Antoinette, 181, 183–84
    Hays, Will Harrison, 207–8, 210, 213–16
    Hopper, DeWolf, 115–17
    Hopper, Hedda, 118–19, 121–22, 125
    Irving, Laurence, 279–82, 285
    Janis, Elsie, 90–92
    Leloir, Maurice, 286–90
    Lloyd, Harold, 36, 38–39
    Loos, Anita, 82, 83f, 84–87
    Loy, Myrna, 150, 156–57
    Marion, Frances, 28
    Miller, Virgil E., 63
    Moore, Colleen, 143, 145, 147–49
    Parrish, Robert, 255, 260
    Parsons, Louella Rose, 229, 231–32, 234
    Pickford, Mary, 18
    Rapf, Maurice, 261, 265–66
    Schulberg, Budd, 158, 165–66
    Scott, Evelyn, 127–28
    Shearer, Norma, 217, 219–20
    Swanson, Gloria, 135–36
    Thackrey, Winfrid Kay, 186, 189, 193–95, 197
    Vidor, King, 107, 109–12
    Wilcox, Daeida, ii, iii
    Wilcox, Horace Henderson, 36, 57–58
    Wilcox ranch, 58
    Winters, Ralph, 292–98
Hollywood Boulevard (Hollywood)
    in 1910, 0f, 7
    about, 67, 101
    Coffee, Lenore, 174–76
    Cudahy mansion, 231
    de Longpré, Paul, 13

de Mille, Agnes George, 101, 104
in the early teens, 7f
Grauman's Egyptian Theatre, vii, 152f, 250f,
    252, 289
Hollywood Bowl, 215
Jerry and Louis, 292
Josef Schenck mansion, 272
Lasky Studio, 128, 207
Main Street, 174–76
moving-picture unit, 104
promenades and paths, 288
Roosevelt Hotel, 270f
sidewalks, promenades and paths, 288–89
Warner Brothers' new studio, 223
Hollywood Bowl, 214–15, 289
Hollywood Club, 59
Hollywood Doesn't Live Here Anymore (Parrish),
    260
Hollywood grapevine, 67
Hollywood High School (1910), 0f
Hollywood Hotel, 0f, 82, 83f, 87, 125, 176, 183,
    219, 248
Hollywood Inn, 13
Hollywood royalty, 18
Hollywood School for Girls, 104
Holofernes, 49, 56, 86
Holt, Jack, 222
"Home Sweet Home," 23
Hoover, J. Edgar, 125
Hopper, Bill, 121, 125
Hopper, DeWolf
    about, 113–18, 114f
    Aitken, Harry, 113, 117n1
    Crane, William, 121
    Fairbanks, Douglas, 115, 121
    Gilbert and Sullivan, 113
    Griffith, David Wark, 115, 117n1
    Hart, William S., 121
    Hollywood, 115–17
    Sennett, Mack, 115, 117n1
Hopper, E. Mason, 211
Hopper, Hedda (Elda Furry)
    about, 113, 117, 120f, 125, 234
    Apfel, Mrs. Oscar, 122–23
    Apfel, Oscar, 122–23
    Catalina Island, 122–23, 124f
    DeMille, Cecil, 118–19
    Fairbanks, Douglas, 118, 121
    Farnum, William, 118, 121–23
    Farrar, Geraldine, 118–19
    Griffith, David Wark, 119, 122
    Hart, William S., 118, 121
    Hollywood, 118–19, 121–22, 125
    Hopper, DeWolf, 118–19, 121–23, 125

Los Angeles Times Syndicate, 125
    Marion, Frances, 125
Hopper, John, 113
Horkheimers, 33
Horsley, David, 36
Horsley, William, 36
Hotel Ambassador, 212
Hotel Wentworth (Pasadena), 3
House Un-American Activities Committee, 125,
    167
How to Write for the Movies (Parsons), 228
Howey, Walter, 143–44, 147, 149
Hughes, Howard Rupert, 176–77, 209, 213
Hum, Jim, 201–2
The Hunchback of Notre Dame, 62
Hunter's Posing Dogs, 127
Hyde Park Hotel, 277
Hyland, Dick, 243

I
Idiot's Delight, 221
Ile de France, 286
In Old Kentucky, 173
In Which We Serve, 302
Ince, Thomas H.
    about, 79, 117, 130, 151, 232
    Hays, Will Harrison, 208–9
    Loy, Myrna, 155
    Parsons, Louella Rose, 229
    Vidor, King, 106, 109
Inceville (town), 79, 106
Inceville studio, 79, 107, 109
The Informer, 260
Intolerance, 46, 55, 60, 109, 111f, 115, 119, 142,
    147–48
Irving, Dorothea, 277
Irving, Harry, 277
Irving, Henry (Sir), 277
Irving, Laurence
    Barry, Leon, 284–85
    Chaplin, Charlie, 282–83
    Crawford, Joan, 283
    Fairbanks, Douglas, 277, 278f, 279–85
    Goldwyn, Samuel, 283–84
    Griffith, David Wark, 281
    Hearst, William Randolph, 283
    Hollywood, 279–82, 285
    Knoblock, Eddie, 277
    Leloir, Maurice, 284–85
    Pickford, Mary, 277, 278f, 279, 285
    Schenck, Joseph, 283
    Woolner, Rosalind, 277
Isherwood, Christopher, 275
It's a Wonderful Life, 60

J

J. W. Robinson's, 187, 189, 192, 194
Jaffe, Sam
  Beverly Hills, 199
  Fairbanks, Douglas, 199
  Fineman, Bernie, 198–202
  Hum, Jim, 201–2
  Jaffe Agency, 203
  Loeb, Edwin, 201
  Lubitsch, Ernst, 202
  MacDonald, Katherine, 198, 200–201
  Paramount Pictures, 198–99, 202
  Preferred Pictures, 198, 202
  Schulberg, B. P., 198–99, 201–3
  Zeidman, Bennie F., 199
Jaffe Agency, 203
Jahrus, Don, 62
Jahrus, Ed, 62
Janis, Elsie (Elsie Jane Bierbower), 89–92
Jannis, Jenny, 89, 92
Jazz Age, v, 97, 141, 149
The Jazz Singer, 228, 267
Jeffries, Mr., 1
Jesse L. Lasky Feature Play Co. *See also* Lasky,
  Jesse L.
  about, 64, 98–99
  DeMille, Cecil B., 64–65, 68
The Jest, 223
Jewell, Austin, 257–59
Jews, ii, iii
Joan of Arc, 118, 130–31
Joan the Woman, 131
Johanna Enlists, iv
John's all-night restaurant, 175
Johnson, Arthur, 8
Johnson, Effie, 11
Jolson, Al, viii, 267
Jones, Jennifer, 203
Jones, Shirley, 34
Joy, Leatrice, ii
Judith (play), 276n1
Judith of Bethulia, 46, 49, 59, 85–86
Julius Caesar, 123

K

The Kaiser—The Beast of Berlin, iv
Kaufman, George, 197, 228
Keaton, Buster, 39, 212
Kennedy, John F., 157
Kennedy, Joseph P., 141
Kerr, Deborah, 276
Kerrigan, Jack, 171–72
Keystone Cops, 16, 79, 174
Keystone studio (Edendale), 79, 136, 138, 140–41

The Kindness of Strangers, 276
Kinemacolor Company, 48–49, 51
Kinetoscope, iii
King, Henry, 31f, 33–34
King of Kings, 72
King of Spain, 19, 57
King Solomon's Mines, 298
Kingston, Winifred, 71
Kirkpatrick, Sidney, 112
Kleine, George, iv
Klieg lights, 175, 228
Knobloch, Edward, 177, 277
Koenig, Bill, 265
Kohner, Paul, 196
Kotch, 299

L

La Cava, Gregory, 197
Lady Godiva, 117
Laemmle, Carl, 221, 264
Laemmle, Rosabelle, 221, 264
The Lamb, 115
Langhanke, Mrs., 223, 225
Langhanke, Otto, 225
Langner, Lawrence, 235, 238
Lasky, Jesse L. *See also* Famous Players-Lasky
  Studios; Jesse L. Lasky Feature Play Co.
  about, 18, 79, 130, 202, 213
  de Mille, Agnes George, 98–99, 101–2
  DeMille, Cecil B., 64, 68, 72
  Hays, Will Harrison, 205, 207–9, 213–15
  Lasky Studio, 174, 189, 191
The Last Command, 275
The Last of Mrs. Cheyney, 221
Le Roy, Mervyn, 102
Lee, Florence (Mrs. Dell Henderson), 8
Lee, Lila, 166
Leezer, Johnny, 54–55
Lehr, Abraham, 207–8, 236
Leloir, Maurice, 286–90, 288f
Lena and the Geese, 40
Lennon, Bert, 155
Lennon sisters, 155
Leonard, Bob, 265
Leonard, Marion, 8
Leonard, Miss, 13
Lesser, Sol, 211, 214
LeSueur, Lucille, 261
Let Us Be Gay, 221
Levee, Mike, 214
Levy, Jake, 292
Levy's Tavern (Spring Street), 78
A Life on Film (Astor), 228
The Lightning Conductor, 127
Little, Tommy, 189, 191–92

The Little American, 72
Little Annie Rooney, 254
The Little Princess, 18, 28
Little Women, 102, 228
Lloyd, Fran, 214
Lloyd, Gaylord, 35
Lloyd, Harold, vii, 35–39, 37f
Loeb, Edwin, 201
Loeb, Joseph P., 235–36
Loew, Marcus, 291
Lois Weber studio, 172
London, Jack, 4, 19
London's West End, 302
Lonesome Luke, 37f
Looney Tunes, 265
Loos, Anita
  about, vii, 81–88, 83f
  Biograph Studios, 81–82, 84
  Brown, Karl, 87
  Dougherty, T. E., 81–82, 84–85
  Emerson, John, 87–88
  Fairbanks, Douglas, 87
  Griffith, David Wark, 82, 83f, 84–87
  Hollywood, 82, 83f, 84–87
  Hollywood Hotel, 82, 83f, 87
  M-G-M, 88
  Pickford, Mary, 81
  Sweet, Blanche, 86
  Walthall, Henry B., 86
Loos, Clifford, 81
Loos, Gladys, 81, 85
Loos, Minnie, 81–82, 84–86
Loos, R. Beers, 81
Lorelei Lee, 87
Lorre, Peter, 203
Los Angeles
  about, 6, 36, 41
  Bertessson, Sergei, 247, 252
  early days, ii, iii, v, vi, vii
  Guy, Alice Ida Antoinette, 181, 182f, 183, 185
  Kinemacolor pictures, 49
  Leloir, Maurice, 287, 289
  Parrish, Robert, 255, 257
  Schulberg, Budd, 162, 164–65
  Scott, Evelyn, 126–27, 128f
  Swanson, Gloria, 134, 136, 141
  Viertel, Salka, 268–73, 275
Los Angeles County's Signal Hill, 182f
Los Angeles Film Exchange, 212
Los Angeles station, 36, 113
Los Angeles Times Syndicate, 234
Los Angeles trolleys, 11
Los Angeles Women's Club, 214
Louis, Willard, 227

Louis B. Mayer Productions, 219, 291. *See also*
  Mayer, Louis B.
Love, Bessie, 147
The Love Boat, 47
The Love Light, 28
Lowe, Edmund, 133
Loy, Myrna (Myrna Adele Williams)
  about, 150–57, 152f
  Academy Award, 157
  Culver City, 150–51, 152f, 153, 155
  Fanchon and Marco, 155–56
  Grauman, Sid, 156, 215
  Hollywood, 150, 156–57
  Ince, Thomas H., 155
  Metro-Goldwyn-Mayer, 151
  U.S. commission for UNESCO, 157
  Westlake, 151, 153–54
  Williams, Della, 150–51, 154–56
  Winebreiner, Harry Fielding, 154
Loyal Order of Moose, 210
Lubin Film Manufacturing Company, 29–32
Lubitsch, Ernst, 4, 197, 202, 232, 271–72, 276n1
Lucretia Lombard, 193, 196
Lumière brothers, iii, 180
Lytell, Bert, 214

M
MacArthur, Charlie, 149, 240–41, 242f, 243,
  245–46, 302
MacArthur, John D., 240
MacDonald, Katherine, 198, 200–201
MacFarlane, Lou, 151, 155
Macintosh, Reginald, 22
Mack Sennett Studios, 136, 174
Macpherson, Jeanie, 6, 141, 231
Madame Butterfly, 23
Mahr, Johnny, 8
Maid Marian, 210
make-over, 3
Male and Female, 72, 165, 176
Malibu beach, 264–65
Malibu Colony, 263f, 265
Malloy, Jack, 79
The Maltese Falcon, 228
Mamoulian, Rouben, 202
The Man in the Iron Mask, 277, 278f, 285–86,
  288f
Manee, Miss, 237
Manhattan Melodrama, 156
Mankiewicz, Herman, 240, 245
Mann, Heinrich, 275
Mann, Thomas, 275
March, Fredric, 203
Marion, Frances (Marion Benson Owens)

about, vii, 4, 18, 27, 231
in 1912, 19–28, 21f
Belletti, Valeria, 236, 238
Dressler, Marie, 94f, 97
Gish, Lillian, 46–47
Griffith, David Wark, 22, 24–25
Hollywood, 28
Hopper, Hedda, 125
Janis, Elsie, 91–92
King, Henry, 33
Morosco, Oliver, 19–20, 23
Pickford, Mary, 22f, 23–28
Sennett, Mack, 20
Mark Hopkins Art Institute, 19
The Marriage Circle, 196
Marsh, Mae, 59
Marsh, Marguerite, 59
Marvin, Arthur, 8
Marx, Groucho, 63
Mascarel, José, 58
Mason Opera House, 178
The Mate of the Schooner Sadie, 30
Matilda, Mme., 151–52
Maugham, Somerset, 177
Max Reinhardt troupe, 275
Mayer, Jerry, 292, 296
Mayer, Louis B. *See also* Louis B. Mayer Productions
about, 166, 292
Coffee, Lenore, 171–73, 179, 206f
Gish, Lillian, 47
Hays, Will Harrison, 203f
Rapf, Maurice, 261
Shearer, Norma, 220
Winters, Ralph, 298–99
Maynard, Gordon, 232
Maynard, Harry, 232
McAvoy, May, 231
McCarthy, Eugene, 157
McCormick, John, 214
McGee, James L., 2
McKenzie, Maurice, 207
McLaughlin, Viva, 150
Meet Me in St. Louis, 228
Meighan, Thomas, 222
Méliès, Georges, iii, 106
Melville, Wilbert, 29, 32
Member of the Crew (Thackrey), 197
Mencken, H. L., 246
The Mender of Nets, 59
Menzies, William Cameron, 249
Meredith, Bess, 231
The Merry Widow, 292
A Message from Mars, 96

Metro Pictures, 210–12, 291
Metro Studios, 188f, 189
Metro-Goldwyn Studios, 291
Metro-Goldwyn-Mayer (Culver City), vi, 112, 151, 210, 220, 232, 291–92
Metropolitan Museum of Art (New York), 290
Metropolitan Opera, 118
M-G-M Studios, 293f
about, 47, 132, 156, 221
Loos, Anita, 88
Miller, Virgil, 60, 62
Rapf, Maurice, 261
Winters, Ralph, 291–92, 294, 297–98
Milady's ablutions, 9
Milestone, Lewis, 241
Miller, Christie, 8, 12
Miller, Virgil E., 61–63, 63f
Million Dollar Theatre (Los Angeles), vii
The Millionaire, 56
Milord's Gillette, 9
Min and Bill, 94f, 97
Miners' Convention, 9
The Minister's Daughter, 29
Miss Information, 92
Mission picture, 12
Mix, Tom, 28, 212, 231
Mme. Matilda's École de Choreographie Classique, 151
Modern Times, 294
Monkey Business, 245
Montgomery, Frank, 3
Montgomery, Robert, 291
Montmartre Café, 229
Moon, Lorna, 72
Moore, Annabelle, iii
Moore, Colleen (Kathleen Morrison)
about, 112, 144f
Brown, Mrs., 147–48
Colleen Moore's Doll House, 149
Gish, Dorothy, 147
Griffith, David Wark, 142–43, 145–46, 148
Hargrave, Homer, 149
Harron, Bobby, 147
Hollywood, 143, 145, 147–49
How Women Can Make Money in the Stock Market, 149
Howey, Walter, 143–44, 147, 149
Morrison, Mrs., 142–43, 145, 147–48
Pickford, Mary, 142, 145
"The Doll House," 149
Vidor, King, 149
Withey, Chet, 147
Moore, Matt, vi
Moore, Mrs. Owen, 91

Moore, Owen, 18, 23, 25, 91–92
Moran, Polly, 97
"More Stars Than There Are in Heaven," 291
Morning Telegraph, 229
Morosco, Oliver, 1, 4n1, 19–20, 23, 59
Morosco, Walter, 4n1
Morosco Stock Company, 35
Morosco Theatre, 4n1, 179
Morrison, Cleeve, 143
Morrison, Mrs., 142–43, 145, 147–48
Morrison, Norma, 148
Moscow Art Theatre, 247, 254
Mother Superior, 280
Motion Picture Actors' Equity, 212
Motion Picture Editors Guild, 298
Motion Picture Home (Woodland Hills), 179, 228
Motion Picture Magazine, 222
Motion Picture Patents Company, i
Motion Picture Producers and Distributors Association (MPPDA), 204–5
Motion Picture Producers' Association, 212
Mountbatten, Lord, 302
moviemakers, independent, v
moviemaking, ii
MPPDA. *See* Motion Picture Producers and Distributors Association
Mr. Blandings Builds His Dream House, 156
Mr. Roberts, 102
Murnau, F. W., 267–69
Museum of Modern Art, 47
Musso Frank's, 175
My Gal Irene, 59
My Man Godfrey, 197
My Story (Astor), 228
Myers, Carmel, 147, 227
Myrtle *(Threads of Destiny)*, 12

N
Naldi, Nita, 222
National Association of Letter Carriers, 210, 215
National Republican Party, 204
Navajo Indian reservation, 181
Nazimova, 183–84
Nearly a Good Picture!, 91
Nearly a Lady, 91
Negri, Pola, 222
Negro hairdresser, 231
Negro housekeeper, 273
Negro porter and waiters, 268
Neilan, Marshall (Mickey), 165
Nemirovich-Danchenko, Vladimir Ivanovich, 247–49, 251–54

New York Academy of Dramatic Arts, 64
The New York Hat, 45, 49
New York Motion Picture Patents Corporation, 6
New York theater, 51
New York Theatre Guild, 235
Newman, Herman, 58
Newman, Vi, 262
newsreels, iv, v, 106, 217
Nichols, George, 8
Nichols, Mrs. George, 8
nickelodeons, iv, 1, 22, 64, 127
Nielan, Marshall "Mickey," 173
Nigh, William, 296–97
A Night in Venice, 252
Niven, David, 276
Noah's Ark, 156
Norma Desmond, 141
Normand, Mabel, 95, 163
Notorious, 246
Novak, Jane, 212
Nuremberg trials, 166

O
Oberammergau, 172
Ocean Boulevard, 179
O'Connell, Reverend, 150
Oklahoma!, 104
In Old California, 12
Old Heidelberg, 35
Olivier, Laurence, 80
On the Waterfront, 166
O'Neill, Joe, 207
Ormston, Frank, 62
Orphans of the Storm, 46
Orpheum Theater, iii
Oscar, Honorary, 18
Osmond, Mr., 29
O'Sullivan, Maureen, 265
O'Sullivan, Tony, 8
Owen, Seena, vi

P
Pacific States Electric Company, 62
Paget, Alfred, 8
The Painted Veil, 275
palace of Versailles, 26
Palm Beach, 6
The Palm Beach Story, 228
Palmer, Mitchell (Attorney General), v
Palmer Raids, v
Paramount Pictures, Inc.
  about, vi, 4, 72, 79, 98, 166
  Jaffe, Sam, 198–99, 202

Schulberg, B. P., 265
Paris Fashions, 240
Parker, Dorothy, 146
Parker, Gilbert (Sir), 177
Parrish, Robert, 276
  about, 255–60
  Academy Award, 260
  Chaplin, Charlie, 255, 256f, 257–60
  Fairbanks, Douglas, 257
  Gish, Lillian, 257
  Griffith, David Wark, 257–60
  Growing Up in Hollywood, 260
  Hollywood, 255, 260
  Hollywood Doesn't Live Here Anymore, 260
  Jewell, Austin, 257–59
  Los Angeles, 255, 257
  Pickford, Mary, 257
Parsons, Harriet, 229
Parsons, John, 229
Parsons, Louella Rose (Oettinger)
  about, 133, 229–39, 230f
  Bow, Clara, 166, 177, 229, 231, 234
  Davies, Marion, 229, 231, 234
  Essanay studio, 229
  Fairbanks, Douglas, 232, 234
  Hollywood, 229, 231–32, 234
  How to Write for the Movies, 228
  Ince, Thomas, 229
  Mix, Tom, 231
  Pickford, Mary, 232, 234
Partners Again, 33
Pasadena, ii, 3, 6, 127, 141, 205, 268, 287
Pasadena train station (Los Angeles), 128f, 247, 279, 287
The Passing Show, 92
The Passion Play, 172
Pathé (Culver City), 39, 217, 239
Pathé camera, 64
patriotism of film industry, iv
Paul Drake, 125
Pavlova, Anna, 104, 127, 154, 179
Peck, Gregory, 34
Pegg, Vester, 76
Peggy, Baby, 212
The Perils of Pauline, 217
Perry Mason, 125
Peter Pan, 148
The Phantom of the Opera, 62
Philharmonic Auditorium (Los Angeles), 178
Photoplay, iv
Photoplay's Gold Medal, 33
Pickfair (Beverly Hills estate), vii, 18, 232, 233f, 281–82
Pickfair Estate, 233f

Pickford, Mary (Gladys Smith)
  in 1910, 15–18
  Academy Award, 18
  Academy of Motion Picture Arts and Sciences, 18
  "America's Sweetheart," 18
  Bertessson, Sergei, 254
  Biograph Studios, 15–16, 18, 18n1
  Bosworth, Hobart, 8–9, 11
  de Mille, Agnes, 103
  DeMille, Cecil B., 64, 72
  dog Zorro, vii
  Dressler, Marie, 96
  Fairbanks, Douglas, vii, 18
  ferry to Jersey City, 8
  Gish, Lillian, 40–41, 45f
  Griffith, David Wark, 15–16, 18, 22
  Griffith, Mrs. D. W., 5–14
  Hays, Will, 210
  Hearst, William Randolph, 9
  interview with, 23–26
  Irving, Laurence, 277, 278f, 279, 285
  Janis, Elsie, 91–92
  Lloyd, Harold, 39
  Loos, Anita, 81
  Marion, Frances, 22f, 23–28
  Moore, Colleen, 142, 145
  Moore, Owen, 18, 23
  Oscar, Honorary, 18
  Parrish, Robert, 257
  Parsons, Louella, 232, 234
  picture, 45f
  in *Ramona*, 17f
  Schulberg, Budd, 165
  Sennett, Mack, 16
  Threads of Destiny, 12
  Walsh, Raoul, 74
  war bonds, iv, 96
  working on script with Frances Marion, 22fig
Pickford-Fairbanks Studio, vi
Pico Boulevard, 59, 270
Pierce Arrow town car, 173
Pike, Robert, 19
The Pink Panther, 299
Pippa Passes, 51, 60
The Spoilers, iv
Pollyanna, 28
Poor Little Rich Girl, 18, 28
Porter, Edwin, iii–iv
Powell, Mr., 8
Powell, William, 156, 222
Power, Tyrone, 33
Preeman, Blanche, 262
Preferred Pictures, 166, 198, 202

Prevost, Marie, 212, 232
Prina, Irma, 235, 239
Private Lives, 302
Production Code, 216
Prohibition Act, 184
Pruett, Max, 207–8, 215
Prynne, Hester, 149
Putnam Building, 29

Q
Quadrangle Pictures, 164
Quality Street, 257
Queen Christina, 275
Queen Elizabeth, iv, 192
Quirk, Billy, 8
Quo Vadis, iv, 85, 298

R
Rapf, Harry, 261, 264, 295
Rapf, Maurice
  about, 166, 261–66
  Davies estate, 263f, 264
  Hollywood, 261, 265–66
  Mayer, Louis B., 261
  Schulberg, Budd, 262, 265–66
  Thalberg, Irving, 261, 264
  vaudeville, 261
  Warner, Jack, 261
Rasputin and the Empress, 60
Reagan, Ronald (Governor), 294
Rebecca of Sunnybrook Farm, 18, 28
Red Dust, 228
Red Headed Woman, 88
Reeve, Arch, 214
Reid, Wallace, 131
Reinhardt, Gottfried, 275–76
Reinhardt, Max, 267, 272, 275, 276n1
Remodeling Her Husband, 46
Resurrection, 249
Revier, Harry, 67–68
Reynolds, Harry, 295–97
Rich, Irene, 227
Riefenstahl, Leni, 166
Rimpau, Billy, 62
Rindge, Mrs., 265
Ritter School of Expression (Culver City), 155
Roach, Hal, 39, 151, 208, 213, 232
Robertson-Cole Studios, 212
Robin Hood, viii, 210
Rodeo, 104
Le Roi Soleil, 285
Roland, Ruth, 212
The Romance of the Redwoods, 72
Romeo and Juliet, 221

Romola, 33
Roosevelt Hotel, 269, 270f, 271
Rosay, Françoise, 273
Rosenberg, B. F., 214
Ross, Bob, 62
Rosse, Herman, 244
Ruggles, Charles, 59
Ruth St. Denis, 151

S
Safety Last, 39
Samuel Goldwyn Company, 235
San Bernardino, 9
San Fernando Valley, v, 71, 103, 110, 130, 174
San Francisco, 6, 20, 168–69, 171, 173, 204
San Francisco, 88
San Francisco Chronicle, 97
San Francisco Earthquake (1906), 5, 19, 153
San Francisco Grand Opera House, 5
San Francisco society's *Blue Book*, 19
San Gabriel, 12
San Gabriel Mission, 6
Sanger, Margaret, v
Santa Barbara Avenue, 79
Santa Fe *Chief*, 145, 158–60
Santa Monica, 261–62, 263f, 265, 270–71, 273, 275, 303
Santa Monica Boulevard, vi, 187, 210, 255, 257
Santa Monica Canyon, 271
Santa Monica Pier, 273
Santschi, Tom, 2, 32
Savage, Henry W., 29
Scarface, 241
The Scarlet Letter, 47, 149
Schenck, Joseph M.
  about, 148, 163, 204, 231
  Bertessson, Sergei, 247, 249, 251
  Hays, Will Harrison, 205, 207–8, 210–11
  Irving, Laurence, 283
  mansion, 272
Schickel, Richard, 13–14
Schlesinger, Leon, 265
School of Athens, 283
Schulberg, Adeline, 158, 203
Schulberg, Budd (Seymour Wilson)
  Abramses, 156, 158, 160, 162–63
  Academy Award, 167
  Alexandria Hotel (Hollywood), 160f, 163–65
  Beverly Hills, 160, 165–66
  Chaplin, Charlie, 163–65
  Famous Players-Lasky, 164–65
  Goldwyn Company, 164
  Griffith, David Wark, 163
  Harvey, Fred, 161

My First Time in Hollywood

Hollywood, 158, 165–66
Jaffe, Sam, 198–99, 201–3
Los Angeles, 162, 164–65
Paramount, 166
Pickford, Mary, 165
Preferred Pictures, 166
Rapf, Maurice, 262, 265–66
Santa Fe *Chief*, 158–62
Sennett, Mack, 163
Stewart, Anita, 163
Swanson, Gloria, 165
Schulberg-Feldman agency, 203
Scott, Evelyn
  Catalina Island, 126
  de Mille, Beatrice (Bibi), 127–32
  de Mille, Cecil, 126–27, 129–32
  de Mille, William, 126–27, 129
  Dix, Beulah Marie, 126–32
  Farrar, Geraldine, 131–32
  Hollywood, 127–28
  Hollywood Boulevard, 128
  Los Angeles, 126–27, 128f
  Sherlock Holmes films, 132
The Scoundrel, 246
Screen Writers' Guild, 212, 266
Seidel, Louise, 266
Selig, William N. (Colonel), 2–3, 5, 36
Selig players, 6
Selig Polyscope Company (Chicago), 2
Selig Zoo, 219
Selwynne, Clarissa, 227
Selznick, David O., 233f, 241, 246
Selznick, Irene Mayer, 241
Sennett, Mack
  Coffee, Lenore, 174
  Dressler, Marie, 95
  Gish, Lillian, 41
  Griffith, Mrs. D. W., 8, 20
  Hopper, DeWolf, 115, 117
  Marion, Frances, 20
  Pickford, Mary, 16
  Schulberg, Budd, 163
  Swanson, Gloria, 135–40
  Walsh, Raoul, 79
Seven Brides for Seven Brothers, 299
Sharkey, Mr., 1
Shaw, Irwin, 260, 276
Shearer, Athole, 217, 221
Shearer, Douglas, 217, 221
Shearer, Edith and Andrew, 217
Shearer, Norma, 291
  about, 195, 197, 218f
  Academy Award, 221
  Arrougé, Martin, 221

Griffith, David Wark, 217
  Hollywood, 217, 219–20
  Louis B. Mayer Company, 219
  Mayer, Louis B., 220
  Metro-Goldwyn-Mayer, 220
  Pathé, 217
  Small, Mr., 219
  Thalberg, Irving, 218f, 220–21
Shelter, Eddie, 8
Sherlock Holmes films, 62, 132
Ship Café, 179
Shore, Allen (Dr.), 216
A Shot in the Dark, 299
Sidney, Sylvia, 166
Siegmann, George, 74
Sills, Milton, 183
Sing Zee Laundry drying yard (Los Angeles),
  x fig
Small, Mr., 219
Smalley, Phillips, 38, 90, 90f, 91, 180
Smith, Gladys, 15, 40. *See also* Pickford, Mary
Smith, Jack (Mary Pickford's brother), 11,
  15–18, 45, 78
Smith, Lottie (Mary Pickford's mother), 15,
  17–18
Soho, 87
Solax Studio, 180, 185
The Song of Bernadette, 34
The Song of the South, 266
Southern California, v, 17, 36, 57, 60, 105, 116,
  127–29, 165
Spanish California, 12
Spanish influenza, 180–81
Spanish Mission (San Francisco), 20
Sparrows, 257
The Spoilers, 32
Spoor, George K. (Essanay), 16, 18n1
The Squaw Man, 64, 66f, 69, 165
St. Denis, Ruth, 104
St. Francis Hotel, 169
St. Johns, Adela Rogers, 2, 22, 27, 112
Stafford, Eddie, 78
Stage Door, 197
Standish, Miles, 1
Stanley, Henry, 30
Stark, Pauline, 147
Stark Love, 56
The Stealers, 217
Stella Dallas, 33, 236
Stern, Jacob, 67–68
Stevenson, Adlai, 157
Stewart, Anita, 163, 165, 172–73
Stewart, James, 291
Strand (New York), iv

Stray, Stella, 68–69
Street of Chance, 179
Stronger Than Death, 183
The Student Prince (musical), 35
Sultan of Turkey, 2
In the Sultan's Power, x fig, 2–4
The Sun Also Rises, 34
Sunny Side Up, 132
Sunrise, 267
Sunset Boulevard (Beverly Hills), 36, 52, 74,
    165, 181, 184, 189, 193, 219, 223, 232, 268
Sunset Boulevard (film), 72, 141
Sunset Inn, 179
Supreme Court (1917), v
Sutherland, Eddie, 193
Swanson, Addie, 133, 135–38, 141
Swanson, Gloria
    about, 133, 137f, 141, 222, 231
    Badger, Clarence, 138, 140
    Beery, Wallace, 133–34, 134f, 136, 141
    Chaplin, Charlie, 133
    Coward, Noël Peirce, 300
    Del Ruth, Mr., 136–37
    DeMille, Cecil B., 72, 141
    Essanay, 135, 139–40
    Griffith, David Wark, 135
    Hayes, Frank, 136–38
    Hollywood, 135–36
    Kennedy, Joseph P., 141
    Keystone studio, 136, 138, 140–41
    Los Angeles, 134, 136, 141
    Mack Sennett Studios, 136
    Queen of the Silent Screen, 141
    Schulberg, Budd, 165
    Sennett, Mack, 135–40
    United Artists, 141
    Vernon, Bobby, 138–40
    Walsh, Raoul, 80
Swanson, Joseph, 133
Swanson, Noah, 135
Sweet, Blanche, 14, 59, 74, 78, 86

T
Talmadge, Constance, 148, 163, 221, 251
Talmadge, Norma, 28, 163, 210–11, 231, 251–52
Talmadge sisters, 163
The Taming of the Shrew, 285
Tarnished Reputations, 180
Tarzan of the Apes, 185
Tashman, Lilyan, 231
Taylor, Elizabeth, 291
Taylor, Robert, 291
Taylor, William Desmond, 112, 163
The Covered Wagon, 56

Teapot Dome scandal, 204
Tearle, Conway, 212
The Ten Commandments, 72, 156
Tender is the Night, 34
Test Pilot, 156
Thackrey, Gene, 197
Thackrey, Sean, 197
Thackrey, Winfrid Kay
    Barker Brothers, 186–87
    Beverly Hills, 187
    Brockway, Les and Ferne, 187, 195
    Conway, Jack, 192–95
    Fairbanks, Douglas, 189
    Hollywood, 186, 189, 193–95, 197
    J. W. Robinson's, 187, 189, 192, 194
    Kohner, Paul, 196
    La Cava, Gregory, 197
    Lasky Studio, 189, 191
    Little, Tommy, 189, 191–92
    Lubitsch, Ernst, 197
    Member of the Crew, 197
    Shearer, Norma, 195, 197
    Warner Bros., 192–93
    Weber-Werness Studios, 187
Thais (opera), 16
Thalberg, Irving
    about, 97, 179, 197
    Hays, Will Harrison, 206f, 208, 214
    Laemmle, Rosabelle, 264
    Rapf, Maurice, 261, 264
    Shearer, Norma, 218f, 220–21, 264
Thalberg, Irving (Mrs.), 221
The Dying Swan, 127, 154, 179
"The Indian Chief" (train), 277
Theatre Owners' Association, 212
Their Own Desire, 132, 221
They Gave Him a Gun, 266
A Thief in Paradise, 236
The Thief of Baghdad, 80, 210
The Thin Man, 156
Thomas Ince Studio (Culver City), vi, 23, 209,
    233f
Thompson, Fred, vii
Thompson, Sadie, 80
Thomson, Fred, iii, 28
Threads of Destiny, 12
Three Musketeers, 285
The Three Sisters, 254
Three Weeks (novel), 177
Tillie's Nightmare, 96
Tillie's Punctured Romance, 95–96
To Hell with the Kaiser, iv
Tol'able David, 33
Top o' the Morning, 29

Tourneur, Maurice, 237
Tracy, Spencer, 34, 266, 291
The Trail of '98, 293
train(s), ii, 6, 8, 15. *See also* California Limited
Triangle studios, 87
A Trip to the Moon, iii, 106
trolleys, Los Angeles, 11
the Trust, ii, v
Tug Boat Annie, 97
Turnbull, Margaret, 104
Twelve O'Clock High, 34
Twentieth Century Limited, 8
20th Century Fox, 62
Two-Faced Woman, 275

U
Uhlfelders, 262
Underworld, 246
Union Station opening (1939), ii
United Artists
    Bertessson, Sergei, 247–49, 250f, 251–53
    Swanson, Gloria, 141
United Studios, 210
Universal City, vi, 130, 174
Universal farm, 232
Universal Pictures, 110, 111f, 112, 164, 174
Universal Studios, 36, 38, 61–62, 189
The Unpardonable Sin, 169
U.S. Amusement Company, 184

V
Van Winkle, Rip, 207
Vance, Miss, 153
Vandyke, Jean, 150
vaudeville
    Brown, Karl, 51
    Coffee, Lenore, 178
    de Mille, Agnes, 98
    DeMille, Cecil B., 64
    Dressler, Marie, 93
    house, 35
    Janis, Elsie, 89
    performers, vi
    Rapf, Maurice, 261
    theaters, iv
Venice Short Line, 151
Victor Victoria, 299
Vidal, Gore, 276
Vidor, Florence, ii, 196
Vidor, King
    about, ii, 4, 108f
    Arto, Florence, 106–7, 108f, 109–10, 112
    Boardman, Eleanor, 112
    Griffith, Corinne, 107, 109

Griffith, David Wark, 109, 111fig
Hill, Elizabeth, 112
Hollywood, 107, 109–12
Ince, Thomas H., 106, 109
Universal, 110, 111f, 112
Vitagraph Company of America, 106–7, 110, 164
Viertel, Berthold, 267–69, 271–73, 275–76
Viertel, Hans, 267, 273, 275
Viertel, Peter, 267, 273, 275–76
Viertel, Salka (Steuermann)
    about, 260, 267–76
    Bing, Herman, 268–69, 271–73
    Guercio, Mr., 274
    Los Angeles, 268–73, 275
    Murnau, F. W., 267–69
    Reinhardt, Gottfried, 275–76
    Reinhardt, Max, 267, 272, 275, 276n1
    Wurtzel, Marion, 273
    Wurtzel, Sol, 273
Viertel, Thomas, 267
Vinard, Madame, 284
Vitagraph Company of America, 106–7, 110, 164
Viva Villa!, 246
A Voice from the Minaret, 211
von Sternberg, Josef, 202, 275

W
Wagner, Mamie, 71
Wallace, Bob, 303
Walsh, Raoul, 73—80, 75f
Walthall, Henry B., 8, 49, 55, 60, 74, 86
Wanger, Walter, 202
War and Peace, 112
war bonds, iv, 96
Ward, Fanny, 166
Warner Brothers Studios, vi, 179, 189, 192–93, 210, 289
Warner Brothers Theater, 267
The Warrens of Virginia, 15, 64
Washington Merry-Go-Round, 197
The Water Lily, 151
Way Down East, 46
The Way of All Flesh, 275
Wayne, John (Marion Morrison), 80
Weber, Lois (Lois Smalley), 4, 21, 26–27, 90f, 91, 171, 180
A Wedding, 47
Weid, Ivar A., 58
West, Charlie, 8
West, Dorothy, 8, 11
West, Mae, 80
West, Mary, 8

Western bar-rooms, 10
Western Costume Company, 213, 225
Western Motion Picture Advertisers, 212
Westerns, 73, 75–77, 79–80
Westlake School for Girls (Los Angeles), 151,
   153–54
The Whales of August, 47
What Makes Sammy Run?, 166
When It Rains It Pours!, 107
White, Pearl, 29
The White Sister, 33
Whitman, Walt, 87
Wife vs. Secretary, 156
Wilcox, Daeida, ii, iii, 36, 57–58
Wilcox, Ella Wheeler, 87
Wilcox, Harvey, ii, iii
Wilcox, Horace Henderson, 36, 57–58
Wilcox ranch, 58
William Fox Studios, 122, 170f
Williams, David, 150
Williams, Della, 150–51, 154–56, 234
Williams, Kathleen, 143
Wilson, 34
Wilson, Gilbert, 92
Wilson, President, 126
The Wind, vi, 47
Winebreiner, Harry Fielding, 154
The Winning of Barbara Worth, 33, 238
Winter Carnival, 266
Winters, Ralph
   Academy Award, 298
   Crawford, Joan, 295, 297
   Culver City, 291, 293–94
   Fairbanks, Douglas, 297
   Garbo, Greta, 292
   Gray, Danny, 293–94, 298
   Hollywood, 292–98
   Levy, Jake, 292
   Mayer, Louis B., 298–99
   M-G-M, 291–92, 294, 297–98
   Motion Picture Editors Guild, 298
   Nigh, William, 296–97
   Rapf, Harry, 295
   Reynolds, Harry, 295–97
Winters, Sam, 291–95
Winters, Teddy, 299
Wise, Robert, 197
Woman's Club (Los Angeles), 105
women, ii
The Women, 88, 221
Women in War, 92
Woods, Frank E., 74–77, 214
Woolner, Rosalind, 277
Workers Leaving the Factory, 180

World War I, iv, v, 92, 96, 131, 240
World War II, 166, 246, 285
Writers Guild, 28
Wurtzel, Marion, 273
Wurtzel, Sol, 208, 273
Wuthering Heights, 246
Wyckoff, Alvin, 54
Wyler, William, 197

Y
"Yes, Sir, That's My Baby," 229
You Bet Your Life, 63
You Can't Take it with You, 60
Young, Clara Kimball, 168–69, 171–73

Z
Zeidman, Bennie F., 199
Ziegfeld, Flo, 217
Zinnemann, Fred, 275
Zukor, Adolph, iv, 18, 72, 165, 204

About the Author

Cari Beauchamp is an award-winning writer, speaker, documentary film-maker, and author of *Without Lying Down: Frances Marion and the Powerful Women of Early Hollywood; Joseph P. Kennedy Presents: His Hollywood Years,* and other books on film history, which have been selected for "Best of the Year" lists by the *New York Times,* the *Los Angeles Times,* Booklist, and Amazon.

Beauchamp wrote and co-produced the documentary film *Without Lying Down* for which she was nominated for a Writers Guild Award. She also wrote the *Emmy*-nominated documentary film *The Day My God Died,* about Nepalese girls sold into sexual slavery, which aired on PBS.

She is the only person to twice be named an Academy of Motion Picture Arts and Sciences Film Scholar and writes for *Vanity Fair* and other magazines. She has appeared in documentaries including *Moguls and Movie Stars* and *The Story of Film* and has spoken about film throughout the United States and Europe, including at the British Film Institute, the Museum of Modern Art, and the Cannes Film Festival. She serves as the Resident Scholar for the Mary Pickford Foundation.

CPSIA information can be obtained at www.ICGtesting.com
Printed in the USA
BVOW10s0010200615

405022BV00009B/60/P